A CULTURAL HISTORY OF WOMEN

VOLUME 2

A Cultural History of Women
General Editor: Linda Kalof

Volume 1
A Cultural History of Women in Antiquity
Edited by Janet H. Tulloch

Volume 2
A Cultural History of Women in the Middle Ages
Edited by Kim M. Phillips

Volume 3
A Cultural History of Women in the Renaissance
Edited by Karen Raber

Volume 4
A Cultural History of Women in the Age of Enlightenment
Edited by Ellen Pollak

Volume 5
A Cultural History of Women in the Age of Empire
Edited by Teresa Mangum

Volume 6
A Cultural History of Women in the Modern Age
Edited by Liz Conor

A CULTURAL HISTORY OF WOMEN

IN THE MIDDLE AGES

Edited by Kim M. Phillips

BLOOMSBURY
LONDON • NEW DELHI • NEW YORK • SYDNEY

Bloomsbury Academic
An imprint of Bloomsbury Publishing Plc

50 Bedford Square
London
WC1B 3DP
UK

1385 Broadway
New York
NY 10018
USA

www.bloomsbury.com

Bloomsbury is a registered trade mark of Bloomsbury Publishing Plc

First published 2013
Reprinted 2013

British Library Cataloguing-in-Publication Data
A catalogue record for this book is available from the British Library.

ISBN: HB: 978-0-8578-5098-0
Set: 978-1-8478-8475-6

Library of Congress Cataloging-in-Publication Data
A catalogue record for this book is available from the Library of Congress.

Typeset by Apex CoVantage, LLC, Madison, WI, USA.
Printed and bound in Great Britain

To all working mothers

CONTENTS

Series Preface ix

List of Illustrations xi

Introduction: Medieval Meanings of Women 1
Kim M. Phillips

1 The Life Cycle: The Ages of Medieval Women 15
Cordelia Beattie

2 Bodies and Sexuality 39
April Harper

3 Religion and Popular Beliefs: Choices, Constraints, and Creativity for Christian Women 59
Katherine L. French

4 Medicine and Disease: The Female "Patient" in Medieval Europe 85
Iona McCleery

5 Public and Private: Women in the Home, Women in the Streets 105
Kim M. Phillips

6 Education and Work: Multiple Tasks and Lowly Status 127
Sandy Bardsley

7 Power: Medieval Women's Power through Authority, Autonomy, and Influence 153
Lois L. Huneycutt

8 Artistic Representation: Women and/in Medieval Visual Culture 179
Marian Bleeke, Jennifer Borland, Rachel Dressler, Martha Easton, and Elizabeth L'Estrange (from the Medieval Feminist Art History Project)

Notes 215

Bibliography 273

Contributors 313

Index 317

SERIES PREFACE

A Cultural History of Women is a six-volume series reviewing the changing cultural construction of women and women's historical experiences throughout history. Each volume follows the same basic structure and begins with an outline account of the major ideas about women in the historical period under consideration. Next, specialists examine aspects of women's history under eight key headings: the life cycle, bodies/sexuality, religion/popular beliefs, medicine/disease, public/private, education/work, power, and artistic representation. Thus, readers can choose a synchronic or a diachronic approach to the material—a single volume can be read to obtain a thorough knowledge of women's history in a given period, or one of the eight themes can be followed through time by reading the relevant chapters of all six volumes, thus providing a thematic understanding of changes and developments over the long term. The six volumes divide the history of women as follows:

Volume 1: A Cultural History of Women in Antiquity (500 B.C.E.–1000 C.E.)
Volume 2: A Cultural History of Women in the Middle Ages (1000–1500)
Volume 3: A Cultural History of Women in the Renaissance (1400–1650)
Volume 4: A Cultural History of Women in the Age of Enlightenment (1650–1800)
Volume 5: A Cultural History of Women in the Age of Empire (1800–1920)
Volume 6: A Cultural History of Women in the Modern Age (1920–2000+)

Linda Kalof, General Editor

LIST OF ILLUSTRATIONS

INTRODUCTION

Figure 0.1: Eve and the Serpent in the Garden of Eden. 8

Figure 0.2: Rogier van der Weyden, *The Annunciation*—detail of the Virgin's face. 10

CHAPTER 1

Figure 1.1: The Ages of Man from the "Wheel of Life." 16

Figure 1.2: The *damoiselle*. 30

Figure 1.3: *Vieille damoiselle*. 31

Figure 1.4: The *espousee* (bride). 34

Figure 1.5: *Vieille* (old woman). 36

CHAPTER 2

Figure 2.1: Wiligelmo da Modena (fl. ca. 1099–1120), *Metope with Hermaphrodite*. 40

Figure 2.2: Lorenzo Maitani (thirteenth to fourteenth centuries), *The Creation of Eve*. 42

Figure 2.3: Man and woman convicted of adultery being punished. 43

Figure 2.4: Scene in a Burgundian bathhouse (brothel) in 1470. 52

Figure 2.5: Lancelot and Guinevere in bed. 56

CHAPTER 3

Figure 3.1: Women in church, Christmas Mass. 60

Figure 3.2: Monk and a woman in the stocks. 63

Figure 3.3: Wedding scene and Adalbert Bishop of Meaux, shaving the tonsure of a nun. 65

Figure 3.4: Priests and nuns in procession. 70

Figure 3.5: Friedrich Herlin, Jacob Fuchsart's wife and daughters in church, outer right wing of the *Nördlingen Altarpiece*. 75

CHAPTER 4

Figure 4.1: Woman gives a patient savich (barley) soup. 89

Figure 4.2: Disease woman. 91

Figure 4.3: Master of the Life of Virgin Mary, *Birth of the Virgin*. 93

Figure 4.4: Santa Clara-a-Velha, Coimbra, Portugal. 98

Figure 4.5: Tomb of Isabel of Aragon, Santa Clara-a-Nova, Coimbra, Portugal. 101

CHAPTER 5

Figure 5.1: Tobit, blind in bed, attended by two women. 107

Figure 5.2: Conversation in front of the fire. 110

Figure 5.3: Market scene: left section with greengrocers and women. 114

Figure 5.4: Birth of Henry VI, from the *Pageant of the Birth, Life and Death of Richard Beauchamp Earl of Warwick*. 116

Figure 5.5: Master of the Jarves Cassone, *Story of Alatiel*. 118

CHAPTER 6

Figure 6.1: Girl assistant in draper's shop. 128

Figure 6.2: *The Education of the Virgin.* 134

Figure 6.3: The Labors of Adam and Eve. 137

Figure 6.4: Apple Harvest, from Pietro de Crescenzi, *Le Rustican* or *Livre des proffitz champestres et ruraulx.* 142

CHAPTER 7

Figure 7.1: Virgin Mary bares her breasts to her son in intercession; Esther begs King Ahasuerus to save the Jewish people. 160

Figure 7.2: Henry IV begs Matilda of Canossa, Countess of Tuscany, to intercede on his behalf with Pope Gregory VII, while Abbot Hugo of Cluny watches. 163

Figure 7.3: Empress Matilda, daughter of Henry I of England, holding a charter. 166

Figure 7.4: Deed by which Margarethe Maultasch, Countess of Tyrol, made over the counties of Tyrol and Goricia to the Dukes of Austria. 168

CHAPTER 8

Figure 8.1: Gislebertus, *The Temptation of Eve.* 182

Figure 8.2: *Virgin and Child as Throne of Wisdom* (Enthroned Virgin and Child). 183

Figure 8.3: *Virgin and Child in Majesty.* 184

Figure 8.4: Giusto de'Menabuoi, *Birth of St. John the Baptist.* 186

Figure 8.5: Limbourg Brothers, Saint Agatha from *The Belles Heures of Jean de France, Duc de Berry.* 188

Figure 8.6: St. Margaret, from the *Psalter-Hours of Yolande de Soissons.* 189

Figure 8.7: St. Eugenia from a capital on north aisle of the nave, Vézelay. 191

Figure 8.8: *St. Radegund Heals a Woman.* 192

Figure 8.9: *Luxuria*. Relief from Saint-Pierre, Moissac. 193

Figure 8.10: Aelgyva and a clerk from the *Bayeux Tapestry*. 194

Figure 8.11: *Patients and Physicians.* 196

Figure 8.12: Tomb of Thomas Beauchamp, Earl of Warwick, and Katherine Mortimer. 198

Figure 8.13: Master of Moulins (Jean Hey), *The Moulins Triptych* (The Bourbon Altarpiece). 200

Figure 8.14: Hildegard of Bingen, inspired by heavenly fire, from the Rupertsburg *Scivias*. 201

Figure 8.15: Donor portrait from *Hours of Mary of Burgundy*. 204

Figure 8.16: Relief carving of the attack on the Castle of Love. 205

Figure 8.17: Tomb sculpture of Eleanor of Aquitaine. 208

Figure 8.18: Blanche of Castile and her son Louis IX, *Bible moralisée*. 209

Figure 8.19: Master of the Cité des Dames and Workshop, *Christine de Pisan Presenting Her Book to Isabeau of Bavaria*. 211

Figure 8.20: Lauds, from the *Très Petites Heures*. 212

Introduction: Medieval Meanings of Women

KIM M. PHILLIPS

> Who are women? Who are they? Are they serpents, wolves, lions, dragons, vipers, or rapacious, devouring beasts and enemies of humanity? Then read this *Art [of Love]*: learn how to invent ruses! Take them forcefully! Deceive them! Insult them! Attack this castle! Men, take care that none of them be released among you and that everything be given over to shame! But by God, they are nonetheless your mothers, your sisters, your daughters, your wives, and your girlfriends: they are you yourselves and you yourselves are they.[1]

Christine de Pizan's rhetorical question "Who are women?" was posed within her defense of women during the so-called *Querelle de la Rose* (1401–2). This debate over the literary and moral merits of *Le Roman de la Rose* (though the quotation above refers to Ovid's *Art of Love*) saw de Pizan and others defend the reputation of womankind against literary men who occupied some of the highest political offices in France. The heated public contest went far beyond literary criticism to offer an unprecedented examination of women's cultural representation.[2] *Le Roman de la Rose (The Romance of the Rose)* was an allegorical dream vision of more than 21,000 lines, begun by Guillaume de Lorris between 1225 and 1230 and finished by Jean de Meun between 1269 and 1278.[3] Despite the poem's great length, the plot is simple: it tells of the protagonist's dream visit to a walled garden where, struck by arrows from the God of Love, he becomes enamored of a lovely lady—the "Rose." His resulting attempts to "pluck" the rose are, however, of minor interest compared with the lengthy dialogues in which the Lover engages with various allegorical figures. It is in the detail of many of these dialogues—which were chiefly the work of Jean de Meun—that de Pizan found the material that offended her. In her opening salvo to the debate, for example, she takes issue with "Reason's" explicit naming of private parts and advocacy of deceit in love affairs; the "Old Woman's" "indecency" and "reprehensible teachings" in the arts of feminine wiles and seduction; "Genius's" warnings to men not to entrust women with their secrets because of the inherent untrustworthiness of the female sex; and much else. Against this she points out the logical inconsistencies of Genius's exhortations at once to "Flee! Flee! Flee the venomous serpent" (woman) *and* to pursue her assiduously, she rubbishes the view of women as essentially untrustworthy ("how many men have they seen accused, murdered, hanged, or reproached in the streets as a result of their wives' accusation?"), and rebuts such defamation with lists of worthy women—biblical and contemporary—who prove women's capability for virtue and wisdom beyond all reasonable doubt.[4] In other words, the antifeminine views found in the *Rose*, according to de Pizan, are not only indecent, they are also illogical and inaccurate.

However, we may turn de Pizan's opening question "Who are women?" to another purpose. It was intended to elicit a moral response, to defy misogynist stereotypes of the female sex as vicious and voracious and emphasize instead not only women's goodness but also men's closeness to and dependency on them: "they are you yourselves and you yourselves are they." She did not intend to raise more fundamental ontological problems, such as: What is the nature of women's existence? What constitutes a woman's being? What, indeed, do we mean when we use this apparently self-evident signifier, "women" (or, in de Pizan's case, *femmes*)? This is not an idle question, nor one with value only to feminist philosophy. Christine de Pizan's question "Who are women?" is of fundamental import to *women's history* because it requires a reply that slows us down for a moment to consider the nature of our subject.

What is the subject of women's history? The answer, one might reply, is obvious: women's history is the study of the past lives of people of the female sex. Everyone knows what a woman is; we want to know her past experiences. Let us then proceed to the archives to find out. Virginia Woolf's list of historical desiderata, from her 1929 essay, implies just this: "What one wants, I thought—and why does not some brilliant student at Newnham or Girton supply it?—is a mass of information; at what age did she marry; how many children had she as a rule; what was her house like, had she a room to herself; did she do the cooking; would she be likely to have a servant?"[5] Woolf wanted to know about Elizabethan middle-class women, but her questions have proved much more widely applicable. Research carried out by social historians has provided the answers to many of Woolf's questions, even though, and not only in the case of medieval European women, the responses are not straightforward. At what age did a medieval woman marry? Well, perhaps at twelve, perhaps at twenty, or perhaps not until she was thirty—depending on her social status and geographic location, as well as on personal circumstances. How many children had she? Perhaps three, perhaps fifteen; again, the answer varies a great deal. What was her house like? It may have consisted of a single smoky room with a dirt floor and a centrally located hearth; alternatively, it may have been a spacious draughty castle with winding staircases, towers, and gardens. Had she a room to herself? Almost certainly not (unless she was Christine de Pizan; see Chapter Five). Did she do the cooking? Probably, except in the houses of magnates where cooking and serving food were too important to be left to women. Would she be likely to have a servant? Yes, indeed, unless she was poor, or she was a servant herself.

Yet questioning "Who are women?" or "What is a woman?" is one way to begin a *cultural* history of medieval women. Cultural history is a rather broad church, the diversity of which has been expertly explored by Peter Burke.[6] He does not wish to limit definitions of *culture* too narrowly—"It seems to be as difficult to define the term as to do without it"[7]—but identifies a number of dominant motifs in cultural history since the late eighteenth century. Many of its earliest proponents focused on elements of high culture (art, literature, ideas—what Roy Wagner termed the *opera house* notion of culture), exemplified in the work of Matthew Arnold, Jacob Burkhardt, and Johan Huizinga, as illustrative of historical zeitgeist (spirit of the age).[8] Subjected to critique from numerous quarters, cultural history, particularly from the 1970s on, took inspiration from anthropology to broaden its base and attend to much wider areas of past human endeavor than could be covered under the opera house model.[9] In the new or anthropological cultural history, no aspect of human experience or imagination is off-limits. Popular cultures, ritual, literacy, food, gestures, death, bodies, and sexualities are among subjects now deemed worthy of serious study, not confined to antiquarian curiosity. It is commonplace, for example, to discuss such subjects as bodies and sexualities as *cultural constructs*, and thus subject to fundamental variation in different historical contexts. Within the realm of the new cultural history, *women* (and indeed *men*) became worthy of reconsideration, through interrogation of gender as a cultural construct. Furthermore, influences from literary studies encouraged historians to reread their traditional sources—court records, chronicles, legal deeds, and so on—as discursive constructions representative of particular and limited viewpoints, rather than transparent windows on a past reality. If there is anything that ties this diverse discipline together, it is the emphasis on attention to shifting meanings. Cultural history is, or very often is, a project of reading sources for the "meaning inscribed by contemporaries,"[10] and although its emphasis on the foreignness of past cultures has sometimes entailed a fascination with the exotic, or other, we do not need to engage in a search for the overtly strange in history in order to be doing cultural history. If, as in L. P. Hartley's often-repeated phrase, "the past is a foreign country," then past women, including medieval ones, are foreigners to us.[11]

The earliest historians of medieval women, in contrast, approached the topic with a fundamental confidence about the nature of their subject, though not about the ease of doing the research. Medieval women were simply people of female sex who lived during the era conventionally termed *the Middle Ages*. It was perceived as not only valid, but valuable—even essential—to write their history as part of the broader effort of women's history to reclaim knowledge about the lives of women in the past and thus redress the drastic imbalance of history that favored men. The task of providing adequate information was perceived by many as challenging, though not necessarily impossible. "The history of women in the middle ages is difficult to write," asserted Christopher N. L. Brooke in his introduction to Derek Baker's groundbreaking 1978 collection.[12] "Why do we know so little about women in the Middle Ages and the Renaissance?" asked Mary Beth Rose in her 1986 volume. Her answer, though, was more optimistic than Baker's view: it is because "until relatively recently, we had never really asked."[13] Yet the remarkable collection of historiographical essays edited by Susan Mosher Stuard in 1987 showed that we have sometimes had rather short memories when it comes to scholarship on medieval women. The authors of the five well-researched contributions to that volume showed how extensive interest in women's medieval experience had been among historians even in the nineteenth century and, to an extent, even to the early modern beginnings of medieval historiography.[14] These essays reminded readers that the study of medieval women can hardly be called a new field. However, fashions wax and wane, and interest in medieval women has had many periods of efflorescence followed by periods of relative quiet. For example, Barbara

Hanawalt suggested that English interest in medieval women, which had by the early twentieth century already produced many studies of working women as well as queens, princesses, nuns, and anchorites, waned from the 1930s to 1950s, and this no doubt contributed to second-wave feminists' sense of medieval women's history as a disregarded subject.[15]

Studies of medieval women's experiences, then, have a long history, and new themes and questions continue to be addressed by scholars. For example, the history of single women—long neglected—has been the subject of recent valuable work.[16] Domestic violence has finally begun to receive detailed attention.[17] Welcome work on Iberian women has extended our sense of geographic diversity in the lives of medieval women.[18] The lives of Jewish and Muslim women in European kingdoms are gaining increased notice.[19] The private lives of families and influence of women, even in the central Middle Ages, continue to be investigated.[20] Historians of medieval women are still delving into archives and finding there remains much more to discover. Moreover, once there, they are increasingly willing to apply new questions and ways of reading to the sources, thus finding new ways to answer questions that may have previously seemed intractable.

Yet we still need to answer de Pizan's question: "Who are women?" or, rather, "What do we mean by 'medieval women'?" That is, how did European people of the era ca. 1000–1500 understand the concept of *woman*? The *Etymologies* of Isidore of Seville (ca. 560–636 C.E.) might seem as good a place as any to look for the answer, although it turns out to be typically idiosyncratic:

> A man (*vir*) is so called, because in him resides greater power (*vis*) than in a woman—hence also "strength" (*virtus*) received its name—or else because he deals with a woman by force (*vis*). But the word woman (*mulier*) comes from softness (*mollities*). . . . These two are differentiated by the respective strength and weakness of their bodies. But strength is greater in a man, lesser in a woman, so that she will submit to the power of the man; evidently this is so lest, if women were to resist, lust should drive men to seek out something else or throw themselves upon the male sex.[21]

It's a curious brand of logic, yet one that is enduringly irresistible, to define an entity by appeal to a purported linguistic origin that, conveniently, can be made to back up a kind of biological essentialism (men are stronger than women), which in turn justifies an existing gender regime (women should submit to the power of men). Isidore could thence have drawn his argument into a social or legal framework (men have the right to rule over women) but, instead, opts for a line that seems rather more unexpected to modern eyes: it is essential that women not be strong enough to resist the sexual advances of men, even when taken "by force," because men's lust would otherwise quickly lead them to another outlet—even to other men!

Isidore adds further detail to his account of woman by turning from the Latin *mulier* to its synonym, *femina*, which he derives

> from the parts of the thighs (*femur*, plural *femora* or *femina*) where the appearance of the sex distinguishes her from a man. Others believe that through a Greek etymology *femina* is derived from "fiery force," because she desires more vehemently, for females are said to be more libidinous than males, both in human beings and in animals. Whence among the ancients excessive love was called feminine (*femineus*) love.[22]

Standing at a turning point between the eras that we, in conventional historical periodization, imagine as ancient and medieval (he has often been called the last scholar of the ancient world), Isidore presents a construction of femininity that would in many respects endure to the end of the fifteenth century at least, even while it lost its most distinctly classical element (that is, the sense that without women to submit to them, men would simply have sex with one another).

In the mid-thirteenth century, the Franciscan scholar Bartholomaeus Anglicus (before 1203–72) drew heavily on Isidore's work in his *De proprietatibus rerum* (ca. 1240), but also on St. Augustine and medical and scientific writing by Aristotle (in its then recent Latin translations) and Constantine the African to compile a much fuller account of sex and gender differences between male and female. In "complexion," a male is hotter and drier than a woman, and therefore possesses the formative virtues of shaping and working, where the cold wet female possesses passive material qualities. The sinews and brawn of men are stronger and able to carry out heavy works and deeds. Their bones, too, are stronger; their joints larger and more "sad" (steadfast); and their hearts are large which causes them to have more blood and spirit, "and so for great abundance of blood a man is more bold and hardy than a woman." His strength of heart and dry complexion means that he does not menstruate; rather any excess moisture in his body is turned into body hairs, or used up in physical labor or through the strength of the heart. From such physical distinctions, Bartholomaeus turns easily to differences in character and intelligence. A male is craftier than a female and knows better how to escape traps and perils; moreover, "he passes a woman in reason, in sharpness of wit and understanding." Citing Augustine on St. Paul, he states that man is set before woman "in dignity and worthiness of the image and likeness of God," and so he surpasses her in authority and sovereignty and she is denied the authority to teach in church.[23] His passage on the *puella* (girl) incorporates general definitions of womanhood: softer, paler, smaller and more pliant than a man in body, brighter and more pleasing of face, lighter in wit, merciful and envious, bitter, guileful, but quick in learning, and hasty in "liking of Venus" (that is, lustful); more feeble than man, more busy in feeding and tending her children; more mild, and more loving, yet also more malicious; prone to lie, yet modest (*schamefast*), and slower in working and moving.[24]

Isidore's vision of woman as, primarily, the weaker sex, defined by their strong sexual appetite and submission to men, was thus built upon and extended by later medieval scholars such as Bartholomaeus with the addition of authoritative notes from scripture, church fathers, and Aristotelian theories of physiology. Ideas about the body thus underlie medieval medical thinking on sex differences, but their proponents would have been puzzled by modern distinctions between sex and gender. It is the coldness and wetness of woman's body, comparative to man's, that creates not only her physical characteristics (such as weakness, sexual ardor, and menstrual flux) but also her character and intellect. Authors such as Bartholomaeus and his English translator John Trevisa seem to have been little troubled by the anomalies and inconsistencies their model imposed; thus, a woman was mild, but also bitter; quick to learn, yet not worthy of authority to teach.

Conspicuously absent from these passages, yet not from wider medieval discourse on femininity, was the figure of Eve. As recounted in the book of Genesis, Eve was created from Adam's rib as a helper fit for him and promptly succumbed to the serpent's temptation, disobeying God's order not to eat the fruit of the tree of knowledge. Eve's culpability for the Fall became a commonplace of medieval theology and literature. In the late fourteenth century, Geoffrey Chaucer put a catchy version of this notion into the mouth of his rebellious Wife of Bath (though she, of course, reviles all such misogynist tropes) when she describes the favorite book of her fifth husband, the one-time scholar Jankin:

> One night Jankin—that's my lord and master—
> Read in his book as he sat by the fire,
> Of Eva first, who through her wickedness
> Brought the whole human race to wretchedness,
> For which Jesus Himself was crucified,

He Who redeemed us all with His heart's blood.
Look, here's a text wherein we plainly find
That woman was the ruin of mankind.[25]

Woman's guilt in bringing sin upon the whole human race was reinforced in many medieval visual representations of the Fall, as it became conventional to depict the serpent as female as shown in Figure 0.1. It was a short step from blaming Eve for the loss of Eden to marking all women as forces for wickedness and chaos, as Marbod, the bishop of Rennes in Brittany (ca. 1035–1123), did in the early twelfth century: "Woman is the unhappy source, evil root, and corrupt offshoot, who brings to birth every sort of outrage throughout the world. For she instigates quarrels, conflicts, dire dissensions; she provokes fighting between old friends, divides affections, shatters families. . . . she dislodges kings and princes from the throne, makes nations clash, convulses towns, destroys cities, multiplies slaughters, brews deadly poisons. She hurls conflagration as she rampages through farmsteads and fields."[26] And on, and on, in this vein.

FIGURE 0.1: Eve and the Serpent in the Garden of Eden. *Mirror of Human Salvation*. Chantilly, Musée Condé, MS 139, fol. 3 recto. France, fifteenth century. Photograph by René-Gabriel Ojéda, courtesy of Réunion des Musées Nationaux/Art Resource, NY.

But it would take a particularly unwary reader not to scent hyperbole, or some other rhetorical play, here. Marbod was one of many medieval intellectuals who were fond of the dialectic practice of posing cases both for and against an argument, and women were sometimes used as their target. Marbod, and other writers such as Jehan le Fèvre, were capable of composing vigorous defamation of the female sex only to turn to its vehement defense in another work (or a few pages later). Thus Marbod's attack on the *meretrix*, which sounds like an exemplum of the worst misogyny, is followed by an encomium on the *matrona* in his next chapter.[27] R. Howard Bloch has controversially argued that medieval misogynist texts were never merely diatribes against the female sex, but rather, because *woman* was the primary focus of language, also offered multilayered explorations of the shortcomings of literature and (male) authors themselves.[28] His ideas were critiqued by many, including Judith Bennett, who found that reducing misogyny to a rhetorical game depreciated its effects upon real women—effects felt by English women squeezed out of the brewing trade in the fifteenth and sixteenth centuries, for example.[29] Yet why should we not allow for both readings? Medieval culture, like any other, was capable of incalculable and interwoven layers of meaning.

We can list numerous virtues as well as vices regularly associated with femininity. Alcuin Blamires's study of medieval literary and philosophical defenses of women identifies several, including chastity, compassion, trustingness, gentleness, courage, guilessness, mercy, pacifism, humility, patience, prudence, piety, kindness, charity, sobriety, moderation, and, most surprisingly, stability (or constancy, unshakability).[30] Alastair Minnis and Eric Johnson in their study of Chaucer's Criseyde add a perhaps unexpected virtue—fear. In attempting to undo earlier authors' calumny against Criseyde as "fickle and wanton," Chaucer "substituted an emotion which, in his view, helped to affirm Criseyde's superlative womanliness."[31] We are used to medieval authors extolling such virtues as feminine peaceweaving skills, mildness, and mercy. These are, for example, inextricably associated with Eve's feminine counterpart and redemption, the Virgin Mary, as shown in Figure 0.2. We may be more surprised to find that for a woman to be fearful was viewed as a fundamental good. Yet, as Minnis and Johnson demonstrate, that imagery is even present in the model of feminine nature held up by Christine de Pizan, though she herself was no shrinking violet:

For women's nature is but sweet and mild,
Compassionate and fearful, timorous
And humble, gentle, sweet, and generous,
And pleasant, pious, meek in times of peace,
Afraid of war, religious, plain at heart.

When angry, quickly she allays her ire,
Nor can she bear to see brutality
Or suffering. It's clear those qualities
By nature make a woman's character.[32]

A cynic, or realist, might comment that nothing could serve a patriarchal culture better than an idealization of feminine fear.

The list of feminine qualities holds some apparent anomalies, for along with timidity, gentleness, and mildness, courage and assertiveness could be prized traits. As Blamires wryly notes, "Medieval culture had a kind of love-hate relationship with the concept of feminine boldness."[33] Authors dealt with the problem, he suggests, by posing women's boldness as a virtue so long as the threats at hand were either to their chastity or to what we might call matters of "national security." Thus figures such as the defiant virgin martyrs, who vigorously repelled the advances of pagan suitors and heroically

FIGURE 0.2: Rogier van der Weyden, *The Annunciation*—detail of the Virgin's face. Oil on wood, Paris, Louvre. Fifteenth century. Photograph by Gérard Blot, courtesy Réunion des Musées Nationaux/Art Resource, NY.

withstood even the most violent torture and mutilations of their own flesh, could stand near the Virgin Mary in a pantheon of Christian feminine exemplars. Such exceptions also account (in part) for the fascination with the Amazons of ancient myth or distant lands and women warrior figures that made regular appearances in chronicles, as well as contemporary women rulers such as Blanche of Castile, queen of France.[34] Admiration for such carefully circumscribed forms of feminine boldness did not by any means imply that wives and daughters living in Christian households were authorized to defy their husbands and fathers.

It is best to make sense of this apparently diverse, and sometimes internally inconsistent, set of feminine virtues and vices by placing them within the framework of what Alastair Minnis has called *structural antifeminism* and Blamires relabels *structural misogyny*.[35] Minnis coins his term by analogy with the modern economist's *structural unemployment*. Like structural unemployment, structural antifeminism acts like a cage to those caught within it; it becomes more than a personal experience (or, in antifeminism's case, outlook) and is self-perpetuating. In a culture suffering from structural antifeminism, legal systems, economic activities, roles within the family, and personal relationships are all affected. It becomes legitimate, for example, for a husband to beat his wife because one of the principles underlying the structure is that the male has rights of governance over the female and this may extend to the use of physical correction or discipline. Because of the imprisoning effects of this structure, "If a medieval writer wished to commend the female sex, she or he inevitably engaged in the traditional gender politics."[36] The concept thus rescues one from the rather bland conclusion that medieval culture saw potential good as well as potential bad in women. If we look again at the list of feminine virtues identified previously (chastity, compassion, trustingness, gentleness, courage, guilessness, mercy, pacifism, humility, patience, prudence, piety, kindness, charity, sobriety, moderation, stability, and fear), we can see that none of these disturbs the traditional gender politics of antifeminism, which prioritized male over female. Quite the reverse: such feminine virtues may overwhelmingly support the status quo. Indeed, they serve antifeminism even more powerfully because they help to veil the facts of underlying antifeminism to the male and female participants in the structure. If a man loves and praises his wife for her gentle, kind qualities and values her moderation and pacifism as a counter to his antagonistic relationships with others—and, indeed, if the wife feels cherished and appreciated for the same qualities—then male rights of governance over women may be further legitimized and structural antifeminism is given license to run indefinitely.[37]

Modern Western feminism has so far found the concept of sexual equality the most effective way to break out of structural antifeminism. Assertions of male and female equality were not unknown in medieval writing but appear mainly in particular theological topoi. St. Paul's assertion in Galatians 3:26–28 of the equality of all in the Christian community ("there is neither Jew nor Gentile, neither slave nor free, nor is there male and female") was explored by Augustine, but perhaps more engaging was the argument that Eve was created from Adam's side rather than from his head or foot as a marker of woman's status as neither man's ruler nor slave but rather companion. "The suggestion of unity, mutuality, and love interpreted in Eve's mode of creation from Adam's *side* was understood as a strategy whereby God meant to rule out absolute gender hierarchy."[38] Blamires notes this interpretation in Hugh of St. Victor's seminal work *De sacramentis* and Peter Lombard's even more important *Sentences*—two mid-twelfth-century works echoed in the fifteenth-century English text *Dives et Pauper*.[39] Apart from such explorations, advocacy of equality of the sexes was so rare as to have been almost unheard of in medieval cultures. Christine de Pizan, in her book of advice for women, opted for a profound pragmatism, advising a married woman to avoid strife with her husband, to "humble herself towards him, in deed and word and by curtseying; she will obey without complaint; and she will hold her peace to the best of her ability." She will attend to her husband's spiritual and physical needs, consult with his doctor, and see that he is well tended by his servants. If he happens to be hard, cruel, and unloving toward her, even having an affair with another woman, a prudent wife will put up with it all, telling herself, " 'You must live and die with him whatever he is like.' "[40] Yet medieval culture was capable of endless subtlety and creativity of interpretation, even within this apparently oppressive gender regime. As Caroline Walker Bynum has so brilliantly demonstrated, the alleged "weakness" and "lowliness" of women could be seen as a virtue, and even appropriated by some men, within a theology which celebrated the humanity, physicality and suffering of the incarnated Christ.[41]

We have thus offered something of an answer to the question of what was a medieval woman, in the sense of the meaning inscribed by contemporaries. There has been little attempt here to move from the realm of ideas about women into the realm of their experiences. Readers will find plenty of material addressing medieval women's social history in the chapters that follow (which survey the dual matters of women's lives and medieval thinking about women) and in the vast scholarly literature on the subject now available and at least partly signaled in this volume's bibliography. This introductory exercise will end by touching on the problem of whether *women* as a collective term remains valid in historical studies.

Not all have been convinced of the value of the study of women in medieval history. Dominique Barthélemy chides "mediocre but prolific writers lacking scientific intention or training" for self-indulgent elaborations of the themes of the "proud and adulated lady, and woman as victim of oppression. But," he continues, "'women' are not a good subject for history in the 'age of cathedrals' or any other period. Social classes were too diverse, and women occupied too many different positions (wives, sisters, mothers, and so on), to permit a unitary treatment. We must examine relations between groups of men, groups of women, and groups of both sexes."[42] His tone is a little more contemptuous than necessary, but the central question is valid: Are women a good subject for study in the medieval or any other period? The linguistic turn of 1980s and 1990s historiography made feminist historians similarly uncertain. When deconstructionist feminist philosophers such as Judith Butler and Denise Riley queried whether the category "women" signified anything more than a set of cultural conventions, it became difficult to justify the project of women's history. How could one write the history of a subject so shifting, amorphous, and slippery?[43]

For a cultural history, the answer to Barthélemy's question must surely be yes, because medieval people clearly identified a category "woman" and associated numerous physical and character traits with her. Once we move beyond ideas about women to women's social, legal, political, economic, and familial experiences, general statements become much more difficult to assert. It has become axiomatic in gender studies to assert the importance of differences within as well as between genders. Thus, factors such as social status, geographic location, age, marital status, and religious vocation must always be taken into account in any study of medieval women.[44] Every contributor to the present collection is attuned to this fact. Yet there were common ideas about women that translated into a certain commonality of experience, even if the shared aspects of femininity were continuously complicated by other facets of identity. Women's status as secondary and subordinate to men of similar standing was practically universal. The guilt of the first woman, Eve, for the Fall, was widely held to stand for women's broader blameworthiness. For those with a little higher learning, women's physically cold and wet natures accounted for a myriad of gendered attributes from menstruation to gullibility. Yet men's closeness to women fostered warm feelings too and also recognition of their essential contribution—as mothers, household managers, business partners and stand-ins, mediators and profferers of wise counsel, or as prayerful and sometimes visionary arbiters of piety. This was not a gender model that advocated equality, much less sameness between men and women, but neither was it simplistically antifeminine. We continue to write medieval women's cultural history—as well as the social, economic, and political histories of their experience—and the voluminous materials we now have to work with, thanks to the labors of countless historians of medieval European women, ensure that our interpretations will become still richer and more subtle. The necessity to embrace differences within as well as between genders—at once to assert the category "medieval woman" at the same time as breaking it apart—may be adapted from Denise Riley's breathtaking account of modern feminist dilemmas:

> That "women" is indeterminate and impossible is no cause for lament. It is what makes feminism; which has hardly been an indiscriminate embrace anyway of the fragilities and peculiarities of the category. What these do demand is a willingness, at times, to shred this "women" to bits—to develop a speed, foxiness, versatility. The temporalities of "women" are like the missing middle term of Aristotelian logic; while it's impossible to thoroughly be a woman, it's also impossible never to be one. On such shifting sands feminism must stand and sway.[45]

It is on such sands, too, that women's history must stand and sway.

To end, as we began: with Christine de Pizan. My battered old 1983 copy of the Picador paperback of her *Book of the City of Ladies* sits by me on the table. A *New York Times* reviewer of the translation, quoted on the back cover, asserts that de Pizan, "while working well within the 15th century mode, has a charming, cunning, angry, thoroughly 20th century voice." It further suggests that the book should bear the label "No Experience Necessary" as one "does not need to be schooled in the Middle Ages to follow, and enjoy, Christine's allegory." It seems doubtful that commentators in the second decade of the twenty-first century would be so confident in any easy equation between fifteenth-century and present-day outlooks, nor so keen to adopt a medieval woman as a spokesperson for contemporary feminism. The caution women's historians have learned to adopt when researching the attitudes and experiences of women of past eras, and hugely increased sensitivity to differences between medieval women as well as between them and women of the present, render such appropriation of past women slightly embarrassing. Let medieval women, then, be foreign to us, even if not unrecognizably other, and engage with their histories not as part of a continuous lineage for modern Western women but to add to our comprehension of the various ways cultures deal with this most fundamental of preoccupations: gender.

CHAPTER ONE

The Life Cycle: The Ages of Medieval Women

CORDELIA BEATTIE

> In the life cycle, as in the Garden of Eden, it is the woman who has been the deviant.
>
> Carol Gilligan, "Woman's Place in Man's Life Cycle"[1]

In recent years, sociologists have criticized the life-cycle theory for its assumption of a series of fixed stages, which everyone passes through, preferring the concept of the *life course*.[2] However, as Deborah Youngs has argued, the cultural expectation in the medieval period was that people would go through life in a predicted order, exhibiting the appropriate behavior for each age.[3] The "ages of man" schema, which divided life into a number of stages, was popular in medieval philosophy, science, literature, and art. If we turn to late-medieval poetry, drama, and art, we see another theme: the "dance of death" in which death could come for any person at any time, which suggests that medieval culture also recognized that not everyone would make it through all the stages. This chapter will discuss how women were represented in both tropes as a way into the topic of how the female life course was viewed in the Middle Ages. Were they seen as "deviants" in comparison with men, as Carol Gilligan—using a very medieval analogy—has argued is the case in much modern psychological theory?

AGES OF MAN, AGES OF WOMAN?

The ages of man schemes varied; by the later Middle Ages, the number of stages ranged from three to twelve, with some preference for seven among English writings and ten in German-speaking areas.[4] Aristotle had divided life into the three stages of youth, maturity, and old age: "Youth is the period of the growth of the primary organ of refrigeration, old age of its decay, while the intervening time is the prime of life."[5] Dante, picking up on this scheme in his *Il convivio* (ca. 1304–7), referred to it as an arc (*arco*) of life with the period of growth (*adolescenza*) lasting until age twenty-five, a period of maturity (*gioventute*) from twenty-five to forty-five with its highest point at age thirty-five, and a period of decline (*senettute*) from forty-five to seventy, although he added a fourth age of *senio* or decrepitude that may last from seventy to eighty.[6]

The arc of life is depicted elsewhere as a wheel, both in psalters and on church walls.[7] In the early fourteenth-century psalter of Robert de Lisle, the wheel is a circle of ten medallions, as shown in Figure 1.1, with the figure at

FIGURE 1.1: The Ages of Man from the "Wheel of Life." *Psalter of Robert de Lisle*. England, ca. 1310. London, British Library, MS Arundel 83, fol. 126 verso. © The British Library Board.

the top—as in depictions of a wheel of fortune—a king, here the *vir perfectus* (perfect man). For Burrow, this is basically a seven-age scheme—infancy, boyhood, adolescence, youth, manhood, old age, and decrepitude (*infans*, *puer*, *adolescens*, *juvenis*, *vir perfectus*, *senex*, and *decrepitus*)—extended by the addition of three further "ages"—dying, dead, and entombed (*infirmus*, *moriens*, and *mortuus*), although banners listing the four ages of *infantia*, *iuventus*, *senectus*, and *decrepitus* are held out by figures in the four corners of the image.[8] All the representations of the ages are male; the only woman depicted is the mother who holds the *infans* on her lap and is the source of the milk to which he refers: "Mitis sum et humilis; lacte vivo puro" (I am tender and lowly; I live on milk alone).[9] In this cycle, man is born, grows up to become the perfect man (a ruler), and then declines. There is no emphasis here on marriage and reproduction, although in some illustrations of encyclopedic texts a young male is depicted embracing a woman; Isidore of Seville had stated in his *Etymologies* that the stage of *adolescencia* (age fourteen to twenty-one) was so named because the individual was mature for procreation.[10]

Elizabeth Sears, in a comprehensive study of medieval depictions of the life cycle, found that artists "would virtually always illustrate the ages of man with men. Only in the fourteenth century and after, in special circumstances, were the parallel lives of women depicted."[11] As Mary Dove has commented, "we need to remind ourselves that 'man' in the Ages of Man is not normally an inclusive term."[12] When we do find examples of life stages being depicted in the feminine form, such as in the pseudo-Aristotelian *Secretum secretorum*, which compared the seasons to stages in the life of a woman, we therefore need to consider carefully what message is being transmitted.

The tradition of drawing links between the ages of man and the four seasons was ascribed to Pythagoras, and as early as ca. 400 B.C.E., a Greek medical treatise attributed to Hippocrates analyzed the four ages of man in terms of four qualities. Spring was linked with childhood and was hot and moist, summer was associated with youth and was hot and dry, autumn related to maturity and was cold and dry, and winter was equated with old age and was cold and moist.[13] This trope can be found in a number of texts, but *Secretum secretorum* was unusual in using a feminine metaphor.[14] The Latin text, a translation of the Arabic *Kitab sirr al-asrar*, is found in about 500 manuscripts dating from the twelfth century onward, and there were also numerous vernacular translations, making it one of the most widely read Arabic treatises of the time.[15] The treatise takes the form of a letter of advice on rulership and routine from Aristotle to his pupil Alexander the Great, and in addition to moral counsel, it provided advice on maintaining health—some of it directed toward time of year, some to time of life. According to the Latin text, in spring the world is like a most beautiful bride, a young girl adorned with many colors on her wedding day ("[Tellus] fit sicut sponsa pulcherrima, speciosa juvencula parata monilibus, ornata variis coloribus, ut appareat hominibus in festo nupciali").[16] In summer, she is like a spouse of perfect age, complete of body and inflamed with heat ("et fit mundus quasi sponsa corpore completa, etate perfecta, calore inflammata").[17] In autumn, she is a woman of full age, indigent in attire, retreating from youth and hastening to old age ("Mundus comparatur femine plene etatis, indigenti vestibus, quasi si recesserit ab ea juventus et festinat senectus").[18] In winter, she is like an old, decrepit woman, stripped of clothing and close to death ("Et tunc est mundus quasi vetula gravida etate decrepita, indumento nuda, morti propinqua").[19] In this treatise, then, woman is positively depicted in the first two ages. In spring, she is very beautiful, but summer is her "perfect age."

The period spanning from the mid-twenties to the mid-forties, usually identified with *iuventus*, was typically considered to be the perfect age of man.[20] Indeed, thirty or thirty-three was usually said to be the perfect age of the body, depending whether Christ's age at his baptism or at his crucifixion was adopted as the ideal.[21] Kim M. Phillips has argued that this view did not apply to females and that their perfect age was maidenhood (teens to early twenties), in late-medieval England at least. It was a stage in which the maiden was seen as sexually and psychologically mature, but she "must also hold onto the virginity required by her pre-marital state" in order to live up to the ideal of perfect womanhood.[22] Phillips cites as an example of the ideal the many representations of the Virgin Mary as a "conventionally desirable young maiden at the moment of her bodily ascension," though she is said to have died at age seventy-two or sixty.[23] In *Secretum secretorum*, it is spring that is depicted as a beautiful young maiden, but summer, the wife, who is said to be of perfect age. Should we make anything of this difference? Perhaps this is about *man's* perfect age: the *Secretum secretorum* texts had an intended male reader (the prince who was being advised), and there was an alternative tradition in which the seasons are personified in male form, which one of the translations of *Secretum secretorum* slips into for spring.[24] However, as Shulamith Shahar has argued, "the link between the symbol and the symbolized is not merely a relationship, not merely descriptive, but a creative one. It imposed a constraining definition upon the body's potentialities."[25] We might therefore profitably consider what message was being sent out by depicting summer, the wife, as of perfect age.

As Phillips also comments, "maidenhood . . . was socially an age of incompletion. In the course of a woman's life it was not hoped that her maidenhood would represent the end or culmination but should instead be a stepping-stone between the shores of childhood and wifehood. In life, if not in imagery, it formed a transitional stage."[26] In the imagery of *Secretum secretorum*, spring is depicted at a point of transition in that it is her wedding day, but she is not yet a wife.[27] Although fewer words were spent describing the appearance of summer, she is said to be "corpore completa"; that is, her body is complete, full, perfect. Is this perhaps a reference to being ready to bear children? While Isidore of Seville stated that the stage of *adolescencia* was so named because the individual was mature for procreation, Vincent of Beauvais's mid-thirteenth-century encyclopedia, *Speculum naturale*, sets the end of *iuventus* at age fifty, the age at which women were widely believed to stop menstruating in the Middle Ages. As Shahar has pointed out, "Needing an obvious biological marker for the end of the youthful stage . . . and finding none in men but only gradual processes, he used the marker which affected only women to define the end of the stage for all."[28] The result of that marker is that the stage then seems to be about procreating. In order to explore this point further, we need to turn to medieval medical views of the development of the female body.

The bride, summer, was also said to be "inflamed with heat." It was thought that children were born with a supply of vital "heat" that dissipated with the years, ending finally with the coldness of decrepitude and death.[29] Summer was the acme of the seasons/ages, being hot and dry. But it should be noted that in medieval scientific thought, heat was seen as "the most fundamental physical difference between the sexes."[30] The superior male was warm and dry, whereas the female was cold and wet. According to Galen, whose views on sexual difference were discussed in universities from the late twelfth century, "the man is more perfect than the woman, and the reason for his perfection is his excess of heat, for heat is Nature's primary instrument."[31] This lack of heat was immediately apparent—it meant the female's reproductive organs were internal rather than external. It also meant females were thought to undergo puberty at an earlier age than males, hence the differences in the ages at which they could marry (twelve for girls, fourteen for boys). A commentator on the thirteenth-century *De secretis mulierum* explained that girls begin to menstruate in their twelfth, thirteenth, and fourteenth years because "at this point the heat of childhood begins to fail" and they need to be purged of excess humidity by way of their menstrual periods.[32] But there was also a belief that females should not conceive for a few years after menarche; for example, Giles of Rome in his *De regimine principum* (ca. 1277–80), which made much use of Aristotle's *Politics*, argued that men and women who procreated too young produced imperfect children who do not live very long, and so he recommended that women wait until they were eighteen and men until they were twenty-one.[33] This sets up a gap between the sexually and psychologically mature maiden of twelve to fourteen, who is capable of marrying and producing a child (spring?), and the female who is seen as physically ready to have a child from age eighteen (summer?).[34]

The characterization of spring as an adolescent—in the four-age scheme, the first stage encompassed the *infans*, *puer*, and *adolescens* of the seven-age scheme—is in line with it being seen as a time that is hot and moist. According to medical literature, the hot and moist qualities necessary for growth made (male) youths generous and hopeful but also victims of passion, leading to loss of reason. Adolescence was characterized as a period of lust.[35] In the *Secretum secretorum* tradition, not only was spring a most beautiful girl, but it was also a time when "the blode meved. . . . It is not bad to vse women ther-yn."[36] Here the text is clearly addressing a male reader. However, the same medical literature also associated all women with lust. Their lack of heat "led commentators to argue that women existed in a condition of perpetual desire."[37] This has implications, as Deborah Youngs has argued, for the different ways in which male and female life stages were viewed:

> For the male, this emotional stage [adolescence] was a temporary life-cycle phase, and, all being well, the adult male's innate rationalism would ultimately triumph. This was not the case with women, who were considered for ever trapped by their lustful bodies and therefore a danger to mankind. As a girl entered her teenage years, her body cooled rapidly and it took on the distinctive characteristics of the adult female, with a body much colder and wetter than the male's. For medical writers, this made women irrational, fickle and indecisive, but did not dampen their sexual ardor.[38]

These negative associations of being cold and/or moist can be seen in the depictions of autumn and winter in the *Secretum secretorum* tradition.

Just as spring was depicted as a transitional moment, autumn—as Dove puts it—"throws retrospective shadows on her perfect age" of summer.[39] The 1422 translation of *Secretum secretorum* by James Yonge, *The Governaunce of Prynces*, makes this point clearly: "Than semyth the worlde as a woman of grete age, than nowe wox a colde and hade need to be hote clothyde, for that the yowuthe is passyde, and age neghyth, Wherfor hit is no mervaile yf beute she hath loste."[40] As youth had gone, so too had her beauty, but old age was also fast approaching; the next stage is anticipated. Yonge likewise elaborates on winter: "In this tyme the world semyth like an olde katte, al overcome with age *and* trauaill, that lyue ne might, for she is al disspoylit of beute and of Streynth *and* vertue" (original emphasis).[41] Not only has the old woman lost her strength and her beauty, but she has also lost her virtue. Although the metaphor here was intended to apply to men too, especially as it was an advice book for princes, it seems telling that the old female body personified autumn and winter, which are described less positively than the first two seasons (Yonge's text actually represents spring as a young man, and some texts did not personify spring, or even summer, despite their source).[42] In a twelfth-century text that uses a masculine metaphor, autumn is seen as bearing the fruits of ripe understanding, fruits that are only produced when the man is no longer young.[43] In the *Secretum secretorum* tradition, though, the focus is on the lost beauty of autumn, rather than on any knowledge that she has acquired over the years. This is in line with much medieval scientific, philosophical, and theological theory, which saw man as associated with the rational and woman with the corporeal.[44]

If we return to the more positive representations in *Secretum secretorum* of spring and summer, it could be argued that the purpose of a woman was to be beautiful to attract a husband so that they could procreate once she had reached her perfect age. Taken to its logical extreme, as Jessica Cooke has argued, this means that "a woman was only useful in the generative stages of her life," and the postmenopausal woman was intrinsically useless.[45] The negative depictions of autumn, but especially winter, fit with a medical (as well as popular) tradition that saw the postmenopausal, old woman as harmful and dangerous.[46] According to *De secretis mulierum*, "the retention of menses engenders many evil humors. The women being old have almost no natural heat left to consume and control this matter, especially poor women who live on nothing but coarse meat, which greatly contributes to this phenomenon. These women are more venomous than others."[47]

The female life course as represented in the *Secretum secretorum* tradition seems quite short when compared with the male life course of the de Lisle image, and not just because ten stages had been compressed to four.[48] In the first stage of spring, she is represented as a maiden on her wedding day, wearing a beautiful gown so that men might admire her. We then see her as a spouse of perfect age in the summer, perhaps only a little older. By the autumn, though, her youth has passed and old age is hastening, and her clothes are purely functional, to keep out the cold. And in the winter, she is an old hag, naked and near to death. It fits well with Aristotle's view that women, like all inferior things, "reach their end more quickly."[49] He blames their lack of heat as this meant that "while within the mother, the female takes longer to develop than the male does; though once birth has taken place everything reaches its perfection sooner in females than in males—*e.g.*, puberty, maturity, old age."[50] So for Aristotle, women died earlier than men. This appears to have been generally the case in the Middle Ages, in part because of maternal mortality but perhaps also because they were more commonly carers for the sick. However, once they had passed childbearing age, "the gap between the life expectation of men and women shrank, and sometimes women's life expectation exceeded that of men."[51] Indeed, Albertus Magnus seemed to feel compelled to disagree with Aristotle on this point, commenting that "the male has a longer life span naturally, but . . . because the length of a natural life span depends on the radical moisture and a tempered heat . . . the female has a longer life span *per accidens*, because she does not work as hard and thus does not consume so much, and she is cleansed more by the menstrual flow and is less debilitated by sexual intercourse."[52] This "accidental" view of life ties in with another genre in the Middle Ages, that of the *danse macabre*.

"WIDOWS, WIVES, AND VIRGINS/AND OTHERS"

The *danse macabre* tradition was popular in the late Middle Ages. The theme is the sudden but inevitable event of death, the great social leveler, as a variety of characters—old and young, rich and poor—are compelled to join in a dance of death. It reveals that while medieval culture did expect people to go through life in a predicted order, it also recognized that not everyone would go through all the stages. The theme can be found in a number of texts in the fourteenth century, such as the Catalan poem *Dansa de la mort*, and is also thought to have had a performative dimension. By the fifteenth century, it had a visual tradition, primarily in northern Europe, in fresco cycles, manuscript illuminations, and woodcut prints, often accompanied by text in verse form.[53] The earliest is thought to be a large mural on the charnel walls of the Church of the Innocents in Paris in 1424–25, accompanied by French verses attributed to Jean Gerson and known as the *Danse macabre des hommes* (hereafter *Dmh*). It was only after 1482 that this text appeared with the *Danse macabre des femmes* (hereafter *Dmf*), in print and manuscript form.[54]

The *Dmf* survives in five manuscripts, one of which contains an illumination of each female figure, and two printed editions.[55] In all these versions, it accompanies the *Dmh*. The male version has between thirty and forty-one roles, ordered "from the most powerful (Pope, Emperor) to the least powerful (Franciscan, Child)," the female one between twenty-eight and thirty-six, but many are not counterparts of male characters.[56] According to Ann Harrison, the *Dmh* "served as a model in general form, tone, and content," but "the choice of some roles [in *Dmf*] must have fallen to the author due to the lack of symmetrical female figures."[57] The profusion of female roles suggests that an analysis of how this model was adapted to apply to women will shed further light on how the female life course was viewed.

I shall discuss the illuminated manuscript that depicts the following thirty-six female characters, which is undated but from the late fifteenth century:[58]

1. Queen [*royne*]
2. Duchess [*duchesse*]
3. Regent [*regente*]
4. Knight's Wife [*femme du chevalier*]
5. Abbess [*abesse*]
6. Squire's Wife [*femme de lescuier*]
7. Prioress [*prieure*]
8. Damoiselle [*damoiselle*]
9. Townswoman [*bourgoisse*]
10. Widow [*femme veufve*]
11. Merchant Woman [*marchande*]
12. Magistrate's Wife [*ballive*]
13. Virgin [*pucelle*]
14. Theologian [*theologienne*]
15. Newlywed [*nouvelle marie*]
16. Pregnant Wife [*femme grosse*]
17. Old Maid [*vieille damoiselle*]
18. Franciscan Nun [*cordeliere*]
19. Friendly Wife or Gossip [*femme dacueil*]
20. Wetnurse [*nourrice*]
21. Shepherdess [*bergiere*]
22. Woman on Crutches [*femme aux potences*]
23. Village Woman [*femme de village*]
24. Old Woman [*vieille*]
25. Regrator or Resaleswoman [*revenderesse*]
26. Prostitute [*femme amoureuse*]
27. Bathhouse Attendant [*garde dacouchees*]
28. Young Girl [*ieune fille*]
29. Nun [*religieuse*]
30. Witch [*sorciere*]

31. Bride [*espousee*]
32. Pampered Wife [*femme mignote*]
33. Chambermaid [*chamberiere*]
34. Recommending Woman [*recommanderesse*][59]
35. Religious Hypocrite [*bigote*]
36. Fool [*sotte*]

Although the list seems to start with the most powerful, from the queen to the prioress, the ordering from then on looks less clear-cut. The opening verse gives some indications as to what factors might have been at work:

Come dames and damoiselles,
From world and cloister
Widows, wives, and virgins [*Veufes mariees et pucelles*]
And others without exception,
Whatever your condition
You all will dance in this Dance.[60]

In the first line, women are addressed as "dames" and "damoiselles." These terms designate high-status women, so social status was still of importance. The second line refers to the division between religious and secular types, so function remained a key element. There is then a reference to women as widows, wives, and virgins, which leads us to expect divisions according to marital status (with the ordering of "Veufes mariees et pucelles" suggesting that life stage was a key factor as the widow is the one we might expect to die first). There is also a reference to "others," so we might anticipate some miscellaneous categories.

The manuscript starts with a number of roles that have a male equivalent (with the exception of the Regent).[61] After that, the next three "additions" are the Widow, the Virgin, and the Newlywed.[62] Is this the introduction of a maid-wife-widow schema? In the printed editions, the ordering is different, and so the new additions run as follows: Widow, Bride, Pampered Wife, Virgin, then Newlywed.[63] What has changed is that in the manuscript the sections dealing with the Bride, the Pampered Wife, the Chambermaid, and the Recommending Woman are interpolated toward the end of the manuscript between the Witch and the Religious Hypocrite, perhaps so that "the dance does not end with a series of essentially negative perspectives on women," as Sandra Hindman has argued.[64] These additional categories and others (such as the Young Girl and the Old Maid) show that if the maid-wife-widow schema is being applied, it is not being done so in its most simple form. Before we explore this, we first need to examine the genealogy of the maid-wife-widow model.

The maid-wife-widow model is usually seen as the dominant classificatory scheme for medieval women, far more relevant for women than the "ages of man" scheme.[65] However, its ubiquity in part stems from the similarities shared by two different models, which are both used in the medieval period: a *life-stage* model of maid-wife-widow and a *hierarchical* model of virgin-widow-spouse, which dates back to discussions of chastity in the writings of the early church fathers. The latter model, as used in the writings of Jerome, Ambrose, and Augustine, is a hierarchy of the saved based on a person's state of chastity at point of death; as John Baldwin has put it, the division is of those who never have done, those who have stopped, and those who do.[66] Based on the parable of the sower in Mathew 13:3–23, virgins merit a hundredfold reward, widows a sixtyfold reward, and the married a thirtyfold reward. This model is about fixed states, the state of chastity that the person occupied at the end of his or her life; it is also a model that might be applied to men as well as women. In contrast, the maid-wife-widow scheme refers to *female* life stages. The maid or virgin (these terms and their variants are often used interchangeably in medieval texts) in this model is the young woman who would usually go on to marry and become the wife and then, if her husband predeceased her, become the widow, and perhaps, if she remarried, return to being a wife.[67] It is thus about *temporary* stages in a woman's life. While such schemes look similar, they are in fact classifying people from very different perspectives.

An early use of the parable of the sower can be found in Cyprian of Carthage's *De Habitu Virginum* (ca. 249): Cyprian asserted that martyrs would receive the hundredfold reward and virgins the sixtyfold.[68] It was when martyrdom became less common after the age of persecutions that it was increasingly displaced from the top of the hierarchy, and, as virgins moved to the top, marriage became the lowest of the three states from the fourth century onward.[69] Bernhard Jussen maintains that it was the writings of Jerome, Ambrose, and Augustine, as part of a dispute with a Roman ascetic called Jovinian, that not only used the virgins-widows-spouses formula but also built up "a stock of rhetorical formulas and images of society, exempla, and associations" around it, with the result that it was "treated for almost a millennium as the vocabulary of the moral order."[70] Jovinian argued against this notion of hierarchy; for him, all baptized Christians, whether virgin, widowed, or married, were equal and would receive the same reward in heaven, whereas Jerome, Ambrose, and Augustine used the hierarchical model to present a case for total clerical celibacy.[71] The images of the intact virgin and the chaste widow were put forward as models to which the clergy should aspire.[72] For Jo Ann McNamara, it was the growing communities of female widows and virgins in the first three centuries, women who dedicated their chastity or virginity to God, that forced the early church to promote first celibacy and then virginity, hence the predominantly feminine imagery in the writings of the church fathers.[73] But the intention of the model was to encompass all of the saved, male and female, and the debate was particularly concerned with the male clergy.

The period from the mid-twelfth century to the fourteenth century is a particularly important one in Christianity's development. In the universities, the new disciplines of biblical studies, theology, and ecclesiastical jurisprudence led to attempts to make sense of inherited texts, such as those of the early church fathers, to coordinate them into systematic accounts and to apply theological principles to the contemporary world.[74] For Pierre Payer, it was in the thirteenth century that theology "came into its own," chiefly at the University of Paris under the influence of Albertus Magnus, Bonaventure, and Thomas Aquinas.[75] The treatises produced were influential across Western Christendom, and in these one can find both the continuation of the tripartite, hierarchical model of chastity and further development. Chastity was now seen as a virtue to be promoted for all of society, whatever their chosen way of life.[76] As a result, chastity was discussed in relation to *temporary, life-cycle phases* as well as lifelong states. Albertus Magnus in his thirteenth-century treatise *De bono* first divides chastity into the three states of virginity, widowhood, and marriage. He considers all these states to apply equally to men as to women. Virginity merits the most attention and is subdivided into four types: first, the innate virginity of infants before the age of reason; second, the virginity of individuals who have not taken a religious vow of chastity; third, virginity that is dedicated to God through a vow or firm proposal; and, fourth, that of foolish virgins (those whose behavior is too extreme or their dress inappropriate). Of these four, he says that only the third type—the lifelong virgin—is worthy of praise, although the first and second have "bodily fairness."[77] The conclusion is that virginity in its ideal form consists of physical integrity, the will to safeguard it, and the dedication of that resolve to God. He points out that "if one inspects the original works (*originalia*) of the saints [Ambrose, Augustine, and Jerome] they will be seen only to speak of virgins who profess virginity for the sake of God."[78]

Some of the religious compilations and manuals of instruction for priests and the laity that proliferated after the Fourth Lateran Council of 1215 similarly make reference to both the threefold model of chastity and possible subdivisions and would have found a wider audience than the treatises of university masters.[79] The late thirteenth-century Anglo-Norman *La Compileison* contains a chapter on "the five degrees of chastity which are found in virginity and in widowhood."[80] Of the five degrees of virginity, the first is "promised by vow to God" and "is the highest before God"; the second also relates to lifelong virginity but unvowed.[81] The third and fourth degrees relate to those who have not decided or have not yet considered whether they will marry or remain virgins. The fifth is of the virgin who intends to marry, and her degree before God is lower than that of a chaste married woman (*bone femme ki est marie*) in that "she does not know whom she wishes to have and the woman who is married does not seek anyone other than him to whom she is joined."[82] (This text feminizes the states of chastity, but this is not the case in all such works.)[83] Vidual chastity is similarly elaborated upon; married chastity was just referred to within the discussions of virginity and widowhood, as illustrated previously. While this text is interested in ranking types of virginity and chaste widowhood, it also makes it clear that not all types of virginity and chaste widowhood are better than married chastity. As in the writings of the church fathers, it is lifelong virginity that is best, and life-stage virgins are actually rated lower than the chaste married: it is better to be a chaste wife than a flighty girl. This is not to say that the religious were not interested in life-stage virginity, but this positive treatment of marriage reflects a broader move in religious discourse by the twelfth century to celebrate the role of marriage in earthly life.[84]

The next example, Guibert of Tournai's *ad status* sermon collection, differs in that it does not purport to be an explicit discussion of chastity, but advice to different groups of people.[85] One of the earliest *ad status* sermon collections is Alan of Lille's late twelfth-century *Ars praedicandi*, which offers summaries of appropriate sermon material, structured according to particular groups. It addresses the poor, the rich, soldiers, public speakers, the learned, prelates, princes, cloistered monks, and the religious, before turning its attention to the married, the widowed, and virgins. The emphasis in the sections for the latter three groups is on chastity: that for the married advises men to avoid sexual sin, even with their wives; that for the widowed advocates chastity for widowed women; and the sermon to virgins recommends lifelong virginity to female virgins, specifically nuns.[86] Guibert of Tournai's text differs in a number of ways, one of which is how he uses the categories of virgin, widow, and spouse. It is a more substantial collection, which offers eighty-eight full sermons, some of which he said were for men, some for women, and some for both sexes (including some for servants).[87] Those for women are divided into four categories: married women (three sermons), widows (one), virgins and young girls (nine), and nuns and the female religious (one). The separation of religious from secular women means that Guibert's nine sermons *ad virgines et puellas*, the largest group of his sermons for women, were by and large aimed at life-stage virgins (in contrast to Alan of Lille's material for virgins). In Jenny Swanson's words, "Two of these [sermons] discuss the need for chastity . . . one discusses the value of literacy and basic medical knowledge, and warns girls against laughing in church, three discuss the perils of make-up and of the interest in fashion and perfume, one covers preparation for marriage, and one the dangers of wealth."[88] The advice proffered, then, is about what conduct was desirable in a young, unmarried woman. The sermons to married women similarly cover practical matters such as managing the household as well as marital chastity, whereas the single sermon to widows focuses on chastity.[89] In this text, while the life-stage model seems to predominate for women, the moral associations of the categories maiden, wife, and widow, particularly the importance of chastity for all three categories, have clearly not been lost.

Thus, it is not that, over time, the life-stage model replaced the hierarchical model.[90] While the two schemes are, at the theoretical level, very different, the more that religious authors sought to interact with the world around them, the more the two intersected. In the texts produced from the mid-twelfth century onward, religious authors wanted to recommend the virtue of chastity to all. Chastity was therefore discussed in relation to temporary phases in a person's life, as well as states to be occupied until death. The result was that there was more than one understanding of the categories virgin, wife, and widow.

We can now return to the *Dmf* to assess the place of the maid-wife-widow schema in the manuscript. It is not just that there are categories that stand outside this tripartite model, but that its constituent parts have been subdivided. In addition to the Virgin, there is also a Young Girl, a Damoiselle, and an Old Maid; we might also include under the umbrella of "virgin" religious women who had likely dedicated their virginity to God, such as the Nun and the Franciscan Nun, but they, like the Abbess, have male equivalents in the *Dmh* and so function here as representatives of religious roles.[91] If we move onto the "wife" part of the maid-wife-widow schema, there are again a number of subdivisions. There is a Bride, a Newlywed, a Pregnant Wife, a Pampered Wife, and a Friendly Wife or Gossip, although the last two are clearly character attributes rather than life stages. There are also the wives of a knight, a squire, and a magistrate, but, as with the religious women, they have male equivalents in the *Dmh* and so function as representatives of social groups. The widow seems more straightforward, although there are a number of figures that represent the older woman here (the Old Woman and the Old Maid, but also the Woman on Crutches and the Witch). In order to understand what lies behind the subdivisions we need to look at some of the characters in *Dmf* in more detail.

Pucelle literally means "maid(en)," but there are indications that she represents the (unvowed) lifelong virgin (the second of the five degrees in *La Compileison*). She has long, flowing hair and is of adolescent appearance, as in the idealized representations of maidens that Phillips has discussed.[92] Her arms are crossed on the breast, left uppermost, a gesture that signified humble submission in religious iconography. Death tells her, "Virginity is very pleasing to God."[93] In the printed editions, she is called *pucelle vierge*, the second term specifying "virgin" as a subset of young girls.[94] By contrast, the Young Girl (*ieune fille*) is more of a child; she is about half the size of Death who tries to lead her away, whereas the Virgin was just a little smaller than Death and most of the female figures are of similar height.[95] Death refers to her "tiny arm" and comments, "Death doesn't spare . . . Big or small."[96] The girl addresses her mother (instead of Death) in three of the five manuscripts and asks her to take care of her doll. The Young Girl, then, can be equated with Albertus Magnus's category of infants, with their innate virginity, or the fourth degree in *La Compileison*, of those who have not yet considered whether they will marry or take a vow. For the *Dmf*, though, it is clearly her age rather than her virginity that is of importance; in the male text the corresponding figure is *enfant*, depicted in a cradle.[97]

Damoiselle is a term that not only referred to an aristocratic lady, but to one that was unmarried and generally young, so a high status maiden; some versions of the *Dmh* feature *le damoiseau*, usually translated as a squire, rather than *l'escuier*.[98] The emphasis in *Dmf* is on the Damoiselle's social status but also her marital eligibility. The text refers to dancing, singing, banquets, and tournaments, suggesting that the Damoiselle was in the midst of her courtship season.[99] She can thus be associated with the virgin who intended to marry, the fifth degree in *La Compileison*. Perhaps of greater interest is the figure known as *vieille damoiselle*, the Old Maid, in that she reminds us that the maid-wife-widow schema depends for its momentum on marriage. If we compare the two images, as shown in Figures 1.2 and 1.3, the Damoiselle wears a style of dress that was much in fashion at the end of the fifteenth century—a long robe with a square collar, wide sleeves, a full skirt, fitted at the waist and worn with a ropelike belt—made of a rich, brocaded cloth, probably satin, and lined with ermine, similar to those worn by the Queen and the Duchess in this manuscript, and a black hat called a *chaperon*.[100] The Old Maid also wears a high-status dress and headdress, but they are very different from those worn by the other women. The narrow-sleeved robe, with a round collar and belted at the waist with a wide-band, and the conical hat date her clothing to before the end of the third quarter of the fifteenth century, suggesting that she bought this clothing in her youth.[101] The text also refers to her "old-fashioned headdresses" and addresses her as "Sa damoiselle du bon temps," a damoiselle from the good old days.[102] The implication is that she had taken part in similar courtly activities to the Damoiselle in the past but had not found a marriage partner. Her face reveals her to be a woman of some age, although she stands upright in contrast to the Old Woman, as shown in Figure 1.5. Death tells her, "Old women are close to death," and she responds, "I have surely overstayed my time."[103] While the Old Maid could also be associated with the virgin who intended to marry, it is clearly her age and marital status that are of import in the *Dmf*.

The figure of the Old Maid is also significant because there are not many medieval representations of older and lifelong single women, despite historical demographers telling us that such women were to be found in the later Middle

FIGURE 1.2: The *damoiselle*. *The Danse Macabre des Femmes*. Paris, Bibliothèque nationale de France, MS fr. 995, fol. 28 verso. © Bibliothèque nationale de France.

FIGURE 1.3: *Vieille damoiselle. The Danse Macabre des Femmes*. Paris, Bibliothèque nationale de France, MS fr. 995, fol. 33 recto. © Bibliothèque nationale de France.

Ages.[104] It has been argued that much of northwestern Europe, from at least the late fourteenth century, had key elements of what John Hajnal called the "north-west European simple household system."[105] In this model, both men and women marry "late" (in their mid to late twenties), they set up their own household on marriage, before marriage they often circulate between households as life-cycle servants (from the age of twelve), and a significant proportion never marries. Single women are found in significant numbers in northwest European towns, where there would have been more employment opportunities for them than in rural areas (nunneries were only really an option for the wealthy). Women in Mediterranean Europe, in contrast, tended to marry in their late teens or early twenties, often straight from their natal households, to men who were usually in their late twenties or early thirties, and there were very few people who never married. Female servants were less numerous in this region and more likely to be very young (under fourteen) or older, married, or widowed. Elite women tended to follow the latter model, regardless of region, although in northwest Europe there is evidence of aristocratic girls going into service in households of comparable status.[106]

When we do find occasional representations of older single women, they largely entail a quiet life of religious contemplation. Christine de Pizan's early fifteenth-century conduct manual, *Le livre des trois vertus* (*The Book of the Three Virtues*), argues that lifelong virgins should behave differently from life-cycle ones: "Just as there is a difference in their intention, there should likewise be a difference in their clothing, circle of friends and way of life, for to those women who have firmly decided never to lose their virginity belongs a most devout and solitary life."[107] Similarly, the Middle English poem, "The Good Wyfe Wold a Pylgremage" (late fifteenth century), advises:

> Yfe þou wylt no hosbonde have, but wher thy maydon croun,
> Ren not about in eueri pley, nor to tawern in tovne.
> Syt sadly in þin arey; let mournynge be þi goun.[108]

The lifelong virgin should act and dress soberly, as if in mourning. However, if we read against the text, paying attention to the behavior that the poem wants to eradicate—as suggested by Felicity Riddy for a similar poem, "What the Goodwife Taught Her Daughter"—then we find a concern that unmarried women would be out on the town, going to pubs and other entertainments.[109] A misericord carved for Bristol Cathedral (then abbey) in 1520 might also be a negative depiction of the never-married woman: a naked woman leads four leashed apes to the jaws of hell, where a devil grabs hold of her.[110] This appears to be an early depiction of what is a popular written motif in the late sixteenth century, that women who reject marriage "lead apes in Hell," suggesting eternal damnation; the nakedness and the apes might imply the sin of lechery.[111] The urban setting of the latter two examples seems significant given what has been outlined about marriage patterns. They perhaps relate to lower status women than the Old Maid of the *Dmf*. Christine de Pizan pointed to the existence of working single women with her comment, "*If it is necessary for them to do any work to make a living or to be a servant anywhere*, they ought to see to it that all their other work comes after they have done their necessary labor of devout prayers in the service of God" (my emphasis).[112]

Are lower status never-married women to be found under the guise of other labels in *Dmf*, then? We might consider the prostitute, for example; Ruth Karras has argued, "In medieval Europe with its strict classification of women as virgins, wives, and widows, any woman who did not fit into one of the three categories risked being equated with members of the only identifiable, demarcated group that did not fit: prostitutes."[113] In this text, she is called *femme amoureuse*, rather than a more pejorative term such as *putain*. Harrison has speculated that this was to correspond with "the rather sympathetic tone of the prostitute's portrait. She is to be pitied as she repents the inordinate pleasures of her misspent youth and curses her seducers."[114] Another reading is that she represents the female counterpart to *l'amoreur*, the lover, who is depicted in the *Dmh*.[115] We might also look at the Chambermaid, who is one of only five figures in the manuscript to be wearing a lower-status costume, namely, a white headdress wound into a turban, white fitted forearm sleeves to allow freedom of movement, and a white apron (the white items could be easily laundered).[116] Although she is included as a type of occupational figure—Death comments that "The servant dies as quickly as the master"—her own response emphasizes that Death is preventing her from taking the next step of marriage: "My mistress promised / To arrange my marriage and give me a dowry, / . . . I will be leaving without doing anything."[117] She thus fits the brief of the life-cycle servant. However, if we want a figure of more comparable age to the Old Maid, we must consider the Old Woman. She is evidently a servant—the text focuses on her stealing from her master—but her marital status is unknown (some widows and even married women can be found in service in this period).[118]

While the Old Maid represents the extreme end of the "maid" spectrum, it could be argued that the Bride, rather than being a subcategory of "wife," actually represents the point of transition from maiden to wife. Indeed, we might compare her to spring in *Secretum secretorum*, a most beautiful young woman adorned with color on her wedding day. The Bride has been described as "the most beautiful woman in the illuminations."[119] She has long golden hair and wears a fashionable, brightly colored dress with a gold belt and on her head is a gold crown, as shown in Figure 1.4. The text reveals that Death appeared on her wedding day to tell her, "you will come to bed in another place," a pointed reference to the fact that the marriage will not be consummated.[120] Although the Bride is about to be married, she is in fact still a maiden and is depicted as such with her unbound hair. The crown might be a wedding crown, with associations of fertility, but it is also a key feature in depictions of ideal maidens, with associations of virginity.[121] "The Good Wyfe Wold a Pylgremage" referred to a "maydon croun."

The Newlywed differs from the Bride in that she is dressed in similar fashion to many of the women in the manuscript—a fashionable gown lined with cloth and a hat that four other women wear—and so does not really stand out.[122] One point of interest is that she is depicted in a bedchamber, as is the Darling Wife, whereas many of the other characters are represented outside.[123] Is that another way of distinguishing her from the Bride, who never made it to the marriage bed? Or is it an allusion to the domestic sphere? The Newlywed comments, "Not even half a year ago / I began to keep house."[124] The bed is of significance to the Darling Wife as it is said that she sleeps until dinner, indeed

FIGURE 1.4: The *espousee* (bride). *The Danse Macabre des Femmes*. Paris, Bibliothèque nationale de France, MS fr. 995, fol. 40 recto. © Bibliothèque nationale de France.

she is depicted wearing her bed cap and gown.[125] The Pregnant Wife appears next in the manuscript (and in the printed editions) and has made it a stage further in married life. She is similarly in fashionable attire but with the addition of an apron, which links the image with those of a number of working women (the Wetnurse, the Shepherdess, the Village Woman, the Saleswoman, the Bathhouse Attendant, and the Chambermaid). This might be a comment on her social status as five of the other apron wearers also wear outfits suitable for lower status women (the Saleswoman is the exception).[126] Or it may be that the apron here conceals (or draws attention to?) her stomach; *la femme grosse* in the 1491 printed edition looks pregnant.[127]

If we take the Bride, together with the Newlywed and the Pregnant Wife, and also the Widow, we have something akin to what Stanley Chojnacki has called, in reference to marriage in Venice ca. 1250–1500, "the uxorial cycle": "from bridehood to mature wife and motherhood to widowhood."[128] In the *Dmf*, the Widow takes up the mantle from the Pregnant Wife in that she refers to her many young children for whom she has to provide. She is not depicted as elderly but some women were widowed at a young age, particularly in those areas and parts of society where women tended to marry older men.[129] Christine de Pizan was widowed at age twenty-five, after ten years of marriage and three children, and lived as a widow until her own death about forty years later.[130] The Widow in *Dmf* is simply a woman who has lost her husband. This reminds us that the maid-wife-widow schema should be taken as a whole. As discussed, medieval culture expected people to go through life in a predicted order, exhibiting the appropriate behavior for that stage, whether the model was from childhood to youth to maturity to old age or from maid to wife to widow. The *danse macabre* tradition, by its very nature, focuses on disruption to life's progress so it is perhaps particularly fitting that the Old Maid features therein.

While the Widow is not depicted as elderly, we have seen already that age as well as marital status is an important factor in the depictions of women in the *Dmf*. The Old Woman is featured as a poor old woman; the earliest manuscript just featured the Woman on Crutches. Death addresses the latter as "poor old woman on crutches" ("pouve viele aux potences").[131] The Old Woman's age is symbolized by her leaning on a stick, as shown in Figure 1.5. The Woman on Crutches, as her name suggests, has two sticks and thus represents a further stage of decrepitude, as winter followed the depiction of autumn in *Secretum secretorum*.[132] But if we are looking for the negative associations that we saw in James Yonge's *Governaunce of Prynces*, of the old woman as lacking in virtue, or in the medical tradition of the old woman as harmful and dangerous, we must turn to the figure of the Witch, also not in the earliest manuscript. She is referred to as old ("vieille sorciere") and is depicted with long, unbound and disheveled hair and wearing a baggy, undistinguished gown, thus cutting an unattractive figure.[133] She is also shown waving a straw broom and standing in front of a fireplace, thus keying into contemporary ideas about satanic rituals.[134] By contrast, the Old Woman is depicted carrying a book under her arm, something that she only has in common with religious figures in this manuscript (the Abbess, Prioress, Theologian, and the Religious Hypocrite).[135] The books seem to suggest learning, but the Old Woman was a

FIGURE 1.5: *Vieille* (old woman). *The Danse Macabre des Femmes*. Paris, Bibliothèque nationale de France, MS fr. 995, fol. 36 verso. © Bibliothèque nationale de France.

servant who stole wine from her master's cellar. Is the addition of a book to her representation meant to suggest wisdom, a trait that accompanies age in the ages of man tradition, for men at least?

The latter point leads me to offer a note of caution. The *Dmf*, like the *Secretum secretorum* texts, was embedded in a tradition that took the male as the norm. As Dove remarked, "Where woman's experiences of the ages is explicitly recognized, it is recognized in terms of its deviation from a masculine norm. The supposition that man's experiences of the ages is normative is remarkably tenacious in writings belonging to the Ages of Man tradition."[136] That tenaciousness means that, when we do find examples of life stages being depicted in the feminine form, like the ones discussed in this chapter, we need to consider what might have been carried over from the masculine norm as well as what is new, or, to adapt Dove's language and refer back to Gilligan's, what is "deviant."

CONCLUSION

In this chapter we have considered ages of menarche and menopause, of marriage and motherhood, of widowhood and death. We have thought about the notion of a perfect age or prime of life and of when women were considered old. We have also contemplated differences according to social status and region. However, where it differs from a social-historical approach to medieval women's life cycle is in its emphasis on interpretive schemes, both at the general level (the ages of man, the virgin-widow-spouse, and the maid-wife-widow schemes) and at the specific (the representation of the seasons in the *Secretum secretorum* tradition and the procession of women in the *Dmf*).[137] An analysis of these schemes has revealed some of the different ways in which the medieval woman's life course could be divided up, depending on what factors were considered important, be it age, sexual status, or marital status. These schemes should not be treated as merely theoretical: they were affected by social reality and had an effect on it in turn. Those that created or adapted an interpretive scheme were engaged in an attempt to understand, or explain, or affect social phenomena. Once in existence, a scheme could affect how others saw and interpreted social phenomena. The cultural preference for a maid-wife-widow model over an ages of (wo)man one signals that sexual and marital status rather than age or mental maturity was seen as of primary importance for women in the Middle Ages. This preference would have had a deep and profound influence on their lives, affecting their experiences of growing up, the roles that they took on in adult life, and their position under the law.

CHAPTER TWO

Bodies and Sexuality

APRIL HARPER

In the Old French fabliau *Du con qui fu fez a la besche* (The Cunt That Was Made with a Shovel), the author ends his description of the devil's creation of female genitalia with a curiously paradoxical statement. Although woman's sexuality, and specifically her physical genitalia are dangerous, "and many good men are destroyed because if it, they are disgraced and confounded by it and they've lost their money because of it," one should never "speak anything but good of women."[1] This contradiction is central to medieval attitudes toward women's bodies and sexuality. It stems from classical authors who were popular and influential in the Middle Ages, such as Tertullian who described women as "the Devil's gateway" and yet also as "Brides of Christ," and Ovid who declared women to be "exquisite hell."[2] Medieval authors similarly commented on the paradox that was woman. Marbod, the eleventh-century Bishop of Rennes, described women as a "compound of honeycomb and poison," an opinion that was echoed in the thirteenth-century chronicle of Salimbene, which defines women as "glittering mud, a stinking rose, sweet poison."[3] The contradiction that seems to define women in the Middle Ages is not only pervasive in literature but also has its roots deeply entwined in theological debate and science of the period. In order to understand how woman became viewed as a dualistic being, it is first necessary to understand how medieval society defined her physically, spiritually, and intellectually, before examining how those definitions became a vehicle for determining women's place and treatment in society.

Much of the image of women's bodies and sexuality was formed by scientific theories and theological views of women. Science, in its attempt to address questions of human nature, attempted to define what was male and female and, in this way, heavily influenced societal, cultural, and even religious views. The influence of Greek and Roman philosophers and physicians on medieval science was profound. The Hippocratic doctrine of the four humors was the cornerstone of medicine and arguably of life; the balance of heat, cold, moisture, and dryness made up not only each individual and accounted for diversity of character, body, and health, but also impacted ideas of sex. The scientific theories medieval authors inherited from ancient texts did not always posit men and women as binary opposites—thus allowing for the possibility of intersexual individuals, or *hermaphrodites*, as shown in Figure 2.1—yet the basic principle of sex difference was that men were hot and women cold.[4] Aristotle cited scientific observation as well as factors such as strength and activity to prove that men were possessed of more heat than women. Using nature as a model, he noted the size and power of the male of each species to reinforce his claims of women's physical inferiority.[5] The Roman physician Galen expanded

FIGURE 2.1: Wiligelmo da Modena (fl. ca. 1099–1120), workshop. *Metope with Hermaphrodite*. Museo Lapidaro, Duomo, Modena, Italy. Photo courtesy of Scala/Art Resource, NY.

Aristotle's views, using his experience with dissection to make the claim that due to her cold nature, the woman was, in effect, an incomplete and inside-out (or, rather, outside-in) man:

> The female is less perfect than the male for one, principal reason: because she is colder . . . think first, please, of a man's sexual organs turned in and extending inward between the rectum and the bladder. If this should happen, the scrotum would necessarily take the place of the uterus, with the testes lying outside, next to it on either side; the penis of the male would become the neck of the cavity that had been formed; and the skin at the end of the penis would become the female pudendum itself. . . . In fact you could not find a single male part left over that had not simply changed its position; for the parts that are inside a woman are outside in man. . . . The man is more perfect than the woman, and the reason for this perfection is his excess of heat, for heat is Nature's primary instrument . . . so too the woman is less perfect than the man in respect to the generative parts. For the parts were formed within her when she was still a fetus, but could not because of the defect in the heat emerge and project on the outside and this . . . provided no small advantage for the race; for there needs must be a female. Indeed, you ought not to think that our creator would purposefully make half the whole race imperfect, and, as it were, mutilated, unless there was to be some great advantage in such a mutilation.[6]

Galen's view of women's bodies did eschew the Aristotelian belief that as an extension of their inferior composition, women must also be intellectually and morally inferior to men. The majority of philosophers and physicians sided with Galen. Soranus, a second-century author of a gynecological text, argued that women differed physically from men only in their generative organs.[7] Augustine (354–430 C.E.) confirmed that men and women differed sexually for a divine purpose.[8] This view held through the twelfth century as illustrated by the philosopher Averroes's claim that men and women were "of one kind" and Thomas Aquinas's assertion that women could not be misbegotten or a blunder of nature, as they were part of God's plan.[9] Any attempt to cast them as a mutation or mistake implied God's creation was flawed, which denied the very nature of God's infallibility. For the majority of medieval intellectuals, the only substantive physical difference between men and women was their genitalia and a woman's ability to give birth. Thus, the only thing that defined a woman in opposition to a man also linked her with motherhood—a defining image and role for a woman's body and sexuality in art, literature, and philosophy.

Though such estimations were prevalent, medieval opinions did vary, and, to a degree, we see Aristotle's assertion of moral and intellectual inferiority present in some academic discussions of women and their bodies. Though woman's physical body did not differ widely from a man's, some argued that its humoral composition had undeniably profound effects. Augustine's contemporary, Jerome (ca. 340–420 C.E.), found it impossible to reconcile the contradiction that a woman's soul could be equal to a man's while housed in an inferior vessel.[10] Indeed, woman was made not from God's hands, nor was she animated by his *pneuma* but was made from man's rib, as depicted in Figure 2.2. She was a copy of an original with the attendant degradation of such. The only acceptable woman was one who shed her femininity and became male. The most central part of that refusal of femininity for Jerome was the rejection of woman's innate vice of lust. Jerome, among many other medieval authorities, saw powerful connections between the image of Eve and her medieval daughters. The lust of women was a central theme in many theological writings.[11] Examples include many of the lives of the Desert Mothers, such as Mary of Egypt, who was not only a prostitute but was also given to such rapacious lust that at times she would not charge her clients in order

FIGURE 2.2: Lorenzo Maitani (thirteenth to fourteenth centuries), *The Creation of Eve*. From the Stories of the Old Testament. Relief. Duomo, Orvieto, Italy. Photo courtesy of Scala/Art Resource, NY.

to satisfy her sexual hunger. Women's extreme sexual nature defined them not only in exempla but also in lexicography. In Isidore of Seville's seventh-century work, the *Etymologiae*, he defines the word *female* as having derived from *femina*, meaning "fiery force" because she lusts so strongly.[12]

Two images of the female body emerge from these sources: the necessarily and natural maternal body and the aberrant, sexual body. By the twelfth century, the division was becoming ever more problematic with the rise of the cult of the Virgin Mary.[13] While the sexual and the maternal bodies of women were always somewhat scientifically linked, the Marian paradox of a virgin mother further fragmented the image of women's bodies and sexuality into spheres of acceptability. The theological writers of the twelfth century, including Aquinas, reinvigorated Augustine's claim as put forth in his *Excellence of Marriage* that sex for procreation was the only sanctioned form of sexual activity.[14] However, both canon and secular law recognized the dangers of condoning any sexual activity, especially in women. Cautionary texts warned husbands of the lustful nature of their wives. By the late Middle Ages, church courts regularly punished adulterous couples, often by means of public humiliation, as shown in Figure 2.3. Authors likewise pondered the dangers of inherent lust for women who were without a husband: the unmarried and the widowed. St. Paul's admonition on the matter was often cited in medieval conduct books and penitential guides: "Now to the unmarried and the widows I say: It is good for them to stay

FIGURE 2.3: Man and woman convicted of adultery being punished. They are led through the streets of the town and preceded by trumpeters. Manuscript from Cîteaux. Bibliothèque municipal, Agen (Lot-et-Garonne), France. Photo courtesy of Scala/White Images/Art Resource, NY.

unmarried, as I am. But if they cannot control themselves, they should marry, for it is better to marry than to burn with passion."[15] Remarriage, however, was not always possible or ideal, especially when transmissions of family titles or land might be forfeited. A widow was in a curious position that was at once fragile in its lack of masculine presence—economically, physically, and legally—but could also be empowering in some circumstances by allowing the widow to represent her late husband.[16] Emphasis was placed on channeling a woman's energies into the fruit of sexual activity—her children.

Motherhood, as defined by canon law, was not only the goal of female sexual activity but also one of the few realms in which women could exercise authority, power, and influence. Historical and literary examples testify to the power of the maternal image of the female body. Perhaps one of the most famous examples was that of Eleanor of Aquitaine who was repeatedly reprimanded in chronicles of the twelfth and thirteenth century for her flagrant sexual activity. In fact, her documented affairs so excited medieval chroniclers that some were even prompted to invent fictitious ones to embellish their texts and reinforced the negative image of the brazenly sexual queen. Descriptions of her alleged affairs in the Holy Land with both her uncle, Raymond of Toulouse, and Saladin describe her as a willing participant and, in the case of the latter, the instigator of the adulterous liaison.[17] A highly embellished retelling of the events is found in the *Récits d'un Ménestrel de Reims*. After describing Eleanor's frustrated attempts to rendezvous with Saladin, this text goes on to recount the French barons' advice to their king: "Let her go, for she is a devil and if you keep her any longer we fear she will kill you. And above all, you have no children with her." The author includes his own opinion that "it would have been better to have walled her up; then he could have kept her lands and avoided the bad things that happened afterwards."[18] Themes of the devilish nature of Eleanor's sexuality are coupled in this text with her failure to give the king a male heir, thus doubly damning her aberrant use of her body and sexuality. Her calculated divorce of the French king and subsequent marriage to the younger English king, Henry II, did nothing to enhance her reputation or change the image of her dangerous sexuality.

However, when examining the depiction of Eleanor, a profound change occurs in her image after her second marriage and more distinctly in her widowhood. The first of these changes becomes evident in the years following her marriage to Henry and with the births of her eight subsequent children, five of whom were male. Though Eleanor and Henry's marriage was turbulent, as a mother, Eleanor had found a more appropriate arena in which to exercise her power. The maternal body of the queen, rather than the sexualized one, allowed her to engage in politics and have an active role in securing the Angevin Empire for her sons. Though Eleanor was unable to cast off her reputation as a daughter of Eve, motherhood allowed a fracturing of her image into a compartmentalized sexualized youth, in which she had wrought the destruction of kings, and an acceptable and powerful, asexual widowhood, in which she acted to secure the lands and honor of her sons.[19]

The dichotomy of women that is so frequently found in medieval chronicles, secular literature, and religious texts was, for a long time, rarely challenged by modern historians, who instead often perpetuated these images of women. Even into the mid-twentieth century, much of the scholarship devoted to medieval women followed this fractional image of them into "the good" (e.g., nonsexual or maternal) and "the bad" (e.g., the sexual). On one hand, medieval women were depicted only as stereotypes and *exempla*—historically passive beings whose marriages cemented political alliances and whose bodies gave birth to the men who shaped history. On the other hand, and perhaps even more damning, are the opinions of many scholars who depict women as "ahistorical" beings; their lives were deemed to be largely private and therefore not of historical import.[20]

In their culturally acceptable role as mothers, women were merely conduits for the forces of history. Those women who defied the stereotype and who actively engaged in public history were often belittled and sexually defamed, even in absence of any historical evidence or accusations by chroniclers of the Middle Ages. An excellent example of such degradation is found in the case of the Empress Matilda who waged a nineteen-year war against her cousin King Stephen for the crown of England, though chroniclers of the period decry her actions in transgressing the bounds of her sex by her masculine behavior, not one accused her of sexual impropriety. The future mother of Henry II may have not acted like a lady or even a mother by medieval standards until deep into her son's reign, when he would declare her to be "great by birth, greater by marriage, and greatest of all in her offspring." And though medieval chroniclers were quick to highlight her every fault down to the masculine tone to her voice, not one cast her as a "daughter of Eve." However, modern historians were quick to posit entirely unfounded sexual relationships between her and her male supporters, such as Brian FitzCount, and some have gone so far as to suggest romantic relationships between her and Stephen as motivation for the war.[21] The message is clearly that even an empress fighting a civil war was not doing so out of standard historical motives of acquisition and power, but out of retribution as a spurned lover, or at the very least, that she was only able to recruit the aid of powerful men through her sexuality. This notion remained prevalent until 1991 with the publication of Marjorie Chibnall's work on the empress, in which she details the loyal and dependent relationship between FitzCount and the old King Henry. FitzCount vowed to support Henry's daughter and wrote letters openly stating his support of the empress based on his loyalty to her father and honoring the promises he and the other barons of England had sworn to the king to support his legitimate daughter in her rule and government.[22] Other powerful women, such as Sybil of Jerusalem, had her role in the governance of the most important crusader state reduced to a mere two lines of text in a recently published, widely respected history of the Crusades, which comments only on her infatuation with a young and "swashbuckling" lord whom she foolishly marries.[23] Sybil's position as a female leader of a frontier principality and, more importantly, as the ruler of Jerusalem, as well as her governance, diplomacy, and relations with her own nobles, are summarily dismissed by the author. Her image was reduced to be little more than a sexually motivated caricature and thus historically devalued. Despite recent efforts to explore her reign more fully, this is still the predominant image of Sybil.[24] Some historians went beyond envisioning women as ahistorical beings and went so far as to label them as an antihistorical force, which often challenged the progressive forces of history such as guilds and communes. In this vein, women acted as vestiges of oppressive, outdated, and family-oriented values rather than as promoters of individualistic or community ideals.[25] In this approach, not even the historically accepted role of mother was historiographically condoned. Many historians of the nineteenth and even the mid-twentieth century seemed to have taken to heart the words of the fabliau with which this chapter begins: "disgraced and confounded" by women's fractured images, they transformed the poet's admonition not to "speak anything but good of women" into a policy of simply not speaking of them at all. Those who did address women did so rarely, almost entirely in the context of men and rarely outside women's roles as wife or mother.[26]

However, by the mid-1980s, a new movement in historiography was gaining acceptance: the history of sexuality. This new movement attracted scholars from across a wide range of disciplines and both integrated and at times defied many traditional historiographical boundaries and spheres. The use of nontraditional sources and reexamination of more standard historical works became necessary to glean the infrequent, imbedded, and often serendipitously discovered evidence used by scholars of sexuality. Women's bodies and their sexuality were a new focus of historical enquiry and debate. The rise of third-wave feminism, which began to find firm footing in the early 1990s, challenged the *essentialist* definition of femininity, which often overemphasized the unanimity of the female experience and the homogenous image of women. Instead, new attention was drawn to the complexities of race, sexual identity, economic and class status, cultural background, and national identity. A more fluid idea of gender that embraced the contradictions and change in the image of women arose and heavily challenged not only modern but also historical interpretations of women's bodies and sexuality.

The fractured image of women's bodies and sexuality led to a study of each of those images, roles, and states. Beginning in the 1990s, the newest generation of historians of sexuality and gender began important work investigating several of those states. Using traditional sources such as hagiography, chronicles, and legal texts, they began to construct images of women outside the traditional molds, questioning the definitions of the female body as primarily maternal and female sexuality as intrinsically linked to male sexuality. They have also, more fundamentally, queried the very notion of sexuality in historical perspective.

On a surface level, this task of separation seems impossible in a medieval context. The key difficulty lies in the fact that in the Middle Ages, women's bodies and social identities were universally coupled with their sexuality. Men's bodies and maturity were linked to legal definitions of age that were often associated with fiscal and judicial concerns, such as the age of maturity or age of inheritance. Women's bodies were likewise connected to legal definitions of maturity, but unlike men, a woman's legal age of maturity was explicitly concerned with her sexuality and the sexual maturation of her body. While men were able to enter apprenticeships at age fourteen and to gain inheritance and enter knighthood at age twenty-one, women's age of maturity was more difficult to establish.[27] In her work on medieval maidenhood (as noted in Chapter One), Kim M. Phillips notes that the age between girlhood and marriage was viewed as a "perfect age" for women.[28] The perfect age for men was depicted in law, literature, and art as an age of full physical maturity as well as a certain psychological maturity beyond the wild years of youth. This age was referred to as *juventus* and could extend from the mid-twenties to the forties.[29] Phillips notes that in contrast, this perfect age for women was far younger and linked to sexual maturity. The ideal nature of maidenhood was reinforced by examples such as images of the Virgin Mary who was, according to the Bible, a mature widow by the time of her death, but in art is depicted as a young woman and according to Voragine's account of the assumption was fourteen when she conceived Christ. On the other hand, virgins and martyrs who died well before their teen years, such as the Pearl Maiden, are aged in their representation to appear to be young women in their early teens.[30] The maiden is especially appealing for the Middle Ages as she possesses "all of the virtues of a woman, but none of the vices." However, the virgin also presented a difficulty for medieval society, for although she was physically inferior to men, she was not always subordinate as she lacked a position as determined by a man in her life. The problem of the virgin became even more complex in the case of maidens who did not leave their virginal state and widows who returned to a sexless state as nuns.[31]

Though widows and virgins were linked through their chastity, very different views of their bodies and sexuality emerged. Though virgins were considered to be blessed for their sacrifice and came close to Jerome's ideal of the masculinized woman who had rejected her lust, widows were considered to be doubly blessed for their sacrifice for having known carnal love and forsaken it. John Chrystosom (ca. 347–407 C.E.) claimed that "the widow starts off inferior only to the virgin; but at the last, she equals and joins her."[32] Though the widow was seen to equal the virgin in her sacrifice, indeed surpassing her in self-control, attitudes to each were different. The widow was often seen to fulfill a role of exemplar within the community. Having proved her ability to live within the world, while rejecting its temptations, the widow was given a more public role and mobility than the virgin. Special communities were established, such as the Order of Widows, which was invested with almost clerical powers and became extremely popular with female religious who desired a more active role within the church.[33] The virgin, however, was imagined to lack such fortitude. Having rejected sex without experiencing it, the virgin was understood to occupy a more tenuous state in which she might easily fall prey to her innate vices and give in to seduction. Virgins were not given the mobility or the public role of the widow but were kept in isolation within their homes under the watchful eye of their parents or within secluded communities. Claustration of virgins was seen as necessary from the earliest rules for communities of nuns. In his *Regula virginum*, Caesarius commands that each nun "must never, up to the time of her death, go out of the monastery."[34] Though certain groups were able to enter the community, including priests, the bishop, close family, and visiting dedicated women, each visit was subject to strict conditions. In Caesarius's rule, there is no mention of monks being prohibited from leaving their monastery, and the only prohibited visitors were women, who "shall never enter the monastery, for it is a reserved place."[35] As Lindsay Rudge notes in her work on female religious life:

> These gender-specific regulations reveal a much more active concern over the contact of female religious with the outside world. In part,

> this no doubt reflects patristic attitudes towards the sexual fallibility of women; as Jerome gleefully pointed out, "Diana went out and was ravished . . . unless you avoid the eyes of young men, you shall depart from my [i.e., Jesus's] bridal chamber and shall feed the goats which shall be placed on the left hand."[36]

The latent lust and dangerous sexuality of widows and especially virgins was a concern that could not be allayed even within the cloister. Though actual cases of nuns violating their vows of chastity were extremely rare, stories of lusty widows permeated medieval literature, and churchmen were quick to cite and even invent stories of concupiscent nuns, such as the infamous nun of Watton, whose pregnancy by a lay brother stood as a terrible warning against the sexual nature of women and the need for claustration.[37]

Tension emerged not only due to concern over women's lustful nature, but also over growing female power within convents as well as within the community. The power and control of land and business exercised by the convents contributed to an overall tension that was felt at a local level under secular widows who continued to manage their households and businesses, challenging masculine power and authority. Although they had attained the status promoted by Jerome to throw off their femininity, virgins and widows still presented a difficulty to medieval society as the definition of woman was so intrinsically linked to her body, as wife and mother. How was a woman to be defined if no longer sexual or linked to the sexual stages of her body? "Women who renounced the sexual life were elevated above their natural abject condition to the degree that they almost constituted a 'third sex,' so much did they differ from females in the thrall of Eve's birth pains and submission to husbands."[38] Marriage acted to place women in an inferior position to men both legally and socially, and thus "sexual functioning itself made women subordinate."[39] Without the clear identity that marriage, sex, and motherhood gave a woman, widows and virgins occupied a mysterious and at times difficult position within medieval society.

The bodies of women who defied sexual definition as determined by their relation to men were not a concern limited only to those women who rejected sex, but also to those whose active, though aberrant sexual bodies could not be discussed in terms of marriage or motherhood: prostitutes and women who engaged in female-to-female intimacy. Though these two groups of women may seem diametrically opposed, in many ways they face the same obstacles in the definitions and tensions that surrounded their bodies and sexuality as at once outsiders and yet also "deviant insiders" of medieval society.[40]

The study of female same-sex desire is a relatively new field and one that has witnessed a dramatic change and not a little controversy.[41] While many pioneers of the field including John Boswell and Jacqueline Murray often alluded to the silent nature of medieval texts regarding female intimacy, recent research has expanded the understanding of the nature of female–female love and has also cast light on a variety of sources for studying the subject, including personal correspondence, poetry, legal cases, and etiquette texts.[42] Though the evidence for female-to-female intimacy in the Middle Ages is less accessible than in later history, it is by no means a silent record, nor were women who engaged in or expressed same-sex desire invisible. The images of female intimacy within these sources are fruitful not only for our understanding of same-sex desire in the Middle Ages, but also for what they tell of medieval attitudes toward the bodies and sexuality of these women. One of the most intriguing forms of evidence is in descriptions of the imagined sex acts. Though letters between female lovers display deep emotional attachment and commitment, male attitudes toward female same-sex relations often point out the ridiculous nature of the union and focus on the sex act, rather than the relationship between individuals. Etienne de Fougères, a court poet for the English king Henry II, mockingly described female intimacy: "These ladies have made up a game . . . they bang coffin against coffin, without a poker to stir up their fire . . . They don't play at jousting but join shield to shield without a lance."[43] Female same-sex activities were no more than amusements and possibly even practice for a future heterosexual encounter, as the English poet John Gower described in his work *Confessio amantis*.[44] The description of coffins being banged against one another is not only a disparaging reference to the triangular shape of the female genitalia, but is also a reference to the humoral nature of a woman as essentially cold, which without the heat of a man's seed, was incapable of creating life.[45] Man carried both heat and life-giving sperm. Female–female sex did not heat the body, nor could it produce offspring and thus, in medical thought, was useless and wasteful. The banging together of empty coffins was a fitting image for the pair of cold, empty wombs. What also emerges, as Jacqueline Murray emphasized, is the medieval phallocentric view of sex. "Without a poker . . . without a lance," these women of Fougères' poem are comical. Unlike his description of male–male sex, which he describes as "vile" and for which he recommends "throwing sticks and stones" and execution, he describes female–female sex as "the beautiful sin."[46] Penalties for acts of female-to-female intimacy varied throughout Europe and were often harshest in areas in which Roman law was prominent. In areas that relied on common law, such as England, a woman who committed a sexual act with another woman was given relatively light penance. For example, in the penitential of Theodore, an Anglo-Saxon penitential guide for priests hearing confessions, the penance given to a woman who engaged in same-sex intercourse was to last three years—the same punishment as for masturbation.[47] However, greater penances were prescribed if the woman was married, as she had transgressed her husband's rightful place and command of her body. Likewise, an ever-greater penalty was prescribed if the sex act involved an instrument of any kind. If replacing her husband's place in bed with a woman was contemptible, replacing his penis with an artificial phallus amounted to the usurpation of his power and contested the God-given hierarchy of gender.[48]

The physical body of women who engaged in female intimacy was imagined to be just as aberrant as her sexuality. Texts which sought to explain the phenomenon of the female-to-female desire described the women involved as masculine in thought, intelligence, and voice. Some warned of great physical strength equal to that of a man, and still others described actual growths that would protrude from the vagina like small penises and would allow a woman to penetrate another woman.[49] Her spiritual state was as aberrant as her body. Often women who were engaged in such same-sex relations, and especially those who employed phallic instruments in sex, were also accused of heresy and, in the later Middle Ages and early modern period, of witchcraft: "The conceptual link between sexual deviance and spiritual deviance is clear: both were perceived as deliberate and willful challenges to the natural order established by God and nature."[50] A usually moderate voice in discussions and debates of sexuality, Hildegard of Bingen (1098–79) declared these women to be "vile . . . and impudently usurped a night that was not theirs. 'They' take up devilish . . . alien ways, they are to me transformed and contemptible."[51] Though women were sexually aggressive according to their humoral makeup, within medieval society and especially within the sex act, women were meant to take a passive role. Churchmen such as Peter of Poitiers warned of terrible consequences for women who defied their natural passivity. Disease, social breakdown, and even the Flood were attributed to women taking active roles within sex and thus transgressing both natural and divine boundaries for their bodies and sexuality.[52] Medieval society often interpreted female intimacy and those who engaged in any form of it to be a threat to marriage, society, vulnerable women, and masculine power structures.

Similar fears were at the heart of the image of another group of women: prostitutes, as shown in Figure 2.4. Though women who engaged in same-sex intercourse and prostitutes may seem to be unrelated and even opposed classifications

FIGURE 2.4: Scene in a Burgundian bathhouse (brothel) in 1470. From Valerius Maximus, *Factorum et dictorum memorabiliorum libri novem*. Staatsbibliothek zu Berlin, Stiftung Preussischer Kulturbesitz. Inv. Dep. Breslau 2, vol. 2, fol. 244 recto. Photograph by Ruth Schacht, Manuscript Division. Photo courtesy of bpk Berlin/Art Resource, NY.

of women, the tensions surrounding the bodies and sexuality of the prostitute were greatly akin to those focused on women who expressed same-sex desire. The prostitute's sin was, for the medieval audience, also centered in the vice of lust. Although the exchange of money for sexual acts was acknowledged by courts as part of the definition of a prostitute, or *meretrix*, for both canon and secular law, the primary characteristic of a prostitute was her promiscuity. The necessary number of sexual partners a woman had to satisfy before she was given the title of *meretrix* was debated, but her willingness to engage in sex without discrimination of partner was key to her definition. *Exempla* are keen to depict women who enter and/or remain in the life of a prostitute to satisfy their formidable lust. Financial motivation is rarely discussed in these stories. Those rare tales in which money is discussed depict the woman's demand for payment not as the incentive for the act, but as an accompanying vice of greed.[53]

Though morally corrupt, the prostitute was seen as a necessary part of medieval society. As Aquinas analogized, even a palace needs a sewer. Without it, the whole palace would become befouled.[54] The prostitute channeled sexual depravity away from proper society. She was thought to act as a safety device for men's rapacious desires and to keep them away from women of good repute. She not only saved virgins from seduction and/or rape, but also acted to preserve the moral goodness of matrons.[55] Although the "unnatural" sex acts men craved, such as oral and anal sex, were deplored in canon law, if a man had to act on such desires, it was best to enact them with a prostitute rather than to force his wife into sin alongside himself.

The prostitute thus acted as an outsider to marriage and even society. As Ruth Mazo Karras notes in her work on the subject, medieval law often reinforced this idea of prostitutes as outsiders by grouping them in laws directed toward other marginal peoples such as criminals and beggars and "others" such as heretics, Jews, and lepers. Along with these groups of outsiders, prostitutes were at once ostracized and also regulated. Prostitutes were often literally outsiders as foreigners or strangers to the towns in which they practiced their trade. In some cases, this was demanded by law in order to ensure local women did not take up the trade and to ensure incestuous sex was not accidentally committed by patrons related to the prostitute. Brothels were also set up to contain the "necessary evil" and ensure the separation of prostitutes from decent society. Laws were passed to stop prostitutes from having their own lovers or from marrying. Laws were also put in place to keep the prostitute from wearing certain items or styles of clothing or to enforce the wearing of certain garments that would mark them out from other women. Although these laws seem to be marking the prostitute as an outsider, they also illustrate her curious position as a "deviant insider" who at once posed a threat to "good" society but also was very much a part of it.[56] While brothels were common, many prostitutes also operated out of more common and socially integrated establishments such as rooms within private homes, taverns, and even their own homes. The prostitute was not always a foreigner, and recent work in the subject draws attention to the fact that prostitution was not always a main occupation or only for single women. Some women would participate in prostitution in order to add to their meager earnings or as a way to supplement a family or husband's income.[57] The prostitute was also invited into society through legal cases in which she was considered an expert in cases of impotency and other sexually based concerns. Ironically, the prostitute was included within Christian society when called on to identify Jews or Muslims in the community who may have acted as her clients. Her occupation would allow her to identify these men due to their circumcision. Likewise, the prostitute was perfectly situated to be part of the gossip center of any town or city. Prostitutes acted as go-betweens for lovers and, in some cases, even gave advice on marriage and the suitability of marriage partners.[58]

The body of the prostitute was likewise treated as both an "outsider and deviant insider." Her overwhelming lust, bodily cravings, and the promiscuousness of her body marked it as separate and possibly contagious in its morally diseased state. However, her body was also the concern of society. Laws regarding prostitution attempted to bring this independent female body into the realm of male authority. Outside the bounds of paternal or matrimonial control, the prostitute represented a peculiarity and a concern for medieval society—an autonomous woman. In reality, the majority of medieval prostitutes would have been under the control of pimps or husbands acting as pimps.[59] Independent prostitutes did not represent modern ideals of female independence. Prostitution was low paying, socially degrading, and dangerous. The tremendous demand for houses of refuge for prostitutes, and the number of single, isolated women who claimed to be prostitutes in order to find a place in these houses, speaks to the perilous and dangerous state of the woman with no familial and particularly masculine ties.[60] While dangerous for women, the independent woman was also dangerous to society and masculine authority. Laws were passed in which prostitutes were made "common women" or held in common by all men. This common identity may have limited her threat to masculine society but did little to protect the prostitutes themselves. For example, as all prostitutes were held in common by men, any prostitutes who were raped could not bring their attackers to trial, as they had agreed to take all men as partners by becoming a prostitute and belonged to all men by law.[61] Her physical body was seen as separate from other women's, and physicians noted that prostitutes were not as fertile as other women.[62] Though this may have been because of the impact of venereal disease or just more widely practiced birth control among prostitutes, the medical treatises do not discuss the causation and leave the image of the prostitute's body as one that is perhaps at its very nature deviant from the norm.

Though the evidence gleaned from court records, charters, and legal texts proves extremely useful for studying women's roles in medieval society, for the historian of women's sexuality, detailed information can prove to be frustratingly intermittent and rare. However, there is a profusion of imagery to be found in less conventional sources. The most accessible and popular vehicle for the transmission of the ideas and ideals of women's bodies and sexuality was literature. The concept of literature as a mirror of society is admittedly inaccurate, as it is subject to artistic license, personal taste, and cultural conventions. Yet, in analyzing the image of women's bodies and sexuality, literature is an invaluable tool for understanding the perception and portrayal of the multi-fractured image of women, its symbolism within medieval society, and its place in the wider scientific, philosophical, and theological discussion.

The twelfth and thirteenth centuries were a watershed for medieval literature. The twelfth-century renaissance had contributed to a rise in literacy, education, and an increase in not only Latin texts but also vernacular works. The influx of classical texts, the diffusion of Arabic artistic and literary topoi, and conventions such as courtly love had a profound impact on literature. The creation and expansion of many of the characters and stories that would be dominant figures and themes in literature took place at this time. New forms of literature were also coming into popularity, including the new genre of the fabliau, which is often discussed for its influence on later writers such as Chaucer and Boccaccio but is also important for its burlesque of the romance genre of literature and its divergent, earthy image of love and sex. Although the prudery of the romance and crudity of the fabliau seem to place the two genres in opposition, the dualistic nature of women's bodies and the latent danger of their sexuality are themes common to both.

The inherently dangerous nature of female sexuality as implied by medieval science and some theology is found in the depictions of the majority of female characters. Women of the Arthurian romances are portrayed as not only dangerous but also deadly and destructive. Morgan Le Fee's sexual jealousy motivates her to abduct Lancelot; Elaine, the Fisher King's daughter, resorts to witchcraft to satisfy her lust; and it is ultimately Guinevere's affair with Lancelot that topples the kingdom. Though destructive, women's sexual cravings are depicted as a matter of fact. In the opening of the *Quest for the Holy Grail* (*Estoire del Saint Graal*), the audience is told that despite Lancelot's determination to lead a chaste life after repenting of his sexual affair with Guinevere, within days of returning to court he has also returned to her arms.[63] Women's natural proclivity to sex is also commented on in the fabliaux. Within the *Blacksmith of Crail* (*Du Fevre de Creel*), a blacksmith notices his apprentice has an unusually large penis. In order to test his wife, the smith speaks of the penis and describes it often in her presence. The wife naturally gives into the enticing prospect of sex with the well-endowed young man, promising him new clothes in exchange for his services, and the story ends with sage advice not to place temptation in front of a woman, for lust is her very nature.[64]

Women's sexual craving often places them as the aggressor in the romances, *lais*, and fabliaux. Women in the lais and fabliaux often orchestrate sexual encounters and even go so far as to bribe young lovers, as the wife of the blacksmith illustrates. Even the romances, which are sparing in details of sexual encounters, often depict women in sexually aggressive behavior. For example, after proving himself worthy of Guinevere's affection by beating her captor in battle, Lancelot is given explicit directions how to avoid her guard and by what means he may visit her bedchamber. When he arrives, it is Guinevere who initiates sex by first kissing Lancelot, whom the text makes clear is a virgin.[65] Although the author takes pains to avoid depicting an act of sex in which

FIGURE 2.5: Lancelot and Guinevere in bed. *Lancelot Romance.* London, British Library, MS Additional 10293, fol. 312 verso, ca. 1300–10. © British Library/HIP/Art Resource, NY.

Lancelot is a passive partner, the implication is that Guinevere is the more experienced and voracious lover. Women are not only typified by their innately lusty bodies and therefore considered dangerous to men in these works, but also viewed as a pollutant to other women. Not wanting to be alone in her sin, Guinevere orchestrates an affair between her companion, Lady Malehaut, and Lancelot's closest friend, Sir Galehaut. Similarly, women within the fabliaux are depicted hiding their friends' lovers in closets, under beds, and in washtubs; distracting suspicious husbands; and even organizing the seduction of other women who attempt to defy their natural lusty state.[66]

The female body, as Isidore of Seville claimed, was defined by "fiery lust." Even the bodies of holy women were suspect as the female body was always given to excess in sexual desire and gluttony, and even in displays of sanctity such as fasting there was a suspicious wildness, a kind of abandon in which women experienced an almost sexual ecstasy through their faith.[67] No matter how she tried, a woman could not shed her body, as advocated by Jerome. The body was central to her definition as a woman and was always illicit. Every Marian aspect of the body had a counterpart in Eve. In literature, attempts to separate a woman from her sexuality resulted in a strange conundrum of literary dissection. Not only was the image of a woman fractured, but in this attempt to fully separate the dual aspects of women, the body itself was divided.[68] While this phenomenon is found subtly executed in the romances and lais, it is most obvious in the genre of the fabliaux. Women are separated from their offending genitalia, which cease to be only metaphorically a weak or wicked aspect of an otherwise good body but, in many of these stories, become a decidedly animated, independent creature from the woman herself. In the fabliau *Li jugemenz des cons* (The judgment of the cunts), three sisters engage in a contest for a young man in which they must describe why each of them would be a preferable lover than either of her sisters. Here the young women compete in the description of their respective genitalia as mouths that "are beardless," "haven't yet grown teeth," and "a hungry young mouth that wants to suckle."[69] The vagina as mouth motif is continued in other fabliaux such as *Le chevalier qui fist parler les cons* (The knight who could make cunts speak) in which a knight brags of his skills in making women's vaginas speak and tell the names of their lovers whom the women's other mouths refuse to share. The knight does not count on the wily nature of the woman though, and is foiled in his plan to make her vagina speak when she plugs it with a cloth.[70] In this story, not only is the woman's genitalia functioning as an independent entity, but it is in opposition to her wishes—it cannot be trusted by her husband or herself. Other fabliaux go as far as depriving the vulva of any human form.

It is depicted in some stories as a snail or even as a mouse that runs away after being used by the wife's lover, leaving the eager husband unable to fulfill his desires.

The dualistic image of women's bodies and their sexuality first presented in *Du con qui fu fez a la besche*, wherein the author ends his description of the creation of female genitalia with the admonition to not speak badly of women, but to be wary of their sexuality, is seemingly contradictory. However, for the Middle Ages, the moral of the fabliau is reflective of the complexity of the image of women's bodies and sexuality. Medieval society and culture defined women through their bodies and through the function of their bodies, menstruation, childbirth, and menopause, which were tied to sexual activity. Ovid's claim that women were a kind of "exquisite hell" is illustrative of medieval culture's struggles with the role of sex as a necessary function within a Christian society and medieval institutions' difficulty in assigning a value to the being that represented in one body the extremes of scientific, theological, and intellectual categorization. Woman's status as the bringer of death through sin and also the bringer of life through salvation, and her possession of an inferior body that yet performs tasks a man's cannot, rendered her image almost indefinable. For the heavily Neoplatonic mindset of medieval culture, obsessed with order and chains of being, this made women suspect creatures yet also objects of infinite desire.

CHAPTER THREE

Religion and Popular Beliefs: Choices, Constraints, and Creativity for Christian Women

KATHERINE L. FRENCH

Scholars have long noted the particular shape of medieval women's religious enthusiasm.[1] As Caroline Bynum explained in the introduction to her book *Holy Feast and Holy Fast*, women's religiosity encompassed four basic themes: "concern for affective religious response, an extreme form of penitential asceticism, an emphasis both on Christ's humanity and on the inspiration of the spirit, and a bypassing of clerical authority."[2] Food and food practices, whether in the form of the Eucharist, lactation, fasting, or feeding the poor, often bound these themes together. While Bynum was most immediately concerned with the experiences of mystics, usually living in communities of other religious women, her observations have influenced scholars interested in the religious lives of laywomen. Among the peasantry and urban bourgeoisie of medieval Europe, whether heretical or orthodox, scholars have also found that food and more generally household and familial cares shaped women's religious practices. As mothers and housewives, women cared for their families, cleaned their houses,

FIGURE 3.1: Women in church, Christmas Mass. *Les Très Riches Heures du Duc de Berry.* France, ca. 1410. Chantilly, Musée Condé, MS 65, fol. 158 recto. Photograph by René-Gabriel Ojéda. Courtesy of Réunion des Musées Nationaux/Art Resource, NY.

and helped with the provisioning and sustenance of those under their care. For orthodox women, these roles translated to the parish where most women practiced Christianity. There they washed the vestments, adorned the mass with hand-made altar cloths, cleaned the church, and offered gifts to the saints in an effort to ease the dangers of childbirth. Heretical women, who often conducted their religious practices in secret, also found their household and family obligations helped promote and protect fellow adherents. These contours of female spirituality and religious practice were so deeply entrenched that they became associated with broader notions of medieval femininity, central to assessing women's behavior.

Despite medieval Christian women's desire for regular and significant religious participation, they were frequently stymied by clerical attitudes toward their bodies and their nature, defined as sinful, lustful, and polluted. The focus on women's inherent sinfulness, which required men's constant supervision, whether by their fathers, husbands, or confessors, was a legacy of the eleventh- and twelfth-century reforms. Women's religious creativity was, therefore, carried out in dialogue with Christian and clerical misogyny. To be sure, women at all levels of society found supportive and concerned men who applauded their devotion and defended their religious practices. Nonetheless, women still operated in a world that did not grant them equal legal status, understood their sex as responsible for the Fall, and believed that their independent actions posed a threat to society and the church. These constraints also shaped women's religious behavior, whether they were in a religious community of their own formation, in a convent, or out in the world, raising a family, and/or working for a living.

GREGORIAN REFORMS AND CHANGING ATTITUDES TOWARD WOMEN

Eleventh-century ecclesiastical religious reforms altered Christian attitudes toward women. The reforms sought the church's independence from political patronage and familial control and a celibate clergy; while women were not the immediate issue, they were central to families, patronage networks, and clerical marriage. Enforcing clerical celibacy, therefore, also meant redefining the nature of women and the social and spiritual status of marriage and the family. Family ties, politics, and patronage had great influence over the church, and eliminating them was no simple matter. Usually referred to as the Gregorian reforms, after Pope Gregory VII (r. 1073–85) who was the most vigorous of the eleventh-century reforming popes, they constituted the first attempt at the total reorganization of the Western church since conversion. Although mostly remembered as a transformation of the papacy from a local political pawn into an international religious and political leader, the Gregorian reforms fundamentally reorganized how the church understood women, thereby altering the role women would have within Christianity.

Until relatively recently, historical discussions of these reforms and the ensuing conflicts cast them as an issue of the church versus the state, or as a clash of wills between Pope Gregory VII and Emperor Henry IV, who violently resisted his loss of patronage over the church.[3] While the stuff of high drama, scholars interested in gender, nonelites, and the spread of ideas have come to understand the reforms as far more than just an ego-driven contest between two powerful and elite men. R. I. Moore has shown that the desire for reform was not only desired by the church hierarchy, bishops, and the pope himself, but also ordinary men and women. Jo Ann McNamara, Megan McLaughlin, and Maureen Miller among others have shown how the issues of clerical celibacy and clerical marriage made the reforms far more than a matter of high politics. As a struggle over whether the church would be under the control of secular leaders or a celibate clergy, and whether it should be based on local liturgical and historical traditions or ones handed down from Rome, these reforms ultimately changed how western Europe understood masculinity and femininity, and lay and clerical lifestyles.[4]

Several scholars have argued that the growing disparity between the wealth of the church and the poverty of most tax and tithe payers generated considerable criticism of the clergy.[5] Laymen and laywomen perceived the clergy as more motivated by wealth and political power than salvation, and they called for a righteous clergy to minister to their needs and forgo the attractions of wealth and worldliness. They worried about the impact of receiving the sacraments from married priests obligated to worldly patrons on their own souls.[6] The call for reform was not only in the mouths of fervent laymen and laywomen. New forms of monastic life dedicated to poverty both individually and corporately provided an alternative example of clerical life, and adherents added their own demands for church reform.

"Purifying" the clergy required severing their ties with noble patronage, wealth, and influence. Landholders were no longer able to appoint the clergy to vacant churches in their own territories, and priests' wives could no longer advocate for their own children. By severing ties with family patronage, the reforms challenged a primary way women had shaped religious policy and practice. While the church had never been comfortable with married priests, they were permitted until the Gregorian reforms.[7] Many reformers believed that abolishing clerical marriage would improve the clergy's morality. Priests should become like monks in their commitment to sexual renunciation, or face punishment such as that shown in Figure 3.2.

Clerical marriage was a long-standing tradition. Priests' wives had special prayers, robes, and roles in the liturgy, and they cared for the sacred space of the church as an extension of their household. Yet priests' wives did not fit into the world envisioned by the reformers, because they transcended the new and increasingly rigid categories that reformers imposed on church organization. Clerical wives, so reformers argued, challenged their priest-husband's

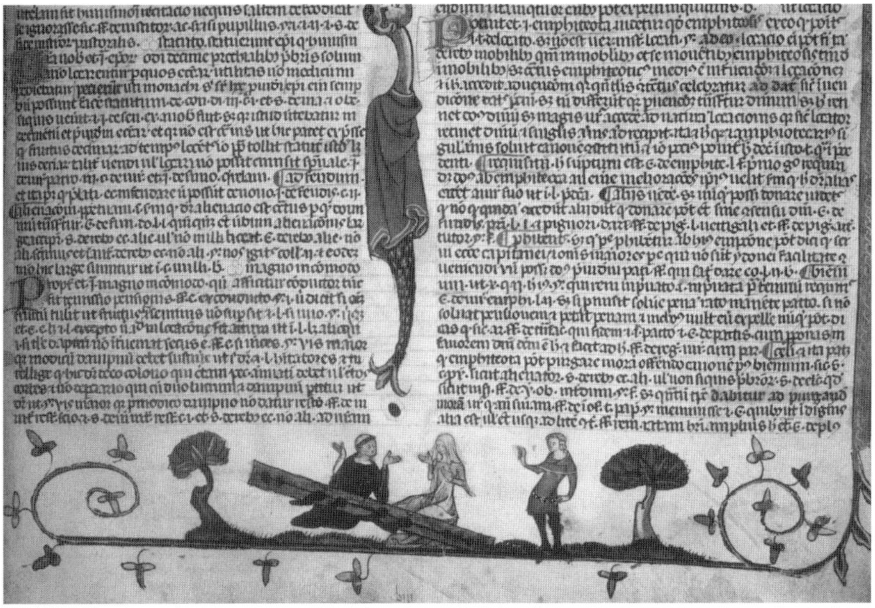

FIGURE 3.2: Monk and a woman in the stocks. *The Smithfield Decretals*. England, ca. 1300–25. London, British Library, MS Royal 10. E. IV, fol. 187 recto. © British Library/Visual Arts Library/Art Resource, NY.

loyalty to the church. Peter Damian (ca. 1007–72) argued that God only recognized three kinds of women: virgins, wives, and widows. Priest's wives, who straddled the line between lay and clerical, did not fit into any of the categories.[8]

By ending clerical marriage, the Gregorian reforms sought to make the clergy more like monks and thus elevate the clergy above the laity as a separate caste. Ending clerical marriage, however, required more than the passage of laws; it required justifications as well. Reformers instituted an extensive campaign that argued that women were a source of pollution and those administering the sacraments must avoid pollution.[9] They were aided by newly rediscovered Greek medical texts that asserted women's physical and emotional inferiority to men.[10] By the twelfth century, it was generally accepted that the ordained clergy were not to marry. Enforcement of this rule was sporadic and often inconsistent, and many village priests continued to live with women.[11] However, they had lost their status as wives and now were described at best as housekeepers or even concubines.

To help in their reform program, clerics also reshaped their understanding of the two iconic women of Christianity: Eve and the Virgin Mary. Eve received sole responsibility for the Fall. Accounts of the Fall focused on her rampant sexuality and the need for Adam to rule her.[12] Eve's counterpart, the Virgin Mary, whose cult expanded greatly in the twelfth century, was equally idealized. A virgin and a mother, she became the intercessor par excellence and offered a safe female image for the celibate clergy to venerate. At the same time, clerics promoted her behavior and life as a model for women, albeit an unattainable one.[13]

Ending clerical marriage profoundly altered the medieval European gender system. Physical strength and heterosexual practices had defined masculinity, but the reformed clergy, now required to be celibate, no longer had such options. Their masculinity was affirmed by the assertion that marriage and procreation were the proper condition for the laity. The church began recognizing marriage as a sacrament and defining and enforcing incest taboos, prohibiting marriage within the fourth degree—that is, between first cousins or closer relatives.[14] Jo Ann McNamara argued that changes in beliefs about marriage asserted even more forcefully women's sinful and inferior nature and affirmed men's responsibility for supervising women.[15]

Although women continued to administer land, wage war, write books, and participate in religious debates and practices, they did so in an atmosphere that was increasingly hostile to their accomplishments and abilities. Clerics found it difficult to understand and accept women as politically astute power brokers. Women's political involvements were described as "manly" because political influence was a masculine virtue, not something a feminine woman could exercise. A woman's desire to protect or advance her family or wield patronage, political power, and influence for her own sake were no longer motives that made sense to these clerical misogynists. When women did exercise political power, it was understood as connected to their sexuality; women sought to influence men because women were sexually insatiable. While women continually found ways around these expectations, or worked effectively through them, the ideals laid out by the Gregorian reforms shaped the lives and experiences of women's religious practices for the rest of the Middle Ages. Motherhood, housekeeping, and subordination were not only the hallmarks of femininity but also became the focus of women's religious behavior.

MONASTIC WOMEN

The religious concerns that motivated calls for reform also inspired men and women to create new forms of religious life. The twelfth century was a particularly vibrant period of religious experimentation. New kinds of religious communities rose up along with the revitalization of existing monasteries.

Monasticism attracted medieval women for a variety of reasons. It offered the chance to serve God and address pious concerns and interests in creative and meaningful ways. It was also an avenue to education and a reprieve from unwanted marriages and pregnancies, and it provided some physical protection. In the ninth and tenth centuries, many convents had fallen victim to the second wave of invasions; with the establishment of some political stability in the eleventh and twelfth centuries, wealthy nobles founded new houses or refounded old ones, and bishops reformed those that had survived. Between 1080 and 1170, the number of monastic houses for women in France and England had grown from about 100 to 400.[16] Moreover, about three-quarters of the houses active in 1170 were independent of the better-known male orders of Cluny or Cîteaux.[17] The Benedictine convent of Bourbourg, in the Low Countries, was one such new convent. Clementia of Burgundy, wife of Count

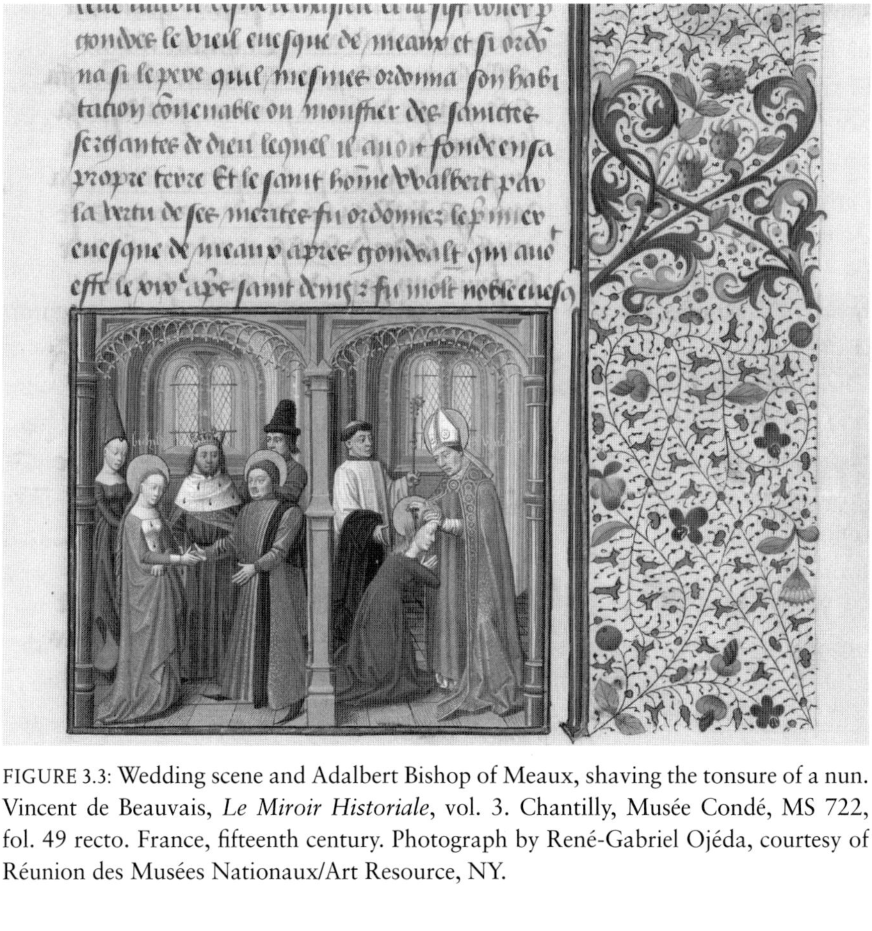

FIGURE 3.3: Wedding scene and Adalbert Bishop of Meaux, shaving the tonsure of a nun. Vincent de Beauvais, *Le Miroir Historiale*, vol. 3. Chantilly, Musée Condé, MS 722, fol. 49 recto. France, fifteenth century. Photograph by René-Gabriel Ojéda, courtesy of Réunion des Musées Nationaux/Art Resource, NY.

Robert of Flanders, founded it sometime around 1200 possibly to celebrate Robert's triumphant return from the First Crusade.[18] These kinds of houses drew their members from elite families. Nuns usually entered as young women or aging widows and left the world behind. At the monastery of Admont, in Bavaria, the monks and nuns shared a house but were separated by a door, with three locks, the keys to which were held by different monks. Typically, the door was only opened when a new nun professed or a nun needed last rites or burial.[19]

The foundation of new convents reflected the religious concerns of the times, and the convents themselves also participated in the revitalized intellectual life of twelfth-century monasticism. Central to this monastic renaissance was the production of manuscripts. Among the more famous manuscripts created by nuns are Hildegard of Bingen's *Wiesbaden Codex* and Herrad of Hohenbourg's *Hortus deliciarum*, both begun at the end of the twelfth century.[20] Both works demonstrated concern for nuns' education and spiritual development. As Alison Beach has shown, however, nuns also produced more mundane texts. Two named nuns at Admont copied booklets containing commentaries on books of the Old Testament.[21] Similarly, monks and nuns at the Premonstratensian house of Schäftlarn in Bavaria collaborated on expanding their library. One scribe named Sophia was active between 1160 and 1180, helping to produce a copy of Augustine's *Commentary on the Psalms*.[22]

By and large, only elites could gain entry into these convents. However, in the twelfth and thirteenth centuries, a women's religious movement attracted both elite and poor women from cities and the countryside.[23] Inspired by itinerant preachers crisscrossing Europe preaching apostolic poverty and a life of Christian service, groups of women (and men) chose to take up lives in imitation of Christ.[24] These women were not enclosed; rather, they performed hard physical labor and worked with the poor and sick. In 1234, for example, a group of women petitioned the bishop of Soissons for a place to live and pray together. He granted them a poor leper hospital in Berneuil, where they cared for the lepers.[25]

Work with lepers, whether feeding, bathing, or even kissing their sores, was one of the ultimate symbols of medieval humility and charity. The leper's diseased body was understood in a variety of ways, including embodying misery and privation. In this way, their suffering was akin to Christ's suffering and sacrifice, and for those who cared for lepers, like the women at Berneuil, caring for lepers was caring for Christ.[26]

Most of these communities remained small and poorly documented; members chose a life of obscurity, labor, and penance. Some communities such as

Fontevraud, however, became quite wealthy and influential. Fontevraud started out as a single house but by the late twelfth century had nearly seventy houses, most in France but at least one in northern Spain and another in England.[27] Fontevraud was founded in 1100 or 1101 by Robert d'Arbrissell, an itinerant preacher from Brittany. He had been active in the Gregorian reforms, "making peace between quarrelers, liberating churches from slavery to the laity, separating the incestuous unions of priest and laity, opposing simony, and manfully opposing all sins."[28] At the death of his bishop, d'Arbrissell turned to preaching about apostolic poverty. As his followers grew in number, he felt compelled to found a house for them, especially the women. He set up a mixed community at the intersection of Anjou, Poitou, and Touraine at Fontevraud. The rules strictly limited contact between the men and women and divided the work of the community according to sex. He "commended the more tender and weaker sex to psalm-singing and contemplation, while he applied the stronger sex to the labors of the active life."[29] Fontevraud was open to men and women of all classes, not just the wealthy, and for the next fifteen years, d'Arbrissell preached in southwestern France expanding his order by setting up new priories and attracting members.

In 1115, believing he was near death, d'Arbrissell returned to Fontevraud to arrange for the future of his order. He had built it for women, and the men living in the house had to agree to this condition or leave. He appointed an abbess, an early follower and widow named Petronilla of Chemillé, because a woman with experience in the world rather than a virgin brought up in the monastery would be more capable of protecting the order's endowments. His rule assumes that the abbess would travel outside the cloister to supervise the priories and oversee the order's property.[30] Fontevraud became so successful that the pope supported it and it attracted wealthy patrons. The English kings Henry II and Richard the Lionheart and Henry's wife Eleanor of Aquitaine were buried there.

Fontevraud was not unique in its focus on women. Another itinerant preacher, Norbert of Xanten (d. 1128), founded the Premonstratensians in 1121, in Prémontré, near Laon, France. It began as a male house, with a nearby attendant female house, but in some areas, such as northwestern Germany, Premonstratensian houses of nuns outnumbered those with monks.[31] Convents were under the ultimate supervision of an abbot or provost, who often lived far away. Within the convent, Premonstratensian nuns were led by a *magistra*. In some communities, such as Meer, the sisters elected their *magistra*. She witnessed property transfers, accepted donations and tithes, negotiated with local bishops and others in the order's hierarchy, and ran the house's charitable works.[32] There could be a great deal of cooperation between Premonstratensian monks and nuns. In 1220, for example, Blysa, a sister at Dünnwald, jointly purchased a vineyard with the male porter of the monastery. The vineyard's proceeds supported candles that burned before the image of the Virgin Mary in the church.[33]

Not all monastic foundations welcomed women with the enthusiasm of Robert d'Arbrissell. The monastery of Cluny, founded in 910 in the Maconnais region of France, had been at the forefront of the Gregorian reforms. It created a centralized and hierarchical monastic order that spread across much of Europe as nobles called upon Cluny to reform the monasteries on their lands. Many women were deeply attracted to Cluny's ascetic lifestyle, but Cluny was slow to set up a house for women. Founded in 1056, a century and a half after the foundation of Cluny, Marcigny was to be, according to Abbot Hugh, a "glorious prison" for all the wives abandoned by men who wanted to join Cluny.[34] Marcigny had room for ninety-nine women, who could enter as unmarried young women or as mature widows. Marcigny's nuns came from some of Europe's most powerful noble houses; William the Conqueror's daughter Adela was a nun at Marcigny.

Marcigny's nuns observed strict enclosure in order to protect them from worldly temptation and to prevent them from tempting the monks. The nuns took this enclosure seriously, coming to view themselves as "penitents immured in a living tomb."[35] When a fire threatened to destroy the convent and the nuns inside, they refused to leave, despite pleas from the monks outside the walls. They trusted God to protect them, and the fire died down before it engulfed the convent.

Marcigny was never as rich or as beautiful as Cluny, and its way of life and liturgy also suffered by comparison. While Cluny elected its own abbot, Abbot Hugh gave the office of abbess of Marcigny to the Virgin Mary and appointed a prioress who had few administrative or liturgical duties. A priest heard confessions and administered the mass, and Cluny oversaw its landed possessions. While Cluny added monastic houses across Europe to its oversight, Marcigny did not. This was not for lack of interest on the part of women, but rather the inability of the enclosed nuns to foster their own growth and Cluny's lack of interest in women's religious vocation. Eventually, other Cluniac houses for women did open, such as one in Bollschwell, Germany, and another at Santa Maria de Cantú, in Italy, but compared to the men's houses, they remained few in number.[36] Cluny accepted the prayers of the Marcigny nuns, praised their piety and virtue, but continued to see the house as filled with women who were by their nature sinful and dangerous.

Ultimately, Cluny's lavish liturgy and enormous wealth and influence attracted criticism and new interpretations of the Benedictine Rule. The Cistercians were the most prominent of Cluny's critics. Led by Bernard of Clairvaux (1090–1153), the Cistercians reinvigorated the self-sufficiency that the Benedictine Rule encouraged, by emphasizing manual labor. Bernard was a dynamic preacher and attracted many men and women to his new monastic ideal. His response to women wishing to join the Cistercians was ambivalent, however. Bernard doubted women could endure the Cistercians' austere lifestyle. Moreover, the Cistercians' governing statutes prohibited monks from having contacts with women, whether they were servants, pilgrims, family members, or nuns. Believing that women were dangerous to the chastity of men, Bernard did not want to compromise the reputation of his monks.[37]

The Cistercians were not able to keep women out of their order. Although they had prohibited the founding of new women's houses by 1225, the Cistercian way of life offered a solution to the church's discomfort with the growing numbers of independent communities of penitential women.[38] Church authorities were distrustful of unsupervised religious women living together on the fringes of society. While these women wanted to pursue a life of apostolic poverty and personal service to Christ, their freedom of movement challenged the church's expectations for women. Moreover, the Fourth Lateran Council, held in 1215, had prohibited the foundation of any new monastic orders for men or women.[39] This meant that women living in communities without the direct supervision of an abbot, or without the structure of an established rule, had to be incorporated into existing orders. Six years after the bishop of Soissons had granted the leper hospital of Berneuil to a group of penitential women, he reformed them under the guidelines of the Cistercian order as the convent of La-Joie.[40] Yet rather than turning control of the house over to the Cistercians, the bishop retained supervisory rights, making their status within the Cistercian order somewhat indeterminate. This process was not uncommon; Anne Lester has found that between 1200 and 1240, a third of the Cistercian convents founded in the archdioceses of Sens and Reims had started out as communities of penitential women.[41]

Enclosure was not a new concept for nuns, but in the twelfth century, bishops increasingly demanded enclosure for them. As the practice spread, religious life changed for nuns.[42] They had to maintain a clerical staff to administer the sacraments, which diminished the power and authority of their own leaders. Enclosure was also a poor strategy for successful fiscal management, and while wealth and worldly riches were not the intended goal of any monastery, many convents found it difficult to survive because of their poverty. Enclosure

FIGURE 3.4: Priests and nuns in procession. London, British Library, MS Additional 39843, fol. 6 verso. France, ca. 1300. © The British Library Board.

prevented nuns from checking on their property, maintaining their legal rights to it, supervising repairs, and collecting rents. Instead, they had to rely on monks to manage their endowments and income, sometimes with disastrous results. Poverty and claustration could also inhibit nuns' educational opportunities and the libraries their houses could support. Closing the gap between monastic and convent education required further monastic intervention. The combination of financial need and declining prestige made many male communities reluctant to have women's houses associated with them.[43] This was to be a recurring problem for religious women up to the end of the Middle Ages. Women remained attracted to a life of apostolic poverty, yet continually found their full participation denied. The orders founded to include women, such as Fontevraud, were also affected by this desire to enclose nuns. The male monks assumed greater financial oversight of Fontevraud's endowments, nuns performed fewer public services, and at the liturgy they were increasingly separated from each other; the nuns were confined to the nave, and the monks to the choir.[44]

The practice of apostolic poverty was readily adaptable to Europe's growing cities. For example, in 1198, Fulk of Neuilly, an itinerant preacher, organized a group of former Parisian prostitutes who wished to live this new life of penitential piety, working with the poor and sick.[45] In an urban context, these practices gave rise to a new form of monastic life. Mendicants lived in the world, owned no possessions, and worked or begged for their sustenance. Urban women who joined these groups of wandering monks confronted the same challenges faced by women in the countryside. Their unenclosed life of intense identification with Christ challenged notions of femininity, and local clerics routinely tried to incorporate them into existing convents to provide appropriate supervision.

Francis of Assisi (1182–1226) and Dominic (Domingo) de Gúzman (1170–1221) were the two most prominent advocates of the mendicant movement. Francis, the son of a wealthy Italian merchant, abandoned his wealth for a life of poverty and begging. Francis believed that in order for the church to return to its original form, it needed to imitate Christ's poverty. In 1210, the pope approved his simple rule of apostolic poverty.[46] Dominic de Gúzman, a Castilian Augustinian canon, had dedicated his life to converting the heretics in the south of France. He had little success but still attracted followers with his simple lifestyle and dynamic preaching. In 1216, the pope approved the mission of Preaching Friars, or the Dominicans, who were to follow the existing rule of St. Augustine and preach the word of God in cities and towns across Europe.[47] In order to have the best-trained preachers, Dominic encouraged all his followers to attend university. Franciscan or Dominican, mendicants supported themselves by begging, preaching, and ministering to the urban poor, activities made possible by the growth of urban populations.

Francis's and Dominic's ideal of poverty and community work through charity and preaching attracted many women. In early communities, men preached and dispensed charity, and women tended the sick in hospices, and performed some manual labor such as spinning. The most prominent of Francis's female followers was Clare Offreduccio (1194–1253), a young noble woman, who fled her family to live at Francis's retreat at San Damiano near Assisi. Clare shared Francis's commitment to poverty, and despite Francis's concerns about unenclosed religious women, the two had a close relationship, with Francis turning to Clare for advice and counsel.[48] Toward the end of his life, when Francis was ill from the stigmata, he wanted Clare to minister to him and provide him with shoes so he could walk.[49] Yet the relationship between the Franciscans and Clare's community at San Damiano remained a problem; Francis did not want to institutionalize his relationship with Clare or her followers, nor was he interested in the other female communities that were imitating Clare's lifestyle.[50]

For the rest of her life, Clare struggled to maintain the privilege of poverty and for recognition as part of the Franciscans. In 1214, Francis proclaimed Clare abbess of the group but demanded claustration. After much persistent petitioning, the pope eventually granted Clare and San Damiano the privilege of poverty, but she was not allowed to found a female order, nor could she affiliate her nuns with the Franciscans. In 1219, Francis assured the pope he would not accept any more female communities.[51] In 1228, two years after Francis's death, the pope renewed the privilege of poverty for the women at San Damiano but insisted that because the Fourth Lateran Council forbade the creation of new monastic orders, the other Clarissen houses follow a Benedictine life. Against their will, those at Santa Maria in Milan had to accept land to support them because the pope feared that "their terrible poverty, caused by the abundant wickedness and flagging charity of many people," would drive the nuns away.[52] In 1253, a few months before her death, Clare wrote a rule for her nuns that included much of the oral rule Francis had given her. In contrast to the hierarchical Benedictine Rule, Elizabeth Petroff argues that Clare's rule was "remarkably democratic," with decisions made by consensus and the abbess the first among equals.[53] The sisters under her rule lived in poverty, worked outside the convent, and observed a vow of silence, preaching only by example, not by words.[54] On Clare's deathbed, Pope Innocent IV in person confirmed Clare's rule for San Damiano and a few other houses. He also confirmed that they were Franciscans, not Benedictines. Ten years after Clare's death, in 1263, Urban IV formally recognized the Poor Clares as a discrete order, but he would not impose Clare's rule on all houses. Complaints from bishops about Clare's followers traveling and begging outside of their cloisters ultimately prevented most Clarrissen houses from preserving the privilege of poverty or begging.

Dominic was more encouraging of Diana d'Andalo's (1201–36) desire to form a companion order to his Preaching Friars. When Diana met Dominic, she was eighteen and already vowed to religion. She took personal vows from Dominic and planned a new convent in Bologna, dedicated to St. Agnes. Dominic supervised the growing numbers of women's houses and created a rule for them. Dominic's successor also supported Diana's efforts but hesitated to affiliate officially with women. After 1228, however, the Dominican chapter general tried to prevent the formation of new convents, fearing they would take energy and resources away from the friars. Dominican leaders were particularly concerned that the supervision of the women distracted friars from their university studies. Nonetheless, the women did not disband, and the Dominicans often paired existing convents with monasteries so that male and female communities could share facilities.

The urban focus of the mendicant's efforts attracted the patronage of merchants, whose own trading networks helped spread Franciscan and Dominican houses for men and women beyond Italy and Spain. Ties with the Hanseatic League helped spread this new form of spirituality to northern Europe. In 1280, Ingrid Elovsdatter took up the life of a Dominican nun and convinced her family to found Sweden's first convent for Dominican nuns in the city of Skänninge.[55]

Despite the desire to enclose and regularize all religious women, urban women chose religious lifestyles that continued to defy simple monastic or secular classification. Some women founded communities of like-minded women, who while dedicated to God were not enclosed in convents. In the English towns of Norwich and Ipswich, there were several communities of "poor women" dedicated to a religious life. In northern Europe, these women were known as beguines; in Iberia, they were known as *beatas*.[56] They had no male leader and followed no formal monastic rule.[57] They tended to pool property, worked together, and pledged themselves to chastity, charity, and poverty. In the Low Countries, beguines often worked in the burgeoning cloth industry. Because of the *beatas*' and beguines' spirituality and economic independence, male ecclesiastics were often suspicious of them, and individual women, such as Marguerite Porete (d. 1310), a French Beguine and author of the mystical tract *Mirror of Simple Souls*, found themselves accused of heresy.[58]

Often under the tutelage of mendicant confessors, some women living in beguinages or as *beatas* or in other penitential communities found themselves receiving mystical visions, an increasingly common form of women's religious experience in the late Middle Ages.[59] Late-medieval mysticism was marked by rigorous self-discipline and self-denial, such as extreme fasting, sleep deprivation, and arduous manual labor. Scholars hypothesize a connection between the rise of women's mysticism in the late Middle Ages and the political, economic, and demographic crises of the period. Perhaps society looked for these women as evidence of a connection to heavenly power and a sign that God had not abandoned the world.[60] While some mystics, such as Catherine of Siena (1347–80), held political influence because of their mystical activities, others simply lived physically difficult lives, punctuated by the doubt and criticism of their confessor or the surrounding community.[61]

Women's bodies played a particularly prominent role in their mystical activity. Female mystics reported the loss of all sense of self when communing with God. Some went into trances, levitated, and had catatonic seizures, miraculous elongation or enlargement of body parts, and ecstatic nosebleeds. Ida of Louvain's (d. 1139) body swelled as if she were pregnant with Christ, while Catherine of Siena reported she could eat nothing but the Eucharist. Male mystics rarely reported these experiences. These experiences took a toll, and for many mystics, patient acceptance of illness and suffering was a major element of their sanctity.[62] The physical and emotional language of mysticism also provided some celibate women with a means to communicate sexual desires and feelings. The writings of the thirteenth-century beguine, Hadewijch of Antwerp, used erotic imagery to describe her intense love and union with God, and Angela of Foligno (ca. 1248–1309) spoke of Christ as her lover. In her raptures, she kissed him and he pressed his body tightly against hers.[63] The physicality of these experiences caused ecclesiastical authorities to doubt the origins of Angela's ecstasies.

Medieval women were continually drawn to the changing trends in religious life and founded a variety of communities where they explored new forms of spirituality and practiced a life devoted to God. The results were a creative and dynamic period of medieval women's spirituality that took many forms, not the least of which was a rise in mystical literature, manuscript production, and aid to the poor—experiences that frequently drew upon women's social and physical roles in families and society. Yet, the growing distrust of women's sexuality and the belief that unenclosed women posed a danger to the spiritual commitment of men made it difficult for women to participate fully in these movements. In 1298, Pope Boniface VIII's decretal *Periculoso* stated that all religious women everywhere must be cloistered. As James Brundage and Elizabeth Makowski argue, *Periculoso* established new standards for women's enclosure. Previous regulations had focused on protecting women from the violent outside world, while *Periculoso* assumed that women's own highly sexual natures made them a danger to men and society and needed to be isolated through enclosure.[64] This decree by no means ended attempts by women to lead active religious lives; however, it did provide the framework for all subsequent attempts to cloister all religious women.

LAYWOMEN AND LOCAL RELIGIOUS PRACTICE

The large crowds of poor men and women who followed itinerant preachers across the countryside and demanded reform of their clergy demonstrate that interest in Christianity was not limited to the nobility or the educated. Because most women did not end up in convents, it was in the context of the parish,

FIGURE 3.5: Friedrich Herlin, Jacob Fuchsart's wife and daughters in church, outer right wing of the *Nördlingen Altarpiece*. Oil on panel. Germany, ca. 1462–65. Stadtmuseum, Nördlingen, Germany. Photograph by Eric Lessing, courtesy of Art Resource, NY.

the basic unit of public worship, that women tried to construct meaningful religious lives for themselves whether in the city or in the countryside.

As Europeans cleared forests and resettled vacated lands following the upheavals of the ninth and tenth centuries, monasteries, bishops, and nobles began establishing parochial boundaries, building churches, and overseeing the performance of the sacraments, the laity's church attendance, and their payment of tithes. Parish formation was also central to the conversion of the Spanish population as the *Reconquista* gathered momentum.[65] R. I. Moore has argued that broadly speaking, in those areas where there were few parishes and thus little ecclesiastical oversight, popular heresy was more common.[66] Yet the foundation of a parish was no guarantee of the quality or consistency of Christian practice within a parish's boundaries, and ecclesiastical authorities found much to criticize about the laity's religious behavior.

The Gregorian reforms increased the centrality of the parish to local religious life. Subsequent church councils, culminating in the Fourth Lateran Council in 1215, required that babies be baptized in their parish churches, preferably by the parish priest. Similarly, while marriages did not require a priest, the church tried to make the priest's blessing a central component of the sacrament and to have the dead buried in parish churchyards.[67] These mandates sometimes challenged local practices and required education of the laity and the parish clergy.

The episcopal statutes that followed the Fourth Lateran Council hint at old practices and the impact of new requirements on communities. For example, between 1252 and 1258, the bishop of Bath and Wells in England's West Country published his own diocesan statutes, which dealt with the administration of the sacraments, condition and contents of parish churches, clerical duties and behavior, and diocesan organization and administration.[68] Not only was the church to be in good condition, but the churchyard needed a wall to prevent animals from digging up the graves, and the laity were forbidden from building booths or stalls in the churchyard or from holding markets, "dishonest games," or fights within its confines.[69] These requirements acknowledged that the church was a center of local social and economic activity, which conflicted with the sacredness of the space defined by the church's reforms.

In the end, these and other such statutes promulgated across Europe required a great deal of the laity. Parishioners had specific financial responsibilities to their parish church's fabric, over and above their tithes. Throughout much of Europe, the laity cared for the nave of their parish church, while the clergy had responsibility for the chancel.[70] The bishop of Bath and Wells specifically stated that "the body of the church is to belong to the parishioners."[71] Moreover, the bishop required a secure and honest custodian to care for the liturgical items.[72] Across Europe, the laity organized themselves, making the parish an important center of corporate Christian activity. Yet status and gender still influenced individual participation, even in small rural parishes where the differences in wealth were less pronounced.

Led by lay leaders variously called churchwardens, *procurators ecclesiae*, *kerkmeesters*, *operai*, *obrers*, or *marguilliers*,[73] parishioners raised and spent money to expand, maintain, and furnish their parish churches. Women were typically excluded from lay leadership positions, and much collective parish decision making. In the mountainous parishes outside of Florence, Italy, many parishes even elected their own priests, but this decision was apparently in the hands of the adult male householders.[74] Nonetheless, by the late fifteenth century, there are some examples of female churchwardens in England.[75] Sometimes women also led individual fund-raising efforts and directed other local initiatives to promote their favorite saint or other pious concern centered on the parish.

Women's domestic and economic roles shaped their daily parish involvement.[76] They cleaned and decorated their churches, much as they cleaned and decorated their houses. In Westminster, England, William Barnowey's wife embroidered a church hanging with an image of the crucifix with Mary and John.[77] Women also did the parish's laundry, mended vestments, brewed ale, cooked food for feasts, and made wax. In Great Dunmow, Essex, the parish widows worked on the May Day and Corpus Christi feasts, supplying some of the ingredients and doing some of the cooking, baking, and brewing. Most women who labored for their parishes were local and invested in the community and its success. Their labor brought them into contact with holy objects and facilitated the performance of the mass, thus involving low-status women in the Eucharistic devotions that were so popular in the late Middle Ages.

Bequests from the dead to pray for their souls offer another chance to see the role of women. While both women and men shared concerns for their soul, they manifested them within the legal and social confines placed on them by medieval society. Women's legal disadvantages regarding land ownership meant that women were more likely to leave goods in their wills than men.[78] Testators left a variety of bequests to their parish churches, from property to household objects. Marie Narrette of Douai left to her parish of St. Jacques the proceeds from the sale of her house to help with church maintenance.[79] Some specifically endowed masses for their soul, such as a widow from Sant' Andrea a Comaggiano, in the Italian Alps, who left a bequest for eight masses to be said on the anniversary of her death for five years. Others, like Agnes Awmbler of Barroby in Lincoln, England, focused on enhancing the veneration of the saints. She left a kerchief to "the image of Our Lady within the choir."[80]

Fertility and childbirth also profoundly shaped women's religious experiences. Childbirth was dangerous for women and their babies, and families, friends, and communities waited anxiously when women went into labor. Rather than passively accept the danger, women prayed to St. Margaret of Antioch, the patron saint of childbirth, and they bought amulets with her image.[81] In the English parish of Ranworth the imagery on the Marian-chapel screen suggests it was dedicated to concerns about family, childbirth, and children.[82] On the screen are St. Margaret and the Holy Kindred: the three daughters of St. Anne, Mary Salome, Mary Cleophas, and the Virgin Mary; and their children saints James the Great, John the Evangelist, Jesus, James the Less, Jude, Simon, and Jose. The young saints play with toy versions of their attributes: John has a toy eagle, and James the Less's fuller's club becomes a bubble pipe.[83] The mothers of Domes, a village near Lyon, France, venerated a local saint named Guinefort because he protected sick children. This saint, inquisitor Stephen Bourbon discovered, was a dog, who had died defending a baby. In the minds of the peasants, he was a martyr, despite Stephen's desire to eradicate this misunderstanding of Christian doctrine.[84]

Because a baby who died without baptism would not be saved, a layperson, even the midwife, could baptize a baby in an emergency. The clergy were increasingly uncomfortable with this possibility and warned that the midwife must say the proper words; otherwise, the baptism would not be efficacious. In an English fourteenth-century instructional manual for parish priests, the author calls home baptisms a "mischance" and warns the priest to

> Teach them all to be cautious and quick
> That they say the words to do the trick,
> And say the words all in a row
> As now I will you show;
> Just this and no more,
> For anything else is women's lore.[85]

Despite the concerns, actual records of midwives baptizing babies are rare. The parishioners in the rural parish of Clunbury, on the Welsh border, complained to their bishop that "certain parishioners came with an infant of William Corvyger's for baptism as it was dying and could not find the said chaplain, and so it was necessary for them to go to the church of Clungonford for the baptism."[86] Even in this moment of crisis, the parishioners apparently preferred a priest to a midwife.

After childbirth, women enjoyed a period of confinement that limited their work and their outside social interactions. Female neighbors, friends, and family members helped out with household chores during this period. When the mother was ready to end her confinement, sometime around four to six weeks, the church had a special liturgy for her called churching. Some scholars understand churching as a ritual of purification that reintegrated the mother back into the community after childbirth. It may have derived from the Jewish ceremony of purification, and medieval people certainly understood that the Virgin Mary went through a Jewish purification ritual, despite her continued purity. Yet many, including the medieval women themselves, also understood churching as a celebration of thanksgiving for a safe delivery.[87] In keeping with this sense of celebration, churches had special decorations, and many husbands hosted churching meals for the neighborhood afterward.[88] Churching could also be a form of social control for un-wed mothers and women pregnant from adultery. For them, churching could be a ceremony of public humiliation rather than celebration. Gilbertra la Cousature, who was pregnant by her parish priest, avoided this humiliation by traveling to Harfleur (Normandy) to be churched by a priest who would overlook both her unmarried status and the fact that she was not his parishioner.[89]

While church statutes laid out the minimum requirements, by the late Middle Ages, the laity increasingly used the parish as centerpiece of their own religious concerns and enthusiasm, adding local saint venerations, side altars and chapels, and other decorations and practices that reflected local priorities. The local environment also found expression in architecture, interior adornment, daily routines, and parish administrations. For example, rural parishes relied on agricultural revenues, such as grain or wool, while urban parishes often rented out property to raise money.[90] These kinds of local variations show how communities incorporated local economies and society into their religious practices.

For urban women the parish was just one of a number of religious venues available in a city. Mendicant confessors, confraternities, public sermons, religious discussions, and private reading gave urban women more religious choices than their rural counterparts. The extremes of wealth and poverty so visible in towns and cities inspired a great deal of criticism of the church's wealth. Groups of devout laypeople sometimes found themselves living outside the theological and legal acceptance of the church. Many groups of heretics started their religious journey inspired by the same charismatic preaching that motivated followers of Robert d'Arbrissell and Francis of Assisi. Uncomfortable with religious enthusiasm, and wary of laypeople assuming religious practices reserved for the clergy, many bishops tried to restrict the laity's religious activities, especially when it came to preaching and men and women living together collectively. Initial accusations of heresy often had more to do with the relationship between an individual cleric and an enthusiastic layperson than a divergent theology. As church authorities moved in on these groups, many fled, and in isolation their theology moved into heresy, demanding an alternative church and advocating heretical beliefs.

Broadly speaking, heretical groups fall into two camps: "proto-Protestant" and dualist. The so-called proto-Protestants, such as the Poor of Lyons or Waldensians, the Lollards of England, and Hussites of Bohemia, shared some beliefs with the Protestants who emerged in the Reformation. They came to doubt the powers of the clergy and sacraments not mentioned in the Bible, and they advocated personal education and study of the Bible, which needed to be translated into the vernacular. Small pockets of Lollards and Waldensians survived into the Reformation and were absorbed into the newer and larger Protestant groups.[91] Dualists, most famously the Cathars, denied that good had defeated evil with Christ's Resurrection, believing that the body and the rest of the physical world were sinful and a creation of the devil. They viewed the sacraments as worthless and denied the Crucifixion and Resurrection, since God would not have taken material form. Only through the strict renunciation of physical experiences such as eating meat, sex, and a comfortable physical life could the soul escape imprisonment in the body and be joined with God.

Scholars have debated whether heretical movements provided women with more freedom and equality than the Latin Church. Cathar theology, like other dualist beliefs, had great anxiety about women's bodies.[92] In Cathar belief, sexuality was the creation of the devil, and women were central in the devil's seduction of the angels away from God. It was because sexual intercourse was a sin that perfects (Cathar clergy) were celibate. Male perfects were not to touch women under any circumstances.[93] These beliefs put Cathar women in a difficult position. Yet Carole Lansing has argued that for women who gave up sex and marriage, Catharism did expand their roles beyond those observed in society at large. Shannon McSheffrey, however, found that English Lollards replicated society's family and work roles, and their theology still understood women as inferior at best and impure and the source of sin at worse.[94]

The Poor of Lyons (or Waldensians) started as an apostolic-poverty movement in the second half of the twelfth century. They were led by a Lyonnaise merchant known to history as Peter Waldes or Waldo. He gave up his career and distributed his wealth to the city's poor and began a career as a preacher, attracting both male and female followers. In order to clarify his exhortations to return to poverty, he had scriptural passages translated into the vernacular. While the church found no fault with his charitable work or his itinerant lifestyle, it was uncomfortable with his preaching and rumors that his female followers were also preaching. In 1184, he was excommunicated for preaching without a license, and he and his followers faced increasing pressure from church officials. When they went underground, they abandoned the cities where they had gained their initial converts and moved into isolated rural areas, setting up their own religious hierarchy.[95] Eventually, Waldensians' theology rejected purgatory, capital punishment, and any doctrines not based in scripture. Waldes's views on women were never explicit. After his conversion, he placed his own two daughters in the convent at Fontevraud, but other women became active followers and promoters of his mission. Female believers learned the same lessons as men and participated in religious discussions. As they went underground, women's control of household resources made them critical to the hiding and feeding of traveling members. Shulamith Shahar's study of Waldensian testimonies before the Inquisition demonstrates that gender was not central to participation in the movement, but that traditional roles were not fully overturned either.[96]

By the mid-twelfth century, another and much more feared heresy, Catharism, had expanded into northern Italy and southwestern France. The Cathar Church was highly organized with its own structures and clerical offices. Cathars divided their communities into two groups: the perfects and the believers. The perfects led ascetic and celibate lives, giving up their possessions, and refusing to eat anything that was the product of sex, such as meat, eggs, or cheese. The majority of Cathars were believers, who supported the perfects but were not as ascetic. They hoped that on their deathbeds they could summon a perfect to carry out the ritual of *consolamentum*, to make them perfects so that they would move directly into the spiritual realm.

One of the reasons for the Cathars' success was that in southern France, local clergy tolerated them and the local nobility supported them as part of an attempt to remain independent of the French king. The count of Foix was a Catholic, but his wife Philippa headed a convent of female perfects. Beatrice, the first wife of Raymond VI, the count of Toulouse, left him and went to a Cathar nunnery, and Raymond's fourth wife, Eleanor of Aragon, became a perfect, thus ending their marriage.[97] Similarly in northern Italy, Catharism thrived in the midst of the political struggles between the pope and the empire. Yet politics were not Catharism's only attraction. The perfects' simplicity, sincerity, and poverty also attracted the respect of those laity who did not join.[98]

Women were a significant portion of those Cathars caught by the Inquisition. In Orvieto, in 1268, a third of those sentenced for heresy were women, most of whom were widows of convicted Cathars.[99] Like the Waldensians, Cathar women provided shelter to believers, mentored young followers, and participated in religious discussions. The French widow Blanche de Laurac not only supported a Cathar convent in her home, but also initiated her five children and numerous grandchildren into the sect.[100] She and her daughter Mabilia also received the *consolamentum* and become perfects themselves.

As perfects, they lived much like beguines in unenclosed all-female houses. Unlike beguines, however, female Cathar perfects also preached and administered the *consolamentum*.

While many Cathars lived openly and even attended their local parish church with their orthodox neighbors, the church feared their growing popularity and tried to reconvert them through intensive preaching by Dominican friars. Frustrated by the lack of success, the papacy finally ordered a crusade to suppress them in 1208.[101] While the crusade did not completely eliminate the Cathars, they were never again as open or as powerful.

In England, the Lollard heretical movement originated in the 1380s from the teachings of Oxford University professor John Wyclif (ca. 1325–84). Lollards sought the formation of a new church, based on the primacy of scripture and a congregation of the predestined.[102] In this new church, the clergy would only preach and teach the word of God; in all other respects, they would be like laypeople. As a result, Lollardy was virulently anticlerical, denying that ordination gave the clergy any special powers or that sacraments not mentioned in the Bible were valid. Adherents repudiated religious practices without scriptural basis, such as pilgrimages, saints, images, and holy days. Like the Waldensians, Lollards emphasized the importance of vernacular works and the ability to read them. Originally, the movement was connected with the university and the gentry, but itinerant preachers spread these ideas across England to urban artisans.

As with other heretic groups, critics accused them of letting women preach and act as clergy.[103] Yet, while individual women did play important roles within the Lollard community, Lollardy did not offer new gender roles for adherents. Women usually became involved in Lollardy as a result of kin who were also members. Mothers introduced their children to the heresy and provided a safe haven in their homes for Lollards to meet and discuss their ideas. Women did play a leading role in Lollard communities; Alice Rowley led conventicles of male and female Lollards in Coventry, converted men and women to her faith, taught members, and was active in the Lollard book trade. Similarly, Joan Smyth sought out new followers, although she mostly worked among other women. Both women, however, were members of Coventry's wealthy merchant elite, and their participation and possible literacy says as much about their high social status as their sex.[104]

Societies' larger gender roles, influenced as they were by the church's teaching on Eve, shaped the religious experiences of ordinary Christian women whether they were in the city or countryside and whether they joined orthodox communities, such as the local confraternity, or heretical groups, such as the

Waldensians. While Christianity, in all its various forms, provided women with a means to address their concerns for motherhood, fertility, marital harmony, and health, the church as an institution continually reminded women that they were ultimately responsible for the Fall. Still, through their local religious communities, women found ways of organizing, participating, and asserting their concerns, so that they never lived out the secluded, invisible, and shame-faced lives that the most misogynist clerics demanded. At the same time, many clerics recognized their interest and spiritual huger and nurtured it with sermons, individual council, and public acclamation. Indeed, these very traits became associated with medieval constructions of femininity.

CONCLUSION

Biblical ideas that women were weak and in need of male supervision created entrenched notions about femininity in the medieval world. As a result, medieval Christian women faced a great deal of opposition when their piety took them outside the direct control of the clerical hierarchy. Yet, as we have seen, these bounds were not constant; they continually shifted as a result of new practices introduced by devout women themselves or by reformers within the church hierarchy. The lesson to be taken from studying medieval Christian women's religious experiences should not be one of victimization or exile, but rather creativity in the face of constraints. Women used their own lives, bodies, and experiences to create meaningful religious practices and to help their communities, no matter on which side of the orthodox/heretical divide they fell.

CHAPTER FOUR

Medicine and Disease: The Female "Patient" in Medieval Europe

IONA MCCLEERY

At some time in the late thirteenth century, a woman called Maria Domingas began to despair of ever conceiving a child. The wife of a rich merchant of the parish of Marvila in the Portuguese town of Santarém, Maria had been bleeding continuously for five years to the despair of expensive doctors. Fearing that Maria would soon die, her mother suggested that she pray at the tomb of the Dominican friar and physician Gil de Santarém (d. 1265). As soon as Maria made a life-long vow to keep vigil at de Santarém's tomb on the eve of his feast, the bleeding began to slacken. Maria eventually conceived and "gave her joyful husband a new baby."[1]

This miracle can be explored on multiple levels. It suggests social networks of family and parish, the prerogatives of patriarchy and inheritance, and the legal situation of women. We can cross-reference descriptions of "bloody flux," explore the symbolism of bleeding, and consider whether the miracle recorder used "bleeding" as a catch-all label for "women's problems." Did he record Maria's story because it resembled that of the bleeding woman in the Gospels who used medicine in vain but then touched Christ's cloak and was cured? Was Maria invented to advertise a new cult?[2] It is also possible to ask more complex questions. Was Maria ill because she was bleeding or because she was unable to conceive? When did her bleeding become viewed as an illness? Did she see menstruation or pregnancy as an illness? Was Maria always viewed as ill because she was female? Medical historians find it difficult to answer questions of this kind with limited sources. They are hesitant about trying to answer questions using cultural methods. This chapter will bring together social and cultural approaches to late-medieval sick women, providing a Portuguese case study.

FROM A SOCIAL TO A CULTURAL HISTORY OF WOMEN'S HEALTH AND HEALING

Over the last twenty years, social historian Monica Green has revolutionized the history of women's health care. She has carried out painstaking archival and manuscript research, greatly enhancing our understanding of theory and practice.[3] Despite these achievements, the sick medieval woman is still an obscure figure. Recent research focuses on the female healer, gynecology, childbirth, and the dead female body. There are cultural histories of the female body but not of sick women.[4] Green, who regularly produces overviews of the history of medicine, is frustrated by cultural historians who analyze medieval attitudes toward the body without much awareness of medical texts or social contexts.[5] The kinds of comparisons sometimes attempted by cultural historians can introduce serious anachronisms. Cultural history is sometimes criticized for its lack of rigor.[6] Yet Green also seems to feel uncertainty about the future development of medical history. She worries it has become isolated from mainstream history. It is also criticized for its lack of rigor.[7] Although still a *very* long way off, especially for some regions of Europe such as the one considered subsequently, there will come a time when the lives of medieval women will be well mapped out socially but culturally will remain terrae incognitae. So what happens next?

As early modernist Mary Fissell argues in an essay that deeply influences this chapter, it is not just a case of documenting health care for women, but of exploring how women made "sense of their lives, of the natural world, of social relations, of their bodies."[8] To develop the field in the future, social historians like Green recognize that they need to go beyond medical treatises and use a much wider range of sources, even if it means drawing on the expertise of others.[9] This shift does not mean abandoning the archival methods that form the bread and butter of social history. It does mean becoming multidisciplinary and collaborative, as in the controversial new discipline of medical humanities, which explores health and healing in all its cultural dimensions, including history, art, music, literature, and philosophy.[10] Cultural history is not an ineffectual way of papering over the cracks in the evidence, as a few historians argue, but can reaffirm the work of many medievalists and early modernists who already work on alternative sources for a better idea of how people understood illness.

Although it is possible to push back further in time for the origins of cultural influences on the history of medieval and early modern medicine, a crucial date was 1985 when the doyen of social history, Roy Porter, published a medical history "from below": the history of the patient rather than of the practitioner. Contained within this influential article was a research agenda that has rarely been fulfilled. Porter's history of the patient included: "the material conditions of communities in times past," "belief systems, images and symbols," "the language of pain," "sufferers' characterizations and classifications of illnesses," and "what did people do when they fell sick?"[11] Thus, at its fullest extent, this agenda encompassed cultural and social history, embracing both empirical and speculative approaches. Porter was vague here about literary and visual sources that could make sense of suffering, though he used them elsewhere. He said little about women, neglected gender issues, took too many things for granted, and relied too much on the concept of the "medical marketplace," a construct of the 1980s that has since been criticized.[12] However, Porter's agenda is still powerful. Its failure to produce the radical step change that it promised was not due to limited sources, as many early modernists demonstrated, but rather to two methodological problems.[13]

Firstly, Porter's research agenda foundered against the rocky shores of multidisciplinarity. A sole researcher cannot produce a total history of the sufferer without ending up with interpretive errors. The second more serious obstacle to the realization of Porter's vision was one that he already tried to downplay in 1985: Michel Foucault's theories about power relations. Porter accepted Foucault's influential idea that a "patient" is the product of the medical "gaze," a subject created by the physician with no independent existence, but he tried to argue for a "sufferers' history" before the patient-practitioner relationship came into being: what did the sick do *before* consulting a healer? Porter suggested that for the premodern period much of Foucault's theorizing about power was less relevant.[14] This *may* be true but the "patient" remains a highly unstable category that is often avoided by medievalists.[15] In contrast, they happily study the female healer but very much still "from below" and not fully integrated into broader health care issues. Many historians still believe that wealthier patients chose academic physicians first and only later turned to what Porter called "the gaggle of herbalists, nurses, wisewomen, bonesetters, ladies of the house, horse-doctors, empirics, itinerant tooth-drawers, peddlers, showmen, witches, clergymen, barbers, charlatans, and so forth."[16] Yet across medieval Europe these people, many of whom were women, may in fact have taken care of most women—and men.

Porter's work was pioneering, paving the way for two generations of scholars who pushed the boundaries much further. What makes the recent work of early modernists Sandra Cavallo, David Gentilcore, and Margaret Pelling so refreshing is that they focus on Porter's "gaggle," repositioning female healers as integral to a community of barbers, "charlatans" and "artisans" or "technicians" of the body, rather than as the dregs of medical practice or a special group.[17] These historians refer to "medical pluralism" when discussing multiple healers and different types of sick people, since it incorporates miracle cures and domestic remedies under the umbrella of medicine without suggesting a hierarchical structure. The idea of artisans of the body allows us to include wig makers, cooks, and valets as part of health care. It helps make sense of images such as Figure 4.1, used as an illustration for barley soup in one manuscript of the *Tacuinum Sanitatis*, a sumptuous health guide from late fourteenth-century Italy. The glimpse of women nursing another woman shows how the domestic environment underpinned health care in the ideal world of its elite readers.[18]

The artisans approach bodes well for the history of women since it redirects the eye of medical historians toward wet nurses, carers, and laundresses, but it has not yet been analyzed for its full implications.[19] Most medical history tends not to be gendered *unless* the subject of research is female healers or childbirth, and then the focus is usually women, not women *and* men as it should be.[20] Consider the following problem: should we include go-betweens and prostitutes as artisans of the body since they were believed to maintain male moral health and sexual hygiene? The figure of the brothel-keeper Celestina in the eponymous Spanish dramatic novel of the late fifteenth century, described as having six trades—"laundress, perfumer, a master hand at making cosmetics and replacing damaged maidenheads, procuress and something of a witch"—seems to be located in a pluralistic medical world, yet so far has attracted limited attention from medical historians perhaps because she is still deemed to be too literary.[21]

It should be possible to return to Porter's original research agenda and apply it more rigorously to the female sufferer. This new cultural history of women's health should no longer be conceived of as a history "from below" since the term implies inferiority or separateness. Women did not play lesser roles than those of men even if some of their social opportunities seem limited

FIGURE 4.1: Woman gives a patient savich (barley) soup. *Tacuinum Sanitatis*. Vienna, Österreichische Nationalbibliothek, Codex s.n. 2644, fol. 44 verso. Verona, end of the fourteenth century. © Österreichische Nationalbibliothek, Vienna.

to us. Medieval women were not passive members of their communities, even if they sometimes failed in their strategies. Women's health should be studied side by side with men's health and properly integrated into the history of political events. Medical historians could also pay more attention to family history, archaeology, and food for an understanding of the living conditions of medieval women.[22] Historians need to recognize, as Isidore of Seville did in the seventh century, that "there pertain to medicine not only those things which display the skill of those to whom the name physician is properly applied, but also food and drink, shelter and clothing and every defence and fortification by which our body is kept safe from external attacks and accident."[23] Finally, we cannot even begin to understand beliefs about suffering if we do not embrace theology, art, and literature.[24]

Historians could, for example, draw on literary methods to become more aware of the narrative techniques of their sources. Can we be sure that pilgrimage meant the same for all of the following? Chaucer's Wife of Bath traveled to St. Thomas's shrine at Canterbury in the late fourteenth century, perhaps because of her deafness, although we are not told this for sure; Margery Kempe (d. ca. 1439), often constructed as mentally ill, traveled to shrines across Christendom; Margaret Paston wished to visit the Marian shrine at Walsingham on hearing that her husband had recovered from a serious illness in 1441.[25] The first source is a literary work, the second was a failed saint's life or early autobiography, and the last is a personal letter, although like Kempe's text it was dictated to a male scribe. A narrative approach to saintly healing can take note of the audience, imagery, and belief systems of these sources, creating a better understanding of this particular health care choice.[26]

Another area where it is crucial to understand cultural metaphors is in the study of disease. Historians often still think that they can produce straightforward epidemiologies of the Plague, but we are reliant on the language and prejudices of medieval chroniclers or, in the early modern period, the compilers of bills of mortality. Recent work has highlighted how dependent these compilers were on female "searchers" in the diagnosis of early modern plague.[27] Porter was already aware of the need to avoid biological determinism, but since 1985, criticisms of retrospective diagnosis have demonstrated how important it is to analyze disease classifications in their own context.[28] If we want to understand what health and illness meant for past sufferers, we have to accept their labels, not impose ours.[29]

Peter Biller's groundbreaking study of medieval population shows that medieval people did try to interpret their society and its problems. There could be much more work along these lines. For example, studies of female life expectancy could explore chroniclers' impressions that women were less susceptible to plague, especially in later outbreaks.[30] Most studies of late-medieval women focus on their economic situation after the Plague; they do not look at female mortality in any kind of detail.[31] It is also important to consider what women suffered from other than plague or gynecological problems. Figure 4.2 shows a "disease woman," one of a widespread series of didactic figures probably used as practical guides to anatomy and physiology. There is no doubt that childbearing is important in the image, but this female also

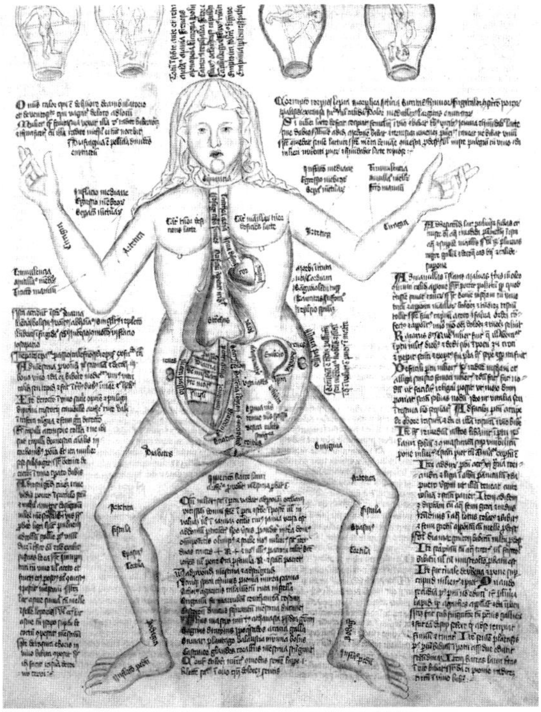

FIGURE 4.2: Disease woman. *Wellcome Apocalypse.* London, Wellcome Library, MS Western 49, fol. 38. ca. 1420–30. © Wellcome Library, London.

has gout and diabetes marked on her limbs, diseases that are usually seen as predominantly male or not part of medieval experience at all. Was all female suffering linked to the womb? Was suffering seen as an intrinsic part of female experience? Biller's analysis of medieval views on human longevity through until the mid-fourteenth century suggests that scholars such as William of Auvergne (d. 1249) or Albertus Magnus (d. 1280) struggled with a series of paradoxes. They believed that women suffered as a result of Eve's sin. Their monthly bleeding was a sign of sinfulness and sickliness—menstruation could be constructed as an illness, and menstrual blood was usually seen as poisonous even transformed into breast milk—but against this was set the strong belief that purgation was beneficial and necessary to female health. A healthy woman was fertile and sexually active; nuns were sometimes perceived to be less healthy due to their celibacy. On the other hand, it was widely argued that childbearing aged a woman and reduced her life expectancy, whereas childless women, although more often ill, lived longer. Against all this was the impression that women generally lived longer than men despite their ailments. Biller cautiously suggests that these paradoxes were the result of learned men trying to weigh up their classical education and religious beliefs against experiences of women in their families and communities. They were not isolated from women as scholars and clerics.[32]

It is very difficult to find female perspectives on menstruation, pregnancy, and ill health to balance these male attitudes. Apart from a tiny number of letters referring to pregnancies and health concerns or a few saints' lives, there is little for us to go on for a female-centered patient history along the lines envisaged by Roy Porter. Most of our sources are still written by men, as with a letter writer in 1480–81 who raised a question mark over the suitability of a bride for Sir William Stonor because of her poor health, suggesting that nevertheless the "beryng of children shuld ease hire infirmyte."[33] This imbalance does not mean that we should therefore dismiss the Middle Ages as misogynistic and medieval women as passive victims. There were of course some very hostile views of women and very real inequalities between men and women, but was gender more of a problem than geographic location, life-cycle stage, social status, or source genre? It is crucial that we analyze the genre of text from whence comes our information on attitudes and behaviors, comparing courtesy literature, fabliaux, sermons, letters, legal cases, and miracles. As a new study of women and law in the Crown of Aragon shows, some women were able to manipulate negative cultural attitudes to benefit their legal situation.[34] Women were acutely aware of their social problems, and they had their own ideas of how to improve them even if they were not always successful. We need more studies of sick women in their communities to illustrate this further.

It is possible to avoid the problems of written sources by looking at material culture and archaeology.[35] Although we cannot determine cause of death from skeletons in most cases, and most pathological traces on the skeleton reflect chronic illness rather than the acute fevers that must have killed the majority of people, archaeological methods can reveal useful data about female diet, longevity, and living conditions. Paleopathologists see little evidence that women were more malnourished or sicker than men, although Anne Grauer acknowledges that frailer members of communities may not have lived long enough for illness to mark their bones. There was a higher incidence of osteoporosis, fractures, and arthritis among older women, something that attracts little attention from medical historians. Archaeological data is as culturally constructed as any other knowledge, and we need to beware of overinterpreting the evidence. However, there is no doubt that archaeology can both complement and contest written texts and, for poorer communities, often provides our only evidence for daily life.[36]

Turning to material and visual culture, it is clear that both have been very influential on the history of medicine. Building on pioneering work by Loren Mackinney and Peter Murray Jones, medieval medical historians now use visual sources in much more sophisticated ways, no longer relegating them to a purely illustrative role but acknowledging them as primary sources in their own right.[37] For the history of women's health, most work has been done on depictions of childbirth, especially the surgical method of removing a fetus from its dead or dying mother misleadingly referred to as Caesarean section, and on artifacts associated with the lying-in period such as the birth trays of Renaissance Italy studied to great effect by Jacqueline Mussachio.[38] For example, one such tray depicts a high-status woman in her chamber receiving visitors and gifts after the birth of her child, which can be seen being bathed in the foreground. The woman is surrounded by domestic possessions and nurtured in an entirely female world. Her situation is closely comparable to contemporary depictions of the births of the Virgin Mary, as shown in Figure 4.3, or John the Baptist. Mussachio and others show that representations of women in birth trays, altar

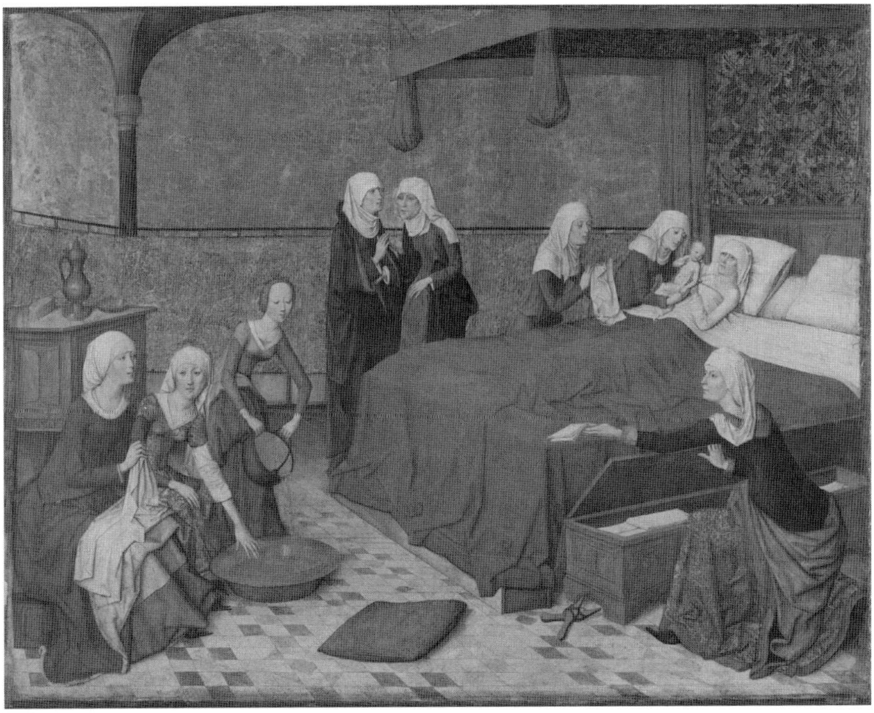

FIGURE 4.3: Master of the Life of Virgin Mary, *Birth of the Virgin*, from a polyptych with scenes from the Life of the Virgin Mary, ca. 1460–65. Alte Pinakothek, Bayerische Staatsgemäldesammlungen, Munich, Germany. Photo courtesy of bpk, Berlin/Art Resource, NY.

pieces, and books of hours can be used both for the study of idealized domestic space and as a method of interpreting the attitudes of women *and* men toward childbearing, since these objects were usually commissioned and exchanged by men.[39] Men may have put pressure on their wives to reproduce through the gift of suggestive religious images, as has been argued for the exquisite book of hours presented to Jeanne d'Evreux (d. 1371) by her husband on their marriage in 1324. This manuscript juxtaposes images of Jeanne with pregnant women in Visitation and Annunciation scenes and can be linked to a succession crisis in the French monarchy.[40]

It is possible to expand this approach to include other types of female images. Kathleen Nolan's work on French royal tombs and seals, for example, looks at queenly manipulation of physical appearance and spatial identity.[41] Medieval art perhaps tells us more about commerce, artistic styles, and patronage than it does about the female self, but medical historians could pay more attention to fashion. As many women today know only too well, fashion can hurt! If we take the plucked hairlines, cosmetics, and tightly corseted waists found in some late-medieval portraits, such as that of Elizabeth Woodville (d. 1492), they seem to present a deceptively familiar image of women sacrificing health for beauty. Or did they represent health, wealth, and fertility in ways unfamiliar to us? Such images did not go without criticism at the time. In the tales written by the Knight of La Tour Landry for his daughters in the late fourteenth century, a dead woman had needles driven into her head and her face covered in burning oil as punishment for plucking her hair and painting her face when alive.[42] In the late fifteenth century, Princess Anne of France (d. 1522) warned against fashion in the courtesy book she wrote for her young daughter Suzanne. Anne told of three princes intent on choosing brides from a noble family. They found that one sister was foolish, another unchaste, and a third "so constrained by her clothing that her heart had been weakened," causing infertility.[43] Monica Green admits that she once had reservations about the beautifying recipes in many medical manuscripts, feeling that they were hardly of life and death import. Yet Montserrat Cabré and Carmen Cabellero-Navas have convinced her that cosmetics were closely related to female health as beautification was a crucial precursor to procreation.[44] As these cautionary tales suggest, beautification was thought to have a profound impact on moral and physical health. Anne of France, herself beset with fertility problems, seems to be telling her daughter that a healthy girl was a fertile girl. Yet in order to present themselves as sexually appealing to men, women risked harming themselves and ruining their chances of childbearing. This is one of the paradoxes that a cultural approach to women's health can explore in more nuanced detail. Incorporating the material, the visual and the literary is not wallpapering over the evidence; if combined with traditional archival evidence, it can build whole new walls.

BEING SICK AND FEMALE IN MEDIEVAL PORTUGAL

The rest of this chapter will explore some of the issues already raised in a historical context that will be new to most people. It is based on long-standing research into medicine in late-medieval Portugal, which has shifted in recent years from a social history based on prosopographical methods undertaken in the archives to one that incorporates narratology, material culture, and network theory. The change in approach is partly motivated by the challenges and opportunities of Portuguese sources. There are few cases of actual medical practice; most documented medical practitioners sat on town councils, received royal privileges, or were embroiled in disputes. In contrast, there are numerous documents, chronicles, and saints' lives recording the behavior of the sick and injured. Material and visual cultures also offer opportunities for research, although it will not be possible to expand on these aspects here.[45]

Like other parts of Europe, Portugal was affected by plague, warfare, and famine in the late Middle Ages, although it is difficult to delineate their effects due to the absence of contemporary chronicles. Economic and legal evidence suggests that combined they had a major impact on the Portuguese population.[46] It is likely that women's labor became more valued at this time due to the reduced workforce, as is argued happened elsewhere, but this needs further research.[47] Women were certainly victims of fifteenth-century violence. In 1435, Catalina Luis was raped by Afonso Lourenço while she lay ill in bed, naked except for her shift. He also wounded her with a razor on the face and left hand, causing her to lose a finger, but still managed to get a royal pardon.[48] In 1446, Pedro de Lisboa was pardoned for murdering the man who killed his seven-months-pregnant sister by setting off a crossbow in the house.[49]

It is possible that Iberian elites were more affected by plague than their northern European counterparts. The traditional warrior ethos of Iberian kings caused them often to be on campaign and thus susceptible to epidemics. King Alfonso XI of Castile, who died besieging Gibraltar in 1350, seems to have been the only European monarch to die of plague during its first outbreak.[50] Portuguese kings and their courts were closely identified with densely populated towns, a legacy of the Muslim past, which may equally have exposed them to disease. Several Portuguese royal women may have succumbed to plague in the late Middle Ages, but the chronicle reports of these deaths demand close cultural analysis and cannot be taken at face value. For example, according to Gomes Eanes Zurara (d. 1474), Queen Philippa, wife of João I of Portugal, died of plague in 1415 just before Portugal launched its first invasion of North Africa. Both in this chronicle and in the philosophical writings of Philippa's son King Duarte (1433–38), her death was a cipher, a trigger for action, a symbolic watershed in political and personal events, and a profoundly religious and chivalric experience.[51] Similarly, chronicler Fernão Lopes (d. ca. 1459) presented the Plague that broke out fifty years earlier during a Castilian siege of Lisbon in 1384 as a morally significant event. Only the Castilian enemy contracted the disease; their Portuguese prisoners of war were immune. Princess Beatriz, eleven-year-old heiress to the Portuguese throne but married to the besieging King Juan of Castile, got the disease (but recovered), indicating that her allegiance had passed from one camp to the other. Disease in these chronicles is a narrative device and should not be used to plot epidemiological patterns.[52]

The life cycles of some Portuguese royal women appear fairly well documented. The aforementioned Queen Philippa, an English princess, bore eight children and had at least one miscarriage. We know the names of a number of her wet nurses.[53] Two children died in infancy, and Philippa nearly took an abortifacient drink during a last dangerous pregnancy in her mid-forties. This episode should not, however, be taken at face value as evidence for abortifacients in late-medieval Portugal. The episode is found in a hagiographical source as the couple miraculously avoided aborting Prince Fernando who later died a martyr's death in a Moroccan prison in 1443 and was viewed as a saint by his family. Philippa's husband wanted to give her the drink but finally dashed down the cup in response to her pious plea that she would rather die than harm the child.[54]

A more complex cultural debate associates Philippa with her daughter Isabel, Duchess of Burgundy (d. 1471). Both women were old by medieval standards when they married in their late twenties or early thirties. A late fifteenth-century guide to French courtly behavior reveals that Isabel of Burgundy had the ritual of purification or churching explained to her at the time of the birth of her first child in 1430. Rita Costa Gomes takes this as evidence for the ceremony in Portugal. However, as Jacques Paviot points out, the original author of the guide, Eleanor de Poitiers (d. 1509), made it clear that procedures had to be explained to Isabel because Portugal was not at all like France.[55] There is very little evidence for churching in southern Europe, although it was widespread in parts of northern Europe well into the modern period. It is unlikely that Isabel's Portuguese wet nurse would have found the ritual familiar.[56] On the other hand, Philippa is known to have introduced the English rite of Sarum, which includes the churching liturgy, into the Portuguese royal court, and since she was a mature woman at the time of marriage, she may have demanded the ceremony as a normal part of her cultural background and passed it on to her daughter.[57] Social historians have cautiously accepted the argument of cultural historians and anthropologists that churching was a female choice, celebrating survival and community, rather than a misogynistic form of social control.[58]

Philippa's daughter-in-law Leonor of Aragon, wife of King Duarte, certainly had great success in surviving childbirth, having nine children at average intervals of thirteen months, except for the last who was born after a stressful period that may have estranged the couple. Duarte usefully plotted the exact date of most of his children's births in his commonplace book, probably for astrological reasons, and recorded a recipe for sore breasts after childbirth which might relate to Leonor's postpartum experience.[59] Leonor's midwife, Caterina Afonso, is the only one documented for the whole of the Portuguese Middle Ages.[60] Three of Leonor's children died in infancy, and one little girl, Felipa, died of plague aged nine. Leonor found herself coregent of her six-year-old eldest son in 1438 and was eventually forced by her husband's ambitious brothers to go into exile in Castile. She died suddenly in 1445, probably in her mid to late thirties. A forthcoming biography will suggest that Leonor died of an infection that killed her sister at the same time, but medical historians should note that Leonor's fertility and sudden death were important political issues; her removal from the stage was politically fortuitous for chroniclers such as Rui de Pina (d. 1520) who suggested poison as the cause of death.[61] This case is a good example of why we should beware retrospective diagnosis and reminds us that political historians should not neglect health and illness.

If we turn to the later fifteenth-century royal family, we find a very different situation with royal fertility. Between the birth of Leonor's last child in 1439 and the end of the century, there were only five legitimate royal births.[62] Two died in infancy; one died in his youth; and Princess Joana (d. 1490), only daughter of King Afonso V (1438–81), refused to marry and led a retired life in the Franciscan convent at Aveiro. She died aged thirty-eight after many illnesses. Her brother João II (1481–95) died aged forty after a long illness that some chroniclers saw as a political poisoning, since it allowed his cousin Manuel to seize the throne.[63] Modern geneticists might link the low fertility and health problems to repeated intermarriage within the royal family, including uncle and niece alliances. At the time, these matches were seen as politically expedient, but royal infertility was a recognized problem. Rui de Pina argued that

Afonso V and his wife Isabel were only able to conceive João II once an emerald ring known to promote chastity shattered on her finger.[64] In 1483, João II sought the help of a ninth-century martyr, St. Domingos de Queimado, at a shrine near Lamego in northern Portugal long associated with fertility.[65] Princess Joana's refusal to marry was strongly opposed by her father and brother as she was second in line to the throne. Our source for Joana's life, however, is a hagiographical work probably written by the nun Margarida Anes in the early sixteenth century. Joana's ascetic lifestyle and physical suffering were perceived by Margarida as empowering saintly experiences not hapless suffering.[66] As with earlier saintly figures, it is possible to argue that Joana's religious vocation, relationship with food, and attitude toward her body gave her some control over her life.[67] However, to reduce her experiences to modern psychology diminishes our understanding of them.

Although normative texts like saints' lives suggest that fasting and hard labor were the order of the day in monasteries, bioarchaeological evidence from the late Middle Ages implies the opposite. One of the best excavated Portuguese cemeteries is that of the Franciscan nunnery of Santa Clara de Coimbra, shown in Figure 4.4, lived in by women drawn from elite society including royalty between the fourteenth and seventeenth centuries. The seventy

FIGURE 4.4: Santa Clara-a-Velha, Coimbra, Portugal. Photograph by Iona McCleery, used with permission.

anonymous women whose remains have been analyzed were longer-lived than their contemporaries in Coimbra (most were over fifty years old), but they had far worse teeth. One early fifteenth-century skeleton even has a rare example of gold bridgework. Nuns had access to the sugar flooding in from the Portuguese colonies from the late fifteenth century; those of Princess Joana's nunnery in Aveiro for all its austerities received ten *arrobas* (ca. 146 kilos) of sugar annually from the island of Madeira.[68] Consequently, nuns had a greater incidence of dental caries and abscesses. The Coimbra skeletons also show signs of age and inactivity: arthritis, osteoporosis, and poor muscle lesions.[69]

Moving away from princesses and privileged nuns, we have less evidence for nonelite beliefs and practices. Portuguese chancery records provide details of lower-status sick people, but they should not be taken at face value. As with the pardon letters studied by Natalie Zemon Davis for early modern France, the narrative devices of these letters require careful cultural analysis.[70] Some letters provide incidental details that a social historian can surely accept as realistic behavior. For example, in 1455, Diego Lourenço from near Lisbon brought sugar and prunes on a visit to his sick sister (and then got into a fight with her husband).[71] Other stories are more manipulative. In 1456, João Vaz from the Algarve felled his mother-in-law by hitting her with a stick in a blow that was meant for his wife. She died two days later, but he claimed that she died more from the fall than the blow because she was old and tired.[72] Some stories are chilling, not only because of what people could get away with, but also because of the casual language. For example, an illegitimate baby was deposited by one grandmother on the doorstep of the other grandmother, mother of the purported father. As neither family would take the child in, "some say it was eaten by pigs."[73] In another case, a poor unmarried mother buried her baby alive. She claimed she changed her mind and went back to get it by which time passersby had heard it and dug it up.[74] These seemingly powerless people had access to the royal court by unknown means and were able to manipulate cultural expectations in order to avoid the death penalty that would have been their lot in most other kingdoms. Instead of execution, they were exiled to Portuguese colonies, thus becoming as much part of the political history of Portugal as the queens described earlier.[75]

As well as chancery records, Portuguese saints' lives are useful sources for the health problems of poorer women, though we should remember that they had a very different purpose and audience. As in France and England, women received only about a third of miraculous cures.[76] Yet if we look closer, women were vocal supporters of cults, accompanying husbands and children to shrines over long distances and encouraging others to visit (as Maria Domingas's mother did in the opening example of this chapter). Miracle cures show that women suffered from a wide range of conditions and had a range of medical as well as religious health care options. In the case of the cult of Gil de Santarém, the healer of Maria Domingas, in 5 percent of cases the women suffered from nongynecological or obstetric conditions such as broken back, carbuncle, throat abscess, deafness, possession, dumbness, cancer of the mouth, paralysis, fistula of the jaw, fever, bladder stones, and inflammation of the ear.[77] By the early sixteenth century, Gil de Santarém was known for providing help in childbirth: his belt was borrowed by Queen Leonor, third wife of King Manuel, in 1520 to help her in childbirth, but in earlier centuries, de Santarém seems to have been better known as a healer of throat and neck problems.[78] Several women in fact came to the Dominican priory in Santarém seeking medical rather than religious healing from the friars and were only later referred to Gil de Santarém's tomb. For example, a poor woman called Maria Soeiro was affected by demonic suicidal thoughts that brought her to "such a state of fear and alarm that she had neither the customary color nor the health of her body, but was consumed by a ghostly pallor and emaciation." Maria confessed regularly to brother Andre, "an experienced physician" whose role here appears to be that of counselor, medical practitioner, and priest. He eventually advised her to visit de Santarém's tomb.[79] Possessed women appear in miracle collections across Europe, of course, but this case is unusual with its blurring of roles and its sense of a "customary" state of health. Other Portuguese cults are more typical. For example, in 1382 at the tomb of Queen Isabel in Coimbra (d. 1336), shown in Figure 4.5, the healing took place of a woman whose seven demons had refused to leave earlier despite several pilgrimages.[80]

The previous miracle stories suggest that women did not turn to the saints to the exclusion of other healers. If we turn to look at healing choices available in Portugal in the late Middle Ages, it is clear that there was a range of practitioners. Jews formed the majority of physicians, treating Christian women despite ecclesiastical prohibitions. Barbers enjoyed higher status than in northern Europe but are not recorded treating women.[81] There was a ward for women dedicated to St. Clare in the hospital of All Saints in Lisbon.[82] Very few women were themselves formally identified as medical practitioners. Before 1495, only one royal medical license out of 300 was granted to a woman: Isabel Martins, a ferryboat operator of Montemor-o-Velho near Coimbra, licensed in surgery in 1454.[83] After 1495, a few more women were licensed but usually as blessers or specialists rather than as general surgeons like Isabel.[84] The increasing number of female healers is probably due to the expansion of royal bureaucracy rather than, as has been suggested, the dearth of educated practitioners after

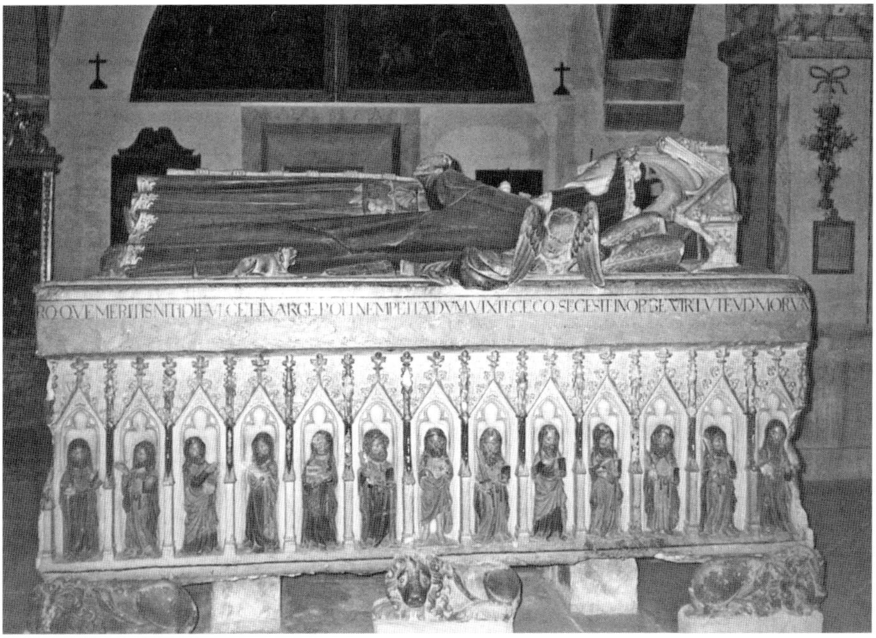

FIGURE 4.5: Tomb of Isabel of Aragon, Santa Clara-a-Nova, Coimbra, Portugal. Photograph by Iona McCleery, used with permission.

the expulsion of Jewish communities in 1496–97.[85] However, the numbers are still tiny. At some point in the late thirteenth century, Maria Martins treated a man for dropsy.[86] Women nursed the plague sick in Oporto and on the island of Madeira in the late-fifteenth and early sixteenth centuries.[87] So far, two female apothecaries and a barber can be documented.[88] Even in 1550, in Lisbon there were only ten nurses of the sick, twenty-five midwives, twelve makers of cosmetics, 324 washerwomen, and twenty *cristaleiras* whose job it was to administer enemas, a peculiarly female job in Portugal.[89]

As time goes on, more female healers may be found, but we need to expand our understanding of women's work to capture them, scrutinizing apparently bland documents more carefully for coded attitudes and values.[90] Connecting some of the aforementioned jobs to medicine requires a return to the concept of *artisans* of the body described previously. Sometimes there is resistance to this broader approach to medicine. After hearing a description of how Queen Isabel of Portugal (d. 1336), canonized in 1625, had treated a wounded leper with an egg white plaster, a conference delegate rejected the suggestion that this was an example of medical knowledge, saying, "well, that's just what women do."[91] Women's knowledge about the body is a contested part of medical history and will continue to be seen as simple domesticity outside the field for some time to come. Another type of artisan has not even entered the debate: the priest's housekeeper. Portuguese priests could apply to the king for permission to have a woman care for them in their old age. For example, in 1440, João Gonçalves was permitted to have a woman in the house to make him medicines as he suffered from gout, stone, and colic. As priestly concubinage was widespread, the woman had to be over fifty for moral reasons. In the case of João Bugalho and his servant Margarida Anes, accorded to him in 1434 when they were both supposed to be over fifty, there seems to have been some impropriety since in 1448 their daughter was legitimated.[92] An excellent example of the priestly carer is Brásia in the satire known as "The Physicians" by Gil Vicente, first performed between 1512 and 1525. The priest for whom Brásia works becomes lovesick, consulting four medics and a friar for advice but also receiving care from his housekeeper. Brásia shares the medics' focus on diet but phrases her views in language reminiscent of the near contemporary figure Celestina.[93] By combining archival and literary sources, it is possible to uncover new kinds of healers in unfamiliar contexts.

CONCLUSION

The observant reader will have noticed that much of this chapter was made up of vignettes from a wide range of sources. It requires a much more collaborative approach to become the kind of total patient history envisaged by Roy Porter. At the same time, it has highlighted problems with sufferers' history: according to whose criteria is somebody suffering? As today, what constituted good health was not standardized. Each case requires microhistorical analysis to take into account local context *and* macrohistorical analysis to compare across Europe and beyond. Bad cultural history is unfortunately often transhistorical, blurring chronological and geographic boundaries. Let us end with a brief example of these issues by returning to the bleeding woman with whom the chapter began.

It might seem easy to start cultural analysis of the bleeding woman by going back to the biblical story that appears to be the point of origin. Yet this tale immediately creates problems since it is actually three stories with significant differences between the Gospels of Matthew, Mark, and Luke. We then have to consider how the stories were interpreted in Christian hermeneutics over the centuries. How were they retold in sermons, church art, and theological writings? Every one of these has a local context, and often it is the circulation of manuscripts that creates the illusion of a bigger picture. How many medieval miracles do we need to study for variations on this theme? Medieval theologians sometimes identified the bleeding woman with Martha, sister of Lazarus and Mary, the latter in her turn merged with Mary Magdalene. Thus, the bleeding woman became the symbol of the active religious life and had siblings also ostracized by pollution but saved by Christ's touch. In the fourteenth century, Álvaro Pais, Franciscan theologian and Bishop of Silves in the Portuguese Algarve, argued that the healing of the woman who touched Christ's robe can be compared to the church bleeding with sin yet cured by the Passion of Christ. The polluted bleeding therefore foretold the holy blood of the Eucharist. Sometimes the bleeding woman was identified with Veronica who traditionally mopped Christ's brow on the way to Calvary, reemphasizing the connection between female and Christological suffering.[94]

In modern biblical exegesis, the bleeding woman is used as a symbol for female exclusion and authority. Modern theologians are interested in her story within a story: in all three versions, Jesus was on his way to heal Jairus's daughter when he met the bleeding woman; healing her meant that the child died before he got there. In Luke, the dead child was twelve years old and the woman had bled for twelve years, suggesting a link between puberty and pathology. The story is also interpreted according to Jewish law, which dictates that women are unclean during menstruation and after childbirth. Therefore, chronic bleeding of any kind means that she cannot go through purification rituals. Bleeding women in medieval Christian miracles invariably bore a child at the end of their ordeal, a nonbiblical addition to the story, but in northern Europe at least their pollution ironically did not end with childbirth but continued another six weeks until churching took place. When exactly therefore were these women thought to be cured?[95]

The apparent continuity of the bleeding woman motif is perhaps what most attracts cultural historians. The problem is that centuries of stories do not help us understand the particular circumstances of Maria Domingas in Portugal. It does not matter whether she really existed; the point is why that miracle, there and then, in that form? In a recent critique of cultural history, Dror Wahrman asked whether societies change over time or whether seemingly new forms of behavior are just old wine in new bottles: is it the same old story in new form?[96] In the case of the bleeding woman, the form does seem to shape the discourse. In medieval miracles, the woman's bleeding became gynecological: this was not stated in the Gospels and even in an early saint's life there was room for nuance; the ninth-century life of St. Leoba identified a bleeding nun's problem as hemorrhoids.[97] Why did the link to gynecology and childbirth develop in these cases? In contrast to miracles, bleeding in medieval chronicles and medical texts was usually acute rather than chronic, a cause of death not long-term ill health. Isabel, the young wife of Afonso V of Portugal, died of bloody flux in 1455. Was this poisoning, as chronicler Rui de Pina suggested, or complications that continued long after childbirth as a modern historian suggests?[98] Again bloody flux was not necessarily gynecological since men could suffer from this condition. How do their symptoms differ? There has been quite a lot of work on the cultural concept of male "menstruation," but the social reality of men's genitourinary problems is sadly neglected.[99]

Does social context matter? Maria Domingas was a woman from the significant royal stronghold of Santarém with its flourishing commercial and religious communities. Her parish of Marvila was one of only five out of fifteen where Gil de Santarém's miracles occurred locally, which might suggest patterns of Dominican missionary activity. The reference to the failure of medicine in Maria's case is not just a motif borrowed from Mark and Luke but resonates in a collection of miracles attributed to a former physician who displayed mixed feelings about medicine but whose brethren practiced it among the laity despite Dominican prohibitions. It is also worth noting that all of de Santarém's surviving vitae were actually written down in the mid-sixteenth century by which time he was known for helping women in childbirth.[100] Did this miracle mean something in particular to local women by that time? Frustratingly it is not possible to find this out. Ultimately, a social investigation into de Santarém's miracles can only go so far. Documents can tell us much about the community in which Maria lived; they say very little about the symbolic significance of her poor health.

It is important to realize finally that the medieval bleeding woman can never be pinned down to one thing, but nor can she float completely free of context. She is both multiple and one at the same time, as is any other sick woman. Philosopher Anne-Marie Mol argues that in modern medicine there can never be a single disease enacted on a single body. We should therefore not expect a neat picture from any historical illness.[101] If we recognize that women and their illnesses can be multiple yet one, transhistorical *and* local, we can bring together cultural and social history in fruitful ways. We need to apply approaches from both fields for the future history of the female patient.

CHAPTER FIVE

Public and Private: Women in the Home, Women in the Streets

KIM M. PHILLIPS

It is anachronistic to draw straightforward associations between *woman* and *home* for the medieval era. The domestic house was a gender neutral or even symbolically masculine space in which women played vital roles as wives, mothers, daughters, sisters, or servants. In some social strata—particularly royal and aristocratic families—and in Mediterranean regions, women appear to have been more likely to spend a large portion of their time confined within the home or even to certain domestic spaces, but this is somewhat different from the demarcation of home as woman's sphere and the wider world of economics, political debate, and governance as men's sphere, as conceived in conservative nineteenth-century ideologies. If we are to stumble down the rocky path of considering public and private and the associated metaphor of separate spheres as they might have applied to medieval women, it is necessary to start by acknowledging that modern conventions are likely to lead us astray.

Divisions between public (political, economic, juridical, intellectual, impersonal) and private (domestic, familial, spiritual, emotional, and intimate) realms need not, in theory, be gendered, but women's history has tended to use the model almost interchangeably with the concept of separate spheres. Amanda

Vickery notes "public and private," "separate spheres," and "domesticity" as key categories of women's history, though she argues that even during their supposed nineteenth-century heyday the separation of spheres probably had greater force in ideology than women's day-to-day lives.[1] The ideal nineteenth-century woman lived to create a pleasant home life for her husband, to offer an exemplum of Christian moral rectitude, and to nurture her children. In its conventional formulation, the separation of spheres occurred in the wake of eighteenth-century industrialization, which fostered greater separation of work—the place of men—and home—the place of women and children. The image of the woman as "the angel in the house" provided vivid illustration of new forms of femininity by the mid-nineteenth century. Though it was more a literary commonplace than a reflection of women's real lives, the vision of the private space of home as the proper place for women existed as a powerful model for nineteenth-century and early twentieth-century gender relations.

Yet it is a vision only uneasily applicable to medieval European women. Medievalists are divided over its relevance to their field of study. For example, Anna Dronzek contends that "medieval Europe . . . made little distinction between the public and private," and that women's subordination in that period cannot be attributed to separate spheres.[2] Shannon McSheffrey shows that historians' habit of considering marriage and sexuality as branches of medieval private life, and their related tendency to label extraecclesiastical conjugal contracts as "clandestine" (thus secret, illicit), misreads medieval understanding of respectable marriage processes in which homes and taverns could quite properly function as places for the public exchange of vows.[3] Conversely, Diane Shaw notes several examples of legal disputes from fourteenth-century London in which citizens attempted to protect their "private business" (*privata*) from the gaze of their neighbors via windows, towers, and apertures.[4] Felicity Riddy suggests, noting frequent associations between the Middle English *privé* and intimate bodily functions such as washing, dressing, defecating, and having sex, that the privacy that citizens wished to preserve concerned matters of potential shame.[5] Such privacy is not necessarily masculine or feminine, though Riddy has elsewhere contended that the most basic physical care of the body, especially in illness and death, was the province of women.[6] Georges Duby relates how the terms *publicus* and *privatus* survived from classical Latin, where *publicus* denoted the realm of the forum, the magistrate, the governor, and property held in common by the people, while *privatus* indicated all that was singular and personal, property held for one's personal use, and the realm of the *domus* where public forms of power gave way to the rule of the *paterfamilias*.[7] While particular elements of this opposition vary depending on

FIGURE 5.1: Tobit, blind in bed, attended by two women. Guyart des Moulins, *Bible historiale,* vol. IV. London, British Library, MS Royal 15. D. 1, fol. 18 recto. The Netherlands, ca. 1470. © The British Library Board.

historical context—such as the modern erosion of the power of the male head over his household—the Roman distinction between what counted as public and private realms held true (according to this account) into the nineteenth century. Duby contends that the fundamental concepts apply similarly to usages of *publicus* and *privatus* in medieval documents, though new usages also arose such as associations between the private and the secret, and therefore morally suspect.

Yet it is debatable how far the distinction applied to physical spaces. For much of the medieval period, political and economic activities took place within the household. A king's court was not only his home but also the chief arena for exercise of justice, meetings with councilors, issuing of laws, diplomatic negotiations, and management of the kingdom's finances. A merchant used his home to store goods and conduct business, while an artisan's front rooms were his workshop and retail outlet. Peasant homes often housed livestock as well as families. With continual blurring of the boundaries between home and production, the realm of the domestic and the realm of affairs, it is invalid to draw any clean lines between public and private in a spatial sense. It is possible, though, that by the fourteenth century a stronger sense of "home" centering on women's roles and the intimate sphere was gaining some purchase.[8]

Medieval Europe from the eleventh to fifteenth centuries therefore presents an interesting opportunity to confront assumptions about gendered spheres. Because other chapters in this volume deal with matters such as women's work roles, opportunities for political influence, and aspects of the religious life (see in particular the chapters by Bardsley, Huneycutt, and French), this chapter focuses on the gendered nature of space for medieval laywomen, in the home and on the street.

We should begin with the peasant majority, as it is often estimated that at least 90 percent of the population of medieval Europe lived in rural settlements and made a basic living from agrarian and pastoral activities, which were sometimes supplemented by crafts and trade.[9] For the vast majority of medieval women, then, home was a relatively simple structure, but its size and layout varied a good deal from place to place.[10] Simple one- or two-room houses were found everywhere. Many were rectangular or oval structures, single storied with a door located on the long side of the building (or on both sides, forming a passage through the house), accommodating the family within one main room with a hearth in its center and a single smaller bedchamber at one end. An expanded variant of this model added a third room or space for livestock or storage at the opposite end. By the fourteenth century, a second story was sometimes built above the chamber, creating a room called a "solar" in English sources, but in many places the standard structure remained single storied. Variants on these basic house types were the "farm," where the relative wealth of the owners allowed for the separation of the homestead into a dwelling house and functional buildings such as byre and barn, and the Mediterranean multiroomed, multilevel house where yard or garden space was often minimal.

Some of the best-known examples of medieval longhouses have been excavated at the deserted Yorkshire village of Wharram Percy, where the majority of peasant dwellings were longhouses, that is, rectangular structures where family and animals were housed under one roof.[11] In sharp contrast with these relatively open, well-spaced houses were the residences of the villagers of Rougiers, perched on a Provençal hilltop, where the topography, strong winds, and enclosure within the walls of a seigneurial castle produced tall narrow houses tightly packed in its winding lanes, without yards or gardens or little more than alleys between houses. Despite the lack of space, the majority of hearths were located on ground outside the houses.[12] When Rougiers residents wished to cook or eat, they did so outside in close proximity to their neighbors.

Within these basic structures, options for privacy or for any kind of separation of spheres were limited. English retirement agreements, drawn up between family members when a male tenant grew too old to carry on with farmwork or an elderly mother was widowed, can touchingly illustrate the closeness of rural family spatial relations. In some houses where a larger number of rooms were available, the retiree was granted one or two rooms and their access (most often a chamber or chamber and solar) and permission to sit by the family hearth in the hall, but in simpler houses, the only option was to share space. This was the case for John Whyting's widow in Wymondham, Norfolk, in 1407, who was granted entry to the home, a place at the hearth, and a bed. Such allocation of space seems to have been based more on age than gender, as older male and female members of families received comparable provisions. The importance of the hearth as the center of domestic life (though possibly showing an urban household) is illustrated in idealized form in the late fourteenth-century Italian health guide, *Tacuinum Sanitatis*, as shown in Figure 5.2. The primary family of parents and children would sleep together in an inner room or, in more complex houses, an upper room or chamber. As indicated in English coroners' inquest records, it was not unusual for the family to share a bed. Barbara Hanawalt notes a case from 1322 in which a bed caught fire from a falling candle, killing a father and son but sparing the mother and other son.[13] Scholarly interest in social and personal uses of buildings is less developed for European areas outside Britain, yet it may be that rather different conventions applied. Peasant housing in villages of the Tierra de Campos region of Castile, for example, had quite a different layout from the common English plan. The houses were frequently divided into a larger number of rooms, variously arranged but sometimes with a hall and kitchen near the front, bedrooms in the middle and in a second floor above the front, and at the rear service areas including cellars, underground granaries, and space for livestock and fowl.[14] These relatively complex buildings, with multiple rooms over more than one level, may have afforded opportunity for greater separation of space, such as differentiation by gender, but the crowded houses at Rougiers (where cooking and eating were apparently done outside) show that this was not necessarily the case.

Hanawalt's important study of peasant families, now more than twenty-five years old, asserted that English coronial evidence on accidental deaths "confirms women's chief sphere of work as the home and men's as the fields

FIGURE 5.2: Conversation in front of the fire. *Tacuinum Sanitatis*. Vienna, Österreichische Nationalbibliothek, Codex s.n. 2644, fol. 100 verso. Verona, end of the fourteenth century. Photo courtesy of Alinari/Art Resource, NY.

and forests."[15] This image of separate gendered spheres of peasant labor has been contested, notably by P.J.P. Goldberg, who suggested that the same evidence could indicate not gendered spheres but rather a gendered division of labor: men's tasks outside the home and village environment (such as carting, milling, and construction) happened to be more dangerous than the jobs undertaken by women away from the home (reaping, milking, weeding, shearing, and binding).[16] Indeed, the breakdown of figures also supplied by Hanawalt suggests that even if one were to view the data in terms of spheres rather than tasks, it only slightly favors the home as women's chief working environment.[17] Where 29.5 percent of women's accidental deaths in her sample took place at home (compared with 11.8 percent of men's), 22 percent of women's accidental deaths (compared with only 18.1 percent of men's) occurred in places

Hanawalt defines as "public areas" (including greens, streets, highways, markets, and churches). Even in places she tellingly labels "work areas" (such as fields, marl pits, and shops), 17.5 percent of women's deaths by misadventure occurred (compared with 37.7 percent of men's). Adding in places under her heading "private property" such as neighbors' or manor houses and taverns (9 percent of women's deaths and 6.2 percent of men's), and "bodies of water" (22 percent of women's deaths and 26.2 percent of men's), we see that 70.5 percent of women's accidental deaths took place outside the family home compared with 88.2 percent of men's. Even if this may be taken to indicate a stronger association between home and women compared with men, the difference is only relative. One wonders whether the shops mentioned were actually often within the home also, and if deaths there were counted in the figures for "Home," whether that would reduce the different connotations for women and men still further.

Shops also complicate any assumptions we might hold about households in towns. A chief feature of many medieval urban houses was their incorporation of both public and private activities, with artisans' workshops or retail shops located under the same roof as familial housing. Frequently these were at the front, ground-floor level with domestic rooms behind and above. In northern towns and cities, houses opened directly onto the street, and the larger ones were multistoried, with basements, ground and first floors and sometimes second floors and attics.[18] Movement between street and front room seems to have often been open and fluid. Some late-medieval French inventories, for example, list chairs "used to prop the door" open or for sitting at or outside the door. In a London church court case from 1472, an apprentice, William Taylbos, tells how he knew that Rose Langtoft, a female servant, did not leave the home of her employer on a specific afternoon from noon to five o'clock but rather stayed within the house (washing clothes in the hall and preparing food in the kitchen, according to her employer's deposition), knowing this "because he sat in the shop openly, next to the street, for that whole time, where he could have seen Rose leaving the house if she were so disposed."[19] This was not necessarily a Europe-wide practice, though. A few decades later (1535), the Venetian ambassador Marino Giustiniano thought it worth commenting on Parisian "men and women, old and young, masters and servants" who sat in their shops, on doorsteps, or in the street.[20] Other English church court records portray young urban women moving between the house and other urban locations: meeting sweethearts in taverns, talking with friends in the street, going to rivers to wash clothes or fetch water, and running local errands.[21] A 1451 inventory from York detailing the contents of the large house of John Stubbes, a barber-surgeon, mentions a "women's *camera*," but as Riddy notes, this appears to have designated a room in which women's work took place rather than a space to which they were restricted.[22] Urban women, including unmarried servant girls, were not necessarily confined to homes, though their spheres of movement were likely generally limited to local neighborhoods.

The houses of urban elites in cities such as Florence and Paris were large and divided into numerous rooms. Merchants, officials, and urban gentry often had "counting rooms," and some also had studies or "writing rooms" within their homes, further indicating a blurring of domestic and business spaces.[23] Any privacy afforded the inhabitants was usually a male preserve (in the *Vita nuova*, Dante tells of shutting himself in his room to cry without being seen, while Petrarch wept over Augustine's confessions in his private chamber), but think also of Christine de Pizan reading the book of Matheolus in her study before her mother called her down for supper.[24] Guillebert de Metz's early fifteenth-century description of Paris portrayed the urban homes of bishops, prelates, parliamentarians, and royal officials as large, lavish, and comfortable. The home of Jacques Duchié—a high-ranking official at the royal Court of Accounts—had peacocks in the courtyard, paintings in the hallway, and rooms full of musical instruments and chess sets. His domestic tastes could indeed be described as "manly": in addition to the music and gaming rooms, a separate chamber was filled with "crossbows, some of which were painted with beautiful figures . . . standards, banners, pennants, bows, picks, *faussars*, *planchons*, axes, guisarmes, mail of iron and lead, shields, bucklers, breastplates, canon and other devices."[25] Home for Duchié was a showpiece for a distinctively aristocratic, French masculinity, not a chintzy realm of women and babies. This Frenchman's *hôtel* was also, in a sense, his castle, as its contents suggested not only domestic comforts but also a fortress's defenses. The house included a square room perched above the rest of the dwelling like a minitower from which one could survey the city while dining comfortably on fine wines and meats. Most intriguingly, and highly suggestive of a sense of the aristocratic urban home as a private (though not feminine) space, is Guillebert's detail of "a window most wonderfully crafted, through which a hollow iron head could be projected out of doors; through this head one could look about and talk to those outside if need be, without revealing oneself."[26]

Still, there was plenty of variety in size, and many urban houses had only two or three rooms; often a single room had to do triple duty as kitchen, hall, and bedroom. Poor families in late-medieval Tuscan towns often lived in one room, while some of the slightly more fortunate rented several rooms located in different parts of a large tenement building, sharing a staircase with other residents and moving from one short one-year lease to another.[27]

Plenty of conservative voices in sermons, exempla, and conduct books warned girls and women to guard themselves against the perceived dangers of the streets. The feminine ideal was of the woman or maiden working diligently within the confines of her home. Preachers told the cautionary tale of Dinah, Jacob's daughter (from Genesis 34), who left home to see women of other places, only to be taken and raped. According to sermon writers, foolish maidens "that walk about in meads and fair places leading dances and singing" only bring it on themselves when they lose their maidenhead. "For it befalls maidens to be in stillness and enclosed, as our Lady Saint Mary was when the angel came to her and found her in a privy chamber and not standing nor walking in the streets."[28] Yet, in actuality, women of all ages and diverse social backgrounds went out into the streets and public places of Europe to work, trade, converse, and play, as depicted in Figure 5.3. David Nicholas notes that in fourteenth-century Ghent, despite legal disqualifications that technically barred women from transacting business without the consent of a husband or male guardian, it was normal and indeed expected that girls would earn their own bread once physically and intellectually capable of it, and married women and widows engaged in all manner of commerce (including, in this medieval European financial hub, money changing) either in partnership with their husbands or independently as a merchant woman—similar to the English *femme sole*—or as a widow. Women traded in the marketplace and could even be members of certain guilds such as the barbers', wagoners', and fruit mongers' (though with certain limitations), and though women apparently could not join the trouser makers' and fishmongers' guilds, they were in any case active in the businesses. Though they "had no political rights," never serving as a guild official or member of the town council, they played wide public roles in an economic sense.[29]

In the houses of the poor and the rich, the hall had the greatest symbolic function as well as multiple uses, yet it was within the great houses and castles of the elite that the hall acquired its deepest associations with power and display. The hall was neither public nor private space in any strict sense of the words. It was overwhelmingly a masculine location in a symbolic sense, but this is not to say no women were found there.[30] It was the space in which the *seigneur* received petitioners, dispensed justice, and fed his retinue and guests. By the fifteenth century, the hall might host set-piece dinners, which were as much a theatrical performance of lordship and homage as they were an occasion to eat. Such displays were visible to the whole household in English great houses,

FIGURE 5.3: Market scene: left section with greengrocers and women. Fresco, Castello d'Issogne, Val d'Aosta, Italy. Fifteenth century. Photo courtesy of Scala/Art Resource, NY.

where the highest and lower social orders dined together under the same roof (though with the magnates grouped at the "high" end, often on a dais), while the clearer segregation of social orders in France was signaled architecturally with a *grande salle* for nobles and clerics located physically above a *salle base* for household members of lower status.[31] The ceremonial nature of life in the halls of noble households was such that at times it even mirrored sacred ritual, as is apparent in detailed ordinances of household ritual surviving from the Burgundian Netherlands and Yorkist England.[32] *The Luttrell Psalter*, made probably between 1325 and 1335 for Sir Geoffrey Luttrell of Lincolnshire, pairs an image of the Last Supper—model for the sacral celebration of the Eucharist—with an image of the manuscript's patron seated for dining at his high table. Mark Gardiner suggests such parallels are apparent also in the architectural arrangement of the hall, which (as many others have also noted) reflects the church layout and separation of food and drink storage places into "pantry" (from *panis*, bread) and "buttery" (from *buttae*, barrels).[33] Earlier practice may have been less elaborate, yet from the mid-thirteenth century, monarchs in Castile, Aragon, and France instituted detailed sets of ordinances for their households, which described the responsibilities of court officials and fostered increasingly elaborate court ceremonial.[34] The important offices (steward, marshal, seneschal, chamberlain, usher, cupbearer, etc.) were as far as we know all filled by men, according to late-medieval ordinances and wage lists in household accounts. As such, some scholars have contended that the houses of the English elite were virtually woman-free zones: for example, examining staff lists in account books, Kate Mertes concluded that "female household members were practically nonexistent." Yet this was not the case; rather, women were less likely to receive a wage or hold an office with an occupational title than male retainers, and thus unlikely to show up in account books.[35] Women seem to have played a stronger ceremonial role in early medieval halls, as indicated by the figure of the "lady with a mead cup" whose duty of offering a drink from the communal cup to visitors was central to forging bonds of hospitality and obligation in many Celtic and Germanic societies. This is vividly portrayed in the Anglo-Saxon poem *Beowulf*.[36] Duby notes that a knight's daughter held the office of butler (*boutellier*, the official in charge of the wine) in a castle at Mons in the early thirteenth century, yet indicates that this was unusual: she inherited the office from her father, and as a canoness, she was sexually off-limits.[37] Part of the literary conceit of the fifteenth-century Middle English poem *The Assembly of Ladies* is in casting noble- and gentlewomen as household officers. While the poem's placement of a lady (Lady Loiaulte) at the head of its fictional household mirrored practice in noble widows' houses, such as those of Cecily, Duchess of York, and Alice Chaucer, Duchess of Suffolk, to have a household staffed entirely by women was "complete fantasy."[38] Noblewomen's roles in managing estates as well as running households are well documented, and their roles as "estate and household administrators . . . represented the acceptable faces of feminine power and influence,"[39] yet while they might head a household, women were not usually its key servants. An English royal ordinance from 1494 indicates that a queen's gentlewomen and ladies could take the place of male servants during childbirth: "no man to come into the chamber where she shall be delivered, save women; and they to be made all manner of officers, as butlers, panters, sewers, carvers, cupbearers; and all manner or officers shall bring to them all manner of things to the great chamber door and the women officers for to receive it in the chamber."[40] A scene of the birth of the future King Henry VI to Catherine of Valois in 1421, shown in Figure 5.4, depicts a woman-only bedchamber with one of the ladies speaking to a man who waits outside the door. In childbirth, the great chamber became a strictly feminine space.

If the medieval noble house was either a masculine or gender-neutral space, and the central space of the hall was symbolically masculine—even though in some instances the position of "lord" was occupied by a woman—other places in the house were more deeply associated with women. In many works of imaginative and prescriptive literature, the chamber was viewed as a feminine space. The medieval historian of the counts of Guines describes spatial divisions in the twelfth-century castle where the lord and lady slept in the great

FIGURE 5.4: Birth of Henry VI, from the *Pageant of the Birth, Life and Death of Richard Beauchamp Earl of Warwick*. London, British Library, MS Cotton Julius E. IV, item 6, fol. 22 verso. England, ca. 1485–90. © The British Library Board.

chamber and their children and servants in an adjoining room. Further chambers were built above the lord's bedchamber—one for the sons to sleep in "if they wished" and the other (near the guardroom) for the elder daughters to sleep in "by necessity."[41] Duby's account of gendered space in high-medieval castles is inconsistent, however. On one page he asserts that high-medieval aristocratic literature portrays maidens as "carefully watched to protect their virginity until the moment when they were conveyed in solemn cortège to the castle of their future spouse" and on another that "the *chambre des dames* was not a place for seduction and amusement but a kind of prison, in which women were incarcerated because men feared them." Yet only a few pages later he describes a literature which portrays the noble household as a hotbed of "private sexuality," with not only older ladies roaming the night corridors looking for a tryst but even the lord's daughters: "With so many unmarried men and women living in close proximity to the lord and his lady, promiscuity was inevitable."[42]

The most detailed study of gendered space in mostly English aristocratic households, by archaeologist Roberta Gilchrist, supports a picture of sexual segregation among the medieval elite. Arguing that the "honour and patrimony of lordship rested on the impermeability of both the castle and the female body," she finds "little doubt that noble and royal women were spatially secluded for at least part of their lives."[43] Her analysis rests on evidence for women's chambers or apartments in six British castles, supplemented by largely literary textual sources depicting intimate, enclosed spaces such as inner chambers and walled gardens as feminine. Amanda Richardson's analysis of the access patterns in a number of English castles points to similar conclusions, showing queens' quarters as often the most deeply embedded and inaccessible parts of the castle complex.[44] Yet to argue for a broad pattern of strictly policed segregation seems too strong, partly because even rooms in the homes of the medieval elite often had a variety of uses (so that, for example, what was a bedchamber by night was also used for dining and receiving visitors by day) and because noble and royal women would be served by male servants for all but their most intimate needs. Gentlewomen and ladies waiting upon high-status women provided companionship and attended to their mistress's dress, body, and bedding, and to some extent assisted with financial and political dealings, but it was left to male servants to bring and serve food, provide lights, clear the rushes, and guard the doors.[45] Household accounts for English queens, including Joan of Navarre, Margaret of Anjou, Elizabeth Woodville, and Elizabeth of York, and noble or gentry women, including Alice de Bryene, Elizabeth Berkeley, and Elizabeth de Burgh, are no doubt typical in their listing of male servants working as chamberlains, ushers, yeomen, grooms, and pages within these female-headed households.[46] Descriptions of both festive and more mundane occasions, moreover, indicate that noble women were not enclosed in private quarters but rather dined alongside their husbands or male fellow servants. For example, when a Dutch lord visited King Edward IV and Elizabeth Woodville in 1472, the guest dined at high table in the company of the king, queen, and many important lords and ladies, and the Dutch male servants dined in an outer chamber with the queen's gentlewomen, the men arrayed along one side of the table and the women along the other.[47] The "Harleian Ordinances" of the 1460s or 70s order male retainers and the gentlewomen of the household to dine at the same table, while in the "Household Book" of the fifth Earl of Northumberland from the early sixteenth century, the countess's female servants—gentlewomen and chamberers—were ordained to sit at the "Knight's board" next to the gentleman usher, yeoman usher, chief clerk of the kitchen, and cofferer.[48] From another cultural context, scenes from Boccaccio's tale of "Alatiel" (*Decameron*, II.7) on a fifteenth-century Italian chest depict mixed dining in an aristocratic setting, as shown in Figure 5.5.

Royal and aristocratic women were not necessarily subject to the strictest sexual control. The courts and great households of England, for example, allowed noblewomen a certain degree of license in their sexual self-expression and more mingling with men than the model of the protected, enclosed woman suggests. Nicola McDonald has shown how dice games devised for noble and

FIGURE 5.5: Master of the Jarves Cassone, *Story of Alatiel*, detail. Museo Correr, Venice, Italy. Fifteenth century. Photo courtesy of Cameraphoto Arte, Venice/Art Resource, NY.

gentry players "encourage a dialogue between women and men, gathered together for the purpose of social entertainment, around matters of secular, and especially sexual, desire." These "challenge our preconceptions about women's leisure habits and cultural tastes," suggesting that "amorous intrigue" was a regular aspect of women's experience in noble houses and that the household itself was in part "an erogenous play-ground in which its members are socialized in forms of conduct that diverge from the dictates of authoritative discourse."[49] In addition to games, men and women of elite northwest European houses regularly exchanged words, glances, and touches at feasts, dances, and tournaments. Naturally, there is a difference between flirtatious encounters and engaging in acts of sexual intercourse, yet the erotic dimension of social engagement in medieval contexts should not be too quickly set aside. Moreover, we should not assume that losing her virginity was necessarily the worst thing that could happen to an aristocratic maiden. For example, in 1387, John of Gaunt's daughter Elizabeth Lancaster, aged twenty-two or twenty-three, had an affair at court with Sir John Holland, the king's constable. Sir John "fell violently in love with her at first sight" and pursued Elizabeth tenaciously (indicating that he had regular contact with her, further contradicting a clear-cut "segregation" model) until she fell pregnant with his child and the two quickly married. *The Westminster Chronicle*, in which this event is described, gives no indication that Elizabeth's reputation was badly harmed by this. Another chronicle, by Henry Knighton, mentions only the wedding and not the premarital affair. Sir John was made an earl and went on to enjoy a string of high-level royal offices.[50] Indubitably, medieval literature and prescriptive texts such as conduct books and sermons made great literary capital out of imagery of the enclosed female body and its homologies with the locked chamber, the remote tower, or the walled garden.[51] Yet romances and other entertaining works such as Arthurian legends also include imagery at odds with a model of feminine seclusion and segregation, such as scenes of courtly maidens disarming, washing, and dressing knights after tournaments or watching them undress for bed, while taking the opportunity to gaze upon and appraise the bodies of the strong men before them. Others tell of damsels taking messages into the heart of battlefields or riding far and wide on the business of their mistresses.[52] Such vignettes may tell us little about women's real experiences, yet they counter the scholarly cliché of a medieval model of enclosed and guarded femininity. On another tack, men of great households also retreated to chambers to talk, play music, sing, and hear stories.[53]

An equation between castle architecture and the female body implies an essentialist understanding of medieval gender relations, imagining elite women as reducible to material entities and as objects of patriarchal possession and control. In elite medieval cultures, women's function and value was much more multilayered than this. Though they seem to have possessed limited freedom of movement both within and beyond the home, they were not rigidly constricted or enclosed. Their ability to move between parts of the house and to intermingle with household members and guests enhanced both the cultural value of the house in its aesthetic and ceremonial aspects and the material prospects of the family through the forging of new alliances.

If privacy was hard to come by in the rooms of medieval houses, rich or poor, perhaps it was to be found in the bed itself. Inventories from late-medieval Europe regularly show the prime importance of the bed among the home's furnishings, whether it belonged to a cook or a king.[54] The grander beds of the late-medieval elite possessed a canopy and side curtains, behind which an individual or couple might seek some privacy. Still, they may not have had the room to themselves, as other family members and servants would often have slept in the same chamber. Perhaps ultimate privacy was offered only by one's clothing. Slight evidence from literary and other texts suggests that couples did not necessarily undress for sex. *The Book of Margery Kempe* notes that the protagonist's husband did not notice that she wore a hair shirt, though they slept together and she bore him children in that time.[55] Women were enjoined by moralists to employ their feminine persuasion within the privacy of the marital bed to influence harsh husbands to greater mercy and kindness. In the thirteenth century, Thomas of Chobham wrote, "Even in the bedroom, in the midst of their embraces, a wife should speak alluringly to her husband, and if he is hard and unmerciful and an oppressor of the poor, she should invite him to be merciful."[56] The image of the husband and wife lying in each other's arms gives a vivid sense of the realm of true medieval privacy.

Stronger support for segregation of men and women is found in written and visual testimony of parishioners' worship in their parish churches or gatherings at open-air sermons. Division of sacred space into male and female domains is well attested in sources deriving from the early centuries of Christianity and may have endured. Certainly, by the fifteenth century, women and men were often seated separately in both Italian and English churches; similarly, a late-medieval German image of women's pews is shown in Figure 3.5 in Chapter 3.[57] However, it is hard to know how much gender divisions were implemented before the introduction of seats and fixed pews, which only occurred near the end of our era. Women of higher status families often engaged in devotions in their own homes, either in bedchambers or private chapels, alone or in the company of other women.[58] The parish church itself could hardly be termed a feminine space; on the other hand, in some monastic and devotional texts, the Christian soul was depicted through feminized imagery of the home. The popular devotional text *De doctrina cordis* (*The Doctrine of the Heart*, composed in the mid-thirteenth century by Hugh of St. Cher for a mostly female audience) presented the heart as the center of moral conduct and as a symbol for the interior self and did so using domestic imagery of the heart as a house and the life of the soul as housework: "Now, Sister, if that thou will worthily receive this blessed champion [Christ, the 'lover-knight'], first thou must make clean thy house of thy heart, and then thou must array it, and afterward keep well the gates of the same house. The broom wherewith the house of thy soul and of thy heart shall be made clean is dread of God." A half-hearted penitent is likened to a lazy servant, who instead of sweeping her house to "put out the filth" merely casts green rushes on the floor.[59] The heart, as seat of the soul, is thus comprehended as a place of feminine labors. The soul itself (in an image that may have been influenced by *De doctrina cordis*, or which might share imagery only by coincidence) is pictured as feminine in a manuscript from the convent of St. Walburg near Eichstätt in Germany. The feminine soul is shown embraced by the Trinity in a cosy heart-shaped house complete with its little flight of stairs and safely fastened front door.[60]

The seclusion of women was taken more seriously in Italian cities, where masculine honor was still more deeply bound to the chastity of women. The reported words of the Alberti patriarch, Giannozzo, though didactic rather than descriptive, are often quoted as emblematic of late-medieval/early Renaissance Italian precepts on gender, respectability, and space:

> The character of men is stronger than that of women and can bear the attacks of enemies better, can stand strain longer, is more constant under stress. Therefore men have the freedom to travel with honor in foreign lands, acquiring and gathering the goods of fortune. Women, on the other hand, are almost all timid by nature, soft, slow, and therefore more useful when they sit still and watch over our things. It is as though nature thus provided for our well-being, arranging for men to bring things home and for women to guard them. The woman, as she remains locked up at home, should watch over our things by staying at her post, by diligent care and watchfulness.[61]

In the palace of the da Varano family in Camerino, central Italy, the ladies of the house accessed the private chapel across the street from the house via a bridge, the Ponte di Madonna, which presumably aided in their seclusion.[62]

In Venice, according to Dennis Romano, "San Marco, Rialto, and the city's streets and canals were essentially male locales," while houses and parish neighborhoods were "viewed as female places and were identified with the private, domestic, and sacred roles that women were expected to play in society."[63] Though the houses and palaces of the elite provided powerful symbolism of paternal lines, houses were run by women (in Francesco Barbero's words from 1415, wives should be like "leaders of bees") and had "special female associations."[64] Romano qualifies the woman/home equation by noting that the ground floor and formal hall were essentially male spaces, devoted as they were to business uses and patrilineal display, yet argues "the bedrooms and perhaps the kitchen" had more female associations, notably concerning childbirth.[65] By the fifteenth century, northern European visitors to Venice commented on the near invisibility of high-status women. Few respectable women were seen in the street, and when they did appear, they were bundled up in cloaks and veils. Even other Italians could be surprised: in 1494, the Milanese traveler Pietro Casola commented that Venetian women were so enveloped in outer garments that "I do not know how they can see where to go in the street."[66] Conversely, when he traveled to the Council of Constance in 1414, the Florentine humanist Poggio Bracciolini was stunned to witness the mixed bathing of men and women at Baden near Zurich. Though the public baths, which were used by "the common folk, men, women, youths, and maidens of no particular quality," were divided by a barrier between the men's and women's pools, Poggio's account indicates not only that he had a clear view of the female bathers but that the male bathers did also: "It is truly laughable to see decrepit old women bathing alongside young beauties, entering the water stark naked while men look on, staring at their natural parts and their buttocks." Private baths in Baden too were only half-heartedly separated by grilles cut with windows, so that men and women "can drink and converse together and look at one another and even touch," while men sit in galleries above to talk and watch, and male and female bathers encounter each other nude or seminaked at the baths' entrances.[67] If Poggio's description is accurate, it indicates an openness to mingling of the sexes and even exposure of the naked body in a northern European location, and also that such breaching of gendered boundaries would have been unthinkable in his native Florence where bathing more likely occurred among mixed family members in private homes.[68]

According to Robert C. Davis, Italian working women could be seen in marketplaces, outdoor workshops, and public piazzas, but in Venice, they covered their faces with a scarf, peeping out through a narrow gap.[69] He argues that the "public arena" of Renaissance-era Italian cities was "repeatedly consecrated as male space" not only through officially sanctioned processions by guild and confraternity members, formal games, and ceremonies, but also through the disruptive activities initiated by working-class men and youths, from relatively innocuous human pyramid contests, swearing, and obscene exposure, to far more threatening behaviors such as ritualized fist fights (*guerre di pugni*), bull baiting (*caccia dei tori*), and perennial rock and stone fights (the *sassaiola*). Women such as laundresses who had by necessity to enter this "masculated" space risked injury or even death.[70] Davis suggests that one feminine response to such a hostile public space was the fashion—especially, but not only, in Venice—for walking out in high wooden clogs (choppines or *zoccoli*) like little elevated platforms bound to each foot. These have been noted from the fourteenth and fifteenth centuries in both Italy and Spain. While attempting to walk in such a precarious fashion might seem only to have exacerbated women's vulnerability in an already hazardous environment, Davis suggests that the added height and splendor (because of the extra yardage of extravagant cloth) enabled by *zoccoli*, combined with women's preference to walk out with groups of ladies up to thirty in number, helped women to reclaim public space for themselves through the sheer impressiveness of the display.[71]

Yet, as with almost every aspect of this topic, the dangers of historical cliché bedevil impressions of spatial seclusion and segregation for Italian women, or the equation of woman and home. In Italian cities, houses were not merely homes but also strongholds of political and economic might. Powerful clans colonized whole quarters, thus expressing their influence through sheer architectural presence. A similar phenomenon has been noted in the Croatian city of Trogir, where "the private house of a noble family, both in its location and even in its design, underpinned the political power of a family in the Commune and fulfilled its political as much as its domestic needs."[72] It is also crucial to acknowledge how social status complicated expectations based on gender in Italy, as we have already seen in relation to northern Europe. Samuel Cohn's studies of working women in postplague Italy show increasing numbers of women and even young girls working unguarded as keepers of sheep and cattle in mountain villages. In urban areas, far from being restricted to domestic service, spinning, food provision, and petty retailing, women were carders, shearers, skinners, and stretchers (all of which were heavy jobs in the Florentine wool industry) and also bakers, vintners, oil merchants, cheese dealers, weavers, cloth finishers, sewers, embroiderers, and dyers. Some headed households based around such occupations as carpentry, goldsmithing, butchery, painting, and cobbling. In other words, Italian women were involved in a wide range of occupations requiring physical strength and/or high levels of skill, many of which were also usually controlled by (male-governed) guilds.[73] In the later medieval context, women of lower and middling status engaged in such a range of economic activity that a simple division of public and private—conceptual or spatial—is inappropriate.[74] It has also often been noted that prostitutes breached notional boundaries of masculine and feminine space, and civic authorities had to come up with regulations to deal with this. In Venice, for example, the Great Council in 1358 bowed to prostitutes' own practice and elected to establish a public brothel in the distinctively "male" space of the Rialto.[75]

If lower-status and nonrespectable women were regularly found in spaces modern historians have named "public" and "male," straightforward assertions of the gendered nature of urban space begin to accrue so many necessary exceptions as to become untenable. Romano's article on gendered space in Venice articulates many such exceptions, even while asserting that in that city "there were two urban settings, one male and one female."[76] We might do better to conclude that gender alone cannot serve as the category for medieval spatial analysis. Such factors as social status, sexual reputation, occupation, and age must also be taken into account. Thomas Kuehn's argument that "gender" is too blunt a category for exploring the nuances of Italian Renaissance legal codes and that "social personhood," which focuses on relations between individuals and emphasizes the conscious and intelligent agency of every person, offers a more helpful framework that could certainly be applied to space.[77]

Venetian women's employment of sartorial props—platform clogs, veils, and scarves—both to protect and promote their presence in the open space of the street reminds us also that space can be defined and policed via means beyond the physical structures of walls and doors. Clothing, and also glances, facial expressions, touch, and gesture serve a powerful function in delimiting realms of enclosure and contact. English girls were taught to walk with straight, upright bodies with gaze fixed firmly forward as a means of maintaining respectability in the street. Christine de Pizan, on the other hand, perhaps because of her Italian heritage, counseled the young women among her readership to maintain a modest downcast gaze.[78] Actual women no doubt found great agency in manipulating social rules of spatial movement and decorum through dress, glances, and attitude, perhaps in the manner of Chaucer's Criseyde. Troilus, Chaucer tells us, has just arrived in Troy and, with his young knights, proud as a peacock, is arrogantly surveying all the women arrayed in the temple, when he first spies Criseyde. Dressed in black, as befits a widow, standing quietly and in humble manner in a small space by the door, she nonetheless looks about with a confident and cheerful air. In silent response to Troilus's lascivious gaze, she glances aside disdainfully, as if to say, "What, may I not stand here?"[79]

CONCLUSION

We should feel uncomfortable with any confident assertion of a gendered separation of spheres in medieval Europe. The editors of a recent essay collection claim that "in most professions the wife organized production at home and the husband organized the trading of the finished goods. He was the one who went out, while she stayed home, although the local marketplace also became a domain for women."[80] While this probably describes daily experiences for numerous men and women, it also has overtones of a modern public/private split that do not sit easily with our period. Let us not forget that oftentimes the husband did not "go out" either, as much of his work was in the home. Moreover, women "went out" or played a role in aspects of public life in ways that we might not always expect. Sylvia Federico's revisionist study of the English "Great Rising" of 1381, for example, finds that women were among the perpetrators of the uprising and that contemporary officials seemed to find nothing implausible in this. Among the female rebels was Julia Pouchere, who roused a mob to destroy the prison at Maidstone and tear down the warden's house. Another, Katherine Gamen, made a timely intervention by untying the rope holding a boat toward which the chief justice, John Cavendish, was dashing to make his escape. Stranded on the riverbank, he was seized and beheaded. Johanna Ferrour was among the chief leaders of the Kentish rebels who burned John of Gaunt's palace of the Savoy and forced the beheading of the archbishop, Simon Sudbury, and treasurer, John Hales.[81] If these anecdotes are accurate, Federico's example may teach us to examine familiar narratives for unfamiliar themes such as medieval women's engagements with their wider worlds. At the same time, we might also seek to learn more about women's daily experiences within domestic settings—particularly in their interactions with one another. The subject of laywomen's quotidian contact with one another, their friendships and enmities—what we might call their *femisociality*—has barely been touched.

Medieval men and women understood notions of public and private, but it is debatable whether they would have conceived of them as neatly divided along gendered lines. If the private is also the inner, the interior, and the upper, then it can variously be associated with the feminine (the segregated, secluded, protected, and suppressed) but alternatively with the masculine (the privileged, comfortable, and at ease). As Sarah Stanbury and Virginia Chieffo Raguin point out, the private space of the medieval parish church, the chancel, was reserved exclusively for the clergy (powerful, masculine, and invested with spiritual authority and sacramental powers), while the public space of the nave was for all laity, including women.[82]

Gendered space in medieval European cities would be better understood by imagining men and women's movements as ripples on a pond. The home would normally represent the central point for both sexes—the dropping place of the imagined stone—but gender would be only one of many factors determining how wide the ripples spread. Depending on several factors, including geography, social status, age, and sexual respectability, a woman's sphere of movement might be mostly confined to the home, garden, and church or might spread wider into fields, marketplaces, and even pilgrimage routes. If we compare men's and women's broad patterns of movement, we will usually find women's to have been more circumscribed, more constrained, than men's, but not well described by the terms *public* and *private*.

CHAPTER SIX

Education and Work: Multiple Tasks and Lowly Status

SANDY BARDSLEY

Imagine a young girl seated on the floor of a house in fourteenth-century London. With miniature pewter jugs, cups, and plates, she serves an imaginary meal for her younger siblings.[1] Is she playing, learning, or working? In the eyes of her mother, she may be doing all three. Modern Western parents must often be reminded that play is the work of children, while medieval parents may have seen fewer boundaries between learning and helping. Although this chapter will separate out education and work—examining differences in each according to social status—the distinction is somewhat artificial and modern since education and work were not discrete categories, especially not for women. Education and work varied by social status, but they also shared a number of characteristics. Focusing on late-medieval England, but with reference to other European contexts, this chapter will first show that women's education tended to be both practical and moral in nature. The second half of the chapter will survey women's work, again focusing on England and incorporating a case study of women's wages after the Black Death of the mid-fourteenth century. Whether peasants, town dwellers, or nobles, women juggled multiple tasks, yet found their labor less valued than that of men.

EDUCATION

Most women learned on the job, and their practical training and work blended together. For both women and men, apprenticeships (whether formal or informal) were more common than schooling followed by employment. A peasant girl learned food preparation from helping to stir the pottage, a daughter of urban craftspeople assisted in her parents' shop from an early age, as depicted in Figure 6.1, and a noble girl trailed her mother as she ordered provisions, managed servants, and oversaw the organization of a household. As girls grew,

FIGURE 6.1: Girl assistant in draper's shop. *Tacuinum sanitatis*. Paris, Bibliothèque nationale de France, MS lat. n.a. 1673. Verona, end of the fourteenth century. Photo courtesy of Scala/White images/Art Resource, NY.

so too did their responsibilities. Moral education accompanied training and work—prayers, songs, and advice manuals demonstrate this intermingling of practical and moral advice. Even while the specifics of education varied between peasant women, townswomen, and noblewomen, practicality and morality remained central.

Education and Peasant Women

Peasants comprised at least 85 percent of the population, even in the late Middle Ages, so the education of most girls consisted of learning the rudiments of household management in small, rural villages.[2] Few were literate: reading, according to the fourteenth-century *Book of the Knight of the Tower*, "is good and profitable . . . to all women," yet only a small minority of girls learned to read, and even fewer could write.[3] Indeed, their lack of literacy obscures the work and training of girls in the countryside as few records supply hints of their work. The best sources, perhaps, are those of coroners' rolls recording accidental deaths, which suggest that tasks were gendered from a young age and that peasant girls learned, like their mothers, to juggle many types of work. While men and boys focused on growing crops and raising animals, their wives and daughters raised children, bought and sold provisions, cooked food, helped in the fields, spun yarn, made clothes, brewed and sold ale, tended chickens, made cheese and bread, and more. Boys were far more likely to meet with accidents while herding animals or fishing, while girls' fatalities happened in the context of drawing water, cooking, or tending fires. Accidents occurring within the household were responsible for almost half of the fatalities of girls between the ages of seven and twelve but less than 10 percent of those of boys. From this, as Barbara Hanawalt has argued, we might extrapolate that girls probably spent considerably more time than their brothers helping their mothers with domestic tasks.[4] As in London, rural children played with miniature jugs, plates, and cauldrons, suggesting that their toys may also have helped orient them toward their future responsibilities.[5]

While mothers were usually their first teachers, girls often spent time as servants in other peasant households.[6] Such service, beginning in adolescence, was in itself a type of practical training and education in the ways of another family. The presence of servants did not imply that a household was of particularly high status nor that the servant was of a low-status peasant family. Rather, it seems that service was almost a way to trade adolescents and help them transition from childhood to adulthood. In theory, at least, servants saved their minimal wages to help establish independent households when they were ready. Whether or not they welcomed it, this period of servanthood may have been a time of relative autonomy for young medieval men and women. While still subject to the rules of their masters and mistresses, adolescents experienced some distance from their parents (after all, many peasants lived in houses consisting of no more than one room, so both physical and emotional proximity were inevitable). The extent to which girls experienced this period as one of education—as opposed to exploitation—probably varied considerably according to the diligence of masters and mistresses. Those with compassionate employers could learn different techniques for managing household work, while others might be confined to undesirable tasks and vulnerable to sexual advances from other members of the household. Because servants' contracts were oral, we know about the conditions of servanthood mostly when something went wrong and came to the attention of the courts—as, for instance, when a servant girl was raped, beaten to the point of serious injury or death, refused wages, or otherwise wronged.[7]

Alongside the practical training received by a peasant girl was a grounding in moral and religious education. Again, most peasant girls probably learned their earliest lessons from their mothers. Joan of Arc, for instance, explained that her mother was responsible for teaching her her prayers, and it seems likely that English peasant girls learned from their mothers too.[8] In churches, girls and women sat or stood together on the northern side of the church. They attended "churchings" together to give thanks for the health of a village mother and child forty days after a safe childbirth. They observed their mothers' devotion to saints who might help them conceive or ensure safe delivery of children, and they may have helped clean the church or launder and mend altar cloths. As they neared adulthood, peasant girls might join maidens' guilds in which their social and religious education took place in the company of other young women.[9] Much religious and moral training of peasant girls thus occurred within a female context. But fathers, masters, village officials, and priests also played a role. As heads of household, fathers participated in setting the moral tone for their family. Few sources provide direct evidence of peasant piety within the household, but we might imagine that families sometimes prayed together, repeated stories they had heard in church, or used religious precepts to reinforce teachings about proper behavior. Girls participated in the life of the parish directly, too: they attended church services, listened to sermons, and, upon reaching the "age of reason" (which could be interpreted as anywhere between about seven and fourteen years), were expected to confess their sins at least once a year.[10] Indeed, lessons came from the church environment itself: even small parish churches could afford a few rudimentary wall paintings. Some of these depicted women, both as saints and as sinners. Some even showed women as humble parishioners, participating in the seven works of mercy.[11] Others emphasized women's propensity to sin, such as depictions of women who gossiped in church while overshadowed by an eavesdropping demon. And messages were reinforced by village officials in local courts, who presented women disproportionately for the crime of "scolding," or speaking in ways deemed loud and inappropriate.[12]

Although literacy played little direct role in the religious and moral education of peasant girls, it was thus present at the margins. Priests, in theory if not always in practice, were required to be literate and some used confessional manuals and collections of sermons to enhance their pastoral roles. On the other hand, priests were not necessarily impartial conduits into textual communities. Some members of the clergy doubtless filtered the messages they conveyed or emphasized some more than others. Surviving sermon manuals suggest that girls would have learned that their femininity made them vulnerable to sin. While both men and women could be guilty of moral misdeeds, women's sins were more directly tied to their inherently weak nature, inherited from Eve.[13] Learning that her status as a female made her inferior to her brothers was arguably the most emphatic lesson taught to a medieval peasant girl. She would have had to work hard to resist this lesson, reinforced as it was by parents, employers, village officials, and the church.

Education and Townswomen

The education of townswomen was similarly both practical and moral. Girls from poorer households might serve as domestic servants for those with more wealth, learning the details of management at the same time as they carried out menial tasks. Daughters of craftsfolk would literally grow up in the workshops of their parents and assist from an early age. A young girl might thread needles for her cobbler parents, for example, or help serve customers. As she grew stronger and more skilled, her responsibilities increased. A few English girls served official apprenticeships, like those apprenticed as silk workers in London, while others were apprentices in all but name. Formal apprenticeships for girls were a little more common elsewhere in Europe—such as Paris or Montpellier—but boys were still more likely to have the terms of their training spelled out in written contracts.[14] Informal contracts were important for girls: often daughters of craftspeople married men from a similar trade, suggesting that skills acquired in their families of origin were of direct use to their new husbands. Their husbands might train them further: widows were frequently permitted to maintain guild membership and were sometimes allowed to train apprentices, which implies that they were acknowledged unofficially as "masters" of trades typically associated with men.[15] Practical education for townswomen was thus widespread, even though it has left few traces in written records.

Advice doled out to women from artisanal families emphasized morality in women's daily work. The French author Christine de Pizan, for instance, urged artisans' wives to keep their households in good moral order. A good wife ought to ensure that "she knows the craft so well that she can direct the workmen if her husband is not there and reprove them if they do not work well." She should see to it that her husband, as well as their workers, works long and hard. A wife should ensure that her children are taught at school and then placed in apprenticeships (Christine de Pizan may be unusual here in refraining from insisting that boys were more deserving of schooling). Finally, she must oversee her children's moral training and be sure that they are not spoiled by too much affection. Both fathers and mothers, according to de Pizan, should be "the source of virtue and good habits," and poorly trained children reflect badly on their parents.[16]

For daughters from richer urban families, practical and moral training were also intertwined. As with peasants, men as well as women played a role in shaping advice for urban girls. The anonymous Goodman (*Ménagier*) of Paris, for example, wrote a manual of instruction for his young wife in the late fourteenth century. While some of his advice is resoundingly down to earth (for instance, how to choose servants or catch fleas), he exhorts his wife continually to pray, attend church, and love God.[17] Moral and practical education were similarly mingled in the fourteenth-century English didactic poem "How the Good Wife Taught Her Daughter." As Felicity Riddy has argued, the poem shows more about the gender ideology of the urban bourgeois household than it does about the behavior of real girls or real mothers and should be interpreted as paternalistic rather than maternalistic. Although the author and his/her gender is unknown, the "Good Wife" narrator encourages her daughter to be modest, pious, and dutiful. She must attend church, rain or shine, and focus on her prayers rather than let her attention wander. Indeed, she may go few other places—not in the town, nor to wrestling matches nor taverns. Instead, she must concentrate on the work of her household, raising children, supervising servants, and managing the household economy. Her premarital interactions with men must be aboveboard, subject to scrutiny from friends. Once married, she must love and honor her husband and cater meekly to his whims, while rebuffing other men. This advice, as Riddy argues, reflects the mixed moral and practical roles that fathers and clerics expected women to play.[18]

Since only a minority of townswomen could read, some poems and instruction manuals may have been intended to be read aloud: Anna Dronzek has argued, for instance, that poems aimed at girls included more aural cues—such as repeated refrains and catchy summaries—than those written for boys.[19] Dronzek also notes that didactic literature for girls made use of more concrete metaphors to align with a girl's knowledge of household duties. *The Book of the Knight of the Tower*, for instance, uses the metaphor of a silver plate with black spots to depict the soul, blemished by sins that must be polished away. Boys, on the other hand, were thought capable of more abstract thought.

Scattered references to literate townswomen show us, however, that at least a few girls must have been taught to read these lessons on their own. Literacy rates are difficult enough to calculate for boys during the Middle Ages. First, we have problems of definition: Does literacy mean the ability to read, or the abilities both to read and to write (since these skills were taught separately)? Second, should literacy be regarded as the ability to read the vernacular language or the ability to read Latin? Third, how can we know who could read or write in an era in which many of the most wealthy employed scribes? Because girls' education was less frequent and less documented, estimates of female literacy are more complicated and patchy still.

Only a few schools and schoolmistresses are mentioned in surviving records. In Paris in 1380, for instance, twenty-one schoolmistresses were licensed to teach girls.[20] In London, girls were occasionally sent to "dame schools" run by women to learn to read in the vernacular.[21] In northwestern Europe, girls were taught the vernacular and sometimes Latin within Beguine communities, though in general Latin literacy was considered far less important for girls than it was for their brothers.[22] Anchoresses occasionally took girls as pupils, too. But formal education was expensive, and few, presumably, could afford it: three months of school fees for a Florentine girl in the mid-fourteenth century cost 5 shillings (a considerable sum by contemporary standards), while five to six years of schooling for a London chandler's daughter in 1390 cost 25 shillings.[23] Not many girls, then, were taught to read in formal schools, but others may certainly have been taught by family members, high-status servants, tutors, or family friends. A townswoman who could read could help her husband in his business. She might also participate in the exchange of books, creating networks between laywomen and religious women such as vowesses, anchoresses, and nuns.[24] Again, moral education was at the heart of this exchange: devotional books were shared among wealthy townswomen during their lifetimes, and at least half of the books specifically mentioned in wills were religious in nature. As with peasant women, education involved learning not only what to do but also how to behave.

Education and Noblewomen

Girls of noble status were most likely to learn the rudiments of literacy, but morality and practical training still comprised the most essential components of their education. Much of this training was overseen by their mothers: both boys and girls of the nobility were often taught to read by their mothers.[25] In other cases, noblewomen hired tutors (especially for their sons) but still played an active role in supervising the content of their children's education and the progress their children made. Mothers such as Marie de Bretagne sponsored works of devotion for their children, selecting stories that resonated with their own notions of appropriate behavior.[26] Similarly, Alice de Condet hired a translator to produce a moral textbook for her son.[27] Indeed, the many surviving images of St. Anne teaching her daughter, the Virgin Mary, to read, as shown in Figure 6.2, suggest that the theme of mothers teaching daughters particularly

FIGURE 6.2: *The Education of the Virgin.* Detail from an antependium with scenes of the life of the Virgin, church of the Dominican Convent at Thetford, Suffolk, England. Painted on oak, ca. 1335. Musée nationale du Moyen Âge—Thermes de Cluny, Paris, France. Photograph by Jean-Gilles Berizzi, courtesy of Réunion des Musées Nationaux/Art Resource, NY.

resonated with the late-medieval nobility.[28] Girls from noble families were also often sent for several years to the houses of other nobles to serve an informal apprenticeship and learn household management from women other than their mothers.[29] But men played a role in the training of noble daughters too: fathers, such as the Knight of the Tower, understood that the comportment of their daughters reflected on the family's aspirations at large, and even though they may have played little direct role in the upbringing of their daughters, they nonetheless expected the final word.

The burgeoning of devotional and vernacular literature in the late Middle Ages brought opportunities to noblewomen to serve, as Susan Groag Bell has expressed it, as "arbiters of lay piety and ambassadors of culture."[30] As readers and patrons, women participated actively in the transmission of texts. Account rolls, wills, and book inscriptions demonstrate that women not only purchased books but also traded them with one another in a network that linked noble- and townswomen, nuns, anchoresses, and vowesses.[31] In some households, such as that of Cecily, Duchess of York, mother of Edward IV, devotional works were read during dinner and discussed among female companions in the evening. Cecily augmented discussions in her household by recounting other works she had heard earlier in the day.[32] Women who read or listened to devotional literature may have received mixed messages. In addition to the familiar exhortations to meek and pious behavior, they also encountered hagiographies of defiant virgin martyrs who faced down their persecutors and resisted male authority.[33] Courtly literature, too, contained contradictory messages for women. While women were often inaccessible, set on a pedestal, they were nonetheless objects of desire. Modern scholars have highlighted, too, the extent to which relationships among women and the convention of cross-dressing undermined the ostensibly conservative messages about female behavior in courtly tales.[34]

Nuns come closer than any other group of women in participating in formal education as we think of it today. Yet many nuns could not read Latin, and even fewer could write. St. Clare of Assisi instructed her nuns, "Let those who do not know how to read not be eager to learn," and made special provision for illiterate nuns when others were reading prayers.[35] As Nicholas Orme has pointed out, the education of most English nuns was much the same as that of noblewomen more generally, with better training in English and French than in Latin. Moreover, English nunneries were relatively few in number—about 146, containing about 3,350 nuns, at their peak in ca. 1300.[36] Although nunneries sometimes took care of children for short periods, English girls often entered convent life as novices when they were in their mid-teens.[37] Most skills of literacy would thus have been acquired before entry. Some nunneries, such as

Barking Abbey, followed the Benedictine custom of issuing a book to each sister to read during the period of Lent; others would have lacked enough books for each nun to have her own. Most of these books, presumably, were in English and consisted of much the same devotional literature as was read by noblewomen outside convents.[38] Even at Syon, one of the best-known nunneries in terms of educational attainment and book owning, an English-language guide was compiled to help nuns fully appreciate the meaning of services in Latin.[39] During the late Middle Ages, monastic education stagnated in most areas for both men and women, while universities became centers of intellectual innovation. Excluded from universities, women's participation in developing new ideas was thus limited. Certainly, some nunneries went through periods of intellectual vitality: in the twelfth century, for instance, scholarship and manuscript copying flourished at German nunneries associated with the Hirsau reform movement and at Hohenbourg, in Alsace, under the abbess Herrad.[40] But for most late-medieval nuns, education meant training in the vernacular and excusal from Latin learning since, in the words of the fifteenth-century translator of Godstow Abbey's records, "it is not their mother tongue."[41] As with noblewomen more generally, education was intimately linked with morality and we know far more about what was transmitted than about the extent to which nuns internalized exhortations to virtue.

Indeed, the potential for divergent readings existed in media addressing the behavior of all medieval women. Peasants saw images of a demon huddled behind women who gossiped in church, yet we do not know whether women interpreted them only as reminders to stay silent and attentive or whether they also saw them as emblems of female friendship. The work of James C. Scott has encouraged scholars to seek "hidden transcripts," that is, to search for agency even in situations of ostensible passivity.[42] The urban Good Wife teaches her daughter to be industrious but thereby opens up the possibility of sloth, while the brave St. Cecilia is at once steadfast in her Christian faith and shrewish in her speech. And the same may have been true of oral teaching. Presumably the peasant daughter muttered under her breath as her mother or mistress instructed her in brewing or spinning, and the noble daughter sighed through repeated lectures on maidenly behavior. The education of women was both practical and moral, but we know far more about how it was delivered than how it was received.

WORK

Just as we know little about what women thought of their education, so too we have few clues about how they perceived their work. Account rolls, statutes, poems, and agricultural manuals make it clear that men saw women's work as less valuable than their own, but women's own opinions are missing from the historical record. Although women's work varied by social status, it shared another characteristic too: women tended to be multitaskers, juggling multiple responsibilities. This was often depicted symbolically in the "Labors of Adam and Eve," as shown in Figure 6.3. Both of these characteristics of women's work—its inferior status and its multifaceted nature—meant that women's work identities tended to be more fractured than those of their husbands.

Work and Peasant Women

Peasant women juggled multiple tasks and demands. Historians of England often point to an anonymous and incomplete poem, known as the "Ballad of the Tyrannical Husband," to exemplify the many types of work a peasant

FIGURE 6.3: The Labors of Adam and Eve. *Mirror of Human Salvation.* Chantilly, Musée Condé, MS 139, fol. 4 recto. France, fifteenth century. Photograph by René-Gabriel Ojéda, courtesy of Réunion des Musées Nationaux/Art Resource, NY.

woman had to do. In this poem, a husband returns from ploughing the fields to find his dinner uncooked and starts to berate his wife for failing to carry out her duties. In his mind, an uncooked dinner suggests that his wife has been gossiping with the neighbors rather than working hard (as he has been). The wife's lengthy retort catalogues the many types of work she must do in a day. Cooking is the least of it: she must look after children; milk the cows and make butter and cheese; feed hens, capons, ducks, and goslings; bake bread; brew ale; make linen from flax; spin yarn; and make cloth.[43] Manuscript illustrations and manorial records add other tasks that the ploughman's wife does not mention: women often worked in the fields alongside their husbands, particularly at harvest and other times when labor needs were most acute. They often grew vegetables and tended fruit trees in the yards surrounding their houses. They fetched water for cooking and drinking and washed their families' clothes in the streams. Women's work helped their families in less tangible ways, too: as they laundered the church's altar cloths and baked communion wafers, for instance, they helped maintain good relationships within the parish. The work of a peasant woman was not always visible, as the ploughman's wife complains, but it was necessary and plentiful. Because their work was so diverse, this section will focus on three types of work in particular: preparation of food and drink, manufacture of clothing, and childrearing.

Peasant women were responsible for growing much of their families' food, and they usually prepared food once it was produced. The medieval English diet was based around cereal grains such as wheat, barley, oats, and rye. Legumes, such as beans and lentils, were also important. These crops were typically sown in large fields, and most of the work involved in tending them was carried out by men. Some families, especially in the later Middle Ages, might be able to supplement their diets with meat, and thus the boys of the household might be sent to pasture sheep or pigs.[44] But much food was also produced within the immediate vicinity of the house, and this work was generally that of women. Archaeologists are teaching us more and more about the *crofts*, or yards, surrounding peasant houses, used for growing vegetables, preparing grain, and raising poultry.[45] Many families subsisted on a pottage based on grains but supplemented with onions, cabbage, and leeks, and flavored with garlic, herbs, or a piece of meat. Eggs, cheese, bread, and fruit might accompany the meal. Those living near the ocean might be lucky enough to eat marine fish, while inland peasants could sometimes catch eels in the rivers or hunt for rabbits or small birds.[46] So while more than half of the calories came from crops grown mostly by men, women's calorific contribution was not at all negligible.

Of course, grains, vegetables, and animal products needed to be cooked to make them palatable, and historians assume that women did the bulk of food preparation.[47] When the ploughman complained that his dinner was not ready, he reflected an assumption that his wife was the one responsible for cooking. In English peasant houses, cooking usually took place over an open fire, and regulation of heat would have been quite difficult. Women collected water from wells or streams and carried it back to the house. At the same time as they gathered ingredients, carried buckets of water, and kept an eye on the pot, women had to ensure that young children did not get too close to the fire: coroners' records show that cooking fires were a real source of danger for infants.[48]

Sometimes peasant women found themselves in the happy position of producing more food products than they needed for their own families and could sell or trade the surplus. Some of this trade took place between neighbors, and we know about it only when something went wrong (as when a neighbor failed to repay the debt—examples abound in manorial court rolls). On other occasions, a family might accumulate enough of a surplus that a woman could carry the extra goods to market and sell them for cash. Most villages were within a few hours' walk of one or more market towns, and these served as important points of connection between the town and the countryside.

An important source of extra income for English peasant women was that of ale brewing. Because the equipment required for making ale was relatively expensive, brewing was typically the preserve of those with a little capital—wives, rather than widows or single women, and members of peasant families with more resources. Prior to the introduction of hopped beer in the late Middle Ages, northern European peasants usually drank weak ale.[49] Without refrigeration, ale spoiled quickly, so it needed to be brewed every few days. As standards of living improved slightly after the Black Death of the mid-fourteenth century, ale became more and more a staple of peasant diets. Historians know more about ale production in England than about most types of work by women because it was regulated by the manorial courts. Ale tasters appointed by the court had to approve each batch before a woman could sell her brew to the community. She also had to pay a small fee each time she brewed and, in some places, had to pay an annual fee akin to a license. On some manors, certain women seem to have established themselves as semi-professional brewsters, while others sold their ale only occasionally. For instance, on the manor of Brigstock (Northamptonshire), thirty-eight women produced about two-thirds of the ale batches documented by the court in the early fourteenth century, while another 273 brewsters produced the other third.[50]

Baking bread, too, was often the specialty of particular women. In many places, peasants were required by their lord or lady to bake their bread in a communal oven (and to pay a fee for the privilege).[51] Thus, loaves were typically baked in large batches and would quickly become stale. Women may have offset this problem somewhat by taking turns to bake bread and trading with one another. Peasant households were thus seldom self-sufficient, and a woman served her family best by participating in what some have called "an economy of make-shifts," making do with scarce resources and borrowing from and lending to others.[52] The ploughman of the poem mentioned earlier derides his wife for gossiping with the neighbors; another reading of her behavior, though, might be that she was maintaining the social relationships that made her family's economy of makeshifts possible.

Women were responsible for their families' nutrition, but also for their clothing. In England, clothing was usually made from woven woolen cloth; the ploughman's wife was fortunate to be able to afford linen.[53] Although her list of tasks implied that she was responsible for weaving flax and wool, many women outsourced this part of the procedure to a professional weaver (typically male)—indeed, the purchase of cloth would have been one of the major expenses for which extra cash was required. But women certainly participated actively in earlier parts of the cloth-making process. They tended, washed, and sheared sheep; they carded wool; and they spun it into yarn using a distaff and a spindle.[54] So ubiquitous was the practice of using a few spare moments to spin that—throughout western Europe—the distaff and spindle became symbolic of women more generally.[55] Women attached raw wool to the long shaft of the distaff and used their fingers to twist it into a thread, wound around the spindle. Allowing the spindle whorl to drop to the ground drew the wool fibers into a twisted thread. Spinning wheels were employed in Europe from the thirteenth century, but peasant women continued to use distaffs and spindles, presumably because of their low cost and their portability.[56] A woman could take advantage of a quiet moment when the baby slept, while a meal was cooking, or while she supervised children outside. Religious authors used the metaphor of spinning when outlining the duties of good wives, and wood-carvers sometimes showed men with distaffs when they wanted to depict the "world upside down" or the inversion of hierarchies.

Childbearing, childbirth, and childrearing also fell to women. A peasant woman might spend many of her fertile years either pregnant or breast-feeding. Indeed, breast-feeding not only helped the health of her child but also made it less likely that she would conceive again immediately, since lactation can have a limited contraceptive effect. Peasant women may have been grateful for the opportunity to space out births, since childbearing was a dangerous business and because performing all their usual tasks while pregnant would have been even more difficult. The population roughly trebled between the years 1000 and 1300, but even so, childhood mortality was high. Most households would have had fewer than three children survive to adulthood.[57] This number represented a considerably higher number of pregnancies, however, since poor nutrition led to miscarriages, stillbirths, and a higher risk of disease in infancy. Accidents were common too: medieval peasant toddlers died by falling into fires, rivers, or wells, or under the wheels of carts.[58] Assisting childbirth was recognized as women's work, and female friends and relatives accompanied a woman through her labor and delivery. Some women developed reputations as midwives, skilled in coaxing a baby from its mother's womb and finding ways to ease the pain of childbirth.[59]

The work of peasant women was more seasonal than that of their sisters in the towns. In spring and summer, women probably spent more time outdoors weeding and tending vegetables. At harvesttime, as depicted in Figure 6.4, they assisted in bringing in crops, picking fruit, or preparing food for other harvesters. Winter would have provided a chance to catch up on spinning and making clothes. Yet despite this seasonal change, certain key elements of a peasant woman's work remained the same: she had to ensure that all members of her household were well fed and clothed.

Case Study: Women's Wages in Post-Plague England

The seasonal nature of women's work has prompted a debate among historians about the extent to which women's labor was valued. In particular, historians have examined women's and men's harvest-time wages following the Black Death of the mid-fourteenth century. In England, the Plague killed somewhere between one-third and one-half of the population. All historians agree that workers were consequently in short supply and—despite efforts by lords to keep wages low—pay rates for both male and female laborers inevitably increased.[60] There is less agreement, however, about whether women's wages increased more than men's; that is, whether women's wages comprised a higher percentage of men's wages after the Plague than previously. As discussed subsequently, some historians have argued that women's labor became more valuable—relative to men's—after the Plague as the workforce was decimated. Some have even suggested that women may have earned equal pay to men in some instances. Others maintain that women's wages increased in about the same proportion as men's and that wage equality was rare or nonexistent.

FIGURE 6.4: Master of the Geneva Boccaccio. Apple Harvest, from Pietro de Crescenzi, *Le Rustican* or *Livre des proffitz champestres et ruraulx*. France, 1459–70. Chantilly, Musée Condé, MS 340, fol. 106 recto. Photograph by René-Gabriel Ojéda, courtesy of Réunion des Musées Nationaux/Art Resource, NY.

This issue has been controversial in part because it plays a role in a broader debate surrounding women's postplague status. Historians such as Caroline M. Barron and P.J.P Goldberg argue that economic opportunities improved significantly in the late fourteenth and fifteenth centuries, constituting a brief "golden age" for women.[61] Others—especially Judith M. Bennett—are skeptical and tend to see women's status as relatively static in the wake of demographic disaster.

Surviving evidence certainly suggests that women appeared in a greater range of rural occupations in the postplague era: one chronicler of the time stated that the Plague caused "such a shortage of servants that men could not be found to work the land, and women and children had to be used to drive ploughs and carts, which was unheard of."[62] But historians do not agree on how to interpret this broader range of occupations. R. H. Hilton, for instance, implied that late-medieval women were afforded "relative independence" by their broad range of occupations.[63] On the other hand, as Mavis E. Mate has pointed out, participation in a wider range of tasks was not necessarily an advantage for women: in her words, "whenever a family could not hire all the labor it really needed, it was the wives and daughters of the household who were likely to pick up the slack."[64] In other words, women were part of a reserve labor force that was pressed into different kinds of service after the Plague, but this did not necessarily improve their standing. Where data survives, it seems that women took up the lowest-status and lowest-paid jobs—driving ploughs and carts rather than, for instance, becoming thatchers or blacksmiths—but we do not know whether the broader range of occupations reflected active choice by women themselves or a response to familial necessity.

Several historians have made passing reference to instances of women and men being paid at seemingly equal rates, but the debate about women's wages began in earnest when Simon A. C. Penn published an article in 1987 asserting, among other things, that the Plague brought about a temporary equality in the wages of male and female harvesters.[65] Harvesttime is the period when the need for labor is most acute: all must participate to ensure that the harvest is brought in before the weather turns and crops are ruined. So it is the time when we might expect to see forces of supply and demand at their most stark. Because of this intense need at harvesttime, workers who demanded wages that employers deemed too high could be prosecuted under the Statutes of Labourers passed soon after the Plague. Penn examined records of prosecutions and found several instances in which women and men were paid what seemed to be the same wage. On the basis of this, he argued that "many female reapers in the years following the Black Death appear not to have been discriminated against when it came to the wages they were being paid for their work."

I queried the argument about wage equality in an article in 1999.[66] When I looked closely at the Statutes of Labourers presentments, I found that both women and men (that is, both female names and male names) received a range of payments and that these two ranges overlapped. That is, the best-paid female workers earned as much as (and sometimes more than) the worst-paid male workers. But the *average* for male laborers was significantly higher than that for female laborers working in the low-status role of reaper and even higher still if the higher-status position of mower (occupied by men only) was taken into account. Indeed, women and men often worked at different tasks even when laboring alongside one another, with the men's jobs being better paid. In grape harvests in France, for instance, women usually picked grapes, while men earned twice as much carrying the baskets of grapes away. In the countryside around Seville, men worked as grain harvesters in July and August, while women earned half as much working as olive harvesters a few months later.[67] When male and female names are listed within the same occupation, therefore, the male names might not be those of healthy adult men but rather those of boys, elderly men, or men with disabilities. Wage discrimination on the basis of age or perceived ability was unfortunately routine in the Middle Ages. Moreover, account rolls from before the Plague and schedules of maximum wage rates published after the Plague suggest that women's wages as a percentage of men's remained remarkably consistent, at somewhere between two-thirds and three-quarters of men's wages.[68]

My argument prompted further discussion. John Hatcher argued that my data focused exclusively on time rates—that is, payment for days or hours worked—and ignored data on piece rates (work paid by product rather than time spent). He is absolutely right; the problem is that we lack reliable and comparable data on piece rates. Hatcher also argued that men are physically stronger than women and that the labor market in late-medieval England was more rational than I had characterized it. "Custom and prejudice, rather than supply and demand," he argued, "can only dictate wages when the occupation is shielded from competition." In my response, I conceded the point about physical strength but argued that other factors, such as stamina, also play a role in one's ability to perform over the course of a day. I acknowledged the logic of supply and demand but maintained that we lack sufficient data to be sure that these economic factors did indeed supersede custom and prejudice in post-Plague England.[69] Gender discrimination, after all, is not an especially logical or rational phenomenon. More work needs to be done, scouring the few available sources for any more hints into post-Plague wages and seeking out new sources. Indeed, this debate exemplifies the difficulties that historians encounter when trying to interpret the sparse sources on women's work.

Work and Townswomen

Townswomen were multitaskers too, although the nature of their husbands' or fathers' work might orient them toward a particular occupation. While most rural men grew crops or raised animals, most urban men participated in crafts or trade. Their wives and daughters helped in craft workshops while juggling household needs such as food preparation and child minding. As in the countryside, women sought extra income for their households, working, for instance, as hucksters (petty retailers), prostitutes, and wet nurses. Unmarried women, especially those newly arrived from the countryside, often found positions as domestic servants where they might carry out a range of tasks akin to those of their rural sisters.[70] As with rural women, the variety of tasks and occupations was vast, and this section will survey only five types of work: within craft workshops, as caregivers, as prostitutes, and within the food and textile industries.

Ample evidence suggests that women worked alongside men in crafts such as shoe making, carpentry, or baking. Yet their tasks within these crafts were often different: women enabled the workshop to function by carrying supplies, tending fires, and dealing with customers. Men, on the other hand, seem to have performed more of the skilled labor.[71] Archaeological investigations from the lay cemetery of a Gilbertine priory in York have found that the arms of lay townsmen were asymmetrical, with one humerus more developed than the other, as might be consistent with repeatedly wielding heavy tools with one arm. Women buried in the monastic cemetery, however, lack the same degree of differentiation between their arms.[72] In the rural cemetery of Wharram Percy, however, the left and right arms of both women and men developed relatively symmetrically, suggesting that both engaged frequently in carrying heavy loads. This suggests that the work of men and women may have been more different in the towns than in the countryside.

Yet whether or not they were routinely swinging hammers or pushing needles through thick pieces of leather, women clearly managed to acquire the skills of the trade. Some guilds allowed women to join as "sisters," receiving fewer privileges than their husbands in return for a lower admission fee. Widows of English guild members had even more rights: they were permitted to oversee workshops and even train apprentices. Yet these entitlements came at a price, which meant that widows seldom numbered more than 5 percent of a guild's members.[73] Widows of guild members were among the most economically vulnerable and held little or no political power within the guild. Moreover, the guild expected a degree of control over their activities and could even influence their choice of partner if they were to remarry. Consequently, many widows seem to have remarried quickly to other members of the guild or to have disbanded their workshops. Trades dominated by women—such as textile work—seldom had guilds of their own. In London, women working in the silk industry seem to have had a quasi-guild status, taking on apprentices or banding together on occasion to write petitions. In some French and German cities, women did participate in guilds of their own, but these were few and far between. Among the higher-status merchants' guilds, women's active role was even smaller.[74] Women's underrepresentation in guilds was probably due to perceptions of their work: guilds were for skilled craftspeople, and for the most part women's work was ipso facto unskilled.

Beyond the guilds, women's work was associated particularly with caregiving. While some French and German towns sought to regulate midwifery by registering midwives and setting out rules for them, English municipalities seem to have paid little heed.[75] The business of midwifery was thus informal and was performed by friends and neighbors rather than professional midwives. Women might also be employed as wet nurses for mothers who lacked milk or had died in childbirth or for members of the urban elite or nobility. Children of the royal family often developed close ties with their childhood wet nurses and caregivers. Because royal courts were frequently on the move and babies found the rigors of travel difficult, royal children and their nurses were settled in one place. Thus, the children typically saw far more of their nurses than they did of their parents, and some of these women became valued members of the household.[76] Others, however, lacked status and were paid little. Foundling hospitals, for instance, hired wet nurses to provide for their charges, and stories of children starving for lack of milk suggest that they sometimes took on more children than they could feed.[77] Other types of caregiving, such as nursing of the sick or elderly, were carried out by religious women, servants, or family members. Hagiographies of female saints, such as Catherine of Siena, often recount tales of these women's patient ministrations to lepers and other sufferers, but the vast majority of mundane caregiving by women has gone unrecorded.

Slightly better documented is women's involvement in prostitution. Seen as a necessary evil and tacitly permitted by even the most pious authorities, prostitution was sometimes regulated by the towns. In London, for instance, prostitutes were confined to the "stews" of Southwark on the southern side of the river and were governed by a set of regulations that protected both prostitutes and their clients. Brothel owners, for example, were not to beat prostitutes, and neither prostitutes nor brothel owners were to approach potential clients in the street.[78] Similar red-light districts for prostitutes were set aside in towns on the Continent, and prostitutes throughout Europe were often required to wear special clothing in order to distinguish them from respectable women.[79] Conditions of work varied considerably: certainly, for many young, single women, perhaps newly arrived from the countryside and lacking safety nets, it was an occupation of last resort. Of fifty-five prostitutes appearing in the courts of fourteenth-century Exeter, 85 percent were single and few had family members in the town.[80] However, we also know of married women who practiced prostitution to help make ends meet in their household budgets and prostitutes of higher status who catered to wealthier clients. Many practiced only part time, piecing together a livelihood from prostitution, laundry, domestic service, and other poorly paid and low-status occupations.[81]

Women who lacked social and economic capital to attract a marriage partner or train in a trade might also work in the food industry. Although men sometimes engaged in this work too, most petty retailers were women. Some used their small yards to raise eggs and sell them in the marketplace, while others gathered shellfish or resold used clothing. Hucksters and tranters made money by carrying food and ale from the countryside to the towns, often in baskets or on their backs.[82] Particularly resented by medieval townspeople were traders who preempted the market by purchasing goods from peasants on their way to the towns and reselling them at higher prices. This practice was known as regrating, and regrators faced fines from borough courts. Women also earned money as cooks, making and selling pasties and other small consumables.

Finally, many women found work within the textile industry, but usually in the lowest-status and most poorly paid positions. Cloth production was highly labor intensive prior to the Industrial Revolution. Even before it was spun, wool needed to be beaten, scoured, washed, and combed, and this was often women's work. Until about the twelfth century, women also wove yarn on vertical looms, but these were eventually replaced by larger horizontal looms operated by men.[83] Master weavers formed guilds and came to enjoy considerable status, especially by contrast with spinsters. Under the "putting-out" system that became common in the late Middle Ages, weavers would buy up raw wool and pay women (and occasionally men) to spin yarn in their own homes. Men also controlled the process of fulling, or felting, the cloth, although women and children might sometimes be paid low wages for stamping on it as it soaked for softening. Men also were responsible for the finishing processes of shearing and dying the cloth. Women were thus confined to the least skilled aspects of the production process.[84] One exception—at least until the fifteenth century—was that of the silk workers in London. Until men took over the trade at the end of the Middle Ages, women controlled the silk production process from beginning to end, including spinning, weaving, and manufacture of garments. London silk women trained girls as apprentices and claimed considerable autonomy, but—as noted previously—lacked a guild of their own.[85]

The work of townswomen was thus a little more focused than that of their rural sisters, but it was still somewhat fragmented and piecemeal. A woman might help her husband in his trade for several hours a day, but she would still need to mind children, prepare food, and ensure that her family was properly clothed. A townsman might be identified as a carpenter or a cobbler, but his wife would be a carpenter's or a cobbler's wife, supporting her husband both in his trade and by liberating him from domestic demands.

Work and Noblewomen

For noblewomen, work meant overseeing the maintenance of the household and managing its relationships with the world beyond. Noblewomen arranged powerful marriages for their children, accepted children of other nobles into their households, oversaw the ordering of supplies, commissioned cultural and religious works, and acted as deputies for their frequently absent husbands. Manuscript illuminations and contemporary literature often portray noblewomen leading lives of leisure. It seems clear from the multiplicity of tasks they juggled, however, that this leisure was often scripted, designed to reflect their families' status. Medieval notions of public and private were quite different from those of today, and many noblewomen were looking out for their families' interests even as they embroidered cloth or entertained guests.

Because their husbands were frequently away, and because many noblemen died before their wives, noblewomen had to know how to manage their lands at a very practical level. Christine de Pizan's advice to noblewomen mixes the moral with the mundane. A noblewoman must be compassionate toward the poor, but she should also avoid hiring shiftless laborers who change masters every season. She should live within her income, but she should also ensure she is not shortchanged by her workers by inspecting their work throughout the day. She should understand the legal status of each piece of land and the various rights owed to the lord for each, since bailiffs and other manorial officials might be more inclined to cheat a woman than a man.[86] In short, she must be capable of running the estate in a manner at least as careful as that of her husband—indeed, she must work harder to ensure that no one took advantage of her.

A noblewoman's position as stand-in for her husband became all the more acute when she needed to protect the rights of her children. Noblewomen who served as regents for minor sons could wield considerable power, yet they were also especially vulnerable. On the Continent, widowed queens holding power on behalf of their sons had to protect realms from jealous uncles and other nobles. The thirteenth-century Blanche of Castile is renowned as a regent who successfully protected the interests of the future Louis IX of France. Louis looked to his mother to hold the kingdom for him again when he went on crusade.[87] In England, Isabella of France served as regent for the future Edward III following the deposition of his father. Isabella faced a multitude of problems, some stemming from her foreign birth, others from her involvement in Edward II's deposition and her affair with Roger Mortimer, and others still from nobles' perceptions of her legitimacy to rule. She was removed, ultimately, by her son, who decided at age eighteen that he could run the kingdom by himself.[88] Noblewomen below the rank of royalty faced similar pressure from land-hungry relatives and ambitious children.

Noblewomen's work involved the raising of children, but not necessarily in the hands-on sense that a peasant woman or townswoman raised her children. A noblewoman may not have changed diapers, but she was ultimately responsible for children's well-being and education. This work began with childbearing. Many noblewomen spent a considerable proportion of their adult years pregnant or recovering from the birth of a child. Because they did not usually breast-feed themselves, they quickly became pregnant once more. A study of the children of English kings between 1066 and 1509 has shown an average of five children per king, but those who died as infants are probably undercounted. William I and his wife Matilda of Flanders, for instance, were parents of four sons, six daughters, and at least one more child of unknown sex.[89] The fifteenth-century Elizabeth Woodville had two sons by her first marriage, then married Edward IV and became mother to a further three sons and seven daughters, a total of twelve children.[90] One of Elizabeth's sons, Thomas Grey, Marquess of Dorset, had fifteen children by his second wife.[91] The drudgery of morning sickness, not to mention the rigors and dangers of childbirth itself, must have been almost routine for these women.

The work of child raising continued with noblewomen's responsibility for children's upbringing. In addition to raising their own children, at least for the first seven years of each child's life, noblewomen often took in children from other households. Boys were schooled in fighting and trained as pages, learning by emulating knights and serving nobles. As Ruth Mazo Karras has argued, women were largely peripheral to this masculine education.[92] Girls, however, were in the charge of noblewomen, learning to manage household accounts, make and mend clothing, oversee the kitchen, and even tend the garden. A noblewoman might feel it incumbent on her to ensure that her charges mixed with other high-born girls, along with parents of potential marriage partners.[93]

Just as a noblewoman might take in the children of others, so too she sought good placements for her own children. Much of a noble mother's job involved launching her children into an appropriate social network and grooming them for the social politics they would encounter beyond the home. Indeed, finding marriage partners for her children was an important responsibility, one often shared with her husband or other relatives. Marriages linked families, so facilitating good marriages was simultaneously a way of maintaining and even raising the family's reputation.

Women also mediated between their families and the world beyond when they served as patrons to artists, authors, and musicians and when they donated money to religious institutions. Recent work on patronage has demonstrated the extent to which women participated in the manufacture of cultural artifacts.[94] For many, this role was an active one. A well-known English example is that of the thrice-widowed Elizabeth de Burgh of Clare, who employed skilled metalworkers, embroiderers, and musicians and founded religious houses and educational institutions. She was also known for her charitable giving, distributing alms to the poor on Maundy Thursday and on the anniversary of her third husband's death.[95] Less wealthy women might still play an important role in patronage by giving donations to the local parish church or to almshouses. These acts of sponsorship and charity made an important statement about the donor and her family: they attested to their piety, wealth, good taste, and good character.

Barbara J. Harris has shown effectively how the definition of power in early Tudor England must be expanded well beyond the level of the royal courts to include the social networking of noblewomen, and much of her argument can be applied to the late Middle Ages as well. As noblewomen entertained one another, trained one another's daughters, found matches for their children, sponsored artists, and gave alms to the poor, they exercised power and performed the multiple types of work that were expected of them.[96]

Women's lives in late-medieval England certainly varied a great deal according to their social status. The education they received and the type of work they performed thus varied too. Yet, in some ways, they were more similar than different. For women of all statuses, education tended to involve a blend of the practical and the moral. While a small minority of women learned to read (and an even smaller proportion learned to write), most were trained in practicalities by observing their mothers. They thus learned the truth of the aphorism that a woman's work is never done: no matter her status, a medieval woman usually juggled many tasks and responsibilities. The young girl who sat on the floor in a London house and played with miniature plates and cups was simultaneously minding her younger siblings and practicing work that she would increasingly take on as she reached maturity. Work, and preparation for work, was central to the identity of medieval girls and women. Yet this work was usually seen as inferior to that of men: women maintained households, families, and craft workshops, while men produced more tangible products that brought greater occupational status. While work was essential to what it meant to be female, it was work that reinforced medieval women's secondary status.

CHAPTER SEVEN

Power: Medieval Women's Power through Authority, Autonomy, and Influence

LOIS L. HUNEYCUTT

When discussing women and power in the Middle Ages, or at any other time, it is important to distinguish among several commonly used terms that denote women's ability to control both their own destinies and those of other people. The simplest form of power is autonomy, or the ability to decide one's own fate and exercise control over one's own body. Both men and women of the Middle Ages (which, in this chapter, covers the early as well as central and later medieval period for the purpose of enhancing comparisons) experienced constraints on the exercise of autonomy. Medieval people often seemed to see themselves as members of families and other cultural groups as much as they were aware of themselves as individuals, and thus their individual identities were often intertwined with those of both their natal and affinal kin to a much greater extent than is the case today in the Western world.[1] Even aristocratic women experienced severe limitations on their personal autonomy. Although they were not supposed to be forced into marriages or nunneries against their wills, particularly after the mid-eleventh century when consent to marriage became a constituent element in a valid marriage, arrangements for girls' futures were often made by their guardians when they were very young. Young women who brooked their families' arrangements would most likely have found themselves without practical alternatives and be compelled to submit to fates to which they had only nominally consented.[2] Some men and women were born into servile conditions, and neither slaves nor serfs were free to go where they chose, nor could they decide not to carry out tasks imposed on them without severe risks and penalties. Slave women were not legally free to refuse to engage in sexual relations with their masters or other free men, and although there were penalties for raping serf women, it was difficult for servile women or their families to prosecute or prove rape when a free man was accused of the crime.[3]

Medical texts of antiquity and the Middle Ages portrayed women as being much more tied to the limits of their bodies than men. Having a female body meant that women dealt with issues of fertility and reproduction in a world where the ability to control either was limited. Women's bodies were also essential to the survival of the young, for there were few or no alternatives to human milk as food for human infants. It is probably the case that most medieval women who were not committed to chastity spent much of the time between menarche and menopause either trying to conceive, pregnant, or lactating, although wealthy families usually hired wet nurses for their offspring. Women's sexual activities and reproductive role were sources of cultural tension. Medical writers from antiquity opined that women needed to experience regular sexual intercourse in order to remain healthy, while Christian didactic literature urged both men and women to remain continent if not chaste.[4] The tension between the perceived biological need for sexual relations and the ideal of chastity often resulted in women being portrayed as obstacles to male Christian perfection, or as one writer termed it, "seductive sirens and sources of sin."[5] Christianity taught that sexual relations were only to be carried out within marriage, but in practice society tolerated male infidelity, and children born outside of marriage were common. Medieval elite families were, however, highly concerned that property be retained within patriarchal lines. Thus, female sexuality and its exercise was highly regulated, limiting women's control of their own bodies much more than was the case for men and their bodies.

Another form of power is the ability to influence and/or compel others to carry out one's will. This form of power (*potestas* in Latin) can be officially recognized and sanctioned, or it can be exercised outside of political or social approval. While women did not usually have the raw physical strength to enforce their will upon others, they did often have the means by which to influence other people. Manipulating the approved role of the role of the medieval mother was one such means. For instance, even when the Carolingian noblewoman Dhuoda (fl. first half of the ninth century) was separated from her children because of political factions in the court of Louis the Pious, she attempted to continue to influence her children through the teaching role of the Christian mother.[6] Christian motherhood, embodied to perfection in Mary, the mother of Christ, could serve to empower women, whose influence over their sons and husbands was often recognized.[7] Texts of the Middle Ages also show women manipulating their sexuality in various ways to influence men's actions so that the women achieve desired outcomes, often in ways that subverted established hierarchies.[8] The medieval world also often saw a kind of inverted power based on ideas of a Christian world order that often placed the lesser over the greater, and the weaker over the stronger. In such a constructed order, women's perceived weakness could itself paradoxically become a source of strength, and women quite low on the social scale could sometimes manipulate these concepts of strength and weakness to achieve desired ends. While Jehanne la Pucelle (Joan of Arc, d. 1431) presents perhaps the most famous and compelling example of the lowly female to influence the outcome of public events, the power of weakness is a constant theme in medieval texts.[9] Since elite medieval women were involved in the commissioning, production, and consumption of texts, they were sometimes influential in shaping the way that texts portrayed women and at the same time, shaped by the cultural attitudes toward women and women's roles that these texts portrayed. Patronage of the visual arts also provided some women with the means of shaping a legacy both for themselves and for their families.[10]

Finally, there is authority (*auctoritas*), which is here defined as holding a legitimately constituted office such as queen, countess, or abbess. The authority of office allowed the occupant of that office to exercise culturally sanctioned forms of power, although both male and female officeholders often overstepped the boundaries of authority in their exercise of raw power. While relatively few women were consecrated to ruling queenship, many did inherit counties or duchies, and those women exercised the most obvious and visible forms of authority and power of any medieval women, so this chapter begins with secular women, including queens, countesses, and other noblewomen and their exercise of authority, and then turns to abbesses and other religious women, who also exercised both legitimately constructed authority as well as the no less important modes of moral suasion and social influence.

Let us turn first to the most visible of medieval women, its queens. In the Middle Ages, the term *queen*, or *regina* in Latin, itself carried multiple meanings. Most of the time, the term was applied to a queen consort, or the wife of a ruling king. If her husband the king had died, she became the dowager queen or the queen mother if her child inherited the throne. If her child was underage and she ruled on behalf of the minor child, she was the queen regent. And in rare cases, a woman succeeded to the throne in her own right, in which case she was the ruling queen, or queen regnant. The queen's role changed over the course of the Middle Ages and also differed depending on the area of Europe she in which she lived. For decades after the 1973 publication of the seminal article by JoAnn McNamara and Suzanne Wemple, "The Power of Women through the Family in Medieval Europe: 500–1100," historians of medieval women tended to accept the periodization offered there. According to McNamara and Wemple, because of the lack of separation of the public and private spheres in the early Middle Ages, women in elite households, and queens especially, were able to exercise what the modern world considers public authority as an extension of their household roles. Women were often present when their male relatives discussed matters of policy and governance, and these women participated in these discussions. With the rise of administrative kingship in the central and later Middle Ages, political deliberation was removed from the household and thus women's presence can no longer be assumed when decisions were made and executed.[11] The growing professionalization of the later medieval court gradually excluded women from exercising either the direct power or indirect influence they had enjoyed in the early medieval period. Recent work, however, has nuanced the McNamara-Wemple thesis. Some have called the public/private model into question entirely, while others have pointed out that some of the most powerful women of the Middle Ages, such as Blanche of Castile (d. 1252), were active long after the rise of administrative kingship had theoretically stripped them of their power. Still others have argued that the growing preference for secure and orderly transmission and titles invariably meant that women would occupy positions of power, and that this fact has seemed to bother modern commentators far more than it did medieval people.[12] But although the McNamara/Wemple thesis can no longer referenced without qualification, it is still useful as a guide to help historians understand a few general trends in the thousand-year period that constitutes the Middle Ages.

Although queenship was an integral part of the exercise of monarchical power, there were few formally constituted roles for a queen consort, and the formal powers that did exist varied over time and space. The queen's success often depended on factors such as her individual interests and abilities, her relationship to the king and his relatives, the financial resources she had at her disposal, and her ability to produce a suitable heir to the throne. In general, while the early medieval queen was highly visible in the court and close to the sources of political power, her status was insecure and depended on her relationships with her male relatives as much as her own abilities. Marriage practices were more fluid than they would later be, and even queens could be divorced or set aside with impunity. By the Carolingian era, Christian familial ideals had made the queen's status somewhat more secure, although she usually still could be replaced if she proved unsuitable or infertile. The period between the mid-eleventh century through the early thirteenth still represents something of a high point in western Europe in the queen's independent authority and ability to control the power structures in place within her realm. But even after the rise of administrative kingship in the later twelfth and thirteenth centuries, individual women serving as queens, countesses, and duchesses left their marks on the political, cultural, and ecclesiastical life of their realms. The rise of primogeniture as a peaceful succession strategy invariably meant that women would inherit property, and with property came titles and power. In most cases at the comital level, female lordship does not seem to have operated too differently from male lordship.[13]

Both in the later Roman world and in early Germanic society, succession practices to kingship, the imperial throne, and individual counties were quite fluid. Monarchs came from a designated bloodline, but smooth father-son succession was not the norm. Especially in Germanic society, which was based on war, it was preferred that the monarch be an adult male with a record as a warrior and with a group of subordinates who supported him in his bid for the throne. If a king died young, leaving only minor sons, he was as likely to be succeeded by an adult brother or other close relative as he was by a son. Kings and other powerful wealthy males had sexual access to many women, and often, as long as a man chose to recognize the sons of any sexual partners, they were accepted as his and theoretically part of the succession pool. In practice, these loose succession practices meant that the death of a ruler was often followed by a violent succession crisis.[14]

Women in early medieval families knew that their status was secure only insofar as they remained in favor with their spouses and their sons. Kings' wives came from a variety of social backgrounds. Some, such as the Visigothic princess Galswintha or the Thuringian Radegund, were "treaty brides" from royal bloodlines who married a foreign king as a seal of a peace treaty between warring groups. Sometimes a king's mistress started life as a slave within his household. However, if she bore children whom the king recognized, these children became part of the royal *stirpes*, and their mothers were sometimes treated with honor and rewarded with treasure. Because many Germanic kings fathered children by several women over the course of their lives, the mothers of these sons had to compete with each other for the king's favor. Women were often given treasure and large areas of land from which they drew enormous revenues. They used these resources to form factions, attract supporters, and thus advance their sons' chances for succession. Early medieval chronicles are full of stories of women who managed to succeed in these trying circumstances, as well as those who did not.[15]

An early example of a woman whose fortunes rose and fell along with those of her male family members was Galla Placidia (d. 450), daughter of the Roman emperor Theodosius the Great. Galla Placidia was captured by the Visigoths under their king Alaric and taken to Gaul in 412 and then to Spain. She married Alaric's brother Ataulf, who became king; bore a son who died early; and prospered as queen of the Visigoths until Ataulf's death. Once her husband died, with no living child and no husband to protect her, Galla Placidia had no secure place in Visigothic society, so she returned to Italy. At her brother's insistence, she then married a Roman general who became Emperor Constantius III. After Constantius died in 421, Galla Placidia fled with her children to Constantinople, where her son's claim to imperial authority was recognized. She served as his regent for more than twelve years between 425 and 437 and remained influential up until her death.[16]

The stories of the Merovingian queens Brunhilde (d. 613) and Fredegunde (d. 597) also illustrate the positions of early medieval queen consorts. Chilperic I, the Neustrian king, married the Visigothic princess Galswintha, only to have her murdered, probably at the insistence of his mistress Fredegunde, who then served as Chilperic's queen. Meanwhile, Chilperic's brother Sigebert, king of the Austrasians, had married Galswintha's sister Brunhilde. In revenge for her sister's murder, Brunhilde arranged to have Chilperic murdered. The ensuing blood feud between the rival queens and their descendants, which led to violent deaths of three generations of Frankish men, drove the political history of early medieval France for more than forty years.[17]

The patterns in the stories of Merovingian women as well as royal women in other areas of early medieval Europe demonstrate how tenuous court life could be, even for a queen. Since marriages were easily made and relatively easily dissolved, women needed wealth in order to attract and retain support. A foreign bride usually came with rich treasures from her natal family. Some of her treasure was given to her husband's family as a gift, but most would be retained to support her during her lifetime and in case of her widowhood. The bridegroom was expected to add to his queen's wealth by gifts given at the time of the marriage. Later, sons, natal relatives, and retainers from her native area would form the nucleus of her support group, and she usually used her wealth to help her form alliances at court, often with influential churchmen or with members of powerful noble families. Women of less exalted status depended on the gifts and whatever they could extract from those for whom they did favors.

A queen who was known to have a good relationship with her husband could secure an influential place at court. Those wishing royal favors would ask the queen to intercede with the king on their behalf. Literary portrayals such as that of Waltheow in the poem *Beowulf* emphasize the wise counsel a trusted woman could offer and depict her as a queen whose ceremonial duties fostered and regularized relationships among the king and attendant nobles. One of the poetic terms often applied to early medieval queens was *peaceweaver*, which pays tribute to her skill at creating and maintaining harmonious relationships among the influential warriors in the kingdom. On the other hand, ignoring or insulting the queen could cause her to turn her husband against the one who had offended her. In *Egil's Saga*, Eirik Bloodaxe's queen's animosity toward the hero leads to him losing his lands and being forced into exile.[18]

Historians have been divided about how to understand the medieval practice of female intercession. There is no question but that the ability of a woman to intercede on behalf of a petitioner with a husband, son, or other powerful person could bring both wealth and prestige to a woman who was perceived to be helpful in bringing about a desired outcome. In one often-cited instance, Bishop Athelwold of Winchester (d. 984) approached King Edgar of England's consort Aelfthryth (d. ca. 1000) asking for help in gaining legal privileges. In return for "her help in his just mission," he gave the queen 50 mancuses of gold in addition to the silver cup and 200 mancuses of gold that he offered the king. When Anselm, Archbishop of Canterbury (d. 1109) ordered England's priests to put aside their wives, and King Henry cooperated by imposing fines on those who failed to comply, a group of 200 priests begged Queen Matilda to intervene on their behalf, although in this instance, they were refused.[19] Literature for medieval women referred to the example of the biblical queen Esther as well as the Virgin Mary as models for intercessory behavior, as shown in Figure 7.1, and it is quite clear that medieval women used these tropes to further their own ends. Intercession is not only important to women. Female intercession served useful social and political purposes. Not only did it provide a vivid reconstruction of the gender hierarchy, it also allowed a king to change his mind without appearing to be weak or indecisive. Justice tempered with mercy was a royal virtue with both male and female connotations that were foregrounded in acts of staged intercession. But since intercession did reinforce the gender hierarchy, it can also be seen as a means of containing women's power, and reinforcing the fact that a woman's power was limited in scope

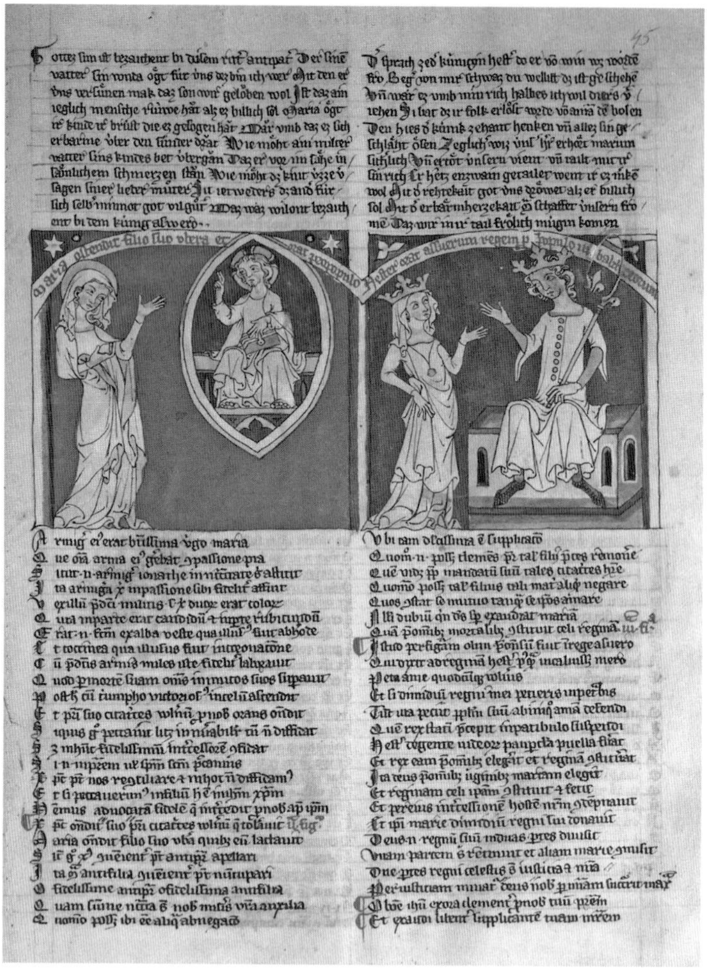

FIGURE 7.1: Virgin Mary bares her breasts to her son in intercession; Esther begs King Ahasuerus to save the Jewish people. *Speculum humanae salvationis*, Austria, Kremsmünster Abbey, Codex Cremifanensis 243, fol. 45 recto. Fourteenth century. Photograph by Erich Lessing, courtesy of Art Resource, NY.

and contingent on a favorable relationship with a more powerful man.[20] Kristen Geaman has recently suggested that in England, at least, queenly intercession should not be seen as an informal female power, but rather a formal one that allowed her to receive a salary at the exchequer in the form of "queen's gold," a surcharge that was leveled on voluntary contributions to the king. It is clear both from earlier studies on eleventh- and twelfth-century queens, and

J. L. Laynesmith's study of the last queens of medieval England that showed little or no intercessory activity on the part of the late-medieval queen at a time when her revenues from queen's gold was also declining, that there is at least a correlation between acts of intercession and receipt of queen's gold.[21]

The informal influence of royal and other aristocratic women is also seen in narrative literature concerning the Christianization of Europe. Beginning with the story of the conversion of the Merovingian Clovis (d. 511), sources often portray queens and as influential in the king's decision to adopt Christianity. These portrayals are formulaic enough to cause concern that the stories reflect more in the way of literary convention than they do historical reality. But Christian queens and other noblewomen did correspond with popes and other churchmen and did often further the cause of Christianity. These women were often patrons of monasteries, reform movements, and ecclesiastical building programs. Many noblewomen entered monasteries after their husbands' deaths, and many daughters of the aristocracy entered into monastic life as consecrated virgins. Some of these women were recognized as saints and thus over time helped add a sense of holiness to further legitimate royal bloodlines.[22]

By the middle of the eighth century, Christian teachings on marriage and the family had begun to permeate the upper ranks of society, and polygyny, or the practice of culturally sanctioned sexual access to many women, including multiple wives, was replaced by serial monogamy, where powerful men were expected to have only one wife at a time. Illegitimate children were generally excluded from full inheritance, and by around the year 1000, primogeniture had begun to replace partible inheritance among the medieval nobility. These changes had mixed effects on women's access to power and authority. There were fewer opportunities for social mobility for the king's mistresses, but legitimate wives enjoyed more security as churchmen insisted that marriages should be both monogamous and indissoluble. With fewer potential male heirs, daughters more often appear as heiresses to both lands and office. Theoretical writings on queenship stressed the necessity of choosing a queen wisely. Sedulius Scottus's *Liber de rectoribus christianis* (*Book on Christian Rulership*) reminded ninth-century rulers to pay attention to the wise counsel of their queens.[23] Carolingian sources confirm that the queen had charge over the royal treasuries. One of Charlemagne's capitularies ordered that his judges fully execute any order that that had come from his queen.[24]

As the queen began to be seen as holding a unique position within the realm, the need arose to mark her accession to queenship formally. Before the ninth century, installation of the queen was not normally a ritual occasion, but Carolingian wives were anointed, often along with their husbands.

About the same time, the Anglo-Saxons developed an inauguration ceremony focused on the ritual enthronement of a new queen. But in Wessex during the ninth century, after a negative experience with a too-powerful queen, it actually became illegal for a woman to be crowned as queen. Alfred the Great's biographer Asser relates that the nobles of the kingdom swore that they would not permit any king to rule over them who allowed a queen to sit beside him on his throne. The West Saxon consort was not called "queen" (*regina*) but only "king's wife" (*regis coniunx*). This situation changed when the Frankish king Charles the Bald (d. 877) agreed to allow his daughter Judith to marry the king of Wessex, with the provision that she had to be crowned and her queenly status recognized.[25] Several ritual orders from Frankish and Anglo-Saxon coronation ceremonies survive and provide clues to early medieval concepts of queenly office. The earliest continental rituals stress the queen's fertility and recognize her potential influence over the king, and the 973 English coronation ritual named the queen as a protector of good religious practice within the realm. The French consecration ceremony became an essential component to kingship in the Capetian years. In a ceremony that became almost a religious ordination, the queen, king, and the heir to the French throne were all promoted to a special elevated status within human society by right of the coronation ritual.[26]

The period from the middle of the eleventh century to the closing years of the thirteenth century saw several women in major European kingdoms claim thrones in their own name, and many other women inherited counties and other territories. For instance, Ermengard of Narbonne (d. 1197), who could not have been over the age of eight at the time that her father was killed at the Battle of Fraga in 1134, inherited that county and oversaw its rule until her retirement in 1192, in the process repelling several attempts by the counts of Toulouse who initially wished to protect Ermengard during her minority.[27] Matilda of Tuscany's (d. 1115) congeries of territories in Italy and Germany allowed her to influence the outcome of military struggles and political events, including the Investiture Controversy played out between Emperor Henry IV and Pope Gregory VII. In her study of the governance of the wealthy counties of Flanders and Hainault, which saw two sisters, Jeanne and Marguerite, holding power successively throughout most of the thirteenth century, Erin Jordan discussed the ways in which women who were granted authority to rule through bloodline and succession to office managed to exercise governing power, often through male lieutenants who served as military commanders.[28]

The role of the queen consort was also augmented in these years. The Norman Conquest of England in 1066 practically demanded that the monarch

FIGURE 7.2: Henry IV begs Matilda of Canossa, Countess of Tuscany, to intercede on his behalf with Pope Gregory VII, while Abbot Hugo of Cluny watches. Miniature from the *Life of Matilda of Canossa.* Eleventh century. Biblioteca Apostolica Vaticana, Vatican Museums, Vatican State. Photo courtesy of Bridgeman-Giraudon/Art Resource, NY.

share power since he could not be on both sides of the channel at once. Both William I (1066–87) and his son Henry (1100–35) had competent, trusted wives who became true partners in the governing of the realm. These women, both named Matilda, judged cases at law, participated in the king's council, chaired the council in the king's absence, issued charters and writs, and corresponded with popes and other leaders of European society. Slightly later, Stephen's queen Matilda of Boulogne (d. 1152) not only headed Stephen's government during his captivity, but also organized a siege and pled his cause before an ecclesiastical council headed by the Bishop of Winchester.[29] The French queen's official role also reached an apogee with the reign of Louis VI

(1108–37) and his consort Adelaide of Maurienne (d. 1154). When Adelaide was queen consort, royal charters were sometimes dated with her regnal year as well as that of Louis. Later, Blanche of Castile served as regent from the time Louis VIII died in 1226 until their son Louis IX came of age in 1234. During that time, she headed off a major baronial rebellion and maintained the peace despite threats from the English. She again served as regent when Louis left the kingdom on crusade, despite her initial objection to her son's crusading activities. Her role was such that Robert Fawtier, a twentieth-century biographer of France's Capetian kings, opined that "for all intents and purposes" Blanche should be counted among the monarchs of medieval France.[30] The work of scholars such as Miriam Shadis and Theresa Earenfight has demonstrated that in the Christian Spanish kingdoms during the central and later medieval period, it was normal for Spanish queens to function as the monarch's alter ego whether or not the queen had provided the king with an heir. The Spanish queens Berenguela (d. 1265) and Maria of Castile (d. 1458) are found serving as lieutenant general during the time that they served Aragon as queen consort.[31]

The papal reform movement beginning in the mid-eleventh century brought the church more fully into the marital lives of European Christians than it had ever before been. While Louis VII of France and Eleanor of Aquitaine were able to procure a separation on grounds of consanguinity, other powerful men found that they could no longer easily divorce or annul marriages that no longer proved useful.[32] Such was the case when Louis's son Philip II "Augustus" (d. 1223) wished to end his marriage to Ingeborg of Denmark. Although Philip claimed that the marriage had never been consummated and was thus not valid, he was unable to secure a papal dispensation for an annulment. Philip later married Agnes of Merania in 1196, despite the fact that Ingeborg was still alive and insisting that she was Philip's rightful wife and queen. Philip's actions led Pope Innocent III to place the kingdom of France under interdict three years later because the king was ignoring the papal order to separate from Agnes. It was not until more than a decade after Agnes died in 1201 that Philip finally became reconciled to Ingeborg.[33]

Perhaps because men theoretically had but one chance to choose a wife and queen, more attention was paid to a woman's suitability for the position in central and later medieval texts. Alfonso X, king of Castile and León (d. 1284), emphasized the importance of a harmonious relationship between the king and queen in his *Siete Partidas*. In a marked departure from early medieval beliefs and practices, Alfonso argued that for a ruler to beget children on women of low status would dishonor the crown (although he himself had illegitimate children). Since the church limited annulments and divorces, Alfonso wrote that queens should be chosen for their lineage, beauty, good habits, and riches they would bring to the realm.[34] Yet, despite cases such as that of Philip II and Ingeborg, in practice the church was usually willing to work with monarchs who wanted to get out of a marriage that proved infertile or unsuitable for other reasons. The "discovery" of a relationship that made the marriage illegal within the strictest interpretation of consanguinity laws was often the legal fiction that allowed a marriage to be dissolved.

There were three major kingdoms also saw ruling queens, or at least an attempt to have a ruling queen, during the first half of the twelfth century. In England, after his only legitimate son drowned in a shipwreck, Henry I had the nobles take an oath to support the claims of his daughter Matilda (d. 1167) should he die before producing another legitimate son. When Henry died, his nephew Stephen managed to claim the throne while Matilda was still on the Continent, but Matilda's attempts to push her claim plunged England into nineteen years of civil war. In the end, although she had come close to being recognized and crowned as a ruling queen, Matilda renounced her claim to rule in return for Stephen's recognition of her son Henry (d. 1189) as his heir. In the Latin kingdom of Jerusalem, Melisende (d. 1161), along with her husband Fulk of Anjou, inherited the throne from her father Baldwin II. As early as 1129, Melisende had witnessed one of her father's charters as the "daughter of the king and the heiress to the kingdom of Jerusalem." When Baldwin was on his deathbed in 1131, he summoned Melisende and Fulk along with their infant son and handed control of the kingdom "to them." Fulk and Melisende had different views of what exactly had been transmitted, and to whom, and each began to form factions among the nobles and churchmen of the kingdom. Eventually, this tension led Melisende's faction, led by her cousin Hugh of Jaffa, to rebel against Fulk, believing that he was trying to usurp sole power in the kingdom. The revolt was unsuccessful, and the chronicler William of Tyre reports that Melisende was so angry with those who had sided with her husband that they were forced to take diligent measures for their own safety.[35] Royal documents issued during their reign confirm that Melisende considered herself a ruler and not just a consort. After Fulk's death she ruled for another thirteen years, and although she is generally listed in modern reference sources as a regent for her minor son, it seems clear that she considered herself at least a coruler and had to be forced to relinquish power when her son reached majority age. The Cistercian abbot Bernard of Clairvaux's letters to Melisende illustrate the malleability of medieval ideas about gender. Since, according to Bernard, God had placed Melisende in a role normally occupied by a man, she must learn to "act as a man by doing all you have to do in a spirit prudent and strong," so that observers would judge from her actions that she was a king rather than a queen.[36] Later in the century, Melisende's granddaughters Sibylla (d. 1190) and Isabella (d. 1192) held the throne in the crusader kingdom, and Isabella was succeeded by her daughter Maria (d. 1212). Finally, Urraca of Leon-Castile (d. 1126) is recognized as the first woman to rule a Spanish kingdom in her own right. Although she was twice married, the title of monarch belonged to her, and she ruled without an official consort after her marriage to Alfonso I of Aragon was annulled in 1112.[37]

FIGURE 7.3: Empress Matilda, daughter of Henry I of England, holding a charter. *Golden Book of St. Albans*, Thomas Walsingham and William de Wylum. London, British Library, Cotton MS Nero D. VII, fol. 7. England, 1380. Photo courtesy of HIP/Art Resource, NY.

McNamara and Wemple were right in asserting that as royal bureaucracies grew and became more professional, it became less necessary for monarchs to depend on family members to participate directly in the business of ruling. They did not take into account, however, the ritual importance of the queen or her other roles and duties that allowed queen consorts and other noblewomen to remain closely associated with the practice of monarchy and lordship. In the later Middle Ages, women generally assumed more ceremonial roles and tended to participate less in the day-to-day business of government. One effect of the rise of professional royal bureaucracies was that royal income was often subsumed into a treasury controlled not by the queen or officials from her household, but by officials who were most likely not personally beholden to or appointed by the queen. After the mid-twelfth century it is not safe to assume that a royal consort had direct control over income from lands or other sources, even if that income were collected in her name. In England, for instance, Eleanor of Aquitaine was the first queen after the Conquest who can be shown to regularly have collected queen's gold, paid to the queen whenever a voluntary fine was paid to the king. The queen's share was one-tenth of that paid to the king and was originally tied to the expectation that the queen would use her influence with the king to reward petitioners. Contemporary evidence points to the conclusion that Eleanor lost control of her resources after the 1173 rebellion against King Henry, and she presumably did not regain control of her income until after Henry's 1189 death. She resumed the collection of queen's gold during the reigns of her sons Richard and John, even though the money was supposed to be collected by the queen consort, possibly until her 1204 death.[38] Likewise, Henry III was able to prevent any revenue going to his wife, Eleanor of Provence, for a time in 1252 when he was angered with her for overstepping her bounds and independently filling a vacant living in Hertfordshire. Actions such as those of Henry II and Henry III serve to illustrate that although the queen consort was part of the institution of monarchy, she ultimately remained subordinate to the king.[39]

Although the autonomy that comes with direct control of resources and the authority that comes from office may have generally lessened over time for medieval queens, it is not only through the exercise of ritually and legally constructed authority that we see medieval women in positions of power. Women also used symbolic means of enforcing their authority and extending their influence through the language of charters and other royal documents as well as through having themselves depicted in traditional monarchical poses in their coinage and seals. Many medieval women in positions of authority used seals to authenticate documents issued in their names. The legends on the seals of individual women often provide clues about the way these women thought about themselves and their positions. Both Kathleen Nolan and Bridgitte Bedos Rezak point out that Bertrada of Montfort (d. 1117), whose marriage to King Philip I had been illegal under canon law and never legitimated by Rome, sealed her documents in widowhood as "Queen of the Franks by God's Grace," perhaps as a conscious attempt on her part to assert her royal status.[40] Although women are usually portrayed standing in their seals, sometimes holding symbols of authority, the Empress Matilda's seal rather optimistically

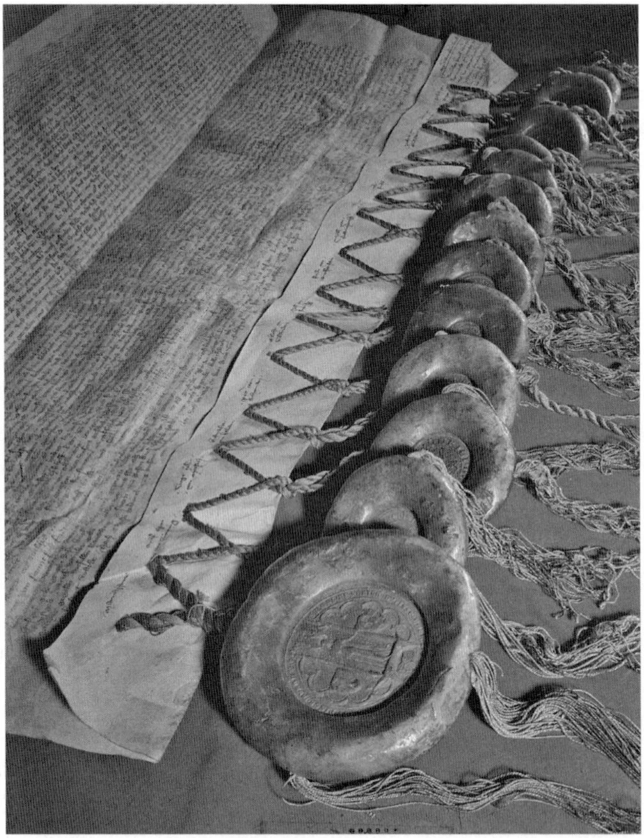

FIGURE 7.4: Deed by which Margarethe Maultasch, Countess of Tyrol, made over the counties of Tyrol and Goricia to the Dukes of Austria. Parchment with seals of Margarethe and fourteen of her squires, January 26, 1363. Haus-, Hof- und Staatsarchiv, Vienna, Austria. Photograph by Erich Lessing, courtesy of Art Resource, NY.

shows her seated, crowned, and holding a scepter in her right hand, just as a king would be portrayed.[41]

Medieval and modern historians alike have recognized that cultural patronage can be a way of asserting and exercising power. The twelfth-century chronicler William of Malmesbury reported that Matilda of Scotland often gave gifts to foreign musicians so that they might "proclaim her dignity abroad."[42] Modern scholars have shown that aristocratic women of the Middle Ages patronized art and literature as a way of shaping their image and legacies. Their carefully crafted images are found in books, stained-glass windows, and even on their tombs. Nolan's study of the Capetian queens of France demonstrates that the these women generally preferred to be buried in monasteries that they themselves had founded rather than in the royal mausoleum at St. Denis, that they specified what kinds of prayers should be said and for whom in return for the gifts that they gave to monasteries, and that women were instrumental in the creation of visual monuments that helped to shape their own historical memories and that of their families.[43] Women also used texts to commemorate their family members. In England, for instance, the widowed queen Edith of Wessex (d. 1075) commissioned a *Life* of her husband Edward the Confessor (d. 1066) that serves as much or more to memorialize her natal family as it does her husband.[44]

The tension between preferring an adult male ruler who could engage in warfare and the desire for direct patrilineal succession continued into the later medieval period. During several succession crises in places as diverse as Sicily and Scotland, women either ruled or transmitted the rights to rule to their sons. Constance of Sicily (1154–98) was born to Beatrice of Rethel after the death of her husband King Roger II and remained single until after her thirtieth birthday. In 1186, she was married to the future German emperor Henry VI. This marriage into the house of Hohenstaufen was controversial with both the nobles of Sicily and the papacy, which feared growing German influence and power in Italian affairs. The unpopularity of Constance's marriage among the great men of Sicily allowed her cousin Tancred to seize the throne in 1189, but in 1190, after Henry and Constance had been crowned as emperor and empress in Germany, they marched south to Sicily and challenged Tancred's rule. It was not until after Tancred's 1194 death that Henry regained the throne in his wife's name. He was crowned in Palermo on December 25 of that year; however, Constance was not able to travel south from Germany in time for the coronation, for she was in her ninth month of pregnancy and was forced to travel more slowly than her husband and his retinue. The future Emperor Frederick II was born on December 26 in the town of Jesi, near Ancona. The fact that Constance was giving birth to her first child at the age of forty must have been a cause for concern at the time. Later sources claim that Constance had been a nun, pulled out of the monastery "as an old hag" in order to secure the succession. Still others claim arranged to deliver her child publicly in a tent set up in the market square in the presence of fifteen bishops, and that she held court the next day, publicly breast-feeding her newborn son. These fantastic stories must have arisen to dispel rumors that the forty-year-old queen had feigned a pregnancy and that the child Frederick was not her biological son, and thus not the legal heir to either Germany or Italy.[45]

In another case of attempted female succession, the royal line of Scotland threatened to fail after the death of Alexander III's last child in 1284, and he persuaded the Scottish Estates to accept his granddaughter Margaret as his heir. Margaret's mother had married the king of Norway, and the younger Margaret had been raised in Norway. However, Margaret was but a three-year-old child when her grandfather died in 1286, and since her stepmother Yolande was thought to be pregnant, it was some time after Alexander's death before Margaret was indeed recognized as the heir of the king. Even after Yolande's child failed to materialize—and accounts differ as to whether she miscarried, delivered a stillborn child, or had never been pregnant at all—the lords of Scotland refused to honor her claim to the throne. This refusal eventually led her father to request the assistance of the English king Edward I, who seems to have been working for a papal dispensation to allow his own son to marry Margaret, despite their close blood relationship. By 1290, Edward had persuaded the Scottish guardians to allow Margaret to travel to Scotland, where presumably a husband would be found for her and she would be crowned queen. Margaret died en route from Norway, leaving the Scottish succession open, which provoked both internal war among the Scots and war with England.[46]

In the cases of Matilda of England and Margaret, "Maid of Norway," it was taken for granted that the daughter of a king could transmit the right to rule to her son, even if it was doubted that she herself would be a suitable monarch. Even this ability to transmit claims to rule was questioned in France, though, when the death of the last male descendant of Philip IV (d. 1314) led to the discovery of the Salic law that prohibited females from transmitting the right to rule to their descendants. Yet later, the Treaty of Troyes of 1420 vested the right to rule following the death of King Charles VI in "our son, King Henry," even though Henry was Charles's son-in-law rather than his son.[47] During the fourteenth and fifteenth centuries, the authority associated with queenship generally became ever more social and ceremonial. Queens set the fashions at court, became extravagant consumers, and were known as patrons of art and literature. Negative reactions when Edward IV (d. 1483) of England's marriage to the commoner Elizabeth Woodville showed that queens were still supposed to come from exalted bloodlines. As late as the fifteenth century, queens could still be used as peaceweavers as evidenced by the marriage of Henry V of England (d. 1422) and Catherine of France (d. 1437) that was supposed to provide a common king and thus lead to the end the Hundred Years' War.

Even in a time when the queen consort possessed little official authority, her potential influence over her husband and her realm should not be discounted. Eleanor of Castile (d. 1290), consort to Edward I of England, helped to popularize the Spanish Dominicans in her new kingdom, and religious dissidents probably followed Anne of Bohemia (d. 1394) into England when she married Richard II. These dissidents helped to fuel reform movements already forming in England. And finally, intercession occasionally still surfaced. Anne pleaded the cause of rebellious Londoners with Richard just as Philippa of Hainault (d. 1369) had interceded with Richard's grandfather Edward III and saved six burghers of Calais from execution.[48]

Family dynamics in the medieval period are often described from a male perspective in which women appear as pawns to be traded in arrangements made among men. Closer examination of texts in which women appear has shown that mothers were often active in forming alliances for their sons and daughters, negotiating the terms of those alliances, and that women maintained long-standing ties to their natal families over several generations, even when they traveled long distances away from their birthplaces. For instance, Adela, Countess of Blois (d. ca. 1137), wife of Count Stephen-Henry of Blois and daughter of William the Conqueror, not only influenced her husband to return to Crusade after he had returned home wounded, but also wielded a great deal of power in northern French politics. Several times she acted as a peaceweaver in disputes among her brother, King Henry I of England (d. 1035), his archbishop Anselm of Canterbury, and the reformer pope Pascal II. Women such as Adela were trained to represent their natal family's interests in new settings and often did so very effectively, making an understanding of the dynamics of marriage and power an essential part of understanding the political and cultural history of the medieval world.[49]

Of course, not all medieval women married. Some remained single because of a lack of opportunity to marry or lack of a dowry. Others were placed into monasteries as child oblates by their family members. These young girls would be educated in the monastery, and upon reaching the proper age to consent, would normally take vows to become fully fledged nuns, or sisters. Although these girls could, and sometimes did, leave the monastery before taking any binding vows, there were usually few practical options for them outside of the cloister in which they had been raised. In addition to the children who were given by their parents, older girls and women could choose to enter the monastery on their own, either before marriage or during their widowhood. For many women, the monastery offered a life of learning, contemplation, and freedom from marriage and childrearing. For others, the monastery served as a place to escape from an undesired match or an unhappy marriage. For a few abbesses of wealthy houses, the monastery provided a position of both power and authority.[50]

Medieval monasticism grew out of models created in late antiquity. Early communities of women dedicated to a life of Christian monasticism could be informal and house centered. St. Macrina (d. 379), from a wealthy family in Caesarea, along with her widowed mother, dedicated herself to virginity and contemplation after her fiancé died before their wedding. They turned their home into a monastery, sharing the work of running the estate with the maid-servants. The *Life of Macrina* speaks of her mother "paying taxes to three different governors" because the family owned property in three provinces. Obviously this family had the means to afford a life of contemplation and study for its female members from its own resources, and it is clear from the text that the women exercised considerable autonomy when it came to making decisions about the course of their own lives. Other early medieval women chose lives of solitude and voluntary poverty. Among the most extreme examples of this phenomenon are the "Desert Mothers" of late antiquity and the early medieval period. Many of their sayings, like the sayings of the better-known Desert Fathers, were uttered in response to questions from pilgrims who encountered them in the deserts of the eastern Mediterranean, remembered by Christian communities, and written down in Coptic, Syriac, Greek, and later, Latin. The phenomenon of the Desert Mothers continued into the medieval period. In a 1983 study, Margot King found 1,100 named recluses in Europe between the sixth and the fifteenth centuries, along with approximately 900 references to unnamed anchoresses and other women who embraced the eremitic, solitary life. The extreme asceticism associated with the life of the Christian recluse gave, to many of those practicing this eremitical lifestyle, prestige and a form of bestowed authority, and the texts extolling their lives often depict people from surrounding communities asked their advice on matters both spiritual and mundane. However, assuming this kind of authority could only come to women who had overcome the weakness associated with the female body, becoming, through extremely rigorous asceticism, "like a man."[51]

Many women in more traditional monastic settings also assumed positions of leadership and responsibility normally exercised by males. The life of Radegund of Thuringia (d. 586) illustrates how religious life could become a haven for women caught up in the political violence of the era. Her father had been king of the German province of Thuringia. When her father was killed by his brother, Radegund was taken into the household of the murderer. After her uncle went to war against the Frankish king, Radegund was transported into Merovingian Gaul by King Clothar I (d. 561) and was married to him. The marriage was never successful, and after Clothar had Radegund's brother murdered, Radegund fled the marriage and, with the help of a sympathetic bishop, was ordained as a deaconess, even though the ordination of women had been forbidden at a series of sixth-century church councils.[52]

In early medieval Ireland, Anglo-Saxon England, and some parts of Gaul, women not only presided over other women as abbesses but were also sometimes in charge of mixed communities of both men and women.[53] Most of the Anglo-Saxon foundations were in the seventh century and were influenced by older continental houses such as Chelles, Faremoutiers, and Jouarre. Eric Fletcher argued that it was customary for seventh-century English kings to send their daughters to one of the houses in Gaul, where they received general education and monastic instruction. Some of these women remained on the Continent; a few rose to the position of abbess in a continental monastery.[54] Others returned home and eventually joined communities in England, many founded either by the princesses themselves or their family members. In England, some of the women who became abbesses were consecrated virgins, but a number of the founders of monastic communities were either widows or women who left marriages after a number of years. The most well-known of these women is probably Hild of Streonshal (later Whitby, d. 680), who was among the first generation of Christians, baptized along with her kinsman King Edwin of Northumbria on Easter Sunday of 627. Hild traveled to Chelles, where she intended to take vows and join her sister, already a professed nun. Recalled to England by Bishop Aidan, she became abbess of Hartlepool before moving to the new foundation at Whitby, where she presided over the synod in 664 that brought England into line with the Roman Church and the continental system of organization. According to Bede, who was born in the later years of Hild's life, "so great was her prudence that not only ordinary folk, but kings and princes used to come and ask her advice in their difficulties and take it." Five of the monks who were educated in the monastery while Hild was abbess later were appointed as bishops, and Barbara Yorke has contended that Hild may be "as significant in the tumultuous church politics of the latter part of the seventh century as some of the male players whose role is more often stressed."[55]

The ability of saintly women to influence powerful men is highlighted in a number of medieval hagiographical texts, including the *Life of St. Leoba.* Leoba (d. 782) was an Anglo-Saxon noblewoman, related to Archbishop Boniface (d. 755), the apostle to the Germans. She entered the religious life as a nun at Wimborne but because of her holy life and wisdom was summoned by Boniface to accompany him on his missionary journeys to Germany. Established at Tauberbischofsheim, she became an abbess and is reported to have performed miracles during her lifetime. When Boniface left Germany to go and preach in Frisia, he left his cowl, a symbol of his authority, with Leoba. Leoba's biographer reports that she was held in veneration by the Frankish kings, including Pepin (d. 783) and Charlemagne (d. 814), as well as by Charlemagne's queen Hiltigard, who "revered her with a chaste affection and loved her as her own soul." According to Leoba's hagiographer, Rudolf of Fulda, Charlemagne summoned Leoba to court on numerous occasions and presented her with gifts "suitable to her station." The queen desired that Leoba "remain continually at her side so that she might progress in the spiritual life and profit by her words and example. But Leoba detested the life at court like poison." Because of her perceived sanctity, she, alone of all women, was allowed to enter into the male monastery at Fulda to pray.[56]

In Ottonian Germany, the abbey of Quedlinburg was founded by Matilda of Ringelheim (d. 968), the widow of Henry the Fowler, and their son Otto, as a memorial to King Henry. The first abbess was Matilda of Ringelheim's granddaughter, also named Matilda, who was installed in 966 at the age of eleven. Successive generations of royal women lived at and ruled over Quedlinburg, which housed many daughters of the nobility who lived as canonesses. During the 980s, Abbess Matilda, her widowed mother, Adelaide (d. 999), and her widowed sister-in-law Theophanu (d. 991) all lived at the abbey and together served as regents for Theophanu's son (and Adelaide's grandson), Emperor Otto III (d. 1002). The abbey was free from local episcopal control and answered only to the pope; in later years, the abbess of Quedlinburg held a seat ex officio in the German Diet.[57]

Perhaps the most influential of all medieval nuns was the German visionary Hildegard of Bingen (d. 1179). The convent provided a site where she could exercise her considerable talents as a theologian, political advisor, composer, playwright, herbalist, healer, and naturalist. Her writings brought her to the attention of many influential men, including Bernard of Clairvaux and Abbot Suger of St. Denis, both advisors to the French king. She corresponded as well with Emperor Frederic Barbarossa and Popes Eugenius III (d. 1153) and Anastasius IV (d. 1154). Hildegard is the only woman whose works were included in the influential nineteenth-century collection of the works of the "church fathers," the *Patrologia latinae*.[58] Obviously, the women who found a voice and positions of power and authority within the institutional structure of the medieval church tended to be women from royal and aristocratic families, and also women gifted with unusual intellectual talents. Yet although Hildegard undeniably possessed one of the greatest intellects of the medieval world, her authority rested as much on the visions that gave her direct access to God as it did on the force of her considerable accomplishments. Hildegard was prone to illnesses and fell sick several times over the course of her life when she was unwilling to carry out directions given to her in her visions or when others prohibited her from doing so. She recovered only when her instructions were followed. Her illness became a source of strength and power, for seeing her in extremis compelled others to carry out orders she believed she had received directly from God.[59]

The belief that a woman had direct access to God through visions, personal holiness, extreme asceticism, or other marks of sanctity often led to her having a voice that would not otherwise be heard. Although the *Life of Leoba* includes several accounts of miracles, it was the probity of her life that drew the Frankish royal family to her, according to her biographer. In other cases, a woman's ability to deny her body, and thus overcome the fragility of her sex, was the marker of her holiness. An extreme example of this kind of asceticism is presented to the reader in the rather troubling text known as the *Life of Christina Mirabilis*. Christina was born in what is now Belgium in 1150, and, according to the text, died several times before the final time, in 1224. Unlike most medieval women of note, Christina was born into a peasant family. In her early twenties, she suffered some sort of seizure that led onlookers to believe that she had died; Christina herself reported that she had been led into through hell, purgatory, and heaven. In the presence of God, she was allowed to choose whether to enter heaven at that time or to return to earth and suffer. Her sufferings would not cause her death but would relieve the sufferings of those in purgatory and would also serve to convert unbelievers on earth and thus save them from hell and purgatory. Upon being reunited with her body, Christina began to subject it to all sorts of privations, ranging from jumping into the near-frozen Meuse River in winter (where the text tells us she remained for weeks at a time), jumping into burning ovens from which she emerged with no signs of being burned, or being chased and torn at by packs of wild dogs. Despite behavior that modern observers can only term *bizarre*, Christina was venerated in her town. Louis, Count of Loos, is said to befriended her, visited for advice, and confessed his sins to her on his deathbed, although Thomas de Cantimpré, the author of the *Life*, is quick to point out that he did so "not for absolution which she had no power to give, but rather that she be moved by this atonement to pray for him."[60] This careful spelling out of the limits of Christina's power raises the question about whether women visionaries were indeed filling priestly roles for those who believed in their saintliness and direct access to God. Christina and her mystic sisters may not have had the authority to carry out the sacrament of penance, but it appears that believers were granting them that power.

Female mysticism and heroic asceticism reached something of a peak in the fourteenth century. Among those who garnered large audiences for her revelations was Catherine of Siena (d. 1380), a Dominican tertiary who worked to recall the papacy to Rome from Avignon and who also called for peace between warring city states in Italy. As a girl, Catherine's father had wished for her to marry her sister's widower; his mind was changed after Catherine refused to eat until he released her from the marriage. She also became seriously ill when her parents initially refused her in her desire to join a group of Dominican laywomen. In the early 1370s, Catherine began dictating a series of letters that were sent to numerous leaders of society, including Pope Gregory XI. Catherine's fasting and other forms of asceticism became a source of concern to those around her. Even her confessor urged her to eat more, but like Christina the Astonishing before her, she claimed that ingesting food made her ill. She considered the stomach pains that she endured as a result of her fasting a form of Christian penance.

Scholars have been divided about how to understand the activities of Christina, Hildegard, Catherine, and others like them. Rudolph Bell saw elements of the modern diagnosis of anorexia nervosa in the behavior of the female saints he studied. Caroline Walker Bynum declined to identify their behavior with modern disease and studied the eating behavior of these saints within the medieval context of a culture of food provision, consumption, and fasting, concluding that modern scholars who associate extreme asceticism only with self-loathing or psychological attempts at control are overlooking the rich relationship between medieval food production/consumption and religious practice. Late-medieval asceticism was not self-hating, but self-empowering as the suffering woman's body became one with that of the suffering Christ.[61]

The paradox of women's suffering and weakness leading to power is nowhere better illustrated than in the life of Jehanne la Pucelle, better known as Joan of Arc. The outlines of Joan's career are well known. Born to a fairly well-to-do peasant family in eastern France during the Hundred Years' War, Joan began hearing voices that she identified as Saints Michael, Catherine, and Margaret. These heavenly voices told her that she must drive the English out of France and secure the coronation of the dauphin, later King Charles VII (d. 1461). With her inspiration, the French armies were able to lift the siege of Orléans as well as win several other victories before Charles was crowned king. Joan's confidence in her own authority was strong, as revealed in several letters that she dictated to the English commanders before the French armies went into action. After ordering the king of England to leave France, and promising to kill those who did not leave, she affirmed: "She comes sent by the King of Heaven, body for body, to take you out of France, and the Maid promises and certifies to you that if you do not leave France she and her troops will raise a mighty outcry as has not been heard in France in a thousand years. And believe that the King of Heaven has sent her so much power that you will not be able to harm her or her brave army."[62] Joan's courage and leadership was celebrated throughout France and captured in a panegyric poem by Christine de Pizan (d. 1430) who saw her as the embodiment of powerful biblical women.[63] Joan was, of course, ultimately captured by the English and burnt at the stake on charges of witchcraft and heresy, although she was found innocent in a retrial shortly after her death.[64] Although Joan is unquestionably the best-known and probably the most effective of the medieval mystics, she is but one of several women whose visions called upon leaders of society to end the Great Schism or drive the English out of France.[65]

The cases of Joan and the other female mystics of the later Middle Ages illustrate the cost that women sometimes paid when they sought to make themselves heard, to exercise autonomy, power, and what they considered authority from God in a world dominated by men. And yet, the story of women and power in the medieval world is not a story of unmitigated oppression. There were times and places in the European Middle Ages where women routinely inherited and ruled vast territories, even major kingdoms. Women identified with biblical models of feminine behavior and used the language of intercession to achieve their ends to the extent that, in England, they were formally rewarded for their intercessory behavior in the form of queen's gold. Women used the written word to shape their legacies and those of their families in the form of literary and artistic patronage. Christianity, while sometimes seen as a force limiting women's autonomy and power, could also enable women to exercise authority as scholars, theologians, abbesses, and mystics. In a place as large as medieval Europe, and over a thousand years, it is difficult to draw any overarching conclusions about women and power. Although the historian Georges

Duby complained that writing the history of medieval women was difficult if not impossible because of the lack of authentic female voices in the medieval record, and it is true that women were never able to exercise authority, power, and autonomy as freely as their male counterparts, powerful women are present in every century and every society that make up the medieval millennium.[66] Once we begin to listen for their voices, we find them almost everywhere.

CHAPTER EIGHT

Artistic Representation: Women and/in Medieval Visual Culture

MARIAN BLEEKE, JENNIFER BORLAND, RACHEL DRESSLER, MARTHA EASTON, AND ELIZABETH L'ESTRANGE (FROM THE MEDIEVAL FEMINIST ART HISTORY PROJECT)

In comparison to men, women were at a social, political, economical, and sexual disadvantage in the Middle Ages. As a result, there is a relative paucity of information about women's lives, especially those from the lower echelons of society. Scholars frequently turn to artistic representations of women in order to fill the gap left in the historical record. A plethora of images from sources such as illuminated manuscripts, frescoes, panel paintings, tapestries, and carved ivories have come down to us and can suggest much about the past. However, it is important to remember that such representations of women, like those of men, were often highly stylized, represented holy or mythical figures, or idealized situations. Thus, to a certain extent, they can tell us more about received ideas than about real life in the Middle Ages.

The objects and images discussed in this chapter are by no means exhaustive but have been chosen to offer a broad range of examples of the different ways in which women were represented in western Europe. The most frequently represented woman at this time was no doubt the Virgin Mary, whose roles encompassed intercessor, mother, Seat of Wisdom, and Queen of Heaven. Yet Mary was a paradox, and her status as both virgin and mother served to emphasize the association of the female sex more generally with corporeality and sexuality: many of the images discussed here, from Eve to the virgin martyrs, *luxuria*, and medical imagery reveal, in various ways, this association. The sensual and sinful body of Eve was diametrically opposed to the intact body of the Virgin Mary. Mary Magdalene was usually depicted wearing red, a reference to her former life as a prostitute, which she left in order to serve Christ. However, whereas Eve was held responsible for women's suffering in childbirth, the biblical saints Elizabeth and Anne were feted for their miraculous conceptions and God-given children. Women's intrinsic role as child bearers also made their bodies an object of study for medical authors, although the images accompanying the texts often reduce the woman to her uterus, a vessel for the child, emphasizing certain contemporary medical ideas about women's relatively passive role in procreation.

Most artistic production in the Middle Ages was collaborative and carried out in monasteries and in town-based workshops, meaning that many artists have remained anonymous. Yet nineteenth-century constructions of the artist as an inspired, singular, male personality have been mapped back onto the Middle Ages where scholars talk of different hands as "masters." Thus, historiographical tendencies as well as the lack of primary evidence make it difficult to discern women's roles as creators of images. Figures such as Hildegard of Bingen and Christine de Pizan who were involved in the production and dissemination of their own works are often cited as exceptions to the rule, yet we should not overlook other instances where women may have produced works of art, even if we do not know their names: the female embroiderers of the *Bayeux Tapestry* discussed here are a case in point.

It is often much easier to discuss women's roles as consumers and patrons of art objects, although the evidence is heavily biased toward aristocratic women whose positions of wealth and power mean that their names and their commissions have been preserved for posterity. Women such as Blanche of Castile and Isabeau of Bavaria, who were at times invested with the authority to govern the kingdom of France, had themselves depicted in manuscripts, sculpture, and stained glass. Although aristocratic women were often pawns on the marriage market, the sumptuous images that they had created of themselves as counselors, patrons, and rulers nevertheless testify to the power they could exercise on both political and artistic levels.

In addition to personal commissions, other art objects such as books of hours, birth trays, and carved ivories were also produced with women in mind or gained particular popularity among groups of female viewers. Books of hours bear witness to women's devotional interests—particularly the importance of saints like St. Margaret, patron saint of childbearing—and often became treasured objects in themselves. Similarly, carved ivory combs and mirror backs usually depicted secular scenes drawn from the literature of courtly love, manuscript copies of which were also popular among female readers.

Women were thus presented with, and in some cases created themselves, a whole variety of images of the female sex. It is tempting for us as modern viewers to use these representations as a window onto some past reality. Yet, we must remain aware of their complexities of production by and within a patriarchal society and an often didactic or instructive use. Nevertheless, placed in their sociohistorical context, medieval depictions of women remain an important source for understanding not only attitudes toward sex and gender but also the power of representation.

BIBLICAL WOMEN

For medieval people, Eve was the first woman. Created from a rib taken out of Adam's side, she remained a thorn in his side thereafter. A sculpture of Eve, originally part of a doorway into the twelfth-century church of Saint-Lazarus at Autun (France), conflates the next several moments in their story into a single image, as shown in Figure 8.1. Stretched out horizontally within the space of the doorway's lintel, Eve reaches back with one arm to pluck a piece of fruit from a tree. A claw grasps the tree's trunk and bends it toward her hand, suggesting that a monstrous figure originally appeared behind Eve, representing the satanic source of her action. The lintel also originally included an image of Adam, in a posture similar to Eve's so that their heads came together in its center. The line of Eve's reaching arm suggests her next action, bringing the fruit forward and offering it to Adam. With her other hand cupped around her chin, she appears to be whispering to him, encouraging him to take a bite. A second foliage frond that curls up and around her head and a third that crosses over her body suggest the significance of their horizontal posture as a result of tasting the fruit of the tree: ashamed, they try to conceal themselves in the trees, hiding from God's eyes in particular. God cannot be avoided, however, and Adam and Eve are expelled from Eden. Eve's gesture to her face is also a conventional sign of grief in medieval art and so indicates her sadness at their loss of paradise.

FIGURE 8.1: Gislebertus, *The Temptation of Eve*. Limestone lintel, Saint-Lazare, Autun, ca. 1130. Musée Rolin, Autun, France. Photograph by Erich Lessing, courtesy of Art Resource, NY.

Aspects of this sculpture also suggest the most common medieval interpretation of the nature of Eve's transgression, as a specifically sexual sin. There is a close relationship between the rounded forms of the fruit on the tree and of Eve's breasts, demonstrating that what Eve offers to Adam is actually her body. In encouraging him to take a bite, she becomes a sexual temptress. Furthermore, the tree that passes in front of her body crosses in front of her genitalia, indicating that the shame that results from this act is sexual shame.[1]

The sexualized, sinful Eve was frequently placed in opposition to the Virgin Mary in medieval theology and art. In the terms of the medieval church teachings, Eve's sin brought death into the world, but Mary's sexless pregnancy brought the possibility of resurrection and eternal life. A comparison of the Autun Eve with a contemporary image of the Virgin holding the Christ Child demonstrates the visual form given to this opposition, as shown in Figure 8.2. Where Eve is stretched out horizontally and her body bends into sinuous curves, Mary sits rigidly upright with her legs and arms bent at sharp angles. Eve's hair and exposed breasts sexualize her body, whereas Mary's body is denied by regular patterns of curving folds. Her body is further obscured by the large form of the child who sits bolt upright in her lap. His size and self-possession are meaningful aspects of this image; an example of a type of Virgin and Child sculpture known as the Throne of Wisdom, the child here represents wisdom and so is shown as a miniature man rather than as an infant.[2] Mary,

FIGURE 8.2: *Virgin and Child as Throne of Wisdom* (Enthroned Virgin and Child). Auvergne, France. Oak, ca. 1150–1200. © The Metropolitan Museum of Art/Art Resource, NY.

then, is the throne. On the one hand, this symbolism associates her with power and authority, which are represented visually by her upright posture and her confrontational gaze. On the other, it identifies her as a mere container for God's child and as an inanimate object rather than a human being.

Images of the Virgin Mary changed over the course of the Middle Ages, as is demonstrated by a comparison of the Throne of Wisdom sculpture with a thirteenth-century ivory statuette of the Virgin and Child shown in Figure 8.3. In contrast to the rigid frontality of both figures in the earlier sculpture, here the child is seated sideways in Mary's lap and turns to reach toward her as she turns and bends her head. She is still heavily swathed in drapery, but her mantle falls open to expose her upper body, and her breasts swell visibly beneath her dress. The child extends a piece of fruit toward her breast, recalling the association between those two forms seen in the Autun Eve, but here as a symbol of maternal nourishment rather than sexual temptation. With his other hand, the child reaches up her to touch her veil: the veil was considered to be

FIGURE 8.3: *Virgin and Child in Majesty*. Paris, Ivory, ca. 1250–60. © The Metropolitan Museum of Art/Art Resource, NY.

a very intimate garment, and so his grasp of it represents his unhindered access to her body.

As well as being an image of intimacy between the mother and child, this statuette would have been an intimate object for a medieval viewer. Where the Throne of Wisdom is approximately two and a half feet tall and would have stood on an altar within a church, the ivory statuette is only seven and a quarter inches tall and was most likely the private possession of an elite individual. Images like this one that belonged to women offered them with idealized images of mother-child bonding and provided them with opportunities to consider their own experiences of motherhood. The associations with power and authority seen in Throne of Wisdom sculpture are here replaced by a more human relationship.

In addition to the relationship with figures of the Virgin Mary, certain aspects of the Eve figure at Autun resonate with the figure of St. Mary Magdalene. Herself a conflation of a number of women who appear in the Gospels, Mary Magdalene was understood to have been a sexual sinner who repented of her sins and became a devoted follower of Jesus. The Autun sculpture's exposed breasts and flowing hair, a strongly sexualized sign in the Middle Ages, point toward Magdalene's early life as a prostitute, while her horizontal posture recalls her prostration at Jesus's feet, where she wiped his feet with her hair. Her prostration also indicates that repentance requires submission and subordination, while her wiping his feet with her hair represents the intimacy with God that the repentant sinner gains. The possibility of reading this sculpture of Eve as representing Magdalene is strengthened by its appearance on a church dedicated to her brother, St. Lazarus, whom Jesus raised from the dead. A now lost tympanum sculpture that was located over the same doorway into the church represented Lazarus's resurrection. Although its exact form is unknown, it likely included a large standing figure of Jesus so that the Eve/Mary Magdalene on the lintel did appear prostrate at his feet. This combination of images would have represented the association of sin with death, as death was understood to be a consequence of Eve's original sin, and likewise of repentance with resurrection.[3]

In addition to Eve, the Virgin Mary, and Mary Magdalene, other biblical women also provided the opportunity to represent the various facets of womanhood as understood in the Middle Ages. For example, depictions of Bathsheba at her bath, spied on by King David, not only evoked David's sin of adultery but also emphasized Bathsheba's beauty and her sexuality. The image in the *Hours of Louis XII* (ca. 1498–99; Los Angeles, J. P. Getty Museum, MS 75) shows her naked to below the waist, with long flowing golden hair reminiscent of that used for depictions of Eve and Mary Magdalene. In such images, the gaze flits from David to Bathsheba to the viewer, often trapping her in the position of object. Yet in the *Hours of Louis XII*, Bathsheba looks coquettishly to one side as if soliciting David's glance. The ambiguity of the gaze in representations of David and Bathsheba thus parallels the difficulty contemporary people had in interpreting Bathsheba's own part in the story: she oscillates between innocent woman and agent of seduction, a paradox that has its origins in the Eve–Mary binary and that structured debates about the nature of women in the Middle Ages.

Two other Biblical women, St. Anne, the mother of the Virgin, and St. Elizabeth, her cousin, offered an alternative image of women that negotiated the Eve–Mary binary. The story of Elizabeth's conception of St. John, as proof of the truth of the Annunciation, is included in the canonical Gospel of Luke. St. Anne's immaculate conception of the Virgin appears in the *Proto-Evangelium of James* and Jacobus de Voragine's *Golden Legend*. Pious, married, and blessed with children in old age and after a period of shameful sterility, the names of St. Anne and St. Elizabeth appear in prayers and charms for childbearing. Their images in books of hours and paintings commissioned by women or couples wishing to conceive are also frequently found, such as in the Visitation miniature from Anne of Brittany's *Très Petites Heures*.[4] Between them, St. Elizabeth and St. Anne (who was said to have been married three times) bore a host of holy children including St. John the Baptist, St. John the Evangelist, St. James the Great, St. James the Less, St. Jude, and St. Simon. This "Holy Kinship" of Christ's relations became an extremely popular subject for manuscript and panel paintings in the Middle Ages. Anne and Elizabeth were also popularly depicted having given birth to their holy children. For example, the Baptistery in Padua contains a fresco cycle recounting the life of St. John the Baptist by Giusto de Menabuoi, as shown in Figure 8.4. It is possible that

FIGURE 8.4: Giusto de'Menabuoi, *Birth of St. John the Baptist*. Baptistery, Padua, Italy, ca. 1375. Photograph courtesy of Scala/Art Resource, NY.

this work was commissioned by Fina Buzzacarini, wife of the ruler of Padua, in 1375 as a thanksgiving for the birth of her son, Francesco, some fourteen years into her marriage.[5] In the frescoes, Fina is depicted with her three older daughters having entered the bedchamber of St. Elizabeth. A woman seated in the foreground turns to present St. John to the women. The fresco thus draws a parallel between Fina and St. Elizabeth, as mothers blessed by God with a son.

SAINTS

Whereas biblical saints were popular devotional subjects, the early Christian virgin martyrs were among the most revered and represented. The basic outlines of their legends are remarkably similar: they are young, beautiful girls devoted to their Christian beliefs, but with the misfortune of attracting the erotic attention of a powerful pagan man. When they refuse to marry or bed their suitors, they are tortured, often in sexually charged ways, and ultimately killed. While all martyrs were interesting to medieval audiences, most of them reminiscent of a time of Christian persecution before the legalization of the faith by Constantine the Great in the fourth century, something about the virgin martyrs particularly captured the imagination of medieval people. They were the subjects of written texts, as well as artistic representations, including manuscript illuminations, sculptures, paintings, and stained glass.

It was quite common to depict virgin martyrs in the throes of their particular tortures; this could even be used as a way of identifying them given the similarities of their narratives. For instance, one of the most graphically represented tortures suffered by the virgin martyrs was the severing of their breasts; Barbara and Margaret are sometimes shown undergoing this torture, and St. Agatha, in particular, has become associated with this gruesome punishment. After Agatha refuses the advances of the pagan consul Quintianus, he responds by sending her to a brothel, stretching her on the rack, throwing her in prison, and rolling her on a bed of burning potsherds and coals, in addition to cutting off her breasts. Despite the rich and complex nature of her legend, however, Agatha is most commonly depicted with her hands bound and the forced mastectomy about to occur. It is likely that the shocking and visceral nature of this type of image would have inspired empathy and devotion in medieval viewers, but it has also been suggested that the sadistic, even erotic, potential of the scene would not be lost on viewers, be they medieval or modern.[6] The depiction of the half-naked St. Agatha in the early fifteenth-century *Belles Heures of Jean de France, Duc de Berry* (New York, The Metropolitan Museum of Art, The Cloisters Collection, MS 54.1.1, fol. 179) is particularly ambivalent, with the well-endowed young woman seeming to arch against the knee of the torturer, who thrusts it into her groin, as shown in Figure 8.5.

St. Margaret of Antioch was another early Christian virgin martyr who was tortured and killed because she would not submit to the advances of a Roman prefect, Olibrius, and renounce her Christianity. Although the narrative associated with St. Margaret shares much with other early Christian martyrs, it is also unique for the miraculous events that occur while she is imprisoned. Two messengers of Satan, an evil man shrouded in black and a dragon, visit her. She

FIGURE 8.5: Limbourg Brothers, Saint Agatha from *The Belles Heures of Jean de France, Duc de Berry*. New York, The Metropolitan Museum of Art, The Cloisters Collection, MS 54.1.1 fol. 179 recto. ca. 1405–8/9. © The Metropolitan Museum of Art /Art Resource, NY.

vanquishes them both, the first by taking him down and standing upon him, and the second by bursting forth from his body after he has swallowed her. Her successful emergence from the dragon's body is what eventually associates Margaret with successful birth and motherhood.[7]

Representations of Margaret abound, especially in the later Middle Ages, and most commonly represent her emerging from the dragon. A representative image can be found in the late thirteenth-century *Psalter-Hours of Yolande de Soissons* (Pierpont Morgan Library MS 729, fol. 262v), as shown in Figure 8.6. Margaret and the dragon are depicted within a historiated initial "D," her head and torso emerging from the back of the winged beast. Margaret is shown with a halo and her hands folded in prayer, reminding the viewer that

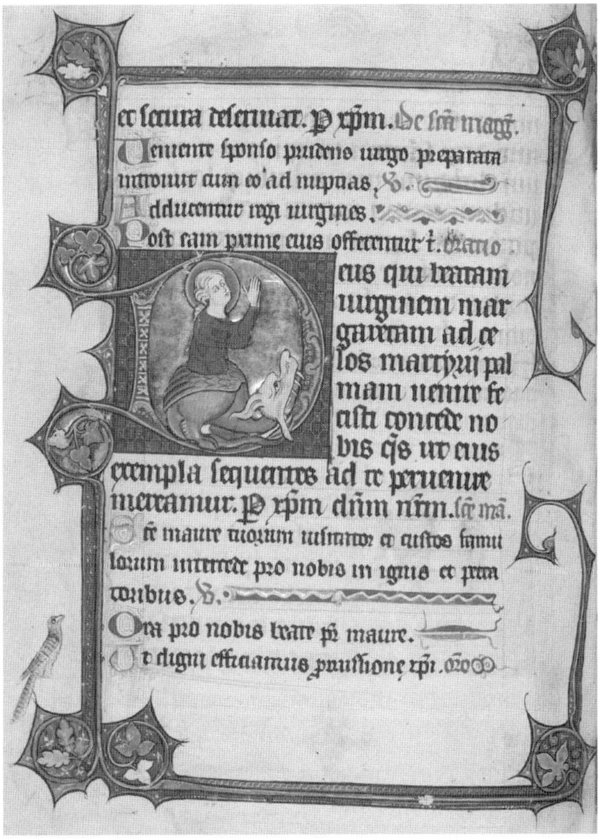

FIGURE 8.6: St. Margaret, from the *Psalter-Hours of Yolande de Soissons*. New York, The Morgan Library and Museum, MS M. 729, fol. 262 verso. ca. 1280–90. © The Morgan Library and Museum.

the saint's devotion and prayer contributed to her successful emergence. This image is one of many saints whose representations are found in the section known as the Suffrages (prayers to various saints). Especially popular in the fifteenth century and often linked to female patrons and readers, many books of hours survive that include Margaret, a logical choice because of her important link to childbirth.[8]

Margaret's victorious action of throwing down and trampling the demon can be read as a heroic transgression of gendered norms, as she displays surprising physical strength in the face of oppression and martyrdom. This power upsets the expectations of female submission, not unlike other female saints who are associated with cross-dressing. In fact, a number of female saints that were popular in the Middle Ages adopted masculinizing strategies as a way of escaping the restrictions of married life, often passing their lives as clerics in monasteries.[9] Significantly, however, in most of these cases, their feminine biological sex (as opposed to their masculine-gendered performance) is exposed at the climax of their stories, usually after they die and their bodies are prepared for burial. There is a notable exception to this sequence of events, however, in the case of St. Eugenia, a cross-dressed cleric who is accused of rape (a common occurrence in the case of the transvestite saints) and brought before the Roman prefect Philip (who is also Eugenia's unsuspecting father). Eugenia herself bares her breasts to expose her female anatomy and thus prove her innocence in an action that itself complicates expected gender roles played by men and women. Eugenia's biological identity fixes her as female, but her active agency in controlling the circumstances of this revelation is in sharp contrast to other more passive transvestite saints, who never protest their innocence in the face of false accusations and whose true identities are only discovered upon their deaths; for example, Marina raises the child she is accused of fathering for five years, begging for food outside the monastery from which she has been exiled until she dies and her real sex is exposed. This blurring of the boundaries of gender takes visual form in the representation of the scene on a capital in the monastic church at Vézelay, where a tonsured Eugenia pulls apart her monk's habit to reveal her breasts, to the astonishment of her accuser and her judge/father, who flank the saint, as shown in Figure 8.7.[10]

By the sixth century, virginity and martyrdom on behalf of Christianity were not the sole requirements for sainthood. Thus, another popular saint, Radegund (ca. 520–587), was not a virgin martyr but a queen who gave up her wealth, left her husband, and founded the nuns' community of Ste.-Croix in Poitiers. However, as an elite woman forced into marriage (as a child she was part of the booty won by her future husband, Clothar), Radegund attempted

FIGURE 8.7: St. Eugenia from a capital on north aisle of the nave, Vézelay. Photograph by Holly Hayes. © Sacred Destinations Images.

to emulate the characteristics and behavior of the virgin saints—by leaving her husband, renouncing her wealth, praying, serving the poor, and undergoing rigorous self-mortification. This made her a model for queens and women of power who exploited her royal connections as well as her wish to follow a religious life.[11] Her impact on the city of Poitiers—establishing the community of Ste.-Croix, acquiring relics of the True Cross to which the convent was dedicated, and performing a number of miracles both before and after her death—was to be further evident in the centuries to come and was crucial in the creation of an important manuscript of her life in the later Middle Ages.

The manuscript of the *Life of Saint Radegund*, made around 1100 and probably commissioned by the nuns of Ste.-Croix, contains twenty-two images (Poitiers, La Médiathèque François-Mitterand, MS 250).[12] While the text of her *Life* is riddled with self-mortification and extreme asceticism, the manuscript's images depict virtually nothing from those moving episodes. Instead, they demonstrate Radegund's important role as convent founder and spiritual intercessor. For example, folio 35r pictures Radegund leaning across her window and toward the woman entangled with a serpentine demon, as shown in Figure 8.8. Radegund does not leave her cell to help this woman, and yet she does not simply reach out her hand to touch her. Despite the small size of the

FIGURE 8.8: *St. Radegund Heals a Woman.* Poitiers, La Médiathèque François-Mitterand MS 250, fol. 35 recto, ca. 1100. © La Médiathèque François-Mitterand, Poitiers. Olivier Neuillé.

window frame, nearly the entire upper half of Radegund's body emerges from the window, with her head above the window's top edge and the sleeve of her garment falling below the bottom. Radegund thus mediates between the sacred space of her cell and the publicly accessible areas that surround it. This emphasis on her role as intercessor between earthly and otherworldly realms reflects the perceptions surrounding female sanctity in the High Middle Ages.

REPRESENTATIONS OF THE FEMALE BODY

The previous discussion of the opposition between Eve and the Virgin Mary has already established the medieval church's association of the female body with sexuality, sin, and death. Those associations may have inspired the creation of a striking figure that appears on the wall of the entrance porch into the church of Saint-Pierre at Moissac (France), as shown in Figure 8.9. Like Eve, this female figure appears naked, and her body is sexualized by her hair

FIGURE 8.9: *Luxuria*. Relief from Saint-Pierre, Moissac, France, ca. 1100. Photograph by Marian Bleeke, used with permission.

and by her exposed breasts. Her breasts are burdened, however, by the heavy forms of serpents that have bitten on to her nipples. The snakes arc up over her arms and then trail down around her legs, where they call attention to a form conventionally identified as a toad that has attached itself to her genitalia. She is accompanied by a demonic figure who grasps her wrist. Placed at the end of a sculpted narrative of the parable of Dives and Lazarus, a story contrasting the heavenly reward of the poor Lazarus with the punishment in hell of the miser Dives, this sculpture has been identified as a personification of *luxuria* (the sin of lust) or a woman suffering torments in hell for her sexual sins. This interpretation of the image is supported by medieval visions of hell that include women being tortured by snakes and toads. Such a horrific, sexually explicit representation of the female body may have had a specific significance for the important monastery of Saint-Pierre in Moissac: it may have been intended to instill fear of women and horror of sex in the monks as a way of promoting their celibacy.[13]

The church's association of women and sexuality with sin and death was not the only discourse on these topics available in the Middle Ages, however. The 230-foot-long embroidery known as the *Bayeux Tapestry* includes one scene that points instead to a secular discourse on female sexuality and its consequences, as shown in Figure 8.10. The embroidery tells the story of the Norman invasion of England in 1066. Although it was probably made by women, its hundreds of figures include only six females, three in its main image space and three in its borders. Despite the inscriptions that name major and minor figures through its images, only one woman is similarly identified. The inscription is highly ambiguous, stating only "where a cleric and Aelgyva"—what? The image suggests some inappropriate sexual contact between them in his violation of her architectural enclosure, his aggressive gesture that touches her cheek, and the mirroring of his gesture by a squatting naked figure with enlarged genitalia in the margin below. This scene appears immediately after one representing a conversation between Harold Godwinson and Duke William of

FIGURE 8.10: Aelgyva and a clerk from the *Bayeux Tapestry*. Musée de la Tapisserie, Bayeux, France. Photograph by Erich Lessing, courtesy of Art Resource, NY.

Normandy, the two contenders for the English throne, and so may represent the subject of their discussion. Aelgyva could represent one of two women of that name who were central to the dispute over the throne: King Cnut's first wife, who was accused of having a son by a priest who she tried to pass off as Cnut's son so that he could accede to the throne; or Cnut's second wife, also known by her Norman name Emma, who was an ancestor of both Duke William and the English king Edward the Confessor and so was key to William's claim to the throne, but who was also accused of adultery.[14] The Aelgyva scene would thus represent the interests of secular male aristocrats in controlling their wives' sexuality, and thus the paternity of his children, in order to ensure patrilineal inheritance.

Despite the negative associations of sexuality and sin, women's bodies were of the utmost importance to different groups in the Middle Ages. Spouses and fathers were often concerned with the reproduction of healthy offspring, preferably male, and both religious and medical authorities were consulted for diseases and ailments of all kinds. A physician may have been able to facilitate a cure, but a priest might also advise a visit to a holy shrine or the repetition of specific prayers. Medical manuscripts were sometimes illustrated, often with images used for prognostics or treatment, such as figures with small red dots on them that reference points for cautery (coagulating blood and destroying tissue with a hot iron) or images of jars with various colored liquids against which a physician might compare a urine sample.[15] Representations of women's bodies in medical imagery are relatively limited, in part because the male body was most often perceived as a stand-in for human beings in general. Extant images of women in manuscripts of a medical nature include those linked directly to childbirth and reproduction. For instance, a medical miscellany (Oxford, Bodleian Library, MS Ashmole 399), includes a schematic diagram of the female reproductive system and a series of images that depict various positions of the fetus in utero. But in addition to these kinds of anatomical depictions, women also appear as patients and even practitioners in medical manuscripts, especially into the later Middle Ages. In sometimes surprisingly frank scenes, women hold out their diseased breasts to physicians, as shown in Figure 8.11, seek advice for genital ailments, attend parturient women in a birthing chamber, and aid patients themselves through administering treatments like cupping, where a cut is a made and a glass bowl is used to suction out the blood or even perform Caesarean sections.[16]

Women's active participation in their bodies' medical matters, such as the services of midwives throughout much of the Middle Ages, is also indicated through a variety of other diverse texts, images, and objects. Images of birthing

FIGURE 8.11: *Patients and Physicians.* London, British Library MS Sloane 1977, fol. 7 verso. Early fourteenth century. © The British Library Board.

scenes, objects like jewelry or charms, and prayers to saints for intervention (such as St. Margaret, St. Anne, and St. Elizabeth; see previous discussion) all contribute to a rich body of material culture that points to women's involvement in the maintenance of health that probably existed outside the text-based and increasingly professionalized and male world of medicine.[17]

WIVES AND MOTHERS

Medieval visual depictions of wives belie their legally and culturally subordinate role in marriage in favor of a deceptive parity with their husbands. This is in contrast to medieval conduct literature in which authors frequently counsel women on their marital obligations to their husbands. Representations of marriage do exist in which the bride inclines her head or lowers her eyes while the groom stands completely upright, but such submissive displays are not consistent enough in these images to be the rule. Marital iconography tends instead to favor the idea of union, echoing the legal and ecclesiastical insistence on mutual consent as a prerequisite for a valid marriage.[18]

Among the images that feature women (and men) in matrimonial roles are certain donor portraits, non-Marian representations of the sacrament of marriage, and paired tomb effigies featuring married couples. Donors are frequently depicted in association with a sacred episode or figure, or both, so that the marital theme is subordinate to the sacred content. Scenes of marriage ceremonies may feature historical or contemporary figures such as Esther and Ahasuerus but may also display literary characters such as Pietro and Agnolella from Boccaccio's *Decameron*.[19] Tombs, on the other hand, commemorate those once alive and offer a prime resource for studying the representation of wives among the elite of medieval western Europe.

Few characteristics distinguish the visual representation of wives from women enacting other social roles such as ruler or mother. All of these categories depend upon the presence of attributes, whether as part of a figure's costume, such as the inclusion of royal regalia, or children in the case of mothers. The female figure's matrimonial status independent from any other role is often signified by a headdress and/or heraldry. Thus, a married or widowed woman wears a veil or other form of head covering while an unmarried woman's hair is not concealed. Heraldic devices also point to married status as the woman's arms are frequently combined with those of her husband; in heraldic terms, they are impaled.[20]

Paired tombs that feature juxtaposed figures of husband and wife begin to appear in medieval Western art as early as the mid-fourteenth century, but the majority date from the last third of the century forward. The stone monument of Thomas Beauchamp, Earl of Warwick, and his wife Katherine Mortimer, dated shortly after 1369 and installed in the chancel of St. Mary's Warwick, displays the couple dressed in standard costumes for their social rank: military for him and close fitting gown with mantle and frilled veil for her, as shown in Figure 8.12. The monument has two features setting it apart from the majority of paired tombs: the couple's hand-holding gesture, in which their right hands are joined, and Katherine Mortimer's position relative to her husband. While the hand-holding gesture is not unique in paired tombs, it is less frequent than the devotional prayer pose, and it foregrounds the matrimonial rather than pious aspect of the monument. This familial emphasis is reinforced by the presence of small figures in the niches decorating the tomb base, which probably represent relatives and associates of the couple.[21] The hand-holding motif evokes representations of marriage ceremonies in which the couple join hands, but, as noted previously, Katherine's covered hair signifies a wife, not

FIGURE 8.12: Tomb of Thomas Beauchamp, Earl of Warwick, and Katherine Mortimer, Collegiate Church of St. Mary, Warwick, ca. 1369. Photograph by Rachel Dressler, used with permission.

a maiden. Yet the hand-holding also points to the tomb's metaphorical dimension since the figures' physical union may symbolize both that of the married couple and the human and divine simultaneously, just as the tomb itself unites the earthly and spiritual realms.[22]

Katherine Mortimer's location to her husband's right also sets this monument apart from other tombs of the time, although it is by no means unique in this regard. In general, the dexter, or heraldic right, is the favored side in any medieval depiction and is usually occupied by the most important figures in a composition. Grooms and husbands are accorded this privileged location in most marriage and paired tomb images, paralleling medieval gender hierarchies. Exceptions might occur when the bride or wife is of higher status as in scenes of the Marriage of the Virgin, where Mary is frequently favored over Joseph.[23] In the case of the Beauchamp tomb, however, it is not clear that Katherine's positioning is related to any indication of status and may result from some other issue entirely.

As a wife, a woman was also expected to bear children, although this would not have been the case for older widows who remarried. Representations of mothers in the Middle Ages are frequently of a religious nature, like the *Birth of St. John* noted above (Padua Baptistery). In this and other images, like those depicting the births of figures such as Constantine and Alexander, the mother is invariably shown lying in an opulent bed assisted by other women, as shown in Figure 4.3 in chapter 4. Sometimes the newborn baby is being bathed, and the mother offered nourishing food. Although it is important to recognize that such images were highly stylized, in that they represent the births of famous figures and, inevitably, a successful outcome, the attention to detail can offer us a partial view of what went on in the space of childbearing. The material culture of childbearing in fifteenth-century Tuscany in particular has left us with a plethora of secular visual material relating to motherhood. For instance, images of childbirth are found on birth trays, or *deschi da parto*, that were given to mothers in Tuscany in the fifteenth century just before or after a birth.[24] Whereas such objects were often given by men and were intended to encourage laywomen in their social roles as wives and mothers, it is also likely that they offered women a form of focus and comfort during a difficult and life-threatening time. A tomb sculpture from 1470s indicates the close link between motherhood and death. Produced by the workshop of Andrea Verrocchio, this sculpture shows Francesca Tornabuoni on the right-hand side, dying in childbirth while surrounded by female assistants. On the left, a woman hands the newborn to Giovanni Tornabuoni surrounded by male friends. The tomb sculpture represents the liminal spaces of birth and death, as well as negotiating the private space of a woman's childbearing and the public space of death and mourning.

Beyond simply giving birth to children, mothers played an increasingly important role in the education of their children in the later Middle Ages. Their model was St. Anne who was frequently represented with a book in hand, as the wise widow teaching her daughter(s) to read.[25] The image of St. Anne holding out an open book to teach her daughters in the fifteenth-century Bolton Hours (York Minster, MS Add. 2, folio 35) would have provided a model of piety and conduct for Margaret Blackburn, the manuscript's owner, when instructing her own daughter(s),[26] as similarly shown in Figure 6.2 in chapter 6. The theme of St. Anne as an educator was particularly exploited by ambitious aristocratic women in their artistic commissions at the end of the fifteenth century. For example, Anne of France, sister of Charles VIII, had herself and her only daughter represented under the protection of St. Anne in the right-hand wing of the monumental *Moulins Triptych*, where she presents them to an image of the Immaculate Conception, as shown in Figure 8.13.[27]

FIGURE 8.13: Master of Moulins (Jean Hey), *The Moulins Triptych* (The Bourbon Altarpiece). Oil on panel, ca. 1498 © Moulins Cathedral, Allier France/The Bridgeman Art Library.

WOMEN AS CREATORS

Looking for women artists in the Middle Ages raises questions concerning what it means for someone to be an artist. For example, as mentioned above, the *Bayeux Tapestry* was probably made by women, most likely a group of English nuns. However, these nuns would have been following a design provided to them by a monk, a design that was intended to express the interests of the patron, Bishop Odo of Bayeux. Who was the artist in this situation? A similar question arises in considering the work of Hildegard of Bingen, a twelfth-century abbess who is recognized today as an important author and composer. Some scholars have argued for identifying Hildegard also as an artist, specifically of the illustrations in certain manuscripts of her visionary works.[28] Such arguments credit Hildegard as the designer of these images, not their physical maker, and identify the images as the expressions of her ideas. She thus takes the roles of the designer and patron in the *Bayeux Tapestry* example, not of the embroiderers.

The arguments for identifying Hildegard as the designer of these images are based on their unusual content, which is best explained by their close connection to Hildegard's texts and so to Hildegard herself; on visual features that may represent the effects of migraine headaches, which could again tie them closely to Hildegard as she reported being sick repeatedly throughout her life; and on an image that seems shows her working process, speaking the words of her text to a scribe and simultaneously sketching on a wax tablet she holds in her lap, as shown in Figure

FIGURE 8.14: Hildegard of Bingen, inspired by heavenly fire, from the Rupertsburg *Scivias* (twentieth-century facsimile of lost original, twelfth century). Photograph by Erich Lessing, courtesy of Art Resource, NY.

8.14. Such sketches may have provided the basis for the fully realized illustrations in these manuscripts. However, this image raises an additional question concerning Hildegard's identification as an artist, for it shows her head engulfed in red flames as a visualization of her claim to divine inspiration. According to this image, Hildegard is not the designer of her illustrations, nor the author of her texts—God is. Indeed, throughout her writings Hildegard described herself as a "weak woman" who was incapable of producing such works on her own.[29] Hildegard's denial of her own authorship raises questions for modern scholars who are unable to accept her claims to divine inspiration. Should such statements be accepted as, at least, genuine expressions of her own self-understanding? Should they be set aside as conventional statements of humility? Or were they strategic statements that were necessary for her to function within a male-dominated world?

An interesting comparison for Hildegard's work comes in the *Hortus Deliciarum*, or Garden of Delights, a richly illustrated encyclopedic text produced by her contemporary and fellow abbess Herrad of Landsberg. Like Hildegard, Herrard has been identified as the designer of the illustrations in this work based on their close relationship to its text. Given the hundreds of images it contained, however, their actual execution must have been the work of many hands. Unlike Hildegard's visionary work, Herrad's text is a compilation that draws from a wide variety of sources, and rather than identifying herself as a mouthpiece for God, Herrad claims only to have been inspired by God in her work of composition, which was done with the aim of instructing the nuns in her community. Indeed, Herrad appears in the final miniature in the text, standing alongside bust-length images of the nuns, holding an inscription that instructs them to turn their attention to contemplation of the divine.[30]

Rather more certain than Hildegard's role as an artist is that of the nuns of the Benedictine abbey of St. Walburg, whose scriptorium produced a series of drawings dated ca. 1500 designed to aid in the devotions of the foundation's inhabitants.[31] At first glance, these drawings seem naïve in execution, yet closer examination reveals a greater sophistication of iconography than is usually ascribed to what has been labeled *Nonnenarbeiten* (Nun's Work), the genre of medieval imagery with which they have been associated. A comparison between this set of around a dozen drawings and contemporary examples from manuscripts, prints, and textiles demonstrates that the nun primarily responsible for their creation seems deliberately to have avoided slavish adherence to any contemporary models. Instead, she wove together certain existing iconographic conventions with idiosyncratic and innovative motifs that foreground the importance of the visual in the nuns' devotions.[32] In essence, the drawings present the body of Christ as the object of the nun's gaze and beyond that as the portal for both entry into the Savior's heart, and into her own.

Like their religious counterparts, there is evidence of secular women engaging in artistic endeavors, especially in the arena of manuscript illustration. A well-known reference to a female Parisian illuminator named Anastaise occurs in Christine de Pizan's *Book of the City of Ladies*; de Pizan describes the artist as unsurpassed in her abilities to paint manuscript borders and the background of miniatures. Because of the stratification of jobs in manuscript illumination, it was common practice for a master to paint the main figures and leave the secondary decoration to others, but in the case of Anastaise, one wonders if her role was restricted because of her gender rather than her artistic abilities. On the other hand, de Pizan herself suffered no such constraints. Left widowed with three children at a young age, to support her family de Pizan became a professional writer, producing highly regarded poetry and prose for a number of patrons, including members of the French court. While the exact nature of her role has been disputed, she was involved in the production of manuscripts of her writings, possibly even extending to the design of the illuminations. She is particularly known for her vigorous defense of women, not only in the allegorical *City of Ladies*, which describes heroic and virtuous women from history, but also in her various written attacks on the misogyny she perceived in *The Romance of the Rose*, a wildly popular dream poem written in the courtly love tradition, recounting the romantic pursuit of the Rose by the Lover. Christine de Pizan particularly addressed the satirical and even vicious attitude toward women evident in the 17,000-line extension to the poem written by Jean de Meun, added several decades later to the original verses penned by Guillaume de Lorris in 1230.[33]

WOMEN AS CONSUMERS AND PATRONS

Christine de Pizan's *City of Ladies* was enormously popular, especially in the libraries of aristocratic women, and it inspired a tapestry series, copies of which were owned by Anne of Brittany and Margaret of Austria.[34] Another type of illuminated manuscript closely associated with women is the book of hours, the prayer book for the laity that was increasingly produced in the later Middle Ages. While the central text of the book of hours was the Latin Hours of the Virgin, and other parts (including a calendar, the Penitential Psalms, and the Office of the Dead) were more or less standard inclusions, the prayer book could be modified and adapted to fit the devotional needs and interests of the user. In addition to this type of textual personalization, books of hours might also include images of their owners. For aristocratic women, they became a kind of commodity as well as an object of devotion.[35] A particularly elaborate example occurs in the *Hours of Mary of Burgundy* (Vienna, Österreischische Nationalbibliothek, Codex Vindobonensis 1857, fol. 14v), where the aristocratic owner is represented twice in the same image, as shown in Figure 8.15. In the foreground, she appears to be seated in an antechamber of a church, intent upon a book of hours that she holds carefully cradled in a bright green cloth, with a lapdog nestled in the folds of her golden gown. In the background, she kneels before the Virgin and Child in an elaborate Gothic church interior, perhaps in a vision of access to the divine accomplished through her pious daily devotions.[36]

In spite of the evidence for female ownership of books of hours, it is not always clear that they had control over their contents; instead, a father or a

FIGURE 8.15: Donor portrait from *Hours of Mary of Burgundy*. Vienna: Österreishische Nationalbibliothek, Codex Vindobonensis 1857, fol. 14 verso. ca. 1475. © Österreishische Nationalbibliothek, Vienna.

husband may have commissioned, purchased, and controlled the production of the manuscript.[37] In addition, it seems that most such manuscripts would have been written and illuminated by men, although there were a few women involved in manuscript production, often as part of a family business. The fourteenth-century *Psalter and Hours of Bonne de Luxembourg*, which includes a double-donor portrait of sorts of Bonne and her husband (who was to become Jean le Bon, king of France) kneeling before Christ on the cross, may very well be the production of the illuminator Jean le Noir and his daughter Bourgot.[38]

Secular ivory objects produced mainly in Paris during the fourteenth century also seem to have been primarily owned by women. In fact, the climax of Jean de Meun's section of the *Romance of the Rose*, so reviled by Christine de Pizan, describes the ultimate seduction of the Rose, which is cast as an attack and forced entry into a barricaded castle: very similar scenes were depicted on ivory mirror backs, combs, and caskets with scenes drawn from the iconography of courtly love. As is the case with manuscripts intended for female users, it is unclear to what extent women might have been involved in the selection of the decoration. Those objects depicting the storming of the "Castle of Love" typically show knights attacking a castle full of women, who ineffectually defend themselves by throwing roses, as shown in Figure 8.16. Other common subjects include scenes from famous romances, with Lancelot and Guinevere or Tristan and Isolde as perhaps the most popular choices, or more anonymous pairs of lovers engaged in various courtship rituals. Although such themes seem innocuous at first glance, they are often underpinned with hints of eroticism and even violence, themes that also appear in courtly literature of the time.[39]

Although the Castle of Love is a fantasy building, it can represent one category of architecture aimed at viewing or use by women. Such structures

FIGURE 8.16: Relief carving of the attack on the Castle of Love. Mirror back, ca. 1320–40. © The Metropolitan Museum of Art/ Art Resource, NY.

demonstrate the significance of gender to the configuration of physical space. In medieval religious spaces like churches and monasteries, limits and controls were constructed, determining who had access to specific areas. Especially in monastic complexes, gender played a role in these determinations, as the archaeological study of nunneries has shown that they have more physical boundaries between the precinct and the inner cloister than monasteries. The dormitories of religious women tend to be the most secluded space in a nunnery.[40]

The so-called Nuns' Church at Clonmacnoise, Ireland, was commissioned by a young woman named Derbforgaill in 1167.[41] She was a member of a family that was deeply involved in the Irish Church: she was the daughter of the king of nearby Meath, a key patron of Clonmacnoise, and her sister Agnes was the abbess at nearby Clonard. In 1152, Derbforgaill was abducted (possibly willingly) as part of a political dispute, which led to the invasion of Ireland by Anglo-Normans in 1169, and some histories suggest that her patronage may have been a form of penance. Although a large and centralized monastic site exists at Clonmacnoise, the Nuns' Church is curiously located at a significant distance from the rest of the precinct, exposed and unprotected some 500 meters away from the main group of buildings. As such, this building seems to epitomize experiences of both isolation and independence for the nuns and their activities in this structure. In contrast to nunneries that are deeply enclosed spaces, this church represents a space where it seems religious women were under less scrutiny and possibly more connected to the surrounding population.

Those women who were able to exercise some control over the art objects they commissioned and owned, or who were able to choose the way in which they themselves were represented, belonged mainly to the ruling classes. Despite the fact that women were usually officially excluded from ruling in their own right, the Middle Ages is littered with examples of women who did in fact do just this. Yet it is only relatively recently that researchers have begun to pay detailed attention to women such as Eleanor of Aquitaine, Blanche of Castile, Margaret of Anjou, and Isabella of Castile.[42] These women and others, including Joan and Margaret, Countesses of Flanders, Elizabeth of Hungary, Joanna of Naples, Anne of France, and Margaret of York ruled in their own right or acted as regents for their fathers, husbands, or sons. Other women such as Mary of Brittany, Abbess of Fontevraux, ruled over religious institutions.[43] All of them wielded a certain amount of power in a world otherwise dominated by men, and they often exploited their positions to exercise a degree of artistic, literary, political, or social patronage.

Like their male counterparts, female rulers were able to draw on a number of strategies to promote their position, notably by associating themselves with illustrious, pious, or regal figures from the antique and biblical past. They employed this method of enhancing their status across a variety of media such as illuminated manuscripts, stained glass, tapestry, sculpture, and panel painting.

Eleanor of Aquitaine (d. 1204) was not only one of the most powerful queens in medieval Europe but also a noteworthy patron of the arts. Married first to the French king Louis VII, and later to Henry II, king of England, Eleanor's political influence spanned many lands. Her spectacular life was marked with momentous events and renown, through which she navigated the complex terrain of going on crusade, dealing with divorce and remarriage, negotiating conflict with her second husband that would result in her imprisonment, and correspondence with key contemporary figures such as Bernard of Clairvaux and Abbot Suger.

Often referred to as "Queen of the Troubadours" in histories of the nineteenth and twentieth centuries, there is little proof that Eleanor was specifically responsible for the commission of literature in the English court.[44] The lack of such documents does not mean she did not foster an environment conducive to writers, singers, or poets, however, who may have also been supported by her husband. She was certainly familiar with these traditions, growing up as she did at the Poitevin court where troubadour poetry was developed. In addition, there is significant visual and material evidence of several artistic commissions and building projects that she supported.

Although she was queen of England for the majority of her adult life, Eleanor always attempted to keep strong ties with Aquitaine and her court at Poitiers, during her installation as ruler between 1168 and 1174, and especially in her later years, when she retired to Fontevraud. An example from her earlier period of residence is the donation of a stained-glass Crucifixion window to the cathedral of Saint-Pierre in Poitiers, which includes a donor portrait of Eleanor and Henry presenting the window. Later examples include the large-scale renovation of the ducal palace at Poitiers, and the commissioning of the tombs of Henry II, their son Richard, Richard's wife, and finally that of Eleanor, as shown in Figure 8.17. These effigies are important as some of the earliest surviving three-dimensional, life-sized effigies of monarchs of France.[45] Eleanor's support of the abbey at Fontevraud began as early as 1170 and increased in later years. She retired there in 1194, after Henry's death, and eventually took the veil.

Although Eleanor's role in the development of courtly literature is now disputed, her tomb sculpture does support perceptions of Eleanor as a both an authoritative and intellectual figure. Completed around 1210, a few years after her death in 1204, this sculpture stands out alongside those she oversaw

FIGURE 8.17: Tomb sculpture of Eleanor of Aquitaine, Fontevraud Abbey, France, ca. 1210. Photograph by Erich Lessing, courtesy of Art Resource, NY.

for her husband and son. With greater three-dimensionality and less angularity than their tombs, her sculpture depicts her as fully alive instead of in deathly repose, holding a book in front of her and in the act of reading.[46] Although it appears her eyes are closed, perhaps signaling spiritual contemplation or prayer, the book's status as open is significant. Probably representing a psalter, the book and Eleanor's activity link her with the increasing popularity of prayer books commissioned by and for elite women in the later Middle Ages. It also evokes the prayers that she no doubt hoped the nuns at Fontevraud would say on her behalf.

Eleanor's legacy is evident not only in her final commissions but also through her offspring. Despite the fact that only two of her eight children survived her, her granddaughter Blanche would go on to be an important royal patron of her own. Blanche of Castile (1188–1252) was the daughter of Alfonso VIII and Eleanor's namesake, known in Spain as Leanor of Castile. In 1200, Eleanor of Aquitaine went to Spain herself to collect her granddaughter for marriage to the future Louis VIII. Serving twice as regent of France

(1226–35, 1248–52), Blanche exercised real political power and significant influence over her children, especially Louis IX (St. Louis) and Isabelle of France.[47] This powerful legacy is evident in the many objects in various media that can be linked to her patronage. Perhaps the best known image now associated with Blanche is the lavish, full-page illumination thought to depict Blanche as regent and her son Louis IX from a *Bible moralisée*, which is now split between the Pierpont Morgan Library (MS M. 240, fol. 8r) and the Tesoro de la Catedral in Toledo, probably made in the late 1230s, as shown in Figure 8.18. This manuscript is one of several extant manuscripts that seem to have been created for Blanche, probably commissioned as a gift to her son.[48]

FIGURE 8.18: Blanche of Castile and her son Louis IX, *Bible moralisée*. New York, The Morgan Library and Museum, MS M. 240, fol. 8 recto, ca. late 1230s. © The Morgan Library and Museum.

Her and her son's patronage of the book arts signal the flourishing of commercial book production at this time.

In this extravagantly luxurious image, four figures are depicted in two registers and separated by trilobed arches resting on narrow columns. The rooflines and towers of a simplified cityscape fill the space above the arches in each register, while the background beneath the arches is resplendent in gold leaf. The clerical author and the scribe or illuminator to whom he dictates are clearly subject to the royal figures above them. Seated on ornate thrones, dressed in fine garments and wearing similar crowns, these two figures are the same size and height, suggesting equal importance. Although Louis holds the scepter and seal of his authority while Blanche's hands are empty, her active gesturing suggests that she speaks in this image while the young Louis looks on and listens to her guidance. Reminiscent of some Gothic images of the Coronation of the Virgin, in which Mary and Christ appear similarly as two royal figures sitting opposite one another on thrones, this image articulates the power and authority held by Blanche as regent through her depiction as valued counselor and wise mother.

In the late thirteenth and early fourteenth century, another queen of France, Isabeau of Bavaria (ca. 1370–1435), wife of Charles VI, played an important role in running the kingdom during the king's frequent attacks of mental illness. History has not been kind to Isabeau, who has frequently been represented as a villainous criminal whose agreement to the Treaty of Troyes led to her disowning her own son, the future Charles VII. Yet, from 1402, she was invested with very real governmental power by her husband, and she was an important patron of the arts.[49] Around 1410, she commissioned a richly illuminated copy of the works of Christine de Pizan, which is now housed in the British Library. This book, known as the Queen's Manuscript (London, BL, MS Harley 4431), was supervised by Christine de Pizan herself, and the frontispiece shows the writer in the process of presenting her work to Isabeau who sits in her bedchamber surrounded by five ladies all wearing sumptuous clothes and with their hair dressed in the fashionable "horn" style, as shown in Figure 8.19. The background of fleur-de-lys and the lozenges of Isabeau's own house allude both to Isabeau's origins and to her status as queen of France. Her reception of Christine de Pizan's book makes it clear that she is a lady of learning who takes an interest in women themselves through her patronage of a female author. In her tomb effigy in the church of St. Denis in Paris, Isabeau is represented as both widow and queen. Her figure parallels that of her husband: in addition to her elaborate widow's headdress, she wears, like him, a crown carved with the French fleur-de-lys; and in her right hand, she holds a scepter, symbol of the earthly power she once wielded.

FIGURE 8.19: Master of the Cité des Dames and Workshop, *Christine de Pisan Presenting Her Book to Isabeau of Bavaria*. London, British Library, MS Harley 4431, fol. 3 recto. ca. 1410–11. © The British Library Board.

In the later fifteenth century, a number of powerful and highly educated women emerged at the French court, emanating from the circle of Anne of France (1461–1522), sister of Charles VIII. Anne's association of herself with St. Anne and her promotion of herself as daughter and sister of the king, and then as the duchess of Bourbon, is evident in the *Moulins Triptych* noted previously. She served as a model for future queens and duchesses such as Anne of Brittany, Louise of Savoy, and Margaret of Austria.[50] All these women employed images of themselves and their favorite saints to help them assert, execute, and maintain their role as rulers and regents. For instance, the Visitation scene in the *Très Petites Heures* (Paris, BnF, n.a.l. 3120) belonging to Anne of Brittany (1477–1514) and noted previously, draws a clear parallel between Anne, who had become queen of France for a second time through her marriage to Louis XII, and the holy mothers of the Visitation scene by depicting Anne's crowned arms at the bottom of the page, as shown in Figure 8.20. Such a mise-en-page was intended to associate Anne with the blessed, biblical mothers and their miraculous conception of illustrious children: as queen of France, Anne too was expected to give birth to a male heir who would be a leader and defend the kingdom of God.

FIGURE 8.20: Lauds, from the *Très Petites Heures*. Paris, Bibliothèque nationale de France, nouvelle acquisition latine, 3120, fol. 40 recto. © Bibliothèque nationale de France.

CONCLUSION

As noted at the beginning of the chapter, medieval visual images are often conventionalized depictions of idealized figures and thus have somewhat limited value as a record of actual human experience. Nevertheless, it is evident from this overview of medieval female imagery that women were actively involved in cultural production whether as subjects, creators, or consumers of representation. These images frequently suggest a close association between women, corporeality, and sexuality, ranging from the opposition of Eve's carnality to

Mary's purity, the eroticized torture of St. Agatha, the motherhood of St. Anne, and the assault on the ladies of the Castle of Love. Thus, most of the images discussed in this chapter take as their subject the female body, its reproductive and erotic potential, and the need for its care and control. This prevailing attitude toward the female gender entailed limitations on women's autonomy and actions; nevertheless, some women such as Hildegard of Bingen, Christine de Pizan, Eleanor of Aquitaine, or Blanche of Castile were clearly able to act within or transcend such restrictions in order to produce and patronize visual and literary productions, and to participate actively in the creative and intellectual discourses of their day. As this chapter confirms, medieval visual culture provided numerous and varied opportunities for the representation and participation of women in its creation.

NOTES

Introduction

1. Christine de Pizan to Pierre Col (October 2, 1402), in Christine de Pizan et al., *Debate of the* Romance of the Rose, ed. and trans. David F. Hult (Chicago: The University of Chicago Press, 2010), p. 182. I wish to offer my heartfelt thanks to the contributors to the present volume, who overcame all kinds of obstacles to produce their essays. I also owe debts of gratitude to Linda Kalof as Series Editor for giving me the chance to edit this volume, for showing saintly patience throughout, and for giving invaluable editorial help most promptly and generously; to all at Bloomsbury for (again) their patience and professionalism; to Lisa Hawos Kerryn Olsen, John Bevan-Smith, and the Faculty of Arts of the University of Auckland for their time and assistance of various sorts; and to the many holders of medieval manuscripts and works of art who kindly gave permission for their images to be reproduced in this volume.
2. The defenders of the *Rose* included Jean de Montreuil, provost of Lille and secretary to powerful men including King Charles VI; Gontier Col, first secretary and notary to the king; and Gontier's brother Pierre, canon of Paris and Tournay. See Joseph L. Baird and John R. Kane, "*La Querelle de la Rose*: In Defence of the Opponents," *French Review* 48 (1974), pp. 298–307; and their edition, *La Querelle de la Rose: Letters and Documents* (Chapel Hill: North Carolina Studies in the Romance Languages and Literatures, 1978), p. 12.
3. Guillaume de Lorris and Jean de Meun, *The Romance of the Rose*, ed. and trans. Frances Horgan (Oxford: Oxford University Press, 1994), p. ix.
4. Christine de Pizan to Jean de Montreuil (June–July 1401), in *Debate*, ed. Hult, pp. 50–63 (at pp. 52–53, 54, 56–57, 59).
5. Virginia Woolf, *A Room of One's Own* (London: Grafton, 1977; originally published 1929), p. 44. My use of the quotation from Woolf is hardly original: see, for example, Joan Wallach Scott, "Women in History: The Modern Period," *Past & Present* 101 (1983), pp. 141–57 (at p. 141).

6. Peter Burke, "Unity and Variety in Cultural History," in *Varieties of Cultural History*, ed. Peter Burke (Cambridge: Polity Press, 1997), pp. 183–212.
7. Burke, "Unity and Variety," p. 183.
8. Burke, "Unity and Variety," pp. 184–88, quoting Roy Wagner, *The Invention of Culture* (Englewood Cliffs, NJ: Prentice Hall, 1975), p. 21.
9. Burke, "Unity and Variety," pp. 191–98; Lynn Hunt, ed., *The New Cultural History* (Berkeley: University of California Press, 1989).
10. Robert Darnton, *The Great Cat Massacre and Other Episodes in French Cultural History* (New York: Vintage, 1984), p. 5.
11. L. P. Hartley, *The Go-Between* (London: Hamish Hamilton, 1953), p. 1.
12. Christopher N. L. Brooke, "'Both Small and Great Beasts': An Introductory Study," in *Medieval Women*, ed. Derek Baker, dedicated and presented to Rosalind M. T. Hill, Studies in Church History, Subsidia 1 (Oxford: Basil Blackwell, 1978), p. 1.
13. Mary Beth Rose, "Introduction," in *Women in the Middle Ages and the Renaissance: Literary and Historical Perspectives*, ed. Mary Beth Rose (Syracuse, NY: Syracuse University Press, 1986), p. xiii.
14. Susan Mosher Stuard, ed., *Women in Medieval History and Historiography* (Philadelphia: University of Pennsylvania Press, 1987). The substantive essays are by Barbara A. Hanawalt on English scholarship, Diane Owen Hughes on Italian, Stuard on French and North American, and Martha Howell (with Suzanne Wemple and Denise Kaiser) on Germanic historiography.
15. Barbara A. Hanawalt, "Golden Ages for the History of Medieval English Women," in *Women in Medieval History and Historiography*, ed. Stuard, pp. 1–24 (quote at pp. 11–12).
16. Judith M. Bennett and Amy M. Froide, eds., *Singlewomen in the European Past 1250–1800* (Philadelphia: University of Pennsylvania Press, 1999); Cordelia Beattie, *Medieval Single Women: The Politics of Social Classification in Late Medieval England* (Oxford: Oxford University Press, 2007).
17. Sara M. Butler, *The Language of Abuse: Marital Violence in Later Medieval England* (Leiden: Brill, 2007).
18. Theresa Earenfight, *The King's Other Body: María of Castile and the Crown of Aragon* (Philadelphia: University of Pennsylvania Press, 2010); Marie Kelleher, *The Measure of Women: Law and Female Identity in the Crown of Aragon* (Philadelphia: University of Pennsylvania Press, 2010).
19. Elisheva Baumgarten, *Mothers and Children: Jewish Family Life in Medieval Europe* (Princeton, NJ: Princeton University Press, 2004); Avraham Grossman, *Pious and Rebellious: Jewish Women in Medieval Europe*, trans. Jonathan Chipman (Hanover: University Press of New England, 2004); Rebecca Lynn Winer, *Women, Wealth and Community in Perpignan, c. 1250–1300: Christians, Jews and Enslaved Muslims in a Medieval Town* (Aldershot: Ashgate, 2006); Suzanne Bartlet, *Licoricia of Winchester: Marriage, Motherhood and Murder in the Medieval Anglo-Jewish Community* (London: Vallentine Mitchell, 2009).
20. Amy Livingstone, *Out of Love for My Kin: Aristocratic Family Life in the Lands of the Loire, 1000–1200* (Ithaca: Cornell University Press, 2010).

21. Isidore of Seville, *The Etymologies of Isidore of Seville*, trans. Stephen A. Barney, W. J. Lewis, J. A. Beach, and Oliver Berghof (Cambridge: Cambridge University Press, 2006), bk. XI.ii.17–19 (p. 242).
22. Isidore, *Etymologies*, XI.ii.24 (p. 242).
23. This partial summary of Bartholomaeus's passage *De masculis* is taken from John Trevisa's late fourteenth-century English translation (spelling modernized): *On the Properties of Things. John Trevisa's Translation of Bartholomaeus Anglicus* De Proprietatibus Rerum*: A Critical Text*, ed. M. C. Seymour et al., 3 vols. (Oxford: Oxford University Press, 1975–88), vol. 1, pp. 306–7.
24. *De puella*, *On the Properties*, vol. 1, p. 302.
25. Geoffrey Chaucer, "The Wife of Bath's Prologue," trans. David Wright, in *Woman Defamed and Woman Defended: An Anthology of Medieval Texts*, ed. Alcuin Blamires (Oxford: Oxford University Press, 1992), lines 713–20 (p. 219).
26. Marbod of Rennes, "The Femme Fatale" *(De Meretrice)*, from "The Book with Ten Chapters," *(Liber Decem Capitulorum)*, chap. III.1, trans. Alcuin Blamires, in *Woman Defamed and Woman Defended*, ed. Blamires, p. 100.
27. Marbod, "The Good Woman *(De matrona)*," trans. Alcuin Blamires, in *Woman Defamed and Woman Defended*, ed. Blamires, pp. 228–32. See also A. J. Minnis, with V. J. Scattergood and J. J. Smith, *The Shorter Poems*, Oxford Guides to Chaucer (Oxford: Clarendon Press, 1995), p. 341.
28. R. Howard Bloch, "Medieval Misogyny," *Representations* 20 (1987), pp. 1–24; in more detail in his book *Medieval Misogyny and the Invention of Western Romantic Love* (Chicago: University of Chicago Press, 1991).
29. Judith M. Bennett, "Misogyny, Popular Culture, and Women's Work," *History Workshop Journal* 31 (1991), pp. 166–88; more fully in her *Ale, Beer, and Brewsters in England: Women's Work in a Changing World 1300–1600* (New York: Oxford University Press, 1996), esp. chap. 7.
30. Alcuin Blamires, *The Case for Women in Medieval Culture* (Oxford: Clarendon Press, 1997), throughout (but see, for example, pp. 37, 137–38 for chastity; p. 16 for compassion and trustingness; pp. 16, 84 for gentleness; p. 37 for courage; pp. 113–19 for guilessness; pp. 113, 126–28 for softness; pp. 83–86 for mercy and pacifism; pp. 37, 90 for humility; pp. 90, 143 for patience; p. 149 for "prudence, piety, kindness, charity, and sobriety or moderation"; and all of chap. 5 and chap. 6, pp. 126–70, for stability).
31. Alastair Minnis and Eric J. Johnson, "Chaucer's Criseyde and Feminine Fear," in *Medieval Women: Texts and Contexts in Late Medieval Britain: Essays for Felicity Riddy*, ed. Jocelyn Wogan-Browne, Rosalynn Voaden, Arlyn Diamond, Ann Hutchison, Carol M. Meale, and Lesley Johnson (Turnhout: Brepols, 2000), pp. 199–216 (at p. 211).
32. *Poems of Cupid, God of Love. Christine de Pizan's "Epistre au dieu d'Amours" and "Dit de la Rose"; Thomas Hoccleve's "The Letter of Cupid,"* ed. Thelma S. Fenster and Mary C. Erler (Leiden: Brill, 1990), pp. 66–67, quoted in Minnis and Johnson, "Chaucer's Criseyde," p. 210.
33. Blamires, *Case for Women*, p. 178.

34. Blamires, *Case for Women*, pp. 179–84.
35. Minnis, *Shorter Poems*, p. 427; Blamires, *Case for Women*, p. 234. Minnis's term will be preferred here, as it is useful to keep *misogyny* for "hatred of women" and use *antifeminism* for women's more general subordination.
36. Minnis, *Shorter Poems*, p. 427.
37. This is old news to many feminists. In 1970 Kate Millett explored a similar point with reference to Hannah Arendt's concept of government imposed by consent (as opposed to its alternative, violence). "Sexual politics obtains consent through the 'socialization' of both sexes to basic patriarchal polities with regard to temperament, role, and status." One of the ways such consent is obtained is through acceptance of gendered temperament, "based on the needs and values of the dominant group and dictated by what its members cherish in themselves and find convenient in subordinates: aggression, intelligence, force, and efficacy in the male; passivity, ignorance, docility, 'virtue,' and ineffectuality in the female." *Sexual Politics* (New York: Doubleday, 1970), p. 70. Blamires quotes the passage also: *Defence of Women*, p. 5.
38. Blamires, *Case for Women*, p. 101.
39. Blamires, *Case for Women*, p. 102.
40. Christine de Pisan, *The Treasury of the City of Ladies, or The Book of the Three Virtues*, trans. Sarah Lawson (Harmondsworth: Penguin, 1985), pp. 63–64.
41. The idea is explored most fully in her *Holy Feast and Holy Fast: The Religious Significance of Food to Medieval Women* (Berkeley: The University of California Press, 1987), but a good place to start is her essay, "'. . . And Woman His Humanity': Female Imagery in the Religious Writing of the Later Middle Ages," in *Fragmentation and Redemption: Essays on Gender and the Human Body in Medieval Religion*, ed. Caroline Walker Bynum (New York: Zone Books, 1992), pp. 151–79.
42. Dominique Barthélemy, "The Aristocratic Households of Feudal France: Kinship," in *A History of Private Life*, vol. 2, *Revelations of the Medieval World*, ed. Georges Duby, trans. Arthur Goldhammer (Cambridge, MA: The Belknap Press of Harvard University Press, 1988), p. 117.
43. See, for example, Denise Riley, *"Am I That Name?" Feminism and the Category of "Women" in History* (Houndmills: Macmillan, 1988); Judith Butler, *Gender Trouble: Feminism and the Subversion of Identity* (New York: Routledge, 1990); Joan Scott, "Introduction," in *Feminism and History*, ed. Joan Wallach Scott (Oxford: Oxford University Press, 1996), pp. 1–13; Toril Moi, *What Is a Woman? And Other Essays* (Oxford: Oxford University Press, 1999). Such developments are succinctly summed up in Mary C. Erler and Maryanne Kowaleski, "Introduction: A New Economy of Power Relations: Female Agency in the Middle Ages," in *Gendering the Master Narrative: Women and Power in the Middle Ages*, ed. Mary C. Erler and Maryanne Kowaleski (Ithaca and London: Cornell University Press, 2003), pp. 1–16 (at pp. 2–3).
44. This is the guiding principle behind some recent collections of essays on medieval gender (masculinity as well as femininity). See, for example, Sharon Farmer and Carol Braun Pasternak, eds., *Gender and Difference in the Middle Ages* (Minneapolis: University of Pennsylvania Press, 2003); Cordelia Beattie and Kirsten

A. Fenton, eds., *Intersections of Gender, Religion and Ethnicity in the Middle Ages* (Houndmills: Palgrave Macmillan, 2011).
45. Riley, "*Am I That Name?*" pp. 113–14.

Chapter 1

1. Carol Gilligan, "Woman's Place in Man's Life Cycle," in *Feminism and Methodology: Social Science Issues*, ed. Sandra Harding (Bloomington/Milton Keynes: Indiana University Press/Open University Press, 1987), pp. 57–73 (at p. 59).
2. Jane Pilcher, *Age and Generation in Modern Britain* (Oxford: Oxford University Press, 1995), pp. 17–21. See also Alice S. Rossi, "Life-Span Theories and Women's Lives," *Signs* 6 (1980), pp. 4–32 (esp. pp. 7–8).
3. Deborah Youngs, *The Life Cycle in Western Europe, c. 1300–c. 1500* (Manchester: Manchester University Press, 2006), pp. 33–34.
4. Youngs, *Life Cycle*, p. 20. For discussion of Jewish schemes, see Michael E. Goodich, *From Birth to Old Age: The Human Life Cycle in Medieval Thought, 1250–1350* (Lanham: University Press of America, 1989), pp. 62–63.
5. Aristotle quoted in J. A. Burrow, *The Ages of Man: A Study in Medieval Writing and Thought* (Oxford: Clarendon Press, 1988), p. 6.
6. See Burrow, *Ages of Man*, pp. 6–7, 32.
7. Burrow, *Ages of Man*, pp. 45–46; Mary Dove, *The Perfect Age of Man's Life* (Cambridge: Cambridge University Press, 1986), pp. 80–85.
8. Burrow, *Ages of Man*, p. 46n104. On the four ages, see Burrow, *Ages of Man*, pp. 12–36.
9. Dove, *Perfect Age*, p. 80.
10. See Elizabeth Sears, *The Ages of Man: Medieval Interpretations of the Life Cycle* (Princeton, NJ: Princeton University Press, 1986), pp. 129–31, plates 65, 67. There was an early sixteenth-century tradition of twelve ages of man in which the man marries in the sixth age and, when integrated into the calendars of books of hours, is sometimes depicted with his wife and child(ren) in the seventh and tenth ages: Sears, *Ages of Man*, pp. 118–19; The Pierpont Morgan Library, "Descriptions of Medieval and Renaissance Manuscripts," MS M.0813, pp. 2–3, http://corsair.morganlibrary.org/msdescr/BBM0813.htm (accessed May 12, 2011). For a representation of October, the tenth age, in which a man is rich enough that he can provide for his wife and children without having to work, see Cordelia Beattie, "Economy," in *A Cultural History of Childhood and Family: In the Early Modern Age*, ed. Sandra Cavallo and Silvia Evangelisti (Oxford: Berg, 2010), pp. 49–67, fig. 3.5.
11. Sears, *Ages of Man*, p. 25. For the parallel images, see Sears, *Ages of Man*, pp. 110–13, plates 45–51.
12. Dove, *Perfect Age*, p. 25.
13. Burrow, *Ages of Man*, pp. 14–15.
14. An early twelfth-century manuscript, which depicts the four ages as women spinning, is even more unusual: Sears, *Ages of Man*, pp. 23–25, plate 6.
15. *Secretum Secretorum: Nine English Versions*, ed. M. A. Manzalaoui, Early English Text Society, original ser. 276 (Oxford: Oxford University Press, 1977), pp. xiv–xlvi;

Opera hactenus inedita Rogeri Baconi, Fasc. V. Secretum Secretorum cum glossis et notulis, ed. Robert Steele (Oxford: Oxford University Press, 1920), pp. xxxi–xxxvii.

16. *Secretum Secretorum*, ed. Steele, at pp. 76–77.
17. Ibid., at pp. 77–78.
18. Ibid., at p. 79.
19. Ibid., at p. 80.
20. Kim M. Phillips, *Medieval Maidens: Young Women and Gender in England, 1270–1540* (Manchester: Manchester University Press, 2003), p. 43.
21. Phillips, *Medieval Maidens*, p. 43; Dove, *Perfect Age*, pp. 53–59.
22. Kim M. Phillips, "Maidenhood as the Perfect Age of Woman's Life," in *Young Medieval Women*, ed. Katherine J. Lewis, Noël James Menuge, and Kim M. Phillips (Stroud: Sutton, 1999), pp. 1–24 (at p. 5).
23. Phillips, *Medieval Maidens*, p. 51 (see also p. 49).
24. Burrow, *Ages of Man*, p. 30; Dove, *Perfect Age*, p. 22. The slip is discussed below.
25. Shulamith Shahar, *Growing Old in the Middle Ages: "Winter Clothes Us in Shadow and Pain"* (London: Routledge, 1997), p. 47.
26. Phillips, *Medieval Maidens*, p. 51.
27. Sociologists who use the concept of the *life course* place an emphasis on the notion of *transition*: Pilcher, *Age and Generation*, p. 20; Tamara K. Hareven and Kathleen J. Adams, eds., *Ageing and Life Course Transitions: An Interdisciplinary Perspective* (London: Tavistock, 1982).
28. Shahar, *Growing Old*, p. 18.
29. Phillips, *Medieval Maidens*, p. 24.
30. Joan Cadden, *Meanings of Sex Difference in the Middle Ages: Medicine, Science, and Culture* (Cambridge: Cambridge University Press, 1993), p. 171.
31. Galen, *Galen on the Usefulness of the Parts of the Body*, ed. and trans. Margaret Tallmadge May (Ithaca: Cornell University Press, 1968), vol. 2, p. 630. See also Cadden, *Meanings of Sex Difference*, pp. 30–37, 108.
32. Pseudo-Albertus Magnus, *Women's Secrets: A Translation of Pseudo-Albertus Magnus's* De Secretis Mulierum *with Commentaries*, ed. Helen Rodnite Lemay (Albany: State University of New York Press, 1992), pp. 69–70 (at p. 70).
33. Aristotle had said males should wait until age thirty-six. See Peter Biller, *The Measure of Multitude: Population in Medieval Thought* (Oxford: Oxford University Press, 2000), pp. 344–47; Phillips, *Medieval Maidens*, p. 26.
34. Phillips comments, "The view that they *should not* conceive for a few years after menarche . . . is well documented in social practice" (original emphasis): Phillips, *Medieval Maidens*, p. 26. For examples, see Phillips, *Medieval Maidens*, pp. 39–42.
35. Youngs, *Life Cycle*, p. 101.
36. *Secretum Secretorum*, ed. Manzalaoui, p. 56 (the "Ashmole" version). See also *Three Prose Versions of the Secreta Secretorum*, ed. Robert Steele, Early English Text Society, extra ser., 74 (London: Kegan Paul, Trench, Trübner & Co., 1898), p. 244 (James Yonge's "The Governaunce of Prynces").
37. Elizabeth Robertson, "Medieval Medical Views of Women and Female Spirituality in the *Ancrene Wisse* and Julian of Norwich's *Showings*," in *Feminist Approaches*

to the Body in Medieval Literature, ed. Linda Lomperis and Sarah Stanbury (Philadelphia: University of Pennsylvania Press, 1993), pp. 142–67 (at p. 147). See also Danielle Jacquart and Claude Thomasset, *Sexuality and Medicine in the Middle Ages* (Cambridge: Polity Press, 1988), p. 81.

38. Youngs, *Life Cycle*, p. 102.
39. Dove, *Perfect Age*, p. 23.
40. *Three Prose Versions*, ed. Steele, p. 245.
41. *Three Prose Versions*, ed. Steele, p. 246.
42. For Yonge on Spring as "a fayre yong man," see *Three Prose Versions*, ed. Steele, pp. 243–44 (Yonge). On lack of personifications, see *Secretum Secretorum*, ed. Manzalaoui, p. 153 (Spring), p. 346 (Spring), p. 347 (Spring); *Three Prose Versions*, ed. Steele, pp. 27–28 (Spring and Summer). Shulamith Shahar found that metaphorical discourses, unlike sermons and fabliaux, which concentrated on the old male body, tended to use the old female body to symbolize or personify "winter, the vices, old age itself and death": Shahar, *Growing Old*, p. 47.
43. Dove, *Perfect Age*, p. 35, citing Hugo de Folieto (d. ca. 1174), *De medicina animae*.
44. See, e.g., Vern L. Bullough, "Medieval Medical and Scientific Views of Women," *Viator* 4 (1973), pp. 485–501.
45. Jessica Cooke, "Nice Young Girls and Wicked Old Witches: The 'Rightful Age' of Women in Middle English Verse," in *The Court and Cultural Diversity: Selected Papers from the Eighth Triennial Congress of the International Courtly Literature Society, the Queen's University of Belfast, 26 July–1 August 1995*, ed. Evelyn Mullally and John Thompson (Cambridge: D. S. Brewer, 1997), pp. 219–28 (at p. 221).
46. Shahar, *Growing Old*, p. 44.
47. Pseudo-Albertus Magnus, *Women's Secrets*, p. 129.
48. Compare the early fifteenth-century miniature of the four ages, which depicts the first age as a boy playing with a toy: Sears, *Ages of Man*, plate 67.
49. Aristotle, *Generation of Animals*, trans. A. L. Peck (London: William Heinemann, 1943), at p. 461.
50. Aristotle, *Generation of Animals*, p. 459.
51. Shahar, *Growing Old*, p. 35. See also Youngs, *Life Cycle*, pp. 28–29; Anne L. Grauer, "Life Patterns of Women from Medieval York," in *The Archaeology of Gender: Proceedings of the Twenty-Second Annual Conference of the Archaeological Association of the University of Calgary*, ed. Dale Walde and Noreen D. Willows (Calgary: The University of Calgary Archaeological Association, 1991), pp. 407–13.
52. Albert the Great, *Questions Concerning Aristotle's* On Animals, Fathers of the Church: Medieval Continuation, vol. 9, trans. Irven M. Resnick and Kenneth F. Kitchell, Jr. (Washington, DC: Catholic University of America Press, 2008), pp. 449–50.
53. Paul Binski, *Medieval Death: Ritual and Representation* (Ithaca: Cornell University Press, 1996), pp. 153–54, 156–57; J. Aberth, *From the Brink of the Apocalypse: Confronting Famine, War, Plague, and Death in the Later Middle Ages* (New York: Routledge, 2001), pp. 205–15; Suzanne F. Wemple and Denise A. Kaiser, "Death's Dance of Women," *Journal of Medieval History* 12 (1986), pp. 333–43 (esp. pp. 336–37).

54. *The danse macabre of Women: Ms. fr. 995 of the Bibliothèque Nationale*, ed. Ann Tukey Harrison, with a chapter by S. L. Hindman (Kent, OH: Kent State University Press, 1994), pp. 7–8, 15. The authorship of the *Dmf* is unknown.
55. *Danse macabre of Women*, ed. Harrison, p. 1.
56. Ibid., p. 8.
57. Ibid., pp. 8, 10.
58. Bibliothèque nationale de France, Paris, MS Fonds français 995; *Danse macabre of Women*, ed. Harrison. Here and elsewhere, I have amended Harrison's translations.
59. "A woman who accumulated and dispensed several types of information, not merely names of servants or nurses, for a fee": Ann Tukey Harrison, "Fifteenth-Century French Women's Role Names," *French Review* 62 (1989), pp. 436–44 (at p. 440). The text of the *Dmf* has her finding accommodation for travelers: *Danse macabre of Women*, ed. Harrison, p. 118.
60. *Danse macabre of Women*, ed. Harrison, p. 46.
61. However, the *Dmh* does not feature a Prior, and the *damoiseau* was often replaced by the *escuier* (Squire). For example, see the 1486 printed edition: Anonymous, *La danse macabre* (Paris: Guy Marchant, 1486), http://gallica.bnf.fr/ark:/12148/btv1b2200008n (accessed June 3, 2011). See also Harrison, "Fifteenth-Century French Women's Role Names," p. 443; Patrick Rossi, *Danse macabre de La Chaise-Dieu: abbatiale Saint-Robert: é´tude iconographique d'une fresque du XVe siècle* (Le Puy-en-Velay: Éditions Jeanne d'Arc, 2006).
62. The theologian is not in every *Dmh*, but for the *clerc théologien*, see Rossi, *Danse macabre*.
63. See Harrison, "Fifteenth-Century French Women's Role Names," p. 437, for the 1486 edition of *Dmf*, which only has thirty-four roles. The 1491 edition has thirty-six: Anonymous, *La danse macabre* (Paris: Guy Marchant, 1491), http://gallica.bnf.fr/ark:/12148/btv1b2200006t (accessed May 7, 2011).
64. Sandra L. Hindman, "The Illustrations," in *Danse macabre of Women*, ed. Harrison, pp. 15–43 (at p. 23). Wemple and Kaiser argue that the printed edition does treat the women in order of social status, but I am unconvinced: Wemple and Kaiser, "Death's Dance of Women," pp. 338–41.
65. For example, see Carla Casagrande, "The Protected Woman," trans. Clarissa Botsford, in *A History of Women in the West*, vol. 2, *Silences of the Middle Ages*, ed. Christiane Klapisch-Zuber (Cambridge, MA: Belknap Press, 1992), pp. 79–84; Margaret Hallissy, *Clean Maids, True Wives, Steadfast Widows: Chaucer's Women and Medieval Codes of Conduct* (Westport, CT: Greenwood Press, 1993); Kim M. Phillips, "Margery Kempe and the Ages of Woman," in *A Companion to* The Book of Margery Kempe, ed. John H. Arnold and Katherine J. Lewis (Cambridge: D. S. Brewer, 2004), pp. 17–34 (esp. pp. 27–33).
66. John Baldwin cited in Giles Constable, *Three Studies in Medieval Religious and Social Thought* (Cambridge: Cambridge University Press, 1995), pp. 252–53.
67. For example, in Trevisa's discussion of *puella*, equivalences are made with "maiden child," "maiden," and "wench," and then between "maid" and "virgo": *On the Properties of Things: John Trevisa's Translation of Bartholomæus Anglicus* De

Proprietatibus Rerum. *A Critical Text*, ed. M. C. Seymour et al., 3 vols. (Oxford: Clarendon Press, 1975–88), vol. 1, pp. 301–2.

68. Saint Cyprian, "The Dress of Virgins," in *Saint Cyprian: Treatises*, trans. Roy J. Deferrari (Washington, DC: Catholic University of America Press in association with Consortium Books, 1958), p. 49 (chap. 21).
69. *Hali Meiðhad*, ed. Bella Millett, Early English Text Society, original ser., 284 (London: Oxford University Press, 1982), p. xxxix; Millett suggests that Athanasius was the first writer to give virgins a hundredfold in his *Epistula ad Amunen monachum* of the early fourth century.
70. Bernhard Jussen, "'Virgins-Widows-Spouses': On the Language of Moral Distinction as Applied to Women and Men in the Middle Ages," *History of the Family* 7 (2002), pp. 13–32 (at p. 15).
71. See David G. Hunter, "Resistance to the Virginal Ideal in Late-Fourth-Century Rome: The Case of Jovinian," *Theological Studies* 48 (1987), pp. 45–64.
72. See Peter Brown, *The Body and Society: Men, Women, and Sexual Renunciation in Early Christianity* (New York: Columbia University Press, 1988), pp. 341–64.
73. Jo Ann McNamara, *A New Song: Celibate Women in the First Three Christian Centuries* (New York: Institute for Research in History and Haworth Press, 1983).
74. See Robert L. Benson and Giles Constable, with Carol D. Lanham, eds., *Renaissance and Renewal in the Twelfth Century* (Oxford: Clarendon Press, 1982); John W. Baldwin, *Masters, Princes and Merchants: The Social Views of Peter the Chanter and His Circle*, 2 vols. (Princeton, NJ: Princeton University Press, 1970).
75. Pierre J. Payer, *The Bridling of Desire: Views of Sex in the Later Middle Ages* (Toronto: University of Toronto Press, 1993), p. 10.
76. Payer, *Bridling of Desire*, p. 160.
77. Albertus Magnus, *De bono*, quoted in Payer, *Bridling of Desire*, at p. 162. See also Kathleen Coyne Kelly, *Performing Virginity and Testing Chastity in the Middle Ages* (London: Routledge, 2000), p. 6. The age of reason (*aetus discretionis*), which was when a person could receive the Eucharist, was not precisely defined with some setting it at seven, some around ten, and others at the age of puberty (Phillips, *Medieval Maidens*, p. 31).
78. Albertus Magnus, *De bono* 3.3.4, ad 9, quoted in Payer, *Bridling of Desire*, p. 252n32.
79. On the manuals, see Leonard E. Boyle, "The Fourth Lateran Council and Manuals of Popular Theology," in *The Popular Literature of Medieval England*, ed. Thomas J. Heffernan (Knoxville: University of Tennessee Press, 1985), pp. 30–43.
80. Jocelyn Wogan-Browne, *Saints' Lives and Women's Literary Culture, c. 1150–1300: Virginity and Its Authorizations* (Oxford: Oxford University Press, 2001), p. 44.
81. Wogan-Browne, *Saints' Lives and Women's Literary Culture*, p. 45.
82. Wogan-Browne, *Saints' Lives and Women's Literary Culture*, pp. 44–45.
83. See Cordelia Beattie, *Medieval Single Women: The Politics of Social Classification in Late Medieval England* (Oxford: Oxford University Press, 2007), pp. 56–58.
84. See J. Witte, Jr., *From Sacrament to Contract: Marriage, Religion, and Law in the Western Tradition* (Louisville, KY: Westminster John Knox Press, 1997), pp. 22–30; Payer, *Bridling of Desire*, pp. 61–72.

85. Guibert of Tournai was a prominent member of the Franciscan order, with connections to the University of Paris, and his sermon collection circulated throughout Europe. See D. L. D'Avray, *The Preaching of the Friars: Sermons Diffused from Paris before 1300* (Oxford: Clarendon Press, 1985), pp. 144–46, 278; Sharon Farmer, *Surviving Poverty in Medieval Paris: Gender, Ideology, and the Daily Lives of the Poor* (Ithaca: Cornell University Press, 2002), p. 167.
86. Alan of Lille, *The Art of Preaching*, trans. Gillian R. Evans (Kalamazoo, MI: Cistercian Publications, 1981), pp. 146–49, 163–68.
87. Guibert de Tournai, *Sermones* (Louvain: Johannes de Westfalia, ca. 1481–83). For Guibert's layout, see *Prediche alle donne del secolo XIII: Testi di Umberto da Romans, Gilberto da Tournai, Stefano di Borbone*, ed. Carla Casagrande (Milan: Bompiani, 1978), pp. 146–47. On the sermons to servants, see Sharon Farmer, " 'It Is Not Good That [Wo]man Should Be Alone': Elite Responses to Singlewomen in High Medieval Paris," in *Singlewomen in the European Past 1250–1800*, ed. Judith M. Bennett and Amy M. Froide (Philadelphia: University of Pennsylvania Press, 1999), pp. 82–105 (esp. pp. 88–91).
88. Jenny Swanson, "Childhood and Childrearing in *ad status* Sermons by Later Thirteenth Century Friars," *Journal of Medieval History* 16 (1990), pp. 309–31 (at p. 322). His second sermon to this group is edited in *Prediche alle donne*, ed. Casagrande, pp. 105–8.
89. For his sermon to widows, see *Prediche alle donne*, ed. Casagrande, pp. 97–105. On the sermons to married women, see D. L. D'Avray and M. Tausche, "Marriage Sermons in *ad status* Collections of the Central Middle Ages," *Archives d'histoire doctrinale et litteraire du Moyen Age* 47 (1981), pp. 71–119, esp. pp. 86–117; the third sermon is edited in *Prediche alle donne*, ed. Casagrande, pp. 93–97.
90. Compare Jussen, "Virgins-Widows-Spouses."
91. For example, see http://gallica.bnf.fr/ark:/12148/btv1b2200008n (accessed June 3, 2011), images 9, 14, and 20.
92. *Danse macabre of Women*, ed. Harrison, p. 77; Phillips, *Medieval Maidens*, pp. 43–51.
93. *Danse macabre of Women*, ed. Harrison, p. 76.
94. Harrison, "Fifteenth-Century French Women's Role Names," p. 442.
95. *Danse macabre of Women*, ed. Harrison, p. 107.
96. Ibid., at p. 106.
97. For example, http://gallica.bnf.fr/ark:/12148/btv1b2200008n (accessed June 3, 2011), image 20.
98. *Danse macabre of Women*, ed. Harrison, pp. 47–48; Harrison, "Fifteenth-Century French Women's Role Names," p. 443.
99. *Danse macabre of Women*, ed. Harrison, p. 66.
100. Hindman, "The Illustrations," pp. 19–20; *Danse macabre of Women*, ed. Harrison, pp. 53, 55.
101. Hindman, "The Illustrations," p. 21.
102. *Danse macabre of Women*, ed. Harrison, p. 84.
103. Ibid.
104. For a discussion of the linked memorial brasses of two never-married women—one in her twenties, the other probably in her fifties—see Judith M. Bennett, "Two

Women and Their Monumental Brass, *c.* 1480," *Journal of the British Archaeological Association* 161 (2008), pp. 163–84.

105. J. Hajnal, "Two Kinds of Pre-industrial Household Formation," in *Family Forms in Historical Europe*, ed. Richard Wall in collaboration with Jean Robin and Peter Laslett (Cambridge: Cambridge University Press, 1983), pp. 65–104 (at p. 69).
106. See Maryanne Kowaleski, "Singlewomen in Medieval and Early Modern Europe: The Demographic Perspective," in *Singlewomen in the European Past 1250–1800*, ed. Judith M. Bennett and Amy M. Froide (Philadelphia: University of Pennsylvania Press, 1999), pp. 38–81 (esp. pp. 39–51). On aristocratic service, see Phillips, *Medieval Maidens*, pp. 109–20.
107. Christine de Pisan, *The Treasure of the City of Ladies, or The Book of the Three Virtues*, trans. Sarah Lawson (Harmondsworth: Penguin, 1995), p. 160. This text had a broad circulation among bourgeois and aristocratic audiences; it circulated in luxury manuscripts, paper manuscripts, and early printed editions, and it was translated into other languages. See Roberta L. Krueger, " 'Nouvelles choses': Social Instability and the Problem of Fashion in the *Livre du Chevalier de la Tour Landry*, the *Ménagier de Paris*, and Christine de Pizan's *Livre des trois vertus*," in *Medieval Conduct*, ed. Kathleen Ashley and Robert L. A. Clark (Minneapolis: University of Minnesota Press, 2001), pp. 49–85 (esp. pp. 51–52).
108. *The Good Wife Taught Her Daughter, the Good Wife Wold a Pylgremage, The Thewis of Gud Women*, ed. Tauno F. Mustanoja (Helsinki: Suomalainen Tiedeakatemia, 1948), p. 175. This poem only survives in a single copy, a household manuscript apparently compiled in the West Midlands, MS Porkington 10: *The Good Wife*, ed. Mustanoja, pp. 131–35.
109. Felicity Riddy, "Mother Knows Best: Reading Social Change in a Courtesy Text," *Speculum* 71 (1996), pp. 66–86 (esp. pp. 85–86).
110. G.L. Remnant, *A Catalogue of Misericords in Great Britain*, with an essay on their iconography by M. D. Anderson (Oxford: Clarendon Press, 1969), p. 47, no. 8; S08 at http://www.misericords.co.uk/bristol.html (accessed June 9, 2011).
111. Malcolm Jones, "Folklore Motifs in Late Medieval Art II: Sexist Satire and Popular Punishments," *Folklore* 101 (1990), pp. 69–87 (esp. p. 75); Amy M. Froide, *Never Married: Singlewomen in Early Modern England* (Oxford: Oxford University Press, 2005), pp. 157–58. Froide argues that the negative figure of the old maid appears in the second half of the sixteenth century but only really takes off in the late seventeenth century in England: *Never Married*, pp. 154–81.
112. de Pisan, *The Treasure of the City of Ladies*, p. 160.
113. Ruth Mazo Karras, "Sex and the Singlewoman," in *Singlewomen*, ed. Bennett and Froide, pp. 127–45 (at p. 127).
114. Harrison, "Fifteenth-Century French Women's Role Names," p. 441.
115. For example, http://gallica.bnf.fr/ark:/12148/btv1b2200008n (accessed June 3, 2011), image 15. Some of the English versions followed discussion of the "amorous squire" with that of the "amorous gentlewoman": *The Dance of Death edited from MSS. Ellesmere 26/A.13 and B.M. Lansdowne 699, collated with the other extant MSS.*, ed. Florence Warren, with introduction, notes, etc., by Beatrice

White, Early English Text Society, original ser., 181 (London: Humphrey Milford, 1931), pp. xxv–vi, 54–56; Aberth, *From the Brink*, p. 210.

116. *Danse macabre of Women*, ed. Harrison, p. 115. On dress and "class" in this manuscript, see Hindman, "The Illustrations," pp. 20–21.
117. *Danse macabre of Women*, ed. Harrison, p. 116. Compare with the ballad in Ashmole MS 48 (ca. 1557–65), which has an ageing servant lament, "For I have bene a meaden so longe, That my tyme wyll be paste or I shall begynne": *Songs and Ballads with Other Short Poems, Chiefly of the Reign of Philip and Mary, Edited from a Manuscript in the Ashmolean Museum*, ed. Thomas Wright (London: J. B. Nichols and Sons, 1860), p. 133 (I owe this reference to Judith Bennett).
118. This phenomenon is more easily documented for Mediterranean Europe: for example, see Christiane Klapisch-Zuber, "Women Servants in Florence during the Fourteenth and Fifteenth Centuries," in *Women and Work in Preindustrial Europe*, ed. Barbara A. Hanawalt (Bloomington: Indiana University Press, 1986), pp. 56–80 (esp. pp. 62–63, 74); Christiane Klapisch-Zuber, *Women, Family, and Ritual in Renaissance Italy*, trans. Lydia G. Cochrane (Chicago: University of Chicago Press, 1985), pp. 172–75. But for widows becoming servants "for meat and drink" in late fifteenth-century London, see, for example, The National Archives, Kew, C 1/63/138, C 1/82/64.
119. *Danse macabre of Women*, ed. Harrison, p.112 n.
120. Ibid., p.112.
121. Phillips, "Maidenhood as the Perfect Age," pp. 7, 9–12.
122. See Hindman, "The Illustrations," p. 20.
123. *Danse macabre of Women*, ed. Harrison, pp. 81, 115; Hindman, "The Illustrations," p. 22.
124. *Danse macabre of Women*, ed. Harrison, p. 80.
125. Ibid., pp. 114–15.
126. Ibid., pp. 82, 91, 93, 97, 101, 105, 117.
127. *Danse macabre of Women*, ed. Harrison, pp. 83, 34 (fig. 2); http://gallica.bnf.fr/ark:/12148/btv1b2200006t (accessed May 7, 2011), image 11. The only character to be depicted with a child is the Wetnurse: *Danse macabre of Women*, ed. Harrison, p. 91. The practice of hiring a nurse so that the mother did not need to breast-feed was common amongst aristocratic families in parts of western Europe and also widespread among the merchants of Florence: Youngs, *Life Cycle*, pp. 47–48; Klapisch-Zuber, *Women, Family, and Ritual*, pp. 133–64.
128. Stanley Chojnacki, "Measuring Adulthood: Adolescence and Gender in Renaissance Venice," *Journal of Family History* 17 (1992), 371–95 (at p. 384).
129. *Danse macabre of Women*, ed. Harrison, pp. 70–71; Youngs, *Life Cycle*, p. 148.
130. de Pizan, *The Treasure of the City of Ladies*, ed. Lawson, pp. 15, 17–18.
131. *Danse macabre of Women*, ed. Harrison, pp. 2, 94.
132. Ibid., p. 95.
133. Ibid., pp. 2, 110, 111.
134. Michael D. Bailey, *Battling Demons: Witchcraft, Heresy, and Reform in the Late Middle Ages* (University Park: Pennsylvania State University Press, 2003), pp. 38–48.

135. *Danse macabre of Women*, ed. Harrison, pp. 61, 65, 79, 121.
136. Dove, *Perfect Age*, at p. 20.
137. Otto Oexle has defined interpretive schemes as "terminological constructs intended to name, organize, and interpret social phenomena": Otto Gerhard Oexle, "Perceiving Social Reality in the Early and High Middle Ages: A Contribution to a History of Social Knowledge," in *Ordering Medieval Society: Perspectives on Intellectual and Practical Modes of Shaping Social Relations*, ed. Bernhard Jussen, trans. Pamela Selwyn (Philadelphia: University of Pennsylvania Press, 2001), pp. 92–143 (at p. 92). For an attempt at both a social-historical and a cultural-historical approach to the female life cycle, see Phillips, "Margery Kempe."

Chapter 2

1. *The French Fabliau: B.N. Ms. 837*, ed. and trans. Raymond Eichmann and John DuVal, 2 vols. (New York: Garland, 1984), vol. 2, pp. 45–47. Eichmann and DuVal's volume supplies an English translation of the largest collection of fabliaux contained in a single manuscript. The fabliaux represent a genre of Old French literature that reached its peak of popularity in the thirteenth century. The writing of fabliaux continued into the fourteenth century and served as the basis of some of Chaucer's *Canterbury Tales* and Boccaccio's *Decameron.* They are short, witty poems written in octosyllabic rhyming couplets and mimic the format of the Aesopic fable, especially in the concluding moral of the story. A complete edited collection of the fabliaux may be found in *Nouveau Recueil Complet des Fabliaux*, ed. Willem Noomen and Nico van den Boogaard, 10 vols. (Assen, the Netherlands: Van Gorcum, 1983–95). For her help with this essay, I would like to thank Kim M. Phillips for her enthusiasm, generosity in sharing sources, patience, and helpful suggestions.
2. Tertullian, "On the Apparel of Women," in *The Ante-Nicene Fathers*, ed. A. Roberts and J. Donaldson, (Buffalo: The Christian Literature Publishing Co., 1885), vol. 4, pp. 14, 37; Ovid, *Amores*, in *Heroides and Amores*, trans. Grant Showerman (Harvard: Loeb Classical Library, 1914), 2.9B. 26 (p. 408).
3. Marbod of Rennes, "The Femme Fatale" *(De Meretrice)*, from "The Book with Ten Chapters" *(Liber Decem Capitulorum)*, chap. III, trans. Alcuin Blamires, in *Woman Defamed and Woman Defended: An Anthology of Medieval Texts*, ed. Alcuin Blamires (Oxford: Oxford University Press, 1992), p. 101; and G. G. Coulton, trans., *From St. Francis to Dante, Translations from the Chronicle of the Franciscan Salimbene, 1221–1288* (Philadelphia: University of Pennsylvania Press, 1972), p. 92.
4. Vern L. Bullough, "Medieval Medical and Scientific Views of Women," *Viator* 4 (1973), pp. 485–501. Also see Joan Cadden, *Meanings of Sex Difference in the Middle Ages: Medicine, Science, and Culture* (Cambridge: Cambridge University Press, 1993); and Helen King, *Hippocrates' Woman: Reading the Female Body in Ancient Greece*, trans. M. B. Debvoise (London: Routledge, 1998).
5. Aristotle, *Historia animalium*, trans. D. W. Thompson, in *The Works of Aristotle*, ed. W. D. Ross, 12 vols. (Oxford: Oxford University Press, 1910), vol. 4, p. 608a.

6. Galen, *On the Usefulness of Parts of the Body (De Usus Partium)*, trans. Margaret Tallmadge May, 2 vols. (Ithaca: Cornell University Press, 1968), vol. 2, pp. 628–630.
7. Soranus, *Gynecology*, ed. Oswei Tempkin (Baltimore: Johns Hopkins University Press, 1991, p. 130). See also Danielle Jacquart and Claude Thomasset, *Sexuality and Medicine in the Middle Ages* (Princeton, NJ: Princeton University Press, 1985), p. 24.
8. Augustine, in *The Works of St. Augustine*, ed. D. G. Hunter, trans. Ray Kearney (New York: New York City Press, 1999), p. 117.
9. Catarina Belo, "Some Considerations on Averroes' Views regarding Women and their Role in Society," *Journal of Islamic Studies* 20 (2009), pp. 1–20 (at p. 8); Thomas Aquinas, *Summa Theologiae*, rev. ed., 5 vols. Bibliotheca de auctore cristianos seccion 2, Teologia y canones 77, 80, 83, 87 (Madrid: La Editorial Catolica, 1955–58).
10. Jerome, *Commentarius in Epistolam ad Ephesios* III.5; see Jacqueline Murray, "Gendered Souls in Sexed Bodies: The Male Construction of Female Sexuality in Some Medieval Confessor's Manuals," in *Handling Sin: Confession in the Middle Ages*, ed. Peter Biller and A. J. Minnis (Woodbridge: York Medieval Press, 1998), pp. 79–93 (at p. 80).
11. See, for example, Saint Jerome, *Select Letters of St. Jerome,* trans. F. A. Wright (London and New York: Loeb Classical Library, 1933), letters 22 (pp. 79–85), 54 (pp. 255–57), and 125 (pp. 405–6).
12. Isidore of Seville, *The Etymologies of Isidore of Seville,* ed. Stephen A. Barney, W. J. Lewis, J. A. Beach, and Oliver Berghof (Cambridge: Cambridge University Press, 2006), XI.ii.23 (p. 242).
13. Miri Rubin, *Mother of God: A History of the Virgin Mary* (New Haven, CT: Yale University Press, 2009).
14. Augustine, "Excellence of Marriage," in *Works*; and Thomas Aquinas, *Summa Theologiae*, III: q. 29.
15. 1 Corinthians 7:8–9.
16. Cindy L. Carlson and Angela Jane Weisl, eds., *Constructions of Widowhood and Virginity in the Middle Ages* (New York: St. Martin's Press, 1999).
17. Eleanor never met Saladin, who was in any case only eleven years old when she accompanied her husband to the Holy Land. The allegation of an affair with Saladin was not only damaging in its adulterous nature, but also breached canon law injunctions against Christians having sexual relations with infidels. See James A. Brundage, *Law, Sex and Christian Society in Medieval Europe* (Chicago: University of Chicago Press, 1987), pp. 207, 461–62, 518.
18. *Récits d'un Ménestrel de Reims au treizième siècle*, ed. Natalis de Wailly (Paris: Renouard, 1876), pp. 4–7.
19. RaGena C. DeAragon, "Wife, Widow, and Mother: Some Comparisons between Eleanor of Aquitaine and Noblewomen of the Anglo-Norman and Angevin World"; Peggy McCracken, "Scandalizing Desire: Eleanor of Aquitaine and the Chroniclers"; and Ralph V. Turner, "Eleanor of Aquitaine in the Governments of Her Sons Richard and John"; all in *Eleanor of Aquitaine: Lord and Lady*, ed. John Carmi Parsons and Bonnie Wheeler (New York: Palgrave MacMillan, 2002), pp. 97–114, 247–264, and 77–96.

20. Many of these themes in medieval scholarship are examined in the essays contained in Susan Mosher Stuard, ed., *Women in Medieval History and Historiography* (Philadelphia: University of Pennsylvania Press, 1987).
21. Nesta Pain, *Empress Matilda: Uncrowned Queen of England* (London: Weidenfeld & Nicolson, 1978, p. 120). It is most telling that the medieval author of the *Gesta Stephani*, a work commissioned by Matilda's rival, still had nothing but praise for the relationship between the empress and Brian FitzCount. Brian's faithfulness as a vassal stood in sharp contrast to the vacillating loyalties of the English nobility in general—a fact the author notes in addition to his bravery and the well-earned fame he had gained through his devotion to the empress. See *Gesta Stephani*, ed. K. R. Potter, revised by R.H.C. Davis, Oxford Medieval Texts (Oxford: Oxford University Press, 1976), p. 134.
22. Marjorie Chibnall, *The Empress Matilda: Queen Consort, Queen Mother, and Lady of the English* (Oxford: Blackwell, 1991), pp. 84–87.
23. T. F. Madden, *The New Concise History of the Crusades* (New York: Barnes and Noble, 2007), p. 72.
24. Helen Nicholson, "'La roine preude femme et bonne dame': Queen Sybil of Jerusalem (1186–1190) in History and Legend 1186–1300," in *The Haskins Society Journal* 15 (2004), pp. 110–25.
25. On this, see Susan Mosher Stuard, "The Three-Decade Transformation: Medieval Women and the Course of History," in *Considering Medieval Women*, ed. Susan Mosher Stuard (London: Ashgate Publishing, 2010), pp. 1–21.
26. *French Fabliau*, ed. Eichmann and DuVal, vol. 2, pp. 45–47. The term *fractured* is perhaps more appropriate than *faceted* when discussing the images of women, their bodies, and sexuality in the Middle Ages and in much modern scholarship. A facet is a deliberately fashioned aspect of a character and is often considered equal to other sides of an object, making up a brilliant whole, while a fracture is the separation of an object into any number of unequal pieces under the force of stress and serves to weaken the strength and image of the whole. The image of women's bodies and sexuality was the subject and subjected to social, intellectual, and economic stress that separated it into any number of pieces that served to weaken the whole.
27. Kim M. Phillips, *Medieval Maidens: Young Women and Gender in England, 1270–1540* (Manchester: Manchester University Press, 2003), pp. 30–36. As Phillips notes, women's age of majority was often linked not to a specified age, but rather to the point at which they could complete the tasks necessary for their position, such as the management of a house. Although some laws stated that a woman might come of age at twenty-one for inheritance purposes, these laws were seldom upheld, and the guardian of a ward, especially a royal ward, could find it advantageous to marry off the girl in his charge earlier. The commonly held idea that girls matured psychologically faster than men, coupled with financial incentives and cultural flexibility, made laws concerning the age of female majority variable.
28. Phillips, *Medieval Maidens*, p. 44.
29. Ruth Mazo Karras, *From Boys to Men: Formations of Masculinity in Late Medieval Europe* (Philadelphia: University of Pennsylvania Press, 2003), pp. 12–15.
30. Phillips, *Medieval Maidens*, pp. 44–49.

31. Cordelia Beattie, *Medieval Single Women: The Politics of Social Classification in Late Medieval England* (Oxford: Oxford University Press, 2007), pp. 40, 43.
32. Carlson and Weisl, eds., *Constructions of Widowhood and Virginity*, p. 2.
33. Ibid., p. 2.
34. Caesarius of Arles, *The Rule for Nuns of St. Caesarius of Arles: A Translation with a Critical Introduction*, ed. M. C. McCarthy (Washington, DC: Catholic University Press of America, 1960), p. 171.
35. Caesarius of Arles, *Regula monachorum*, Morin II, 149–155, in *Césaire d'Arles. Oeuvres monastiques, II, Oeuvres pour les moines* SC 398, ed. A. de Vogüé and J. Courreau (Paris: CERF, 1994), p. 11.
36. Lindsay Rudge, "Texts and Contexts: Women's Dedicated Life from Caesarius to Benedict" (PhD thesis, University of St. Andrews, 2006), p. 81 (citing Jerome, *Epist.* 22, "Ad Eustochium"). See also Jane Tibbets Schulenburg, "Strict Active Enclosure and Its Effects on the Female Monastic Experience (ca. 500–1100): Patterns of Expansion and Decline," *Signs* 14 (1989), pp. 261–92, at p. 273.
37. Giles Constable, "Aelred of Rievaulx and the Nun of Watton: An Episode in the Early History of the Gilbertine Order," in *Medieval Women*, ed. Derek Baker (Oxford: Blackwell, 1981), pp. 205–26.
38. Carlson and Weisl, eds., *Constructions of Widowhood and Virginity*, p. 2n8.
39. Ibid., p. 2.
40. Mary Elizabeth Perry, "Deviant Insiders: Legalized Prostitutes and a Consciousness of Women in Early Modern Seville," *Comparative Studies in Society and History* 27 (1985), pp. 138–58.
41. The use of *lesbian* in reference to female same-sex unions and female-to-female intimacy in the Middle Ages is highly debated. Historians, anthropologists, and sociologists need to consider whether in using *lesbian* they import modern and chiefly Western ideas of sexuality into another culture. While some historians, including Jacqueline Murray and John Boswell, have argued that *gay* and *lesbian*, though of modern construction, are appropriate in discussing premodern cultures, others, including Elizabeth Wahl, Valerie Traub, Kim M. Phillips, and Barry Reay, find they can be misleading. The use of the term *lesbian* has also resulted in a modern understanding and therefore a limited view of what constituted acts of female-to-female intimacy. By abandoning modern concepts of sexuality and analyzing sources for evidence of, in Traub's words, "intense emotional investment and compelling erotic attraction," expressed variously as "love, passion, appetite, lust" and manifesting variously as "caresses, kisses, bodily penetration, and passionate verbal addresses expressing longing, loss, devotion, frustration, pleasure, and pain," claims of silence in medieval texts regarding female intimacy become unsustainable. Valerie Traub, *The Renaissance of Lesbianism in Early Modern England* (Cambridge: Cambridge University Press, 2002), p. 13, as cited in Kim M. Phillips and Barry Reay, *Sex before Sexuality: A Premodern History* (Cambridge: Polity Press, 2011), p. 90.
42. Jacqueline Murray, "Twice Marginal and Twice Invisible: Lesbians in the Middle Ages," in *Handbook of Medieval Sexuality*, ed. Vern L. Bullough and James A. Brundage (New York: Garland Publishing, 1996), pp. 191–222.

43. Etienne de Fougères, *Livre des Manières,* trans. R.L.A. Clark, in *Same Sex Love and Desire among Women in the Middle Ages*, ed. Francesca C. Sautman and Pamela Sheingorn (New York: St. Martin's Press, 2001), pp. 166–67.
44. John Gower, *The English Works of John Gower*, ed. G. C. Macaualy (London: Oxford University Press, 1900), bk. 4, lines 479–505 (p. 314).
45. Aristotle, *Generation of Animals*, trans. A. L. Peck (Cambridge, MA: Loeb Classical Library, 1942), bk. 1, chap. 19 (p. 103).
46. Murray, "Twice Marginal," p. 210.
47. Ibid., p. 197.
48. Ibid., pp. 202–3.
49. Ibid., p. 201.
50. Ibid., p. 203.
51. Hildegard of Bingen, *Scivias*, trans. Mother Columba Hart and Jane Bishop (New York: Paulist Press, 1990), p. 279.
52. Pierre J. Payer, *The Bridling of Desire: Views of Sex in the Later Middle Ages* (Toronto: University of Toronto Press, 1993), pp. 77, 79, 220a.
53. See "Life of St. Mary" in *Holy Women of Byzantium: Ten Saints' Lives in English Translation*, ed. Alice-Mary Talbot (Washington, DC: Dumbarton Oaks Research Library, 1996); Ruth M. Karras, "Holy Harlots: Prostitute Saints in Medieval Legend," *Journal of the History of Sexuality* 1 (1990), pp. 3–32.
54. Ruth M. Karras, "Prostitution in Medieval Europe," in *Handbook of Medieval Sexuality*, ed. Bullough and Brundage, pp. 243–60, at p. 245.
55. Little consideration was given to the possibility that many prostitutes became such as a result of their own rape, which had deprived them of an honorable marriage.
56. The concept of the *deviant insider* is explored in Perry, "Deviant Insiders."
57. Karras, "Prostitution," pp. 243–60.
58. Perry, "Deviant Insiders."
59. Ruth M. Karras, *Common Women: Prostitution and Sexuality in Medieval England* (Oxford: Oxford University Press, 1996), pp. 40, 62, 74.
60. Karras, "Prostitution," p. 254.
61. Karras, "Prostitution," p. 251.
62. Jacquart and Thomasset, *Sexuality and Medicine*, pp. 25, 63–64.
63. *The Vulgate Version of the Arthurian Romances Edited from Manuscripts in the British Museum*, ed. H. O. Sommer, 8 vols. (Washington, DC: Carnegie Institute, 1908–16), vol. 6, p. 11.
64. *Du Fevre de Creel*, in *French Fabliau*, ed. Eichmann and DuVal, pp. 134–40.
65. *The Vulgate Version,* ed. Sommer, vol. 3, p. 412.
66. See *Du Cuvier*, in *French Fabliau*, ed. Eichmann and DuVal, vol. 2, pp. 143–49.
67. Carolyn Walker Bynum, *Holy Feast and Holy Fast: The Religious Significance of Food to Medieval Women* (Berkeley: University of California Press, 1987), p. 117.
68. E. Jane Burns, "Knowing Women: Female Orifices in the Old French Fabliaux," *Exemplaria* 4 (1992), pp. 81–104.

69. *Li jugemenz des cons*, in *French Fabliau*, ed. Eichmann and DuVal, vol. 2, pp. 49–55, lines 123, 132–135, 149–150.
70. *Nouveau Recueil Complet des Fabliaux*, ed. Noomen and van den Boogaard, vol. 3, pp. 45–173.

Chapter 3

1. I want to thank Anne Lester for sharing her unpublished paper with me, and Sandy Bardsley for her wise comments.
2. Caroline Walker Bynum, *Holy Feast and Holy Fast: The Religious Significance of Food to Medieval Women* (Berkeley: University of California Press, 1987), p. 17.
3. Gerd Tellenbach, *Church, State, and Christian Society in the Time of the Investiture Controversy*, trans. R. F. Bennett (Oxford: Basil Blackwell, 1966).
4. See for example, R. I. Moore, *The Origins of European Dissent*, 2nd ed., Medieval Academy Reprints for Teaching, vol. 30 (Toronto: University of Toronto Press, 1994); Jo Ann McNamara "Canossa and the Ungendering of the Public Man," in *Render Unto Caesar: The Religious Sphere in World Politics*, ed. Sbrina Petra Ramet and Donald W. Treadgold (Washington, DC: American University Press, 1995), pp. 131–50; Jo Ann McNamara, "The *Herrenfrage*: The Restructuring of the Gender System, 1050–1150," in *Medieval Masculinieties*, ed. Clare A. Lees (Minneapolis: University of Minnesota Press, 1994), pp. 3–30; Megan McLaughlin, "The Bishop as Bridegroom: Marital Imagery and Clerical Celibacy in the Eleventh and Early Twelfth Centuries," in *Medieval Purity and Piety: Essays on Medieval Clerical Celibacy and Religious Reform*, ed. Michael Frassetto (New York: Garland Publishing, 1998), pp. 209–38; Maureen C. Miller, "Masculinity, Reform, and Clerical Culture: Narratives of Episcopal Holiness in the Gregorian Era," *Church History* 72 (2003), pp. 25–52.
5. Lester K. Little, *Religious Poverty and the Profit Economy* (Ithaca: Cornell University Press, 1979); Moore, *Origins*, pp. 45–53.
6. Moore, *Origins*, p. 52.
7. Dyan Elliott, "The Priest's Wife: Female Erasure and the Gregorian Reform," in *Fallen Bodies: Pollution, Sexuality, and Demonology in the Middle Ages* (Philadelphia: University of Pennsylvania Press, 1999), pp. 81–106.
8. Ibid., p. 83.
9. Ibid., pp. 81–106.
10. Joan Cadden, *Meanings of Sex Difference in the Middle Ages* (Cambridge: Cambridge University Press, 1993).
11. Jennifer Thibodeaux, "Man of the Church or Man of the Village? Gender and the Parish Clergy in Medieval Normandy," *Gender & History* 18 (2006), pp. 380–99.
12. This assumption is widespread; see, for example, Augustine, "From the Literal Meaning of Genesis," in *Woman Defamed and Woman Defended: An Anthology of Medieval Texts*, ed. Alcuin Blamires (Oxford: Oxford University Press, 1992), pp. 79–81; Gratian, "From the Decretum," in *Woman Defamed and Woman Defended*, ed. Blamires, pp. 83–87.

13. Miri Rubin, *Mother of God: A History of the Virgin Mary* (New Haven, CT: Yale University Press, 2009), pp. 121–37, esp. p. 133.
14. Georges Duby, *The Knight, the Lady, and the Priest*, trans. Barbara Bray (New York: Pantheon, 1983).
15. McNamara, "The *Herrenfrage*," pp. 15–21. See also the hypermasculine image of the postreform clergy; Miller, "Masculinity, Reform, and Clerical Culture."
16. Bruce L. Venarde, *Women's Monasticism and Medieval Society: Nunneries in France and England, 890–1215* (Ithaca: Cornell University Press, 1997), p. 54.
17. Ibid.
18. Ibid., p. 67.
19. Alison Beach, "Claustration and Collaboration between the Sexes," in *Monks and Nuns, Saints and Outcasts*, ed. Sharon Farmer and Barbara H. Rosenwein (Ithaca: Cornell University Press, 2000), p. 60.
20. Madeline Caviness, "Artist," in *Voice of the Living Light: Hildegard of Bingen and Her World*, ed. Barbara Newman (Berkeley: University of California Press, 1998), pp. 110–24; Fiona Griffiths, *The Garden of Delights: Reform and Renaissance for Women in the Twelfth Century* (Philadelphia: University of Pennsylvania Press, 2006).
21. Beach, "Claustration and Collaboration," p. 65.
22. Ibid., p. 70.
23. Herbert Grundmann, *Religious Movements in the Middle Ages*, trans. Steven Rowan (Notre Dame, IN: Notre Dame University Press, 1995), pp. 75–88.
24. Grundmann, *Religious Movements*, p. 8.
25. Anne E. Lester, "From the Margins to the Center: Religious Women and the Cistercian Order in Thirteenth-Century Northern France" (unpublished paper, Brown University, March 2009, used with permission); Anne E. Lester, *Creating Cistercian Nuns: The Women's Religious Movement and its Reform in Thirteenth-Century Champagne* (Ithaca, NY: Cornell University Press, 2011), p. 97.
26. Catherine Peroux, "The Leper's Kiss," in *Monks and Nuns, Saints and Outcasts*, ed. Farmer and Rosenwein, pp. 172–88.
27. Venarde, *Women's Monasticism*, p. 63.
28. Penny Schine Gold, "Male/Female Cooperation: The Example of Fontevrault," in *Distant Echoes: Medieval Religious Women*, ed. John A. Nichols and Lillian Thomas Shank (Kalamazoo: Cistercian Publications, 1984), p. 151.
29. Gold, "Male/Female Cooperation," p. 152.
30. Penny Schine Gold, *The Lady and the Virgin: Image, Attitude, and Experience in Twelfth-Century France* (Chicago: University of Chicago Press, 1985), pp. 97–102.
31. Shelley Amiste Wolbrink, "Women in the Premonstratensian Order of Northwestern Germany, 1120–1250," *Catholic Historical Review* 89 (2003), pp. 387–408, at p. 393.
32. Ibid., pp. 397–98.
33. Ibid., p. 394.
34. Jo Ann McNamara, *Sisters in Arms: Catholic Nuns through Two Millennia* (Cambridge, MA: Harvard University Press, 1996), p. 218.

35. Ibid.
36. Ibid., p. 219.
37. Ibid., pp. 227, 246.
38. Elizabeth Freeman, " 'Houses of a Peculiar Order': Cistercian Nunneries in Medieval England, with Attention to the Fifteenth and Sixteenth Centuries," *Cîteaux: Commentarii Cistercienses* 55 (2004), pp. 244–51; Elizabeth Freeman, "Cistercian Nuns in Medieval England: Unofficial Meets Official," in *Elite and Popular Religion*, ed. Kate Cooper and Jeremy Gregory, Studies in Church History 42 (Woodbridge: Boydell Press for the Ecclesiastical History Society, 2006), pp. 110–19; Lester, "From the Margins to the Center," p. 9.
39. McNamara, *Sisters in Arms*, p. 304.
40. Lester, "From the Margins to the Center"; Lester, *Creating Cistercian Nuns*, p. 130.
41. Lester, "From the Margins to the Center."
42. McNamara, *Sisters in Arms*, pp. 289–92; Penelope D. Johnson, *Equal in Monastic Profession: Religious Women in Medieval France* (Chicago: University of Chicago Press, 1991), pp. 150–63.
43. Johnson, *Equal in Monastic Profession*, pp. 207–28.
44. Venarde, *Women's Monasticism*, p. 164; Gold, *Lady and the Virgin*, pp. 105–8.
45. Constance Berman, "Cistercian Nuns and the Development of the Order: The Abbey of Saint-Antoine-des-Champs Outside Paris," in *The Joy of Learning and the Love of God: Studies in Honor of Jean Leclercq*, ed. E. Rozanne Elder (Kalamazoo, MI: Cistercian Publications, 1995), pp. 121–56.
46. John Moorman, *A History of the Franciscan Order* (Oxford: Oxford University Press, 1968), pp. 16–18.
47. C. H. Lawrence, *Medieval Monasticism*, 3rd ed. (London: Longman, 2001), pp. 252–53.
48. Clara Gennaro, "Clare, Agnes, and Their Earliest Followers: From the Poor Ladies of San Damiano to the Poor Clares," in *Women and Religion in Medieval and Renaissance Italy*, ed. Daniel Bornstein and Roberto Rusconi, trans. Margery J. Schneider (Chicago: University of Chicago Press, 1996), p. 41.
49. Elizabeth Alvilda Petroff, *Body and Soul: Essays on Medieval Women and Mysticism* (New York: Oxford University Press, 1994), p. 68.
50. Gennaro, "Clare, Agnes, and Their Earliest Followers," p. 42.
51. Lezlie Knox, "Audacious Nuns: Institutionalizing the Franciscan Order of Saint Clare," *Church History* 69 (2000), pp. 42–47.
52. Gennaro, "Clare, Agnes, and Their Earliest Followers," p. 48.
53. Petroff, *Body and Soul*, p. 69.
54. Ibid., pp. 68–76.
55. Tore Nyberg, "On Female Monasticism and Scandinavia," *Medieval Scandinavia* 13 (2000), pp. 181–97, at p. 191.
56. Norman Tanner, *The Church in Late Medieval Norwich, 1370–1532* (Toronto: Pontifical Institute of Mediaeval Studies, 1984), pp. 64–66, 130–31; Robert Gilchrist and Marilyn Oliva, *Religious Women in Medieval East Anglia* (Norwich: Centre of East Anglian Studies, 1993), pp. 17, 71–74, 95–96.

57. Walter Simon, *Cities of Ladies: Beguine Communities in the Medieval Low Countries, 1200–1565* (Philadelphia: University of Pennsylvania Press, 2003).
58. J. M. Robinson, *Nobility and Annihilation in Marguerite Porete's* Mirror of Simple Souls (Albany, NY: SUNY Press, 2001).
59. There is a large literature on late-medieval female mystics. For starters, see Valerie M. Lagorio, "The Medieval Continental Women Mystics: An Introduction," in *An Introduction to the Medieval Mystics of Europe*, ed. Paul Szarmach (Albany: SUNY Press, 1984), pp. 161–94; Petroff, *Body and Soul.*
60. Donald Weinstein and Rudolph Bell, *Saints and Society* (Chicago: University of Chicago Press, 1982), pp. 220–26.
61. Thomas Luongo, *The Saintly Politics of Catherine of Siena* (Ithaca: Cornell University Press, 2006).
62. Bynum, *Holy Feast*, pp. 33–47, 246–51.
63. Petroff, *Body and Soul*, pp. 182–203, 211–15.
64. James A. Brundage and Elizabeth A. Makowski, "Enclosure of Nuns: The Decretal of *Periculoso* and Its Commentators," *Journal of Medieval History* 20 (1994), pp. 143–55.
65. R. I. Burns, "The Parish as Frontier Institution in Thirteenth-Century Valencia," *Speculum* 37 (1962), pp. 244–51.
66. Moore, *Origins*, p. 74.
67. James A. Brundage, *Law, Sex, and Christian Society in Medieval Europe* (Chicago: University of Chicago Press, 1987), pp. 494–503; Shannon McSheffrey, *Marriage, Sex, and Civic Culture in Late Medieval London* (Philadelphia: University of Pennsylvania Press, 2006), pp. 21–47; Christiane Klapisch-Zuber, "Zacharias, or the Ousted Father: Nuptial Rites in Tuscany between Giotto and the Council of Trent," in *Women, Family, and Ritual in Renaissance Italy*, trans. Lydia G. Cochrane (Chicago: University of Chicago Press, 1988), pp. 178–212; Katherine L. French, *The People of the Parish: Community Life in a Medieval English Diocese* (Philadelphia: University of Pennsylvania Press, 2001), p. 28.
68. French, *People of the Parish*, p. 29.
69. Ibid., p. 30.
70. Beat Kümin, "The European Perspective," in *The Parish in English Life: 1400–1600*, ed. Katherine L. French, Gary G. Gibbs, and Beat Kümin (Manchester: Manchester University Press, 1997), p. 24; Burns, "Parish as Frontier Institution," pp. 249–50.
71. French, *People of the Parish*, p. 30.
72. Ibid.
73. Kümin, "The European Perspective," p. 25.
74. Samuel L. Cohn, "Piety and Religious Practice in the Rural Dependencies of Renaissance Florence," *English Historical Review* 114 (1999), pp. 1121–42, at p. 1138.
75. Katherine L. French, "Women Churchwardens in Late Medieval England," in *The Parish in Late Medieval England*, ed. Clive Burgess and Eamon Duffy (Donington, Lincolnshire: Shaun Tyas/Paul Watkins Publishing, 2006), pp. 302–21.
76. See Sandy Bardsley's contribution to this volume (chapter 6).

77. French, *The Good Women of the Parish: Gender and Religion after the Black Death* (Philadelphia: University of Pennsylvania Press, 2008), p. 34.
78. French, *Good Women*, pp. 37–48; Giovanna Benadusi, "Investing the Riches of the Poor: Servants and Their Last Wills," *American Historical Review* 109 (2004), pp. 805–26; Martha C. Howell, "Fixing Movables: Gifts by Testament in Late Medieval Douai," *Past & Present* 150 (1996), pp. 3–45.
79. Howell, "Fixing Movables," pp. 12–13.
80. Cohn, "Piety and Religious Practice," p. 1135; French, *Good Women*, p. 43.
81. Wendy R. Larson, "Maternal Patronage of the Cult of St. Margaret," in *Gendering the Master Narrative: Women and Power in the Middle Ages*, ed. Mary C. Erler and Maryanne Kowaleski (Ithaca: Cornell University Press, 2003), p. 100.
82. French, *Good Women*, p. 135.
83. Eamon Duffy, "Holy Maydens, Holy Wyfes: The Cult of Women Saints in Fifteenth and Sixteenth Century England," in *Women in the Church*, ed. W. J. Sheils and Diana Wood (Oxford: Basil Blackwell, 1990), pp. 175–96.
84. Jean-Claude Schmitt, *The Holy Greyhound: Guinefort, Healer of Children since the Thirteenth Century* (Cambridge: Cambridge University Press, 1983).
85. French, *Good Women*, p. 57.
86. Ibid., p. 58.
87. Paula M. Rieder, *On the Purification of Women: Churching in Northern France, 1100–1500* (New York: Palgrave/Macmillan, 2006), pp. 3–6.
88. Becky R. Lee, "Men's Recollections of a Woman's Rite: Medieval English Men's Recollections regarding the Rite of the Purification of Women after Childbirth," *Gender & History* 14 (2002), pp. 224–41.
89. Rieder, *Purification of Women*, p. 140.
90. Cohn, "Piety and Religious Practice," pp. 1121–42; Katherine L. French, "Parochial Fund-Raising in Late Medieval Somerset," in *The Parish in Late Medieval England*, ed. Burgess and Duffy, pp. 115–32.
91. J.A.F. Thomson, *Later Lollards, 1414–1520* (Oxford: Oxford University Press, 1965); Gabriel Audisio, *The Waldensian Dissent: Persecution and Survival, c. 1170–1570* (Cambridge: Cambridge University Press, 1999), pp. 161–214.
92. Elisabeth Schüssler Fiorenza, *In Memory of Her: A Feminist Theological Reconstruction of Christian Origins* (New York: Crossroads, 1983).
93. Malcolm Lambert, *Medieval Heresy: Popular Movements from the Gregorian Reform to the Reformation* (Oxford: Blackwell, 1992), p. 107; Carol Lansing, *Power and Purity: Cathar Heresy in Medieval Italy* (New York: Oxford University Press, 1998), pp. 81–134.
94. Lansing, *Power and* Purity, pp. 116–25; Shannon McSheffrey, *Gender and Heresy: Women and Men in Lollard Communities, 1420–1530* (Philadelphia: University of Pennsylvania Press, 1995). See also Shulamith Shahar, *Women in a Medieval Heretical Sect: Agnes and Huguette the Waldensians* (Woodbridge: Boydell Press, 2001); John Hine Mundy, *Men and Women at Toulouse in the Age of the Cathars* (Toronto: Pontifical Institute of Medieval Studies, 1990); Richard Abels and Ellen Harrison, "The Participation of Women in Languedocian Catharism," *Medieval Studies*

41 (1979), pp. 215–51; Peter Biller, "Cathars and Material Women," in *Medieval Theology and the Natural Body*, ed. Peter Biller and Alastair Minnis (York: York Medieval Press, 1997), pp. 61–107.

95. Audisio, *Waldensian Dissent*, pp. 36–37.
96. Shahar, *Women in a Medieval Heretical Sect*, pp. 46–65.
97. Malcolm Lambert, *The Cathars* (Oxford: Blackwell, 1998), pp. 59–63.
98. Lansing, *Power and Purity*, pp. 151–57.
99. Ibid., pp. 117.
100. Lambert, *The Cathars*, pp. 77–79.
101. Ibid., pp. 102–7.
102. Margaret Aston, *Lollards and Reformers: Images and Literacy in Late Medieval Religion* (London: Hambledon, 1984), pp. 197–200; McSheffrey, *Gender and Heresy*, pp. 8–10.
103. Margaret Aston, "Lollard Women Priests?" *Journal of Ecclesiastical History* 31 (1980), pp. 441–61.
104. McSheffrey, *Gender and Heresy*, pp. 109–23.

Chapter 4

1. Andre de Resende, *Aegidius Scallabitanus: Um Diálogo sobre Fr. Gil de Santarém*, ed. Virgínia Soares Pereira (Lisbon: Fundação Calouste Gulbenkian, 2000), pp. 550–53.
2. Iona McCleery, "*Multos ex Medicinae Arte Curaverat, Multos Verbo et Oratione*: Curing in Medieval Portuguese Saints' Lives," in *Signs, Wonders, Miracles: Representations of Divine Power in the Life of the Church*, ed. Kate Cooper and Jeremy Gregory, Studies in Church History 41 (Woodbridge: Boydell, 2005), pp. 192–202.
3. Monica H. Green, *Women's Healthcare in the Medieval West: Texts and Contexts* (Aldershot: Ashgate, 2000); Monica H. Green, *Making Women's Medicine Masculine: The Rise of Male Authority in Pre-Modern Gynecology* (Oxford: Oxford University Press, 2008); *The Trotula: A Medieval Compendium of Women's Medicine*, ed. Monica H. Green (Philadelphia: University of Pennsylvania Press, 2001).
4. For example, Katharine Park, *Secrets of Women: Gender, Generation and the Origins of Human Dissection* (New York: Zone Books, 2006); *The Material Culture of Sex, Procreation and Marriage in Pre-Modern Europe*, ed. Anne McClanan and Karen Rosoff Encarnación (New York: Palgrave, 2002).
5. Monica H. Green, "Bodies, Gender, Health, Disease: Recent Work on Medieval Women's Medicine," *Studies in Medieval and Renaissance History* (3rd ser.), 2 (2005), pp. 1–46. See also Monica H. Green, "Bibliography on Medieval Women, Gender and Medicine (1989–2009)," *Digital Library of Sciència.cat*, February 2010, Universitat de Barcelona, http://www.sciencia.cat/biblioteca/documents/green_CumulativeBib_Feb2010.pdf (accessed March 3, 2010).
6. Peter Burke, *What Is Cultural History?* (Cambridge: Polity, 2004); Peter Mandler, "The Problem with Cultural History," *Cultural and Social History* 1 (2004), pp. 94–117; Dror Wahrman, "Change and the Corporeal in Seventeenth- and

Eighteenth-Century Gender History; or, Can Cultural History Be Rigorous?" *Gender & History* 20 (2008), pp. 584–602.

7. Monica H. Green, "Gendering the History of Women's Healthcare," *Gender & History* 20 (2008), pp. 487–518; Monica H. Green, "Integrative Medicine: Incorporating Medicine and Health into the Canon of Medieval European History," *History Compass* 7 (2009), pp. 1218–45. For debates about medical history, see *Locating Medical History: the Stories and their Meanings*, ed. Frank Huisman and John Harley Warner (Baltimore: Johns Hopkins University Press, 2004); George Weisz, "Making Medical History," *Bulletin of the History of Medicine* 80 (2006), pp. 153–59; Roger Cooter, "After Death/After-'Life': The Social History of Medicine in Post-Postmodernity," *Social History of Medicine* 20 (2007), pp. 441–64; Jonathan Toms, "So What? A Reply to Roger Cooter's 'After Death/After-"Life": The Social History of Medicine in Post-Postmodernity,'" *Social History of Medicine* 22 (2009), pp. 609–15.
8. Mary Fissell, "Making Meaning from the Margins: The New Cultural History of Medicine," in *Locating Medical History: The Stories and their Meanings*, ed. Frank Huisman and John Harley Warner (Baltimore: Johns Hopkins University Press, 2004), pp. 364–89 (at p. 365).
9. Monica H. Green and Daniel Smail, "The Trial of Floreta d'Ays (1403): Jews, Christians and Obstetrics in Later Medieval Marseille," *Journal of Medieval History* 34 (2008), pp. 185–211.
10. Brian Dolan, "History, Medical Humanities and Medical Education," *Social History of Medicine* 23 (2010), pp. 393–405.
11. Roy Porter, "The Patient's View: Doing Medical History from Below," *Theory and Society* 14 (1985), pp. 175–98.
12. Flurin Condrau, "The Patient's View Meets the Clinical Gaze," *Social History of Medicine* 20 (2007), pp. 525–40.
13. Lucinda Beier, *Sufferers and Healers: The Experience of Illness in Seventeenth-Century England* (London: Routledge, 1987); Mary Fissell, *Patients, Power and the Poor in Eighteenth-Century Bristol* (Cambridge: Cambridge University Press, 1991); Barbara Duden, *The Woman Beneath the Skin: A Doctor's Patients in Eighteenth Century Germany*, trans. Thomas Dunlap (Cambridge MA: Harvard University Press, 1991); Gianna Pomata, *Contracting a Cure: Patients, Healers, and the Law in Early Modern Bologna* (Baltimore: Johns Hopkins University Press, 1998); Michael Stolberg, *Experiencing Illness and the Sick Body in Early Modern Europe*, trans. Leonhard Unglaub and Logan Kennedy (Basingstoke: Palgrave Macmillan, 2011); Alisha Rankin, "Duchess Heal Thyself: Elisabeth of Rochlitz and the Patient's Perspective in Early-Modern Germany," *Bulletin of the History of Medicine* 82 (2008), pp. 109–44.
14. Porter, "Patient's View," pp. 181–82.
15. Exceptions are Michael McVaugh, *Medicine before the Plague: Patients and Practitioners in the Medieval Crown of Aragon, 1285–1345* (Cambridge: Cambridge University Press, 1993); John Henderson, *The Renaissance Hospital: Healing the Body and Healing the Soul* (New Haven: Yale University Press, 2006).
16. Porter, "Patient's View," p. 188.

17. Sandra Cavallo, *Artisans of the Body in Early Modern Italy: Identities, Families and Masculinities* (Manchester: Manchester University Press, 2007); David Gentilcore, *Medical Charlatanism in Early-Modern Italy* (Oxford: Oxford University Press, 2006); Margaret Pelling, *The Common Lot: Sickness, Medical Occupations and the Urban Poor in Early Modern England* (London: Longman, 1998).
18. Cathleen Hoeniger, "The Illuminated *Tacuinum Sanitatis* Manuscripts from Northern Italy *c.* 1380–1400: Sources, Patrons and the Creation of a New Pictorial Genre," in *Visualizing Medieval Medicine and Natural History, 1200–1550*, ed. Jean Givens, Karen Reeds, and Alain Touwaide (Ashgate: Aldershot, 2006), pp. 51–81.
19. Mary Fissell, "Introduction: Women, Health and Healing in Early-Modern Europe," *Bulletin of the History of Medicine* 82 (2008), pp. 1–17; Carole Rawcliffe, "A Marginal Occupation? The Medieval Laundress and Her Work," *Gender & History* 21 (2009), pp. 147–69; Rebecca Winer, "Conscripting the Breast: Lactation, Slavery and Salvation in the Realms of Aragon and Kingdom of Majorca, *c.* 1250–1300," *Journal of Medieval History* 34 (2008), pp. 164–84.
20. Becky Lee, "A Company of Women *and* Men: Men's Recollections of Childbirth in Medieval England," *Journal of Family History* 27 (2002), pp. 92–100.
21. *The Celestina: A Fifteenth-Century Spanish Novel in Dialogue*, ed. Lesley Byrd Simpson (Berkeley: University of California Press, 2006), p. 17. See Michael Solomon, *The Literature of Misogyny in Medieval Spain* (New York: Cambridge University Press, 1997); Jean Dangler, *Mediating Fictions: Literature, Women Healers and the Go-Between in Medieval and Early-Modern Iberia* (Cranbury, NJ: Associated University Presses, 2001). Celestina is not mentioned explicitly in Montserrat Cabré, "Women or Healers? Household Practices and the Categories of Health Care in Late Medieval Iberia," *Bulletin of the History of Medicine* 82 (2008), pp. 18–51.
22. Louise Tilly, "Women's History and Family History: Fruitful Collaboration or Missed Connection?" *Journal of Family History* 12 (1987), pp. 303–15; Felicity Riddy, "Looking Closely: Authority and Intimacy in the Late Medieval Urban Home," in *Gendering the Master Narrative: Women and Power in the Middle Ages*, ed. Mary C. Erler and Maryanne Kowaleski (Ithaca: Cornell University Press, 2003), pp. 212–28; Peregrine Horden, "Family History and Hospital History in the Middle Ages," in Peregrine Horden, *Hospitals and Healing from Antiquity to the Later Middle Ages* (Aldershot: Ashgate, 2008), article VI; Anne Grauer and Patricia Stuart-Macadam, eds., *Sex and Gender in Paleopathological Perspective* (Cambridge: Cambridge University Press, 1998); Christopher Woolgar, "Food and the Middle Ages," *Journal of Medieval History* 36 (2010), pp. 1–19.
23. Isidore of Seville, *The Etymologies of Isidore of Seville*, trans. Stephen Barney, W. J. Lewis, J. A. Beach, and Oliver Berghof (Cambridge: Cambridge University Press, 2006), p. 109.
24. Marcia Kupfer, *The Art of Healing: Painting for the Sick and the Sinner in a Medieval Town* (University Park: Pennsylvania State University Press, 2003); Stephen Harper, *Insanity, Individuals and Society in Late-Medieval English Literature:*

The Subject of Madness (New York: Edwin Mellen, 2003); Jeremy Citrome, *The Surgeon in Medieval English Literature* (Basingstoke: Palgrave Macmillan, 2007).

25. Geoffrey Chaucer, *Riverside Chaucer*, ed. Larry Benson, 3rd ed. (Boston: Houghton Mifflin, 1987), pp. 30–31; Margery Kempe, *The Book of Margery Kempe*, ed. Lynn Staley (New York: Norton, 2001); Norman Davis, ed., *Paston Letters and Papers of the Fifteenth Century*, 2 vols. (Oxford: Oxford University Press, 1971–76), vol. 1, pp. 218–19.
26. Scholars of medieval hagiography have done this for a long time and now influence modern historians: see Jacalyn Duffin, *Medical Miracles: Doctors, Saints and Healing in the Modern World* (Oxford: Oxford University Press, 2009). However, there is much less interest in medical motifs in letters and chronicles.
27. Richelle Munkhoff, "Searchers of the Dead: Authority, Marginality, and the Interpretation of Plague in England, 1574–1665," *Gender & History* 11 (1999), pp. 1–29; Deborah Harkness, "A View from the Streets: Women and Medical Work in Elizabethan London," *Bulletin of the History of Medicine* 82 (2008), pp. 52–85.
28. Jon Arrizabalaga, "Problematizing Retrospective Diagnosis in the History of Disease," *Asclepio* 54 (2002), pp. 51–70; Andrew Cunningham, "Identifying Disease in the Past: Cutting the Gordian Knot," *Asclepio* 54 (2002), pp. 13–34.
29. See Emily Cockayne, *Hubbub: Filth, Noise and Stench in England, 1600–1770* (New Haven: Yale University Press 2007), for a study that does not impose modern terms of analysis but explores how street lighting, personal hygiene, occupational health, and building regulations were debated in the language of the time.
30. Peter Biller, *The Measure of Multitude: Population in Medieval Thought* (Oxford: Oxford University Press, 2000). A survey of the extracts in Rosemary Horrox, ed., *The Black Death* (Manchester: Manchester University Press, 1994), suggests that plague killed indiscriminately in the first epidemic in 1347–52 but affected women less when it returned in 1361. For archival evidence supporting these impressions, see Samuel Cohn, *The Black Death Transformed: Disease and Culture in Early Renaissance Europe* (London: Arnold, 2003), pp. 210–12.
31. P.J.P. Goldberg, *Women, Work and Lifecycle in a Medieval Economy: Women in York and Yorkshire, c. 1300–1520* (Oxford: Clarendon, 1992); Mavis Mate, *Daughters, Wives and Widows after the Black Death: Women in Sussex, 1350–1535* (Boydell: Woodbridge, 1998); Samuel Cohn, "Women and Work in Renaissance Italy," in *Gender and Society in Renaissance Italy*, ed. Judith Brown and Robert Davis (London: Longman, 1998), pp. 107–26; Stephen Rigby, "Gendering the Black Death: Women in Later Medieval England," *Gender & History* 12 (2000), pp. 745–54; Katherine L. French, *The Good Women of the Parish: Gender and Religion after the Black Death* (Philadelphia: University of Pennsylvania Press, 2008).
32. Biller, *Measure of Multitude*, pp. 253–95; Monica H. Green, "Flowers, Poisons and Men: Menstruation in Medieval Western Europe," in *Menstruation: A Cultural History*, ed. Andrew Shail and Gillian Howie (Basingstoke: Palgrave Macmillan, 2005), pp. 51–64.
33. Christine Carpenter, ed., *Kingsford's Stonor Letters and Papers, 1290–1483* (Cambridge: Cambridge University Press, 1996), p. 382.

34. Marie Kelleher, *The Measure of Women: Law and Female Identity in the Crown of Aragon* (Philadelphia: University of Pennsylvania Press, 2010).
35. It should, however, be noted that objects and images can be read as texts, and artifacts are often difficult to interpret without supplementary documentation: Richard Grassby, "Material Culture and Cultural History," *Journal of Interdisciplinary History* 35 (2005), pp. 591–603.
36. Biller, *Measure of Multitude*, pp. 292–93; Anne Grauer, "Life Patterns of Women from Medieval York," in *The Archaeology of Gender*, ed. Dale Walde and Noreen Willows (Calgary: University of Calgary Archaeological Association, 1991), pp. 407–13; Charlotte Roberts and Margaret Cox, *Health and Disease in Britain: From Prehistory to the Present Day* (Stroud: Sutton, 2003), pp. 278–85.
37. Loren MacKinney, *Medical Illustrations in Medieval Manuscripts* (Berkeley, University of California Press, 1965); Peter Murray Jones, *Medieval Medical Miniatures* (London: British Library, 1984), reissued as *Medieval Medicine in Illuminated Manuscripts* (London: British Library, 1998); *Visualizing Medieval Medicine and Natural History, 1200–1550*, ed. Jean Givens, Karen Reeds, and Alain Touwaide (Aldershot: Ashgate, 2006).
38. Renate Blumenfeld-Kosinski, *Not of Woman Born: Representations of Caesarean Section in Medieval and Renaissance Culture* (Ithaca: Cornell University Press, 1990); Jacqueline Musacchio, *The Art and Ritual of Childbirth in Renaissance Italy* (New Haven: Yale University Press, 1999).
39. See also Adrian Randolph, "Gendering the Period Eye: *Deschi da Parto* and Renaissance Visual Culture," *Art History* 27 (2004), pp. 538–62; Elizabeth L'Estrange, *Holy Motherhood: Gender, Dynasty and Visual Culture in the Later Middle Ages* (Manchester: Manchester University Press, 2008), pp. 32–40.
40. Madeline Caviness, "Patron or Matron? A Capetian Bride and a Vade Mecum for her Marriage Bed," *Speculum* 68 (1993), pp. 333–62; Joan Holladay, "The Education of Jeanne d'Evreux: Personal Piety and Dynastic Salvation in her Book of Hours at the Cloisters," *Art History* 17 (1994), pp. 585–611.
41. Kathleen Nolan, *Queens in Stone and Silver: The Creation of a Visual Imagery of Queenship in Capetian France* (New York: Palgrave Macmillan, 2009).
42. Geoffroy de la Tour Landry, *The Book of the Knight of the Tower*, trans. William Caxton (London: Early English Text Society, 1971), pp. 76–78.
43. Anne of France, *Lessons for My Daughter*, trans. Sharon Jansen (Cambridge: D. S. Brewer, 2004), pp. 37–38, 41–42.
44. Green, "Bodies, Gender, Health and Disease," p. 4; Cabré, "Women or Healers?"; Carmen Cabellero-Navas, "The Care of Women's Health and Beauty: An Experience Shared by Medieval Jewish and Christian Women," *Journal of Medieval History* 34 (2008), pp. 146–63.
45. Surviving tombs, sculptures, altar paintings, relics, and books of hours are suggestive of attitudes toward spiritual and physical health. There are also intriguing documentary references to long-lost objects, such as a mirror that cured paralysis belonging to Princess Mafalda (d. 1257): Filomeno Soares da Silva, ed., *Cartulário de D. Maior Martins: seculo XIII* (Arouca: Associação da Defesa do Património Arouquense, 2001), p. 165. See p. 98 for an emerald ring that promoted chastity.

46. Mário da Costa Roque, *As Pestes Medievais Europeias e o Regimento Proveitoso Contra ha Pestenença* (Paris: Fundação Calouste Gulbenkian/Centro Cultural Português, 1979); João Pedro Ferro, "Para o Estudo da População Portuguesa Medieval: O Caso de Alenquer," *História* 122 (1989), pp. 38–65; Ana Maria Rodrigues, "A População de Torres Vedras em 1381," *Revista de História Económica e Social* 25 (1989), pp. 15–46; Ole Benedictow, *The Black Death, 1346–1353: A Complete History* (Woodbridge: Boydell, 2004), pp. 77–90, 283–94.
47. Maria Helena da Cruz Coelho, "A Mulher e o Trabalho nas Cidades Medievales Portuguesas," in *Homens, Espaços e Poderes: Séculos XI–XVI*, vol. 1, *Notas do Viver Social* (Lisbon: Livros Horizonte, 1990), pp. 37–59; Vitaline Cardoso Ferreira, "A Presença da Mulher na Legislação Medieval Portuguesa," 2 vols. (MA diss., University of Lisbon, 2006); Iria Gonçalves, "Regateiras, Padeiras e Outras Mais na Lisboa Medieval," in *Lisboa Medieval: Os Rostos da Cidade*, ed. Luís Krus, Luís Felipe Oliveira and João Luís Fontes (Lisbon: Livros Horizonte, 2007), pp. 11–29.
48. *Chancelarias Portuguesas: D. Duarte*, ed. João José Alves Dias, 4 vols. (Lisbon: Centro de Estudos Históricos, Universidade Nova, 1998–2002), vol. 3, pp. 477–79.
49. Pedro de Azevedo, ed., *Documentos das Chancelarias Reais Anteriores a 1531 Relativos a Marrocos*, 2 vols. (Lisbon: Academia das Sciências, 1915–34), vol. 1, pp. 321–22. For the problems with interpreting pardon letters, see p. 99.
50. Pedro López de Ayala, *Crónicas*, ed. José Luis Martín (Barcelona: Planeta, 1991), pp. 7–9.
51. Gomes Eanes de Zurara, *Crónica da Tomada de Ceuta*, ed. Reis Brasil (Mem Martins: Europa-América, 1992); Jennifer Goodman, *Chivalry and Exploration, 1298–1630* (Woodbridge: Boydell, 1998), pp. 134–48; Iona McCleery, "Both 'Illness and Temptation of the Enemy': Understanding Melancholy in the Writings of King Duarte of Portugal (1433–38)," *Journal of Medieval Iberian Studies* 1 (2009), pp. 163–78.
52. Fernão Lopes, *Crónica de D. João I*, 2 vols. (Oporto: Livraria Civilização, 1963–68), vol. 1, pp. 309–15; Iona McCleery, "Medical 'Emplotment' and Plotting Medicine: Health and Disease in Late Medieval Portuguese Chronicles," *Social History of Medicine* 24 (2011), pp. 125–41.
53. Manuel Lopes de Almeida, Idalino da Costa Brochado, and António Dias Dinis, eds., *Monumenta Henricina*, 15 vols. (Coimbra and Lisbon: Comissão Executiva do V Centenário da Morte do Infante D. Henrique, 1960–74), vol. 1, pp. 289–90 (Maria Vasques); vol. 3, p. 151 (Mécia Gonçalves); vol. 4, p. 232 (Mécia Lourenço); vol. 6, p. 127 (wife of Rodrigo Esteves).
54. João Álvares, *Obras*, ed. Adelino de Almeida Calado (Coimbra: Acta Universitatis Conimbrigensis, 1960), pp. 6–7.
55. Rita Costa Gomes, *The Making of a Court Society: Kings and Nobles in Late Medieval Portugal*, trans. A. Aiken (Cambridge: Cambridge University Press, 2003), pp. 387–89; Jacques Paviot, "Les *Honneurs de la Cour* de d'Éleonore de Poitiers," in *Autour de Marguerite d'Écosse: Reines, Princesses et Dames du XVe Siècle*, ed. Geneviève Contamine and Philippe Contamine (Paris: Champion, 1999), pp. 163–79.

56. Isabel and her husband rewarded Mor Gonçalves and another wet nurse, Anne, for their services during the 1430s: *Portugal et Bourgogne au XVe Siècle*, ed. Jacques Paviot (Lisbon and Paris: Centre Culturel Calouste Gulbenkian/Commission Nationale pour les Commémorations des Découvertes Portugaises, 1995), pp. 91, 103–4.
57. Mário Martins, "O Bispo-Menino, o Rito de Salibúria e a Capela Real Portuguesa," in *Estudos de Cultura Medieval*, 3 vols. (Lisbon: Editorial Verbo, 1969), vol. 3, pp. 237–52.
58. Peter Rushton, "Purification or Social Control? Ideologies of Reproduction and the Churching of Women after Childbirth," in *The Public and the Private*, ed. Eva Gamarnikov, David H. J. Morgan, June Purvis, and Daphne Taylorson (London: Heinemann, 1983), pp. 118–31; Becky Lee, "The Purification of Women after Childbirth: A Window onto Medieval Perceptions of Women," *Florilegium* 14 (1995–96), pp. 43–55; Gail Gibson, "Blessing from Sun and Moon: Churching as Women's Theatre," in *Bodies and Disciplines: Intersections of Literature and History in Fifteenth Century England*, ed. Barbara Hanawalt and David Wallace (London: Minnesota University Press, 1996), pp. 139–54; Joanne Pierce, " 'Green Women' and Blood Pollution: Some Medieval Rituals for the Churching of Women after Childbirth," *Studia Liturgica* 29 (1999), pp. 191–215; Becky Lee, "Men's Recollections of a Women's Rite: Medieval English Men's Recollections regarding the Rite of the Purification of Women after Childbirth," *Gender & History* 14 (2002), pp. 224–41; Paula Rieder, *On the Purification of Women: Churching in Northern France, 1100–1500* (New York: Palgrave Macmillan, 2006).
59. João José Alves Dias, ed., *Livro dos Conselhos de El-Rei D. Duarte (Livro da Cartuxa)* (Lisbon: Editorial Estampa, 1982), pp. 146, 257. The suggestion about the last birth was a personal communication from Ana Maria Rodrigues of the University of Lisbon who is currently working on a biography of Leonor.
60. *Chancelaria de D. Afonso V*, bk. 19, fol. 91, Arquivos Nacionais da Torre do Tombo (ANTT), Lisbon. It is likely that attendance at childbirth was not yet a formal occupation in Portugal.
61. Rui de Pina, *Crónicas*, ed. Manuel Lopes de Almeida (Oporto: Lello & Irmão, 1977), p. 693. The suggestion of an infection comes from Ana Maria Rodrigues in a personal communication.
62. Afonso V and his wife Isabel had João (1451), Joana (1452–90), and Joao II (1455–95); João II and his wife Leonor had Afonso (1475–91), killed in a riding accident; King Manuel and his first wife, Isabel, had Miguel (1498–1500).
63. Fernando da Silva Correia, "A Causa da Morte da Infanta Santa Joana: uma História Clínica do Século XV," *A Medicina Contemporânea* 23–24 (1942), offprint; Fernando da Silva Correia and Júlio Dantas, "O Julgamento da Rainha D. Leonor: Seguido de Três Relatórios Médicos," *Occidente* 19 (1943), offprint. For a modern description of the king's death, see Luís Adão da Fonseca, *João II* (Lisbon: Círculo de Leitores, 2005), pp. 173–78.
64. *Pina,* Crónicas, pp. 768–69.
65. João Vasconcelos, ed., *Romarias: Um Inventário dos Santuários de Portugal*, 2 vols. (Lisbon: OLHAPIM, 1996–98), vol. 2, pp. 381–82. João II's presence in the region was explicitly for fertility reasons according to Pina, *Crónicas*, pp. 925–26.

66. António Gomes da Rocha Madahil, ed., *Crónica da Fundação do Mosteiro de Jesus de Aveiro e Memorial da Infanta Santa Joana Filha del Rei D. Afonso V* (Aveiro: Francisco Ferreiro Neves, 1939).
67. Caroline Walker Bynum, *Holy Feast and Holy Fast: The Religious Significance of Food to Medieval Women* (Berkeley: University of California Press, 1987); Aviad Kleinberg, *Prophets in Their Own Country: Living Saints and the Making of Sainthood in the Later Middle Ages* (Chicago: University of Chicago Press, 1992).
68. Fernando Jasmins Pereira, ed., *Documentos Sobre a Madeira no Século XVI Existentes no Corpo Cronológico: Análise Documental*, 2 vols. (Lisbon: Arquivo Nacional da Torre do Tombo, 1990), vol. 1, pp. 86, 189.
69. Célia Rodrigues Lopes, "As Clarissas de Coimbra dos Séculos XIV a XVII: Paleobiologia de uma Comunidade Religiosa de Santa Clara-a-Velha" (MA diss., University of Coimbra, 2001).
70. Natalie Zemon Davis, *Fiction in the Archives: Pardon Tales and their Tellers in Sixteenth-Century France* (Stanford: Stanford University Press, 1987). No trace of the medieval Portuguese system of criminal justice survives below the level of the royal pardon: Luís Miguel Duarte, *Justiça e Criminalidade no Portugal Medievo (1459–1481)* (Lisbon: Fundação Calouste Gulbenkian, 1999); Isabel Ribeiro de Queirós, "Theudas e Mantheudas: A Criminalidade Feminina no Reinado de D. João II Através das Cartas de Perdão (1481–1485)," 2 vols. (MA diss., University of Oporto, 1999).
71. *Documentos das Chancelarias Reais*, vol. 2, pp. 251–52.
72. *Documentos das Chancelarias Reais*, vol. 2, pp. 585–86.
73. Possidónio Laranjo Coelho, ed., *Documentos Inéditos de Marrocos: Chancelaria de D. João II* (Lisbon: Imprensa Nacional, 1943), pp. 286–87.
74. *Documentos Inéditos de Marrocos*, p. 353.
75. We do not know to what extent colonial exile was perceived as a death penalty due to the likelihood of disease and injury.
76. Pierre-André Sigal, *L'Homme et le Miracle dans la France Médiévale, XIe–XIIe siècle* (Paris: Cerf, 1985), pp. 242, 259–61, 300–1; Ronald Finucane, *Miracles and Pilgrims: Popular Beliefs in Medieval England*, new ed. (New York: St. Martin's Press, 1995), p. 143. The same proportion of women is reported in José Mattoso, "Saúde Corporal e Saúde Mental na Idade Média Portuguesa," in *Fragmentos de uma Composição Medieval* (Lisbon: Estampa, 1987), pp. 233–52. For some insight, see Kathleen Quirk, "Men, Women and Miracles in Normandy, 1050–1150," in *Medieval Memories: Men, Women and the Past, 700–1300*, ed. Elisabeth Van Houts (Harlow: Longman, 2001), pp. 53–71.
77. My own findings based on the eighty miracles in Resende, *Aegidius Scallabitanus*.
78. Resende, *Aegidius Scallabitanus*, p. 360.
79. Ibid., p. 316–17.
80. José Joaquim Nunes, ed., "Livro que Fala da Boa Vida que Fez a Reynha de Portugal, Dona Isabel," *Boletim da Segunda Classe da Academia das Sciências de Lisboa* 13 (1918–19), pp. 1293–1384 (at pp. 1382–83); Iona McCleery, "Isabel of Aragon (d. 1336): Model Queen or Model Saint?" *Journal of Ecclesiastical History* 57 (2006), pp. 668–92.

81. Jewish practitioners and barbers will feature prominently in my forthcoming monograph.
82. Irisalva Moita, *V Centenário do Hospital de Todos os Santos* (Lisbon: Correios de Portugal, 1992).
83. *Chancelaria de D. Afonso V*, bk. 15, fol. 99, ANTT, Lisbon.
84. Maria Gomes was licensed for healing in 1517, and Joana Martins, described as poor, old, and harmless, was pardoned for blessing children with "damaged mouths" in 1522: *Chancelaria de D. Manuel*, bk. 25, fol. 165v, ANTT, Lisbon; *Chancelaria de D. João III*, bk. 46, fol. 144v, ANTT, Lisbon.
85. Saúl António Gomes, "Higiene e Saúde na Leiria Medieval," in *III colóquio sobre a história de Leiria e da sua região* (Leiria: Câmara Municipal, 1999), pp. 9–43; Manuela Mendonça, "A Reforma da Saúde no Reinado de D. Manuel," in *1as Jornadas de História do Direito Hispânico: Actas* (Lisbon: Academia Portuguesa da História, 2004), pp. 221–41.
86. Resende, *Aegidius Scallabitanus*, pp. 341–42.
87. *Vereações*, bk. 5, fols. 26–26v, 162 and bk. 6, fol. 4, Arquivo Histórico Municipal, Oporto; José Pereira da Costa, ed., *Vereações da Câmara Municipal do Funchal: Primeira Metade do Século XVI* (Funchal: Secretária Regional de Turismo e Cultura/Centro de Estudos de História do Atlântico, 1998), pp. 139–40.
88. Margarida Anes was a *boticaira* to whom houses in Lisbon were leased in 1390: José João Alves Dias, ed., *Chancelarias Portuguesas: D. João I*, 11 vols. (Lisbon: Centro de Estudos Históricos, Universidade Nova de Lisboa, 2004–6), vol. 1, p. 227. Maria Nunes, apothecary of Lamego, set a legal precedent in an adoption case in 1326: Martim de Albuquerque and Eduardo Borges Nunes, eds., *Ordenações del-Rei D. Duarte* (Lisbon: Fundação Calouste Gulbenkian, 1988), p. 387. Both women were widows, suggesting that wives involved in their husbands' occupations may never have been documented. The only female barber, Caterina Anes of Oporto, documented in 1518, was a barber's widow: *Chancelaria de D. Manuel*, bk. 39, fols. 100–101, ANTT, Lisbon.
89. Cristóvão Rodrigues de Oliveira, *Lisboa em 1551: Sumário em que Brevemente se Contêm Algumas Coisas assim Eclesiásticas como Seculares que Há na Cidade de Lisbon*, ed. José da Felicidade Alves (Lisbon: Livros Horizonte, 1987), pp. 99–100, 136–38.
90. Darlene Abreu-Ferreira, "Work and Identity in Early Modern Portugal: What Did Gender Have to Do with It?" *Journal of Social History* 35 (2002), pp. 859–87.
91. "Livro que Fala da Boa Vida," ed. Nunes, pp. 1378–79.
92. Both cases are discussed in Margarida Garcez Ventura, *Igreja e Poder no Século XV: Dinastia de Avis e Liberdades Eclesiásticas (1383–1450)* (Lisbon: Edições Colibri, 1997), pp. 536–37.
93. Maximiano Lemos, *O Auto dos Físicos de Gil Vicente: Comentârio Médico* (Oporto: Tipografia Enciclopédia Portuguesa, 1921).
94. Álvaro Pais, *Estado e Pranto da Igreja*, ed. and trans. Miguel Pinto de Meneses, 8 vols. (Lisbon: Instituto Nacional Investigação Científica, 1988–98), vol. 3, pp. 256–57; Barbara Baert, "'Who Touched My Clothes?': The Healing of the Woman with the Haemorrhage (Mark 5: 24–34; Luke 8: 42–48 and Matthew 9:

19–22) in Early Medieval Visual Culture," *Konsthistorisk Tidskrift/Journal of Art History* 79 (2010), pp. 65–90; Giles Constable, *Three Studies in Medieval Religious and Social Thought* (Cambridge: Cambridge University Press, 1998), pp. 1–142; Grant Lemarquand, *An Issue of Relevance: A Comparative Study of the Story of the Bleeding Woman (Mk 5:25–34; Mt 9:20–22; Lk 8:43–48) in North Atlantic and African Contexts* (New York: Peter Lang, 2004), appendix I; Kupfer, *Art of Healing*, pp. 105–7.

95. For modern debates, see Baert, "Who Touched My Clothes?"; Lemarquand, *Issue of Relevance*; Joan Branham, "Bloody Women and Bloody Spaces: Menses and the Eucharist in Late Antiquity and the Early Middle Ages," *Harvard Divinity Bulletin* 30 (2002), http://www.hds.harvard.edu/news/bulletin/articles/branham.html (accessed May 22, 2011); Elaine Lawless, "Transforming the Master Narrative: How Women Shift the Religious Subject," *Frontiers: A Journal of Women Studies* 24 (2003), pp. 61–75.
96. Wahrman, "Change and the Corporeal," p. 590.
97. Rudolf, "The Life of St. Leoba," in *Soldiers of Christ: Saints and Saints' Lives from Late Antiquity and the Early Middle Ages*, ed. Thomas Noble and Thomas Head (University Park: Pennsylvania State University Press, 1995), pp. 255–77 (at p. 271).
98. Pina, *Crónicas*, pp. 770–71. The suggestion of childbirth complications comes from Ana Maria Rodrigues.
99. Willis Johnson, "The Myth of Jewish Male Menses," *Journal of Medieval History* 24 (1998), pp. 273–95; Irven Resnick, "Medieval Roots of the Myth of Jewish Male Menses," *Harvard Theological Review* 93 (2000), pp. 241–63; Ana Maria Rodrigues, "Entre a Sufocação da Madre e o Prurido do Pénis: Género e Disfunções Sexuais no *Thesaurus Pauperum* de Pedro Hispano," in *Rumos e Escrita da História*, ed. Maria de Fátima Reis (Lisbon: Edições Colibri, 2007), pp. 33–44.
100. Iona McCleery, "Saintly Physician, Diabolical Doctor, Medieval Saint: Exploring the Reputation of Gil de Santarém in Medieval and Renaissance Portugal," *Portuguese Studies* 21 (2005), pp. 112–25.
101. Annemarie Mol, *The Body Multiple: Ontology in Medical Practice* (Durham: Duke University Press, 2002).

Chapter 5

1. Amanda Vickery, "Golden Age to Separate Spheres? A Review of the Categories and Chronology of English Women's History," *The Historical Journal* 36 (1993), pp. 383–414. Among a vast literature on gendered "separate spheres" in modern contexts, see in particular Carol Smith-Rosenberg, "The Female World of Love and Ritual: Relations between Women in Nineteenth-Century America", *Signs* 1 (1975), pp. 1–29; and Leonore Davidoff and Catherine Hall, *Family Fortunes: Men and Women of the English Middle Class, 1780–1850* (Chicago: University of Chicago Press, 1987). Classic critiques include Vickery's 1993 article; Linda Kerber, "Separate Spheres, Female Worlds, Woman's Place: The Rhetoric of Women's History," *Journal of American History* 75 (1988), pp. 9–39; and more recently,

Kim Warren, "Separate Spheres: Analytical Persistence in United States Women's History," *History Compass* 5 (2007), pp. 262–77.

2. Anna Dronzek, "Private and Public Spheres," in *Women and Gender in Medieval Europe: An Encyclopedia*, ed. Margaret Schaus (New York: Routledge, 2006), pp. 670–71 (at p. 670).
3. Shannon McSheffrey, "Place, Space, and Situation: Public and Private in the Making of Marriage in Late-Medieval London," *Speculum* 79 (2004), pp. 960–90.
4. Diane Shaw, "The Construction of the Private in Medieval London," *Journal of Medieval and Early Modern Studies* 26 (1996), pp. 447–66 (esp. pp. 453–57). Parts of her argument are briefly critiqued by McSheffrey, "Place, Space and Situation," p. 989.
5. Felicity Riddy, " 'Burgeis' Domesticity in Late-Medieval England," in *Medieval Domesticity: Home, Housing and Household in Medieval England*, ed. Maryanne Kowaleski and P.J.P. Goldberg (Cambridge: Cambridge University Press, 2008), pp. 14–36 (at p. 33).
6. Felicity Riddy, "Looking Closely: Authority and Intimacy in the Late Medieval Urban Home," in *Gendering the Master Narrative: Women and Power in the Middle Ages*, ed. Mary C. Erler and Maryanne Kowaleski (Ithaca: Cornell University Press, 2003), pp. 212–28. She and Sarah Rees Jones have elsewhere engaged with Jürgen Habermas's exploration of relations between public, private, and intimate spheres as they might apply to medieval contexts: Sarah Rees Jones and Felicity Riddy, "The Bolton Hours of York: Female Domestic Piety and the Public Sphere," in *Household, Women, and Christianities in Late Antiquity and the Middle Ages*, ed. Anneke B. Mulder-Bakker and Jocelyn Wogan-Browne (Turnhout: Brepols, 2005), pp. 215–60 (at p. 218n5, citing Habermas's *The Structural Transformation of the Public Sphere* [Cambridge: Polity Press, 1989]).
7. Georges Duby, "Introduction: Private Power, Public Power," in *A History of Private Life*, vol. 2, *Revelations of the Medieval World*, ed. Georges Duby, trans. Arthur Goldhammer (Cambridge, MA, and London: Belknap Press of Harvard University Press, 1988; originally published 1985), pp. 3–31 (at pp. 3–6).
8. Maryanne Kowaleski and P.J.P. Goldberg note the *OED*'s earliest entries for *domesticity* and *domestic* as 1726 and 1521, respectively: "Introduction. Medieval Domesticity: Home, Housing and Household," in *Medieval Domesticity*, ed. Kowaleski and Goldberg, p. 2n10; but Riddy's article, " 'Burgeis' Domesticity," in the same collection, pp. 14–36, makes a case for English domestic sensibility from the fourteenth century. Barbara A. Hanawalt states that the English word *home* originally referred to a wider village community and only in the fourteenth century came to have the familiar meaning of family residence: *The Ties that Bound: Peasant Families in Medieval England* (Oxford: Oxford University Press, 1986), p. 31.
9. Even in the late Middle Ages, the proportion of the rural to urban population was approximately 85:15, while in some regions as much as 95 percent of the population was rural. See Gérard Sivéry, "Social Change in the Thirteenth Century: Rural Society," in *The New Cambridge Medieval History*, vol. 5, *c. 1198–c. 1300*, ed. David Abulafia (Cambridge: Cambridge University Press, 1999), pp. 38–49 (at p. 38); and Jean-Pierre Leguay, "Urban Life," in *The New Cambridge Medieval History*, vol. 6,

c. 1300–c. 1415, ed. Michael Jones (Cambridge: Cambridge University Press, 2000), pp. 102–23 (at pp. 103–4).

10. The following summarizes points made in Jean Chapelot and Robert Fossier, *The Village and House in the Middle Ages*, trans. Henry Cleere (London: B. T. Batsford, 1985; originally published in 1980), pp. 183–246. Another helpful survey of diverse types of rural housing is in Philippe Contamine, "Peasant Hearth to Papal Palace: The Fourteenth and Fifteenth Centuries," in *History of Private Life*, vol. 2, ed. Duby, pp. 425–505 (at pp. 444–60). A more analytical survey, but for England only, is in Jane Grenville, *Medieval Housing* (London: Leicester University Press, 1997), pp. 121–56.
11. Maurice Beresford and John Hurst, *Wharram Percy: Deserted Medieval Village* (New Haven and London: Yale University Press, 1990); see also Chapelot and Fossier, *Village and House*, pp. 197–209.
12. Chapelot and Fossier, *Village and House*, pp. 183–97, where Rougiers is noted as "very typical of villages in Provence and, no doubt, over a much wider geographic area" (quote at p. 196).
13. For retirement agreements see Elaine Clark, "Some Aspects of Social Security in Medieval England," *Journal of Family History* 7 (1982), pp. 307–20; for beds, see Hanawalt, *Ties that Bound*, p. 152. These examples are cited alongside archaeological findings in N. W. Alcock, "The Medieval Peasant at Home: England, 1250–1550," in *The Medieval Household in Christian Europe, c. 850–c. 1550: Managing Power, Wealth, and the Body*, ed. Cordelia Beattie, Anna Maslakovic, and Sarah Rees Jones (Turnhout: Brepols, 2003), pp. 449–68 (esp. pp. 450–55).
14. Hipólito Rafael Oliva Herrer, "The Peasant *Domus* and Material Culture in Northern Castile in the Later Middle Ages," in *Medieval Household in Christian Europe*, ed. Beattie, Maslakovic, and Rees Jones, pp. 469–86 (at pp. 477–81).
15. Hanawalt, *Ties that Bound*, p. 145 (and for girl and boy children mirroring their parents' tasks as they grew older, see pp. 157–61).
16. P.J.P. Goldberg, "The Public and the Private: Women in the Pre-Plague Economy," in *Thirteenth Century England III*, ed. Peter R. Coss and S. D. Lloyd (Woodbridge: Boydell, 1991), pp. 75–89 (at pp. 75–78).
17. Hanawalt, *Ties that Bound*, appendix, table 1, p. 271.
18. Contamine, "Peasant Hearth to Papal Palace," pp. 460–70, surveys mainly French urban examples including many aristocratic urban residences. Grenville, *Medieval Housing*, pp. 157–93, concentrates on houses of the English middling sort (mainly artisans and retailers); see also David Clark, "The Shop Within? An Analysis of the Architectural Evidence for Medieval Shops," *Architectural History* 43 (2000), pp. 58–87.
19. Shannon McSheffrey, ed. and trans., *Love and Marriage in Late Medieval London* (Kalamazoo: Medieval Institute Publications, 1995), pp. 59–65 (at p. 64).
20. Examples quoted in Contamine, "Peasant Hearth to Papal Palace," p. 463.
21. See some examples in McSheffrey, ed. and trans., *Love and Marriage*, pp. 45, 55, 58–59.
22. P. M. Stell and Louise Hampson, eds., *Probate Inventories of the York Diocese, 1350–1500* (York: York Minster Library, 1999), p. 175 (with associated goods in the garden, the room contained hay, a tub with lime, a bucket, a steeping vat, two boards, and firewood); see also Riddy, " 'Burgeis' Domesticity."

23. Contamine, "Peasant Hearth to Papal Palace," pp. 466–69; for some English examples, see Clark, "Shop Within," p. 74.
24. For Dante and Petrarch, see Philippe Braunstein, "Toward Intimacy: The Fourteenth and Fifteenth Centuries," in *History of Private Life*, vol. 2, ed. Duby, pp. 535–630 (at p. 616); Christine de Pizan, *The Book of the City of Ladies*, trans. Earl Jeffrey Richards (London: Pan, 1983), p. 3.
25. Guillebert de Metz, *Description de la Ville de Paris au XVe Siècle*, ed. Le Roux de Lincy (Paris: Auguste Aubrey, 1804), pp. 67–68, following the translation in Contamine, "Peasant Hearth to Papal Palace," pp. 469–70.
26. Quoted in Contamine, "Peasant Hearth to Papal Palace," pp. 469–70.
27. Charles de La Roncière, "Tuscan Notables on the Eve of the Renaissance," in *History of Private Life*, vol. 2, ed. Duby, pp. 157–309 (at p. 172).
28. Quoted in G. R. Owst, *Literature and Pulpit in Medieval England* (Oxford: Oxford University Press, 1966), p. 119; see also Kim M. Phillips, *Medieval Maidens: Young Women and Gender in England, 1270–1540* (Manchester: Manchester University Press, 2003), pp. 81–82.
29. David Nicholas, *The Domestic Life of a Medieval City: Women, Children, and the Family in Fourteenth-Century Ghent* (Lincoln and London: University of Nebraska Press, 1985), pp. 84–104.
30. In an unpublished paper, Anna Dronzek made the case for aristocratic households as imbricated with masculine identities: "No Separate Spheres: The Household as Masculine and Feminine Space in Late Medieval England" (paper presented to the North American Conference on British Studies, Baltimore, November 2002).
31. Mark Girouard, *Life in the French Country House* (London: Cassell and Co., 2000), p. 42.
32. On the Burgundians, see Peter Arnade, *Realms of Ritual: Burgundian Ceremony and Civic Life in Late Medieval Ghent* (Ithaca: Cornell University Press, 1996), for example, pp. 16–17; for the Yorkists, Kim M. Phillips, "The Invisible Man: Body and Ritual in a Fifteenth-Century Noble Household," *Journal of Medieval History* 31 (2005), pp. 143–62.
33. Michael Camille, *Mirror in Parchment: The Luttrell Psalter and the Making of Medieval England* (London: Reaktion Books, 1998), pp. 84–90; R. K. Emmerson and P.J.P. Goldberg, " 'The Lord Geoffrey had me made': Lordship and Labour in the Luttrell Psalter," in *The Problem of Labour in Fourteenth-Century England*, ed. James Bothwell, P.J.P. Goldberg, and W. M. Ormrod (York: York Medieval Press, 2000), pp. 43–63; Mark Gardiner, "Buttery and Pantry and Their Antecedents: Idea and Architecture in the English Medieval House," in *Medieval Domesticity*, ed. Kowaleski and Goldberg, pp. 37–65.
34. Malcolm Vale, *The Princely Court: Medieval Courts and Culture in North-West Europe, 1270–1380* (Oxford: Oxford University Press, 2001), pp. 202–6; Marta Vanlandingham, *Transforming the State: King, Court, and Political Culture in the Realms of Aragon (1213–1387)* (Leiden: Brill, 2002), chaps. 7 and 8.
35. Kate Mertes, *The English Noble Household, 1250–1600: Good Governance and Politic Rule* (Oxford: Basil Blackwell, 1988), p. 57; also C. M. Woolgar, *The Great Household in Late Medieval England* (New Haven: Yale University Press, 1999), pp. 34–36; compare Phillips, *Medieval Maidens*, pp. 109–20.

36. Michael J. Enright, *Lady with a Mead Cup: Ritual, Prophecy and Lordship in the European Warband from La Tène to the Viking Age* (Dublin: Four Courts Press, 1996) (see pp. 1–37 for a summary of his argument).
37. Georges Duby, "The Aristocratic Households of Feudal France," in *History of Private Life*, vol. 2, ed. Duby, pp. 35–155 (at pp. 73–74).
38. D. A. Pearsall, ed., *The Floure and the Leafe and The Assembly of Ladies* (London: Nelson, 1962); Janet M. Cowen and Jennifer C. Ward, " 'Al myn array is bliew, what nedith more?': Gender and the Household in *The Assembly of Ladies*," in *Medieval Household in Christian Europe*, ed. Beattie, Maslakovic, and Rees Jones, pp. 107–26 (at p. 119).
39. Louise J. Wilkinson, "The *Rules* of Robert Grosseteste Reconsidered: The Lady as Estate and Household Manager in Thirteenth-Century England," in *Medieval Household in Christian Europe*, ed. Beattie, Maslakovic, and Rees Jones, pp. 293–306 (quote at p. 294).
40. "Articles Ordained by King Henry VII for the Regulation of His Household. 31st Dec 1494," in *A Collection of Ordinances and Regulations for the Government of the Royal Household* (London: Society of Antiquaries, 1790), p. 125.
41. Duby, "Aristocratic Households," pp. 61–62.
42. Ibid., pp. 69, 77 (also 78–79), 81–82.
43. Roberta Gilchrist, *Gender and Archaeology: Contesting the Past* (London: Routledge, 1999), chap. 6, pp. 109–145 (quotes at pp. 139 and 144). In this chapter, Gilchrist modifies the argument for sexual segregation made in an earlier study, "Medieval Bodies in the Material World: Gender, Stigma and the Body," in *Framing Medieval Bodies*, ed. Sarah Kay and Miri Rubin (Manchester: Manchester University Press, 1993), pp. 43–60, by noting that women's seclusion in youth might be replaced by greater visibility and ease of movement in later life or widowhood and acknowledging the potential for fluidity of movement, male and female, between the more open and more enclosed elements of the castle (such as hall and chamber, open space, and gardens). Yet the primary argument is for an ideology and practice of gendered segregation.
44. Amanda Richardson, "Gender and Space in English Royal Palaces *c.* 1160–*c.* 1547: A Study in Access Analysis and Imagery," *Medieval Archaeology* 47 (2003), pp. 131–65.
45. Phillips, *Medieval Maidens*, pp. 113–19.
46. A. R. Myers, ed., *Crown, Household and Parliament in Fifteenth Century England* (London: Hambledon, 1985); Nicholas Harris Nicolas, ed., *Privy Purse Expenses of Elizabeth of York. Household Accounts of Edward the Fourth* (London: William Pickering, 1830); Jennifer C. Ward, *English Noblewomen in the Later Middle Ages* (London and New York: Longman, 1992), p. 52.
47. C. L. Kingsford, trans., "The Record of Bluemantle Pursuivant," in *English Historical Documents, 1327–1485*, ed. A. R. Myers (London: Eyre and Spottiswoode, 1969), pp. 1176–77.
48. MS Harleian 6815, fols. 28v–29r and 31v, British Library, London; Thomas Percy, ed., *The Regulations and Establishment of the Household of Henry Algernon Percy at his Castles of Wreshill and Likinfield in Yorkshire* (London: W. Pickering, 1827), p. 301. See also Phillips, *Medieval Maidens*, pp. 117–18, 163.

49. Nicola McDonald, "Fragments of *(Have Your) Desire*: Brome Women at Play," in *Medieval Domesticity*, ed. Kowaleski and Goldberg, pp. 232–58 (quotes at pp. 249, 251).
50. L. C. Hector and Barbara Harvey, eds. and trans., *The Westminster Chronicle 1381–1394* (Oxford: Oxford University Press, 1982), p. 192 (see also pp. 294, 392–94, 414); Henry Knighton, *Knighton's Chronicle*, ed. and trans. G. H. Martin (Oxford: Oxford University Press, 1995), p. 342.
51. Numerous examples are summarized in Margaret Hallissy, *Clean Maids, True Wives, Steadfast Widows: Chaucer's Women and Medieval Codes of Conduct* (Westport, CT: Greenwood Press, 1993), in a chapter titled "The Good, the Bad, and the Wavering: Women and Architectural Space," pp. 89–111.
52. For examples of the former, see *Merlin, or The Early History of King Arthur*, ed. Henry B. Wheatley, Early English Text Society, original ser. 10, 21, 36, and 112 (London, 1865–99; reprinted as 2 vols., Liechtenstein: Kraus, 1973), pp. 225, 466, 499, and 607; and William Caxton, *Caxton's Blanchardyn and Eglantine, c. 1489*, ed. Leon Kellner, Early English Text Society, extra ser., 58 (London: Trübner, 1890), p. 50, lines, 21–32. For examples of maidens riding onto the battlefield or far and wide, see J. Douglas Bruce, ed., *Le Morte Arthur: A Romance in Stanzas of Eight Lines*, Early English Text Society, extra ser. 88 (London: Trübner, 1903), lines 2048–85, 2608–715; and W. A. Wright, ed., *Generydes: A Romance in Seven-Line Stanzas*, Early English Text Society, original ser. 55 and 70 (London: Trübner, 1873–78), lines 5596–702.
53. A. R. Myers, ed., "The Black Book," in *The Household of Edward IV* (Manchester: Manchester University Press, 1959), p. 129.
54. Several examples are given in Contamine, "Peasant Hearth to Papal Palace," pp. 489–99; see also de La Roncière "Tuscan Notables," pp. 184–87.
55. Margery Kempe, *The Book of Margery Kempe*, trans. B. A. Windeatt (Harmondsworth: Penguin, 1985), p. 47.
56. Quoted in Sharon Farmer, "Persuasive Voices: Clerical Images of Medieval Wives," *Speculum* 61 (1986), pp. 517–43 (at p. 517).
57. Katherine L. French, "The Seat under Our Lady: Gender and Seating in Late Medieval English Parish Churches," pp. 141–60, and Corine Schlief, "Men on the Right—Women on the Left: (A)symetrical Spaces and Gendered Places," pp. 207–49 (esp. pp. 225–30), both in *Women's Space: Patronage, Place, and Gender in the Medieval Church*, ed. Virginia Chieffo Raguin and Sarah Stanbury (Albany: State University of New York Press, 2005); Margaret Aston, "Segregation in Church," in *Women in the Church*, ed. W. J. Sheils and Diana Wood, Studies in Church History 27 (Oxford: Blackwell, 1990), pp. 237–94.
58. Diana M. Webb, "Woman and Home: The Domestic Setting of Late Medieval Spirituality," in *Women in the Church*, ed. Sheils and Wood, pp. 159–73; Diana Webb, "Domestic Space and Devotion in the Middle Ages," in *Defining the Holy: Sacred Space in Medieval and Early Modern Europe*, ed. Andrew Spicer and Sarah Hamilton (Aldershot: Ashgate, 2005), pp. 27–47.
59. Denis Reveney, "Household Chores in *The Doctrine of the Hert*: Affective Spirituality and Subjectivity," in *Medieval Household in Christian Europe*, ed. Beat-

tie, Maslakovic, and Rees Jones, pp. 167–85 (quotes at pp. 173 and 175, spelling slightly modernized).

60. Jeffrey F. Hamburger, *Nuns as Artists: The Visual Culture of a Medieval Convent* (Berkeley: University of California Press, 1997), pp. 137–76.
61. Leon Battista Alberti, *I libri della famiglia*, trans. Renée Neu Watkins as *The Family in Renaissance Florence* (Columbia: University of South Carolina Press, 1969), pp. 207–8.
62. Fiorelli Paino, "The Palazzo of the da Varano Family in Camerino (Fourteenth–Sixteenth Centuries): Typology and Evolution of a Central Italian Aristocratic Residence," in *Medieval Household in Christian Europe*, ed. Beattie, Maslakovic, and Rees Jones, pp. 335–58 (at pp. 347–48).
63. Dennis Romano, "Gender and the Urban Geography of Renaissance Venice," *Journal of Social History* 23 (1989), pp. 339–53 (quote at p. 342).
64. Ibid., p. 342.
65. Ibid., p. 343.
66. Quoted in Robert C. Davis, "The Geography of Gender in the Renaissance," in *Gender and Society in Renaissance Italy*, ed. Judith C. Brown and Robert C. Davis (London and New York: Longman, 1998), pp. 19–38 (at p. 21).
67. Quoted in Braunstein, "Toward Intimacy," pp. 603–6.
68. De La Roncière, "Tuscan Notables," pp. 201, 232.
69. Davis, "Geography of Gender," pp. 22–23.
70. Ibid., pp. 23–31.
71. Ibid., pp. 33–37.
72. Irena Benyovsky, "Noble Family Clans and Their Urban Distribution in Medieval Trogir," in *Medieval Household in Christian* Europe, ed. Beattie, Maslakovic, and Rees Jones, pp. 19–33 (quote at p. 27). For a summary of similar practices in northern Italian cities, see de La Roncière, "Tuscan Notables," pp. 237–38.
73. Samuel K. Cohn, Jr., "Women and Work in Renaissance Italy," in *Gender and Society*, ed. Brown and Davis, pp. 107–26.
74. Yet in an earlier study, Cohn suggested that lower-status women's movement and actions in the Florentine streets and legal activity in the courts were strongly curtailed in the fifteenth century compared with the fourteenth. His data suggest that "women in the mid-Quattrocentro were less inclined and less able to circulate as freely through the streets of Florence, meeting other women and even men outside the home, as they had in the late Trecento": Samuel K. Cohn, Jr., "Women in the Streets, Women in the Courts, in Early Renaissance Florence," in *Women in the Streets: Essays on Sex and Power in Renaissance Italy* (Baltimore and London: The Johns Hopkins University Press, 1996) (a revised version of an essay first published in Italian in 1981), pp. 16–38 (quote at p. 35).
75. Romano, "Gender and the Urban Geography," p. 345.
76. Ibid.
77. Thomas Kuehn, "Person and Gender in the Laws," in *Gender and Society*, ed. Brown and Davis, pp. 87–106 (esp. p. 89).
78. For English examples, see Kim M. Phillips, "Bodily Walls, Windows, and Doors: The Politics of Gesture in Late Fifteenth-Century English Books for Women," in

Medieval Women: Texts and Contexts in Late Medieval Britain: Essays for Felicity Riddy, ed. Jocelyn Wogan-Browne, Rosalynn Voaden, Arlyn Diamond, Ann Hutchison, Carol Meale, and Lesley Johnson (Turnhout: Brepols, 2000), pp. 185–98; for Christine, see *City of Ladies*, trans. Richards, p. 256. Francesco de Barberino's early fourteenth-century *Del Reggimento e Costumi di Donna* counseled maidens to keep their eyes downcast in public lest one's feelings be communicated: see summary in Alice A. Hentsch, *De la littérature didactique au moyen âge, s'addressant spécialement aux femmes* (Cahors: Coueslant, 1903), pp. 105, 106.

79. Geoffrey Chaucer, "Troilus and Criseyde," in *The Riverside Chaucer*, 3rd ed., ed. Larry D. Benson (Oxford: Oxford University Press, 1987), pp. 475–77 (quote at line 292, spelling modernized).
80. Anneke B. Mulder-Bakker and Jocelyn Wogan-Browne, "Introduction Part II: Medieval Households," in *Household, Women, and Christianities*, ed. Mulder-Bakker and Wogan-Browne, pp. 125–31 (at p. 128).
81. Sylvia Federico, "The Imaginary Society: Women in 1381," *Journal of British Studies* 40 (2001), pp. 159–83 (examples at pp. 167–68). In contrast, David Nicholas found women played little role in the mid-fourteenth-century Ghent uprisings: Nicholas, *Domestic Life*, p. 103.
82. Sarah Stanbury and Virginia Chieffo Raguin, "Introduction," in *Women's Space: Patronage, Place, and Gender in the Medieval Church*, ed. Virginia Chieffo Raguin and Sarah Stanbury (Albany: State University of New York Press, 2005), pp. 1–21 (at p. 5).

Chapter 6

1. Toys such as these have been excavated in London. An example of a pewter jug found on the Thames foreshore may be seen in the Museum of London (Accession Number 98.2/159).
2. See discussion of population estimates in Edward Miller and John Hatcher, *Medieval England: Towns, Commerce and Crafts 1086–1348* (London: Longman, 1995), pp. 395–96.
3. Geoffroy de La Tour Landry, *The Book of the Knight of the Tower*, ed. M. Y. Offord, trans. William Caxton, Early English Text Society, supplemental ser. 2 (London: Oxford University Press, 1971), p. 122.
4. Barbara A. Hanawalt, *The Ties that Bound: Peasant Families in Medieval England* (New York: Oxford University Press, 1986), pp. 157–60, 273. Hanawalt's arguments have been challenged by P.J.P. Goldberg, among others, who has proposed that gender differences in mortality rates may reflect the danger of various tasks rather than their location per se: "The Public and the Private: Women in the Pre-Plague Economy," in *Thirteenth-Century England III*, ed. P. R. Coss and S. D. Lloyd (Woodbridge: Boydell, 1991).
5. Geoff Egan, "Miniature Toys of Medieval Childhood," *British Archaeology* 35 (June 1998), pp. 10–11.
6. For discussion of servanthood, see, for instance, P.J.P Goldberg, *Women, Work, and Life Cycle in a Medieval Economy: Women in York and Yorkshire c. 1300–1520* (Oxford: Clarendon Press, 1992), pp. 158–202.

7. Kim M. Phillips, *Medieval Maidens: Young Women and Gender in England, 1270–1540* (Manchester: Manchester University Press, 2003), pp. 120–22, 130–32.
8. Judith M. Bennett, *A Medieval Life: Cecilia Penifader of Brigstock, c. 1295–1344* (Boston: McGraw Hill College, 1999), p. 44.
9. Phillips, *Medieval Maidens*, pp. 185–94; Katherine L. French, *The Good Women of the Parish: Gender and Religion after the Black Death* (Philadelphia: University of Pennsylvania Press, 2008), pp. 118–56.
10. This requirement resulted from the Fourth Lateran Council of 1215. For discussion of how the age of reason was variously interpreted, see Nicholas Orme, *Medieval Children* (New Haven: Yale University Press, 2001), pp. 214–21.
11. French, *Good Women of the Parish*.
12. Sandy Bardsley, *Venomous Tongues: Speech and Gender in Late Medieval England* (Philadelphia: University of Pennsylvania Press, 2006).
13. Ruth M. Karras, "Gendered Sin and Misogyny in John of Bromyard's Summa Predicantium," *Traditio: Studies in Ancient and Medieval History, Thought, and Religion* 47 (1992), pp. 233–57.
14. See, for instance, Kathryn L. Reyerson, "The Adolescent Apprentice/Worker in Medieval Montpellier," *Journal of Family History* 14 (1992), pp. 353–70.
15. Phillips, *Medieval Maidens*, pp. 132–34; Ilana Krausman Ben-Amos, "Women Apprentices in the Trades and Crafts of Early Modern Bristol," *Continuity and Change* 6 (1991), pp. 227–52; Caroline M. Barron, "The 'Golden Age' of Women in Medieval London," *Reading Medieval Studies* 15 (1989), pp. 35–58 (at p. 52n1).
16. Christine de Pizan, *A Medieval Woman's Mirror of Honor: The Treasury of the City of Ladies*, ed. Madeleine Pelner Cosman, trans. Charity Cannon Willard (New York: Persea, 1989), pp. 209–11.
17. Le Ménagier de Paris, *The Good Wife's Guide: A Medieval Household Book*, trans. Gina L. Greco and Christine M. Rose (Ithaca: Cornell University Press, 2009).
18. Felicity Riddy, "Mother Knows Best: Reading Social Change in a Courtesy Text," *Speculum* 71 (1996), pp. 66–86.
19. Anna Dronzek, "Gendered Theories of Education in Fifteenth-Century Conduct Books," in *Medieval Conduct*, ed. Kathleen Ashley and Robert L. A. Clark (Minneapolis: University of Minnesota Press, 2001), pp. 135–59 (at p. 141).
20. Caroline M. Barron, "The Education and Training of Girls in Fifteenth-Century London," in *Courts, Counties and the Capital in the Later Middle Ages*, ed. Diana E.S. Dunn (Stroud: Sutton; New York: St. Martin's Press, 1996), pp. 139–53 (at pp. 141–42).
21. Barron, "The Education and Training of Girls."
22. Walter Simons, *Cities of Ladies: Beguine Communities in the Medieval Low Countries,1200–1565* (Philadelphia: University of Pennsylvania Press, 2001).
23. Judith Bryce, "Les Livres des Florentines: Reconsidering Women's Literacy in Quattrocento Florence," in *At the Margins: Minority Groups in Premodern Italy*, ed. Stephen J. Milner (Minneapolis: University of Minnesota Press, 2005), p. 137n24; Sylvia L. Thrupp, *The Merchant Class of Medieval London, 1300–1500* (Ann Arbor: University of Michigan Press, 1962), p. 171.

24. Mary C. Erler, *Women, Reading, and Piety in Late Medieval England* (Cambridge: Cambridge University Press, 2002).
25. M. T. Clanchy, "Learning to Read and the Role of Mothers," in *Studies in the History of Reading*, ed. G. Brooks and A. G. Pugh (Reading: Centre for Teaching of Reading, 1984), pp. 33–39.
26. Judith K. Golden, "Images of Instruction, Marie de Bretagne, and the Life of St. Eustace as Illustrated in British Library Ms. Egerton 745," in *Insights and Interpretations: Studies in Celebration of the Eighty-Fifth Anniversary of the Index of Christian* Art, ed. Colum Hourihane (Princeton, NJ: Princeton University in association with Princeton University Press, 2002), pp. 60–84.
27. Susan M. Johns, *Noblewomen, Aristocracy and Power in the Twelfth-Century Anglo-Norman Realm* (Manchester: Manchester University Press, 2003), pp. 42–43.
28. Pamela Sheingorn, " 'The Wise Mother': The Image of St. Anne Teaching the Virgin Mary," in *Gendering the Master Narrative: Women and Power in the Middle Ages*, ed. Mary C. Erler and Maryanne Kowaleski (Ithaca: Cornell University Press, 2003), pp. 105–34.
29. Nicholas Orme, *From Childhood to Chivalry: The Education of the English Kings and Aristocracy 1066–1530* (London: Methuen, 1984), pp. 58–60.
30. Susan Groag Bell, "Medieval Women Book Owners: Arbiters of Lay Piety and Ambassadors of Culture," *Signs* 7 (1982), pp. 742–68.
31. Erler, *Women, Reading, and Piety.*
32. Felicity Riddy, " 'Women Talking about the Things of God': A Late Medieval Sub-Culture," in *Women and Literature in Britain, 1150–1500*, ed. Carol M. Meale, 2nd ed. (Cambridge: Cambridge University Press, 1996), pp. 104–27 (at p. 110).
33. Karen A. Winstead, *Virgin Martyrs: Legends of Sainthood in Late Medieval England* (Ithaca: Cornell University Press, 1997).
34. E. Jane Burns, *Courtly Love Undressed: Reading through Clothes in Medieval French Culture* (Philadelphia: University of Pennsylvania Press, 2002).
35. In Emilie Amt, ed., *Women's Lives in Medieval Europe: A Sourcebook* (New York: Routledge, 1993), pp. 244, 238.
36. Nicholas Orme, *Medieval Schools: From Roman Britain to Renaissance England* (New Haven: Yale University Press, 2006), pp. 275–76.
37. Marilyn Oliva, *The Convent and the Community in Late Medieval England: Female Monasteries in the Diocese of Norwich, 1350–1540* (Woodbridge: Boydell, 1998), pp. 45–46.
38. Erler, *Women, Reading, and Piety*, pp. 31–32.
39. Orme, *Medieval Schools*, p. 128.
40. Marie Luise Ehrenschwentner, " 'Puellae litteratae': The Use of the Vernacular in the Dominican Convents of Southern Germany," in *Medieval Women in Their Communities*, ed. Diane Watt (Cardiff: University of Wales Press, 1997); Alison Beach, *Women as Scribes: Book Production and Monastic Reform in Twelfth-Century Bavaria* (Cambridge: Cambridge University Press, 2004); Fiona J. Griffiths, *The Garden of Delights: Reform and Renaissance for Women in the Twelfth Century* (Philadelphia: University of Pennsylvania Press, 2007).

41. P.J.P. Goldberg, ed. and trans., *Women in England, c. 1275–1525* (Manchester: Manchester University Press, 1995), p. 266.
42. Especially his *Domination and the Arts of Resistance: Hidden Transcripts* (New Haven: Yale University Press, 1990).
43. Goldberg, *Women in England,* pp. 169–70.
44. Hanawalt, *The Ties that Bound*, pp. 40, 124–40, 158.
45. For just one example among many, see Jennifer Browning, Tim Higgins, with contributions from Patrick Clay, Paul Courtney, Angela Monckton, and Deborah Sawday,"Excavations of a Medieval Toft and Croft at Cropston Road, Anstey, Leicestershire," *Transactions of the Leicestershire Archaeological and Historical Society* 77 (2003), pp. 65–81. This excavation yielded evidence that different areas of the croft were used for preparing different types of food.
46. For varieties of food eaten by peasants, see Christopher Dyer, *Standards of Living in the Later Middle Ages: Social Change in England, c.1200–1520* (Cambridge: Cambridge University Press, 1989), pp. 151–60. Note that consumption patterns changed a little in the postplague era with greater availability of wheat, meat, and bread.
47. See, for instance, Hanawalt, *The Ties that Bound*, p. 145.
48. Hanawalt, *The Ties that Bound*, pp. 175–76, 179–81.
49. While the poorest of peasants drank water, the better-off peasants preferred the taste of weak ale: Judith M. Bennett, *Ale, Beer, and Brewsters: Women's Work in a Changing World, 1300–1600* (New York: Oxford University Press, 1996), pp. 9–10. The spread of hopped beer as a commercial enterprise, beginning in the thirteenth century in Northern Germany, is traced by Richard W. Unger, *Beer in the Middle Ages and the Renaissance* (Philadelphia: University of Pennsylvania Press, 2004), pp. 53–106.
50. Bennett, *Ale, Beer, and Brewsters*, p. 19.
51. H. S. Bennett, *Life on the English Manor: A Study of Peasant Conditions 1150–1400* (Cambridge: University of Cambridge Press, 1937), pp. 135–37.
52. This term was originally used by Olwen Hufton to describe the economy of French peasants (in *The Poor of Eighteenth-Century France, 1750–1789* [Oxford: Clarendon Press, 1974]) but has been much used elsewhere since.
53. Veronica Sekules, "Spinning Yarns: Clean Linen and Domestic Values in Late Medieval French Culture," in *The Material Culture of Sex, Procreation, and Marriage in Premodern Europe*, ed. Anne L. McClanan and Karen Rosoff Encarnación. (New York: Palgrave, 2002), pp. 79–91.
54. Ruth Mazo Karras usefully surveys the gendering of the textile industry and its changes over time in " 'This Skill in a Woman Is By No Means to Be Despised': Weaving and the Gender Division of Labor in the Middle Ages," in *Medieval Fabrications: Dress, Textiles, Clothwork, and Other Cultural Imaginings*, ed. E. Jane Burns (New York: Palgrave, 2004), pp. 89–104. See also Diane Hutton, "Women in Fourteenth-Century Shrewsbury," in *Women and Work in Pre-Industrial England*, ed. L. Charles and L. Duffin (London: Croon Helm, 1985), pp. 83–99. For mention of women as sheep washers and sheepshearers, see, for instance, James E. Thorold Rogers, *A History of Agriculture and Prices*, 7 vols. (Oxford: Clarendon Press, 1866–1902), vol. 1, p. 280.

55. Frances M. Biscoglio, "'Unspun' Heroes: Iconography of the Spinning Woman in the Middle Ages," *Journal of Medieval and Renaissance Studies* 25 (1995), pp. 163–84.
56. John H. Munro, "Medieval Woolens: Textiles, Textile Technology, and Industrial Organisation, *c.* 800–1500," in *The Cambridge History of Western Textiles*, ed. David Jenkins (Cambridge: Cambridge University Press, 2003), vol. 1, pp. 181–227 (at pp. 201–2). Spinning wheels are mentioned in York documents from the late fourteenth century: for instance, Goldberg, *Women, Work, and Life Cycle*, p. 118.
57. For discussion of population growth, see Edward Miller and John Hatcher, *Medieval England: Rural Society and Economic Change 1086–1348* (London: Longman, 1978), pp. 28–33. Medieval life expectancy at birth was startlingly low—perhaps as low as 20 years—even for the most privileged sectors of the population (John Hatcher, "Mortality in the Fifteenth Century: Some New Evidence," *Economic History Review* (2nd ser.), 39 [1986], pp. 19–38; Barbara Harvey, *Living and Dying in England 1100–1540: The Monastic Experience* [Oxford: Oxford University Press, 1993], pp. 114–29.)
58. Hanawalt, *The Ties that Bound*, pp. 180–82.
59. Carole Rawcliffe, *Medicine and Society in Later Medieval England* (Stroud: Alan Sutton, 1995), pp. 194–204.
60. Among many examples, see, for instance Rogers, *History of Agriculture and Prices*, vol. 1, pp. 265–82; Mavis E. Mate, *Daughters, Wives and Widows after the Black Death: Women in Sussex, 1350–1535* (Woodbridge: Boydell Press, 1998), pp. 11–12. Historians do not always agree about the extent of these increases in real wages: see John Hatcher, "England in the Aftermath of the Black Death," *Past & Present* 144 (1994), pp. 3–35.
61. Barron, "The 'Golden Age' of Women in Medieval London"; Goldberg, *Women, Work and Life Cycle*, passim; Bennett, *Ale, Beer, and Brewsters*, passim; and Judith M. Bennett, "Confronting Continuity," *Journal of Women's History* 9 (1997), pp. 73–94.
62. *Eulogium*, compiled at Malmesbury Abbey, quoted in Rosemary Horrox, ed., *The Black Death* (Manchester: Manchester University Press, 1994), p. 64.
63. R. H. Hilton, "Women in the Village," in his *The English Peasantry in the Later Middle Ages* (Oxford: Clarendon Press, 1975), pp. 95–110, at p. 105.
64. Mavis E. Mate, *Women in Medieval English Society* (Cambridge: Cambridge University Press, 1999), p. 33.
65. Simon A. C. Penn, "Female Wage-Earners in Late Fourteenth-Century England," *Agricultural History Review* 35 (1987), pp. 1–14.
66. Sandy Bardsley, "Women's Work Reconsidered: Gender and Wage Differentiation in Late Medieval England," *Past & Present* 165 (1999), pp. 3–29.
67. Mercedes Borrero Fernández, "Peasant and Aristocratic Women: Their Role in the Rural Economy of Seville at the End of the Middle Ages," in *Women at Work in Spain: From the Middle Ages to Early Modern Times*, ed. Marilyn Stone and Carmen Benito-Vessels (New York: Peter Lang, 1998), pp. 11–31 (at p. 15); E. Perroy, "Wage Labour in France in the Later Middle Ages," *Economic History Review* (2nd ser.), 8 (1955–56), pp. 234–36.

68. Bardsley, "Women's Work Reconsidered," pp. 19–27.
69. John Hatcher, "Debate—Women's Work Reconsidered: Gender and Wage Differentiation in Late Medieval England," *Past & Present* 173 (2001), pp. 191–98; Bardsley, "Debate—Women's Work Reconsidered: Gender and Wage Differentiation in Late Medieval England—Reply," *Past & Present* 173 (2001), pp. 199–202.
70. In fourteenth-century Exeter, for instance, servants comprised 37 percent of working women appearing in court rolls and other documents: see Maryanne Kowaleski, "Women's Work in a Market Town: Exeter in the Late Fourteenth Century," in *Women and Work in Preindustrial Europe*, ed. Barbara A. Hanawalt (Bloomington: Indiana University Press, 1986), pp. 145–64 (at pp. 148, 153–54).
71. For discussion of men's and women's typical roles within crafts, see Karras, "This Skill in a Woman"; Bennett, *Ale, Beer, and Brewsters*; and Hutton, "Women in Fourteenth-Century Shrewsbury."
72. Simon Mays, "A Biomechanical Study of Activity Patterns in a Medieval Human Skeletal Assemblage," *International Journal of Osteoarchaeology* 9 (1999), pp. 68–73.
73. Maryanne Kowaleski and Judith M. Bennett, "Crafts, Gilds, and Women in the Middle Ages: Fifty Years after Marian K. Dale," in *Sisters and Workers in the Middle Ages*, ed. Judith M. Bennett, Elizabeth A. Clark, Jean F. O'Barr, B. Anne Vilen, and Sarah Westphal-Wihl (Chicago: University of Chicago Press, 1989), pp. 11–39.
74. Kowaleski and Bennett, "Crafts, Gilds, and Women in the Middle Ages."
75. Rawcliffe, *Medicine and Society*, pp. 198–99.
76. Rawcliffe, *Medicine and Society*, p. 199; John Carmi Parsons, "Que Nos in Infancia Lactauit: The Impact of Childhood Care-Givers on Plantagenet Family Relationships in the Thirteenth and Early Fourteenth Centuries," in *Women, Marriage, and Family in Medieval Christendom: Essays in Memory of Michael M. Sheehan, C.S.B*, ed. Constance M. Rousseau and Joel T. Rosenthal (Kalamazoo: Western Michigan University, 1998), pp. 289–324.
77. Philip Gavitt, "Infant Death in Late Medieval Florence: The Smothering Hypothesis Reconsidered," in *Medieval Family Roles: A Book of Essays*, ed. Cathy Jorgensen McItnyre (New York: Garland, 1996), pp. 137–53; Leah L. Otis, "Municipal Wetnurses in Fifteenth Century Montpellier," in *Women and Work in Preindustrial Europe*, ed. Barbara A. Hanawalt (Bloomington: Indiana University Press, 1986), pp. 83–93.
78. Ruth Mazo Karras, "The Regulation of Brothels in Later Medieval England," in *Sisters and Workers in the Middle Ages*, pp. 100–134.
79. Leah Lydia Otis, *Prostitution in Medieval Society: The History of an Urban Institution in Languedoc* (Chicago: University of Chicago Press, 1985), pp. 25–26; Joëlle Rollo-Koster, "From Prostitutes to Brides of Christ: The Avignonese 'Repenties' in the Late Middle Ages," *Journal of Medieval and Early Modern Studies* 32 (2002), pp. 109–44, at p. 112; Ruth Mazo Karras, *Common Women: Prostitution and Sexuality in Medieval England* (Oxford: Oxford University Press, 1996), pp. 21–22.
80. Kowaleski, "Women's Work in a Market Town," p. 154.
81. Karras, *Common Women*, pp. 53–57.
82. R. H. Hilton, "Lords, Burgesses and Hucksters," *Past & Present* 97 (1982), pp. 3–15; Hilton, "Women Traders in Medieval England," *Women's Studies* 11 (1984), pp. 139–55.

83. Eleanora M. Carus-Wilson, "The Woollen Industry," in *The Cambridge Economic History of Europe*, vol. 2, *Trade and Industry in the Middle Ages*, ed. M. M. Postan, Edward Miller, and Cynthia Postan (Cambridge: Cambridge University Press, 1987), pp. 613–90 (at pp. 637–38); Miller and Hatcher, *Medieval England: Towns, Commerce and Crafts*, pp. 94–95; Munro, "Medieval Woolens."
84. Karras, "This Skill in a Woman."
85. Kowaleski and Bennett, "Crafts, Gilds, and Women in the Middle Ages."
86. de Pizan, *A Medieval Woman's Mirror of Honor*, pp. 170–74.
87. Joseph F. O'Callaghan, "The Many Roles of the Medieval Queen: Some Examples from Castile," in *Queenship and Political Power in Medieval and Early Modern Spain*, ed. Theresa Earenfight (Aldershot: Ashgate, 2005), pp. 21–32, at p. 29.
88. J. S. Bothwell, "The More Things Change: Isabella and Mortimer, Edward III, and the Painful Delay of a Royal Majority (1327)," in *The Royal Minorities of Medieval and Early Modern England*, ed. Charles Beem (New York: Palgrave Macmillan, 2008), pp. 67–102.
89. Josiah Cox Russell, *British Medieval Population* (Albuquerque: University of New Mexico Press, 1948), p. 165. Birth rates among urban and peasant families are much harder to calculate: see Russell, pp. 167–69.
90. Michael Hicks, "Elizabeth (*c.* 1437–1492)," in *Oxford Dictionary of National Biography* (Oxford: Oxford University Press, 2004), http://www.oxforddnb.com/view/article/8634 (accessed May 19, 2010).
91. T. B. Pugh, "Grey, Thomas, First Marquess of Dorset (*c.* 1455–1501)," in *Oxford Dictionary of National Biography* (Oxford: Oxford University Press, 2004), http://www.oxforddnb.com/view/article/11560 (accessed May 19, 2010).
92. Ruth Mazo Karras, *From Boys to Men: Formations of Masculinity in Late Medieval Europe* (Philadelphia: University of Pennsylvania Press, 2003), pp. 29–30.
93. Jennifer C. Ward, *English Noblewomen in the Later Middle Ages* (London: Longman, 1992), pp. 96–97.
94. See, for instance, essays in June Hall McCash, ed., *The Cultural Patronage of Medieval Women* (Athens: University of Georgia Press, 1996).
95. Frances A. Underhill, "Elizabeth de Burgh: Connoisseur and Patron," in McCash, ed., *The Cultural Patronage of Medieval Women*, pp. 266–87; Jennifer C. Ward, "English Noblewomen and the Local Community in the Later Middle Ages," in *Medieval Women in Their Communities*, ed. Diane Watt (Toronto: University of Toronto Press, 1997), pp. 186–203.
96. Barbara J. Harris, "Women and Politics in Early Tudor England," *The Historical Journal* 33 (1990), pp. 259–81.

Chapter 7

1. See Colin Morris, *The Discovery of the Individual, 1050–1200* (first published 1972; Toronto: Medieval Academy of America, 1987), and the important qualifications of Caroline Walker Bynum in *Jesus as Mother: Studies in the Spirituality of the High Middle Ages* (Berkeley: University of California Press, 1982), pp. 82–106.
2. The work of Georges Duby, Michael Sheehan, and David Herlihy, while dated, is still the starting place for any serious inquiry into medieval marriage. See Duby, *Medieval*

Marriage: Two Models from Medieval France, trans. Elborg Foster (Baltimore: The Johns Hopkins University Press, 1978); Sheehan, *Marriage, Family and Law in Medieval Europe: Collected Studies*, ed. James K. Farge (Toronto: Toronto University Press, 1997); and Herlihy, *Women, Family, and Society in Medieval Europe: Historical Essays 1978–1991*, ed. A. Molho (Providence: Berghahn Books, 1995). See also David D'Avray, *Medieval Marriage: Symbolism and Society* (Oxford: Oxford University Press, 2005).

3. For rape, abduction, and female slavery, see David R. Wyatt, *Slaves and Warriors in Medieval Britain, 800–1200* (Leiden: Brill, 2009); see also, Susan Mosher Stuard, "Ancillary Evidence for the Decline of Medieval Slavery," *Past & Present* 149 (1995), pp. 3–28. See James A. Brundage, *Law, Sex, and Christian Society in Medieval Europe* (Chicago: University of Chicago Press, 1990), esp. pp. 127–34, 167–73, 517–36. Secondary literature on rape in medieval Europe is plentiful, but the topic has been handled in a much more detailed and nuanced way by literary scholars than by legal scholars and historians of late. Exceptions include Kim M. Phillips, "Written on the Body: Reading Rape from the Twelfth to the Fifteenth Centuries" in *Medieval Women and the Law*, ed. Noël James Menuge (Woodbridge: Boydell and Brewer, 2000); and Angeliki E. Laiou, ed., *Consent and Coercion to Sex and Marriage in Ancient and Medieval Societies* (Washington, DC: Dumbarton Oaks, 1998). For the later Middle Ages, see Jeremy Goldberg, *Community Discord, Child Abduction, and Rape in the Later Middle Ages* (New York: Palgrave, 2007). For the literary treatments, see first, Kathryn Gravdal, *Ravishing Maidens: Writing Rape in Medieval French Literature and Law* (Philadelphia: University of Pennsylvania Press, 1991); and Corinne Saunders, *Rape and Ravishment in the Literature of Medieval England* (Cambridge: D. S. Brewer, 2001). I have not yet been able to examine Albrecht Classen, *Sexual Violence and Rape in the Middle Ages: A Critical Discourse in Premodern German and European Literature* (Berlin: De Gruyter, 2011), nor the new edition of Ruth Mazo Karras, *Sexuality in Medieval Europe: Doing unto Others* (New York: Routledge, 2005; 2nd ed. 2011). Karras discusses rape in passim, and the first edition included extensive and useful notes for anyone interested in further reading on the subject.
4. See Joan Cadden, *Meanings of Sex Differences in the Middle Ages: Medicine, Science, and Culture* (Cambridge: Cambridge University Press, 1993); and also, April Harper and Caroline Proctor, eds., *Medieval Sexuality: A Casebook* (New York: Routledge, 2007).
5. B. P. Prusak, "Woman: Seductive Siren and Source of Sin? Pseudepigraphal Myth and Christian Origins," in *Religion and Sexism: Images of Woman in the Jewish and Christian Traditions*, ed. Rosemary R. Reuther (New York: Simon and Schuster, 1974), pp. 89–116.
6. Dhuoda, *Handbook for her Warrior* Son, ed. and trans. Marcelle Thiébaux (Cambridge: Cambridge University Press, 2007).
7. See Paul Strohm, "Queens as Intercessors," in Paul Strohm, *Hochon's Arrow: The Social Imagination of Fourteenth-Century Texts* (Princeton, NJ: Princeton University Press, 1992), pp. 95–119 (esp. pp. 99–102), and three essays by John Carmi Parsons: "The Queen's Intercession in Thirteenth-Century England," in *Power of the Weak:*

Studies on Medieval Women, ed. Jennifer Carpenter and Sally-Beth MacLean (Urbana: University of Illinois Press, 1995), pp. 147–77; "The Intercessory Patronage of Queens Margaret and Isabella of France, *Thirteenth Century England*, vol. 6 (Woodbridge: The Boydell Press, 1995), pp. 145–56; and "The Pregnant Queen as Counselor and the Medieval Construction of Motherhood," in *Medieval Mothering*, ed. John Carmi Parsons and Bonnie Wheeler (New York: Garland, 1996), pp. 39–61. Anneke Mulder-Bakker and Kristen Geaman have questioned the interpretation of intercession as a substitution for more direct participation in royal government. See Mulder-Bakker, "Jeanne of Valois: The Power of a Consort," in *Capetian Women*, ed. Kathleen Nolan (New York: Palgrave, 2003), pp. 253–69; and Geaman, "Queen's Gold and Intercession: The Case of Eleanor of Aquitaine," *Medieval Feminist Forum* 46 (2010), pp. 10–33.

8. As two among many possible examples, the Anglo-Norman chronicler Orderic Vitalis describes how the wives of Norman warriors, "consumed by fierce lust," threatened to leave their absent husbands and take other lovers unless the men who were fighting in England returned home immediately to fulfill their marital debt. Some of the men "returned to Normandy to oblige their wanton wives," but in the process lost their claims to land in England. See Orderic Vitalis, *The Ecclesiastical History of Orderic Vitalis*, ed. and trans. Marjorie Chibnall, 6 vols. (Oxford: Clarendon Press, 1969–85), vol. 3, pp. 219–21. William of Malmesbury, Orderic's contemporary, describes how King Philip of France was manipulated by his mistress (later wife) Bertrada of Montfort's sexual charm to the extent that "while aiming at universal domination himself, he was quite content to be dominated by her." William of Malmesbury, *Gesta Regum Anglorum*, ed. and trans. R.A.B. Mynors, R. M. Thomson, and M. Winterbottom, 2 vols. (Oxford: Clarendon Press 1988–99), vol. 1, p. 235. For examples of clerical writers urging women to use their sexuality to influence men in church-approved directions, see Sharon Farmer, "Persuasive Voices: Clerical Images of Medieval Wives," *Speculum* 61 (1986), pp. 517–43.
9. The theme of "power in weakness" was explored in the volume of essays edited by Carpenter and MacLean, *Power of the Weak*.
10. See Susan Groag Bell, "Medieval Women Book Owners: Arbiters of Lay Piety and Ambassadors of Culture," *Signs* 7 (1982), pp. 742–68; June Hall McCash, ed., *The Cultural Patronage of Medieval Women* (Athens: University of Georgia Press, 1996); Kathleen Nolan, *Queens in Stone and Silver: The Creation of a Visual Imagery of Queenship in Capetian France* (New York: Palgrave, 2009); Loveday Lewis Gee, *Women, Art, and Patronage from Henry III to Edward III, 1216–1377* (Woodbridge: The Boydell Press, 2002); Therese Martin, "The Art of a Reigning Queen as Dynastic Propaganda in Twelfth-Century Spain," *Speculum* 80 (2005), pp. 1134–71; and Therese Martin, *Queen as King: Politics and Architectural Propaganda in Twelfth-Century Spain* (Leiden: Brill, 2006).
11. Jo Ann McNamara and Suzanne Wemple, "The Power of Women through the Family," *Feminist Studies* 1 (1973), pp. 126–41; reprinted with minor revisions in *Women and Power in the Middle Ages*, ed. Mary Erler and Maryanne Kowaleski (Athens: University of Georgia Press, 1988), pp. 83–102. See also McNamara, "Women and Power through the Family Revisited," in *Gendering the Master*

Narrative: Women and Power in the Middle Ages, ed. Mary C. Erler and Maryanne Kowaleski (Ithaca: Cornell University Press, 2003), pp. 17–30.

12. Two essays in *Capetian Women*, ed. Nolan, are illustrative here: Miriam Shadis, "Blanche of Castile and Facinger's 'Medieval Queenship': Reassessing the Argument," pp. 137–61; and Kimberly LoPrete, "Historical Ironies in the Study of Capetian Women," pp. 271–86.
13. Medieval queenship is now a topic with a huge and growing bibliography. There are several foundational essay collections, including John Carmi Parsons, ed., *Medieval Queenship* (New York: St. Martin's Press, 1993); Louise Olga Fradenburg, ed., *Women and Sovereignty* (Edinburgh: Edinburgh University Press, 1993); and Anne J. Duggan, ed., *Queens and Queenship in Medieval Europe* (Woodbridge: The Boydell Press, 1997). The pioneering modern study is that of Pauline Stafford, *Queens, Concubines and Dowagers: The King's Wife in the Early Middle Ages* (Athens: University of Georgia Press, 1983). Stafford's contributions to the field of queenship studies, both in theoretical works and in biographical works such as *Queen Emma and Queen Edith: Queenship and Women's Power in Eleventh-Century England* (Oxford: Blackwell, 1997), is unparalleled. Likewise, the important work of John Carmi Parsons in establishing queenship studies in its own right should not be overlooked. See his edited volume, *Medieval Queenship,* as well as his biographical study, *Eleanor of Castile: Queen and Society in Thirteenth-Century England* (New York: St. Martin's Press, 1995). Since the mid-1990s, numerous biographies of individual queens have appeared, primarily in England, France, and Spain; many of these works are cited as they appear in the discussion. Scandinavian queenship is the focus of William Layher, *Queenship and Voice in Medieval Northern Europe* (New York: Palgrave, 2010). Literary scholars and art historians have also made important contributions. See, for instance, Stacy S. Klein, *Ruling Women: Queenship and Gender in Anglo-Saxon Literature* (Notre Dame: Notre Dame University Press, 2006); Peggy McCracken, *The Romance of Adultery: Queenship and Sexual Transgression in Old French Literature* (Philadelphia: University of Pennsylvania Press, 1998); and Joan Holladay, "Fourteenth-Century French Queens as Collectors and Readers of Books: Jeanne d'Evreux and Her Contemporaries," *Journal of Medieval History* 31 (2006), pp. 69–100, and "The Education of Jeanne d'Evreux: Personal Piety and Dynastic Salvation in Her Book of Hours at the Cloisters," *Art History* 17 (1994), pp. 585–611. It is a sign of the progress of the study of medieval women that not even all of the most important works of the last twenty years could possibly be cited in a chapter of this length.
14. See Pauline Stafford, "Sons and Mothers: Family Politics in the Early Middle Ages," in *Medieval Women*, ed. Derek Baker (Oxford: Basil Blackwell for the Ecclesiastical History Society, 1978), pp. 79–100.
15. See, among others, Lisa M. Bitel, *Women in Early Medieval Europe, 400–1100* (Cambridge: Cambridge University Press, 2002); Janet L. Nelson, "Queens as Jezebels: The Careers of Brunhild and Balthild in Merovingian History," in *Medieval Women*, ed. Baker, pp. 31–78, as well as many of Nelson's articles collected in *Politics and Ritual in Early Medieval Europe* (London: The Hambledon Press, 1986), and *Rulers and Ruling Families in Early Medieval Europe: Alfred, Charles*

the Bald, and Others (Aldershot: Ashgate, 1999); Suzanne Fonay Wemple, *Women in Frankish Society: Marriage and the Cloister 500–900* (Philadelphia: University of Pennsylvania Press, 1981); and Valerie L. Garver, *Women and Aristocratic Culture in the Carolingian World* (Ithaca: Cornell University Press, 2009).

16. Hagith Sivan's new biography of Galla Placidia appeared just as this chapter was finalized: *Galla Placidia: The Last Roman Empress* (New York: Oxford University Press, 2011). See also the older biography by Stewart Irwin Oost, *Galla Placidia Augusta: A Historiographical Essay* (Chicago: University of Chicago Press, 1968).
17. These narratives have been discussed by many historians, including Suzanne Wemple in *Women in Frankish Society*, esp. pp. 64–65, and Edward James, *The Franks* (Oxford: Basil Blackwell, 1988), but by no one more engagingly than the sixth-century chronicler Gregory of Tours, *The History of the Franks*, ed. and trans. Lewis Thorpe (Harmondsworth: Penguin Books, 1974).
18. For the role of women in Beowulf and the northern sagas, see among many others, Helen Damico, *Beowulf's Wealhtheow and the Valkyrie Tradition* (Madison: University of Wisconsin Press, 1984); Michael J. Enright, *Lady with a Mead Cup: Ritual Prophecy and Lordship in the European Warband from La Tène to the Viking Age* (Dublin: Four Courts Press, 1995); Mary Dockray-Miller, "The Masculine Queen of Beowulf," *Women and Language* 21 (1998), pp. 31–38; and Dorothy Carr Porter, "The Social Centrality of Women in Beowulf: A New Context," *The Heroic Age* 5 (2001), http://www.heroicage.org (accessed September 1, 2011); and Jenny Jochens, *Old Norse Images of Women* (Philadelphia: University of Pennsylvania Press, 1996).
19. I discuss these two instances, among others, in Lois L. Huneycutt, *Matilda of Scotland: A Study in Medieval Queenship* (Woodbridge: The Boydell Press, 2003), p. 37 and pp. 82–84.
20. See Huneycutt, "Intercession and the High-Medieval Queen: The Esther Topos," in *Power of the Weak*, ed. Carpenter and MacLean, pp. 126–46, and in the same volume, John Carmi Parsons, "The Queen's Intercession in Thirteenth-Century England," pp. 147–77. Also Lois L. Huneycutt, "Intercession," in *Women and Gender in Medieval Europe: An Encyclopedia*, ed. Margaret Schaus (New York: Routledge, 2006), pp. 406–7.
21. See Geaman, "Queen's Gold and Intercession: The Case of Eleanor of Aquitaine"; Huneycutt, *Matilda of Scotland*, pp. 57–63; and J. L. Laynesmith, *The Last Medieval Queens* (Oxford: Oxford University Press, 2004), pp. 7, 32, 95, 106, 139, and for queen's gold, pp. 223, 239–40.
22. Sean Gilsdorf, ed. and trans., *Queenship and Sanctity: The Lives of Mathilda and the Epitaph of Adelheid* (Washington, DC: Catholic University of America, 2004). See also Patrick Corbet, *Les saints ottoniens. Sainteté dynastique, sainteté royale et sainteté féminine autour de l'an mil* (Sigmaringen: Thorbecke, 1986).
23. Sedulius Scottus, *De Rectoribus Christianis (On Christian Rulers): An Edition and English Translation*, ed. and trans. R. Dyson (Woodbridge: The Boydell Press, 2008), p. 79.
24. Discussed in McNamara and Wemple, "Power of Women through the Family" (1988), pp. 90–91.

25. Asser, "Life of Alfred the Great," in *Alfred the Great: Asser's Life of Alfred and Other Contemporary Sources,* ed. and trans. Simon Keynes and Michael Lapidge (Harmondsworth: Penguin, 1983), p. 71.
26. For the early medieval period, a starting point is Janet Nelson, "Inaugurations Rituals," in *Politics and Ritual in Early Medieval Europe*, p. 307. See also Pauline Stafford, whose essays on women and power have been collected in *Gender, Family, and the Legitimisation of Power* (Aldershot: Ashgate, 2006). See also Laura Gathagan, "The Trappings of Power: The Coronation of Mathilda of Flanders," *The Haskins Society Journal* 13 (1999), pp. 21–39. For the French coronation in the later medieval and early modern period, see Richard A. Jackson, *Vive le roi: A History of the French Coronation from Charles V to Charles* X (Chapel Hill: University of North Carolina Press, 1984).
27. See Frederic L. Cheyette, *Ermengarde of Narbonne and the World of the Troubadours* (Ithaca: Cornell University Press, 2001).
28. Erin L. Jordan, *Women, Power, and Religious Patronage in the Middle Ages* (New York: Palgrave, 2006).
29. For Matilda of Scotland, consort of Henry I, see Huneycutt, *Matilda of Scotland.* There is no modern biographical monograph on Matilda of Boulogne, but see Heather J. Tanner, "Queenship: Office, Custom, or Ad Hoc? The Case of Queen Matilda III of England (1135–1152)," in *Eleanor of Aquitaine: Lord and Lady*, ed. Bonnie Wheeler and John Carmi Parsons (New York: Palgrave Macmillan, 2002), pp. 133–58; and Patricia A. Dark, "'A Woman of Subtlety and a Man's Resolution': Matilda of Boulogne in the Power Struggles of the Anarchy," in *Aspects of Power and Authority in the Middle Ages*, ed. Brenda M. Bolton and Christine E. Meek (Turnhout: Brepols, 2007), pp. 147–64.
30. Robert S. Fawtier, *The Capetian Kings of France: Monarchy and Nation, 987–1328*, trans. Lionel Butler and R. J. Adam (London: Macmillan, 1960), pp. 27–29.
31. Scholars of the medieval Iberian Peninsula have produced a number of important studies in recent years. See, for instance, Theresa Earenfight, ed., *Queenship and Political Power in Medieval and Early Modern Spain* (Aldershot: Ashgate, 2005) and *The King's Other Body: Maria of Castile and the Crown of Aragon* (Philadelphia: University of Pennsylvania Press, 2009). See also Nuria Silleras-Fernandez, *Power, Piety, and Patronage in Late Medieval Queenship: Maria de Luna* (New York: Palgrave, 2008); Miriam Shadis, *Political Women in the High Middle Ages: Berenguela of Castile and Her Family* (New York: Palgrave, 2009); and Iona McCleery, "Isabel of Aragon (d. 1336): Model Queen or Model Saint," *Journal of Ecclesiastical History* 57 (2006), pp. 668–92.
32. For the divorce, see two essays in Wheeler and Parsons, eds., *Eleanor of Aquitaine*: James A. Brundage, "The Canon Law of Divorce in the Mid-Twelfth Century: Louis VII c. Eleanor of Aquitaine," pp. 213–21; and Constance Brittain Bouchard, "Eleanor's Divorce from Louis VII: The Uses of Consanguinity," pp. 223–36.
33. For Ingeborg, see George Conklin, "Ingeborg of Denmark, Queen of France, 1193–1223," in *Queens and Queenship*, ed. Duggan, pp. 39–52; and Kathleen S. Schowalter, "The Ingeborg Psalter: Queenship, Legitimacy, and the Appropriation of Byzantine Art in the West," in *Capetian Women*, ed. Nolan, pp. 99–135.

34. Discussed in O'Callaghan, "The Many Roles of the Medieval Queen: Some Examples from Castile," in *Queenship and Political Power*, ed. Earenfight, pp. 21–32.
35. William of Tyre, *A History of Deeds Done beyond the Sea,* ed. and trans. Emily Atwater Babcock and A. C. Krey, 2 vols. (New York: Columbia University Press, 1943), vol. 2, p. 76. The best study of Melisende remains Hans Eberhard Mayer, "Studies in the History of Queen Melisende of Jerusalem," *Dumbarton Oaks Papers* 26 (1972), pp. 94–182.
36. Bernard of Clairvaux in *Patrologiae Cursus Completus,* ed. J.-P. Migne (Paris: Migne, 1862), vol. 182, p. 557.
37. See Bernard F. Reilly, *The Kingdom of Leon-Castilla under Queen Urraca: 1109–1126* (Princeton, NJ: Princeton University Press, 1982); and Martin, *Queen as King,* and "Art of a Reigning Queen."
38. Ralph V. Turner, *Eleanor of Aquitaine: Queen of France, Queen of England* (New Haven and London: Yale University Press, 2009), pp. 250, 261. See also Margaret Howell, "The Resources of Eleanor of Aquitaine as Queen Consort," *English Historical Review* 102 (1987), pp. 372–93.
39. Margaret Howell, *Eleanor of Provence: Queenship in Thirteenth-Century England* (Oxford: Blackwell, 1998), pp. 262–64.
40. Nolan, *Queens in Stone and Silver*, p. 21; Brigitte Bedos Rezak, "Women, Seals, and Power," in *Women and Power in the Middle Ages*, ed. Erler and Kowaleski, pp. 61–82 (at p. 63).
41. Marjorie Chibnall, *The Empress Matilda: Queen Consort, Queen Mother, and Lady of the English* (Oxford: Blackwell, 1991), plate 5 (following p. 116).
42. William of Malmesbury, *Gesta Regum Anglorum,* vol. 1, p. 176.
43. Nolan, *Queens in Stone and Silver.*
44. Frank Barlow, ed. and trans., *The Life of King Edward Who Rests at Westminster*, 2nd ed. (Oxford: Oxford University Press, 1992).
45. David Abulafia, *Frederick II: A Medieval Emperor* (Harmondsworth: Penguin, 1988), p. 89; John Julius Norwich, *The Normans in Sicily: The Magnificent Story of the "Other" Norman Conquest* (Harmondsworth: Penguin, 1992), pp. 748–50; and S. H. Steinberg, "A Portrait of Constance of Sicily," *Journal of the Warburg Institute* 1 (1938), pp. 249–51. There is as yet no modern scholarly monograph on Constance, but see the interesting and idiosyncratic reflections of Mary Taylor Simeti, *Travels with a Medieval Queen* (New York: Farrar, Straus and Giroux, 2001), who retraced Constance's journey south.
46. See G.W.S. Barrow, "A Kingdom in Crisis: Scotland and the Maid of Norway," *Scottish Historical Review* 69 (1990), pp. 120–41; Knut Helle, "Norwegian Foreign Policy and the Maid of Norway," *Scottish Historical Review* 69 (1990), pp. 142–56; and Norman Reid, "Margaret, 'Maid of Norway' and Scottish Queenship," *Reading Medieval Studies* 8 (1982), pp. 75–96.
47. Treaty of Troyes, quoted in F. A. Ogg, *A Source Book of Mediaeval History,* (New York: American Book Company, 1907), p. 443.
48. See Parsons, *Eleanor of Castile.* For Queen Philippa and the burghers of Calais, see Strohm, "Queens as Intercessors," pp. 99–105. For Anne of Bohemia, see Bell, "Medieval Women Book Owners," pp. 760, 764–65; and Strohm, pp. 105–19.

49. See Kimberly LoPrete, *Adela of Blois: Countess and Lord (c. 1067–1137)* (Dublin: Four Courts Press, 2007). Also, more generally, John Carmi Parsons, "Mothers, Daughters, Marriage, Power: Some Plantagenet Evidence, 1150–1500," in *Medieval Queenship*, ed. Parsons (New York: St. Martin's Press, 1993), pp. 63–78.
50. First and foremost, anyone interested in medieval religious women should consult Jo Ann McNamara, *Sisters in Arms: Catholic Nuns through Two Millennia* (Harvard: Harvard University Press, 1996); and Jane Tibbetts Schulenberg, *Forgetful of Their Sex: Female Sanctity and Society, c. 500–1100* (Chicago: University of Chicago Press, 2001).
51. Margot King, "The Desert Mothers: A Survey of the Female Anchoritic Tradition in Western Europe," *Fourteenth Century Mystics Newsletter* 9 (1983), pp. 12–25. King's use of the term *Desert Mothers* is rather loose, extending to any solitary/enclosed woman. See also Laura Swan, *The Forgotten Desert Mothers: Sayings, Lives, and Stories of Early Christian Women* (New York: Paulist Press, 2001).
52. For the councils and the status of the female deacon in sixth-century Francia, see Wemple, *Women in Frankish Society*, pp. 140–43.
53. For Ireland, see Lisa M. Bitel, *Land of Women: Tales of Sex and Gender from Early Ireland* (Ithaca: Cornell University Press, 1996), esp. chap. 8.
54. For instance, Anna, king of the East Angles, sent both his daughter and his step-daughter to Faremoutiers, and each later served as abbess there. See Eric Fletcher, "The Influence of Merovingian Gaul on Northumbria in the Seventh Century," *Medieval Archaeology* 24 (1980), pp. 69–82 (at p. 78).
55. Bede, *Ecclesiastical History of the English People,* ed. and trans. D. H. Farmer, Ronald E. Latham, and Leo Shirley Price, rev. ed. (Harmondsworth: Penguin, 1991), pp. 243–47; and Barbara Yorke, *Nunneries and the Anglo-Saxon Royal Houses* (London: Continuum, 2003), p. 163. See also Sarah Foot, *Monastic Life in Anglo-Saxon England, c. 600–900* (Cambridge: Cambridge University Press, 2006), pp. 278–79.
56. Rudolf of Fulda, "The Life of St. Leoba, by Rudolf, a Monk of Fulda," in *The Anglo-Saxon Missionaries in Germany, Being the Lives of SS. Willibrord, Boniface, Leoba and Lebuin together with the* Hodoepericon *of St. Willibald and a Selection from the Correspondence of St. Boniface*, ed. and trans. C. H. Talbot (London and New York: Sheed and Ward, 1954).
57. Gilsdorf, ed. and trans., *Queenship and Sanctity*; Corbet, *Les saints ottoniens*; and John W. Bernhardt, *Itinerant Kingship and Royal Monasteries in Medieval Germany, c. 936–1075* (Cambridge: Cambridge University Press, 2002), pp. 142–43.
58. Hildegard of Bingen, *Sanctae Hildegardis Abbatissae Opera Omnia*, Patrologia Latina, ed. J.-P. Migne, 221 vols. (Paris: Migne, 1855), vol. 197.
59. There is an enormous modern bibliography on Hildegard. For a start, see the work of Barbara Newman, including *Sister of Wisdom: St. Hildegard's Theology of the Feminine* (Berkeley: University of California Press, 1987) and Newman, ed., *Voice of the Living Light: Hildegard of Bingen and Her World* (Berkeley: University of California Press, 1998); and also Sabina Flanagan, *Hildegard of Bingen: A Visionary Life* (New York: Routledge, 1989). A selection of Hildegard's works can be

found in Hildegard of Bingen, *Selected Writings,* ed. and trans. Mark Atherton (Harmondsworth: Penguin, 2001).

60. Thomas de Cantimpré, *The Life of Christina Mirabilis,* trans. Margot H. King (Toronto: Peregrina Press, 1989; 2nd ed. 1997), p. 40.
61. Rudolph M. Bell, *Holy Anorexia* (Chicago: University of Chicago Press, 1987); and Caroline Walker Bynum, *Holy Feast and Holy Fast: The Religious Significance of Food to Medieval Women* (Berkeley: University of California Press, 1987), esp. pp. 294–96. For a modern treatment of the religious aspects of anorexia that takes into account the Bynum thesis, see Mary Michelle Lelwica, *Starving for Salvation: The Spiritual Dimensions of Eating Problems among American Girls and Women* (New York: Oxford University Press, 2002).
62. Letter of Joan of Arc to the King of England, March 22, 1429, trans. Belle Tuten, from M. Vallet de Vireville, ed., *Chronique de la Pucelle, ou Chronique de Cousinot* (Paris: Adolphe Delahaye, 1859), pp. 281–83.
63. Christine de Pisan, *Ditié de Jehanne d'Arc,* ed. Angus J. Kennedy and Kenneth Varty (Oxford: Society for the Study of Mediaeval Languages and Literature, 1977).
64. Joan of Arc is one of the few medieval women for whom there exists an extensive bibliography. See Régine Pernoud and Marie Véronique Clin, *Joan of Arc: Her Story,* trans. Jeremy duQuesnay Adams (New York: Palgrave, 1999); Deborah A. Fraioli, *Joan of Arc and the Hundred Years War* (New York: Greenwood, 2005); and the excellent collection of essays edited by Bonnie Wheeler and Charles T. Wood, *Fresh Verdicts on Joan of Arc* (New York: Routledge, 1996). For the military aspects of her career, see Kelly DeVries, *Joan of Arc: A Military Leader* (New York: Sutton Publishing, 1999). For the early theological debate on her mission, see Fraioli, *Joan of Arc: The Early Debate* (Woodbridge: The Boydell Press, 2002). For her trial and the posthumous retrial, see Daniel Hobbins, ed. and trans., *The Trial of Joan of Arc* (Cambridge, MA: Harvard University Press, 2007); and Pernoud, ed. and trans., *The Retrial of Joan of Arc: The Evidence for Her Vindication* (originally published New York, 1955; reprint San Francisco: Ignatius Press, 2007).
65. See Anne Llewellyn Barstow, "Joan of Arc and Female Mysticism," *Journal of Feminist Studies in Religion* 1 (1985), pp. 29–42.
66. For example, Georges Duby, "Affidavits and Confessions," in *A History of Women in the West,* ed. Christiane Klapisch-Zuber, vol. 2, *Silences of the Middle Ages* (Cambridge, MA: Belknap Press), pp. 483–91, at p. 483. For a succinct and insightful discussion of Duby's difficulties with women's history, see Ann Kettle, "Review of Georges Duby, *Women of the Twelfth Century*" (review 73), *Reviews in History,* https://www.history.ac.uk/reviews/review/73 (accessed September 1, 2011).

Chapter 8

The individual authors were responsible for the topics covered in this chapter as follows: Marian Bleeke (Eve, the Virgin Mary, Luxuria, Aelgvfa, and Hildegard of Bingen); Jennifer Borland (St. Margaret, St. Radegund, Women and Medicine, Eleanor of Aquitaine, Blanche of Castile, and Female Users of Architecture); Rachel Dressler (Representations of Wives, Conclusion, and project facilitator); Martha

Easton (St. Agatha, St. Eugenia, Women as Creators and Consumers); and Elizabeth L'Estrange (Introduction, Bathsheba, St. Anne, St. Elizabeth, and Representation of Mothers).

1. O. K. Werckmeister, "The Lintel Fragment Representing Eve from Saint-Lazare, Autun," *Journal of the Warburg and Courtauld Institutes* 35 (1972), pp. 3–7; Georges Duby, *Women of the Twelfth Century*, vol. 3, *Eve and the Church* (Chicago: University of Chicago Press, 1998), pp. 29–47.
2. Ilene H. Forsyth, *The Throne of Wisdom: Wood Sculptures of the Madonna in Romanesque France* (Princeton, NJ: Princeton University Press, 1972); Miri Rubin, *Mother of God: A History of the Virgin Mary* (New Haven: Yale University Press, 2009).
3. Linda Seidel, *Legends in Limestone: Lazarus, Gislebertus, and the Cathedral of Autun* (Chicago: University of Chicago Press, 1999), pp. 103–4; George Duby, *Women of the Twelfth Century*, vol. 1, *Eleanor of Aquitaine and Six Others* (Chicago: University of Chicago Press, 1997), pp. 21–41.
4. Marianne Elsakkers, "In Pain You Shall Bear Children: Medieval Prayers for a Safe Delivery," in *Studies in the History of Religions*, ed. Anne-Marie Korte (Leiden: Brill, 2001), pp. 179–209.
5. Cordelia Warr, "Painting in Late Fourteenth-Century Padua: The Patronage of Fina Buzzacarini," *Renaissance Studies* 10 (1996), pp. 139–55.
6. Martha Easton, "Saint Agatha and the Sanctification of Sexual Violence," *Studies in Iconography* 16 (1994), pp. 83–118; Madeline Caviness, *Visualizing Women in the Middle Ages: Sight, Spectacle, and Scopic Economy* (Philadelphia, University of Pennsylvania Press, 2001), pp. 82–124.
7. Jennifer Borland, "Violence on Vellum: Saint Margaret's Transgressive Body and Its Audience," in *Representing Medieval Genders and Sexualities in Europe: Construction, Transformation, and Subversion, 600–1530*, ed. Elizabeth L'Estrange and Alison More (Aldershot: Ashgate, 2011). See also Renate Blumenfeld-Kosinski and Timea Klara Szell, *Images of Sainthood in Medieval Europe* (Ithaca: Cornell University Press, 1991), p. 285; and Brigitte Cazelles, *The Lady as Saint: A Collection of French Hagiographic Romances of the Thirteenth Century* (Philadelphia: University of Pennsylvania Press, 1991), p. 218.
8. Wendy R. Larson, "Who Is the Master of this Narrative? Maternal Patronage of the Cult of St. Margaret," in *Gendering the Master Narrative: Women and Power in the Middle Ages*, ed. Mary C. Erler and Maryanne Kowaleski (Ithaca and London: Cornell University Press, 2003), pp. 94–104.
9. Martha Easton, "'Why Can't a Woman Be More Like a Man?' Transforming and Transcending Gender in the Lives of Female Saints," in *The Four Modes of Seeing: Approaches to Medieval Imagery in Honor of Madeline Harrison Caviness*, ed. Evelyn Staudinger Lane, Elizabeth Carson Pastan, and Ellen M. Shortell (Burlington, Ashgate, 2009), pp. 333–47.
10. Kirk Ambrose, *The Nave Sculpture of Vézelay: The Art of Monastic Viewing*, Studies and Texts 154 (Toronto: Pontifical Institute of Mediaeval Studies, 2006), pp. 39–44.
11. Véronique P. Day, "Recycling Radegund: Identity and Ambition in the Breviary of Anne De Prye," in *Excavating the Medieval Image: Manuscripts, Artists, Audiences:*

Essays in Honor of Sandra Hindman, ed. David S. Areford and Nina A. Rowe (Aldershot: Ashgate, 2004), pp. 151–77.

12. Magdalena Elizabeth Carrasco, "Spirituality in Context: The Romanesque Illustrated Life of St. Radegund of Poitiers (Poitiers, Bibl. Mun., Ms 250)," *Art Bulletin* 72 (1990), pp. 414–35.
13. Emile Mâle, *Religious Art in France, the Twelfth-Century: A Study of the Origins of Medieval Iconography*, trans. Marthiel Matthews (Princeton, NJ: Princeton University Press, 1978), pp. 372–76; Ilene Forsyth, "Narrative at Moissac: Schapiro's Legacy," *Gesta* 41 (2002), pp. 71–93.
14. Madeline Caviness, "Anglo-Saxon Women, Norman Knights, and a 'Third Sex' in the Bayeux Embroidery," in *The Bayeux Tapestry: New Interpretations*, ed. Martin K. Foys, Karen Eileen Overbey, and Dan Terkla (Woodbridge: The Boydell Press, 2009), pp. 89–93.
15. Peter Murray Jones, "Image, Word, and Medicine in the Middle Ages," in *Visualizing Medieval Medicine and Natural History, 1200–1550*, ed. Jean A. Givens, Karen M. Reeds, and Alain Touwaide (Aldershot, UK, and Burlington, VT: Ashgate, 2006), pp. 1–24.
16. In manuscripts such as British Library MS Sloane 1977 and Bodleian Library MS Laud. Misc. 724. On Caesarean sections, see Renate Blumenfeld-Kosinski, *Not of Woman Born: Representations of Caesarean Birth in Medieval and Renaissance Culture* (Ithaca and London: Cornell University Press, 1990).
17. See Elizabeth L'Estrange, *Holy Motherhood: Gender, Dynasty and Visual Culture in the Later Middle Ages* (Manchester: Manchester University Press, 2008); Monica H. Green, *Making Women's Medicine Masculine: The Rise of Male Authority in Pre-Modern Gynaecology* (Oxford: Oxford University Press, 2008).
18. A good overview of medieval marriage history and law is provided by Edwin Hall, "On Marriage Law and Ceremony," in *The Arnolfini Betrothal: Medieval Marriage and the Enigma of Van Eyck's Double Portrait* (Berkeley, Los Angeles, and London: University of California Press, 1994), chap. 2, pp. 13–47. For its symbolic dimensions, see D. L. D'Avray, *Medieval Marriage: Symbolism and Society* (Oxford: Oxford University Press, 2005). See also Conor McCarthy, "The Principle of Consent," in *Marriage in Medieval England: Law, Literature and Practice* (Woodbridge: The Boydell Press, 2004), chap. 1; and the essays in Philip L. Reynolds and John Witte, Jr., eds., *To Have and to Hold: Marrying and Its Documentation in Western Christendom, 400–1600* (Cambridge: Cambridge University Press, 2007).
19. Hall, *Arnolfini Betrothal*, pp. 70–77.
20. Thomas Woodcock and John Martin Robinson, *The Oxford Guide to Heraldry* (Oxford: Oxford University Press, 1988), pp. 120–26.
21. Anne McGee Morgenstern, *Gothic Tombs of Kinship in France, the Low Countries, and England* (University Park, PA: The Pennsylvania State University Press, 2000), pp. 122–25.
22. D'Avray, *Medieval Marriage*, pp. 7–9.
23. Corine Schleif, "Men on Right—Women on the Left: (A)symmetrical Spaces and Gendered Places," in *Women's Space: Patronage, Place, and Gender in the*

Medieval Church, ed. Virginia Chieffo Raguin and Sarah Stanbury (Albany: The State University of New York Press, 2005), pp. 207–49.

24. Jacqueline Marie Musacchio, *The Art and Ritual of Childbirth in Renaissance Italy* (New Haven: Yale University Press, 1999).
25. Pamela Sheingorn, "The Wise Mother," *Gesta* 32 (1993), pp. 69–80.
26. Patricia Cullum and Jeremy Goldberg, "How Margaret Blackburn Taught Her Daughters: Reading Devotional Instruction in a Book of Hours," in *Medieval Women: Texts and Contexts: Essays for Felicity Riddy*, ed. Jocelyn Wogan-Browne, Rosalynn Voaden, Arlyn Diamond, Ann Hutchison, Carol Meale, and Lesley Johnson (Turnhout: Brepols, 2000), pp. 217–36.
27. Elizabeth L'Estrange, "Sainte Anne et le mécénat d'Anne de France" and "Le mécénat d'Anne de Bretagne," in *Patronnes et mécènes en France à la Renaissance*, ed. K. Wilson-Chevalier (St-Étienne: Presse Universitaire de St-Étienne, 2007), pp. 135–54, 169–94.
28. Madeline Caviness, "Artist: To See, Hear, and Know All at Once," in *Voice of the Living Light: Hildegard of Bingen and Her World*, ed. Barbara Newman (Berkeley: University of California Press, 1998), pp. 110–24; and "Hildegard as Designer of the Illustrations to Her Works," in *Hildegard of Bingen: The Context of Her Thought and Art*, ed. Charles Burnett and Peter Dronke (London: Warburg Institute, 1998), pp. 29–42.
29. Barbara Newman, *Sister of Wisdom: St. Hildegard's Theology of the Feminine* (Berkeley: University of California Press, 1987), pp. 2–3, 35, 182–85; Sabina Flanagan, *Hildegard of Bingen (1098–1179): A Visionary Life* (London: Routledge, 1989), pp. 13–14, 42, 53–54.
30. Herrad of Landsberg, *Hortus Deliciarum (Garden of Delights)*, commentary and notes by A. Straub and G. Keller, ed. and trans. Aristide D. Caratzas (New Rochelle, NY: Caratzas Brothers Publishers, 1977).
31. Jeffrey F. Hamburger, *Nuns as Artists: The Visual Culture of a Medieval Convent* (Berkeley and Los Angeles: University of California Press, 1997).
32. Hamburger, *Nuns as Artists*, p. 214.
33. Barbara K. Altmann and Deborah L. McGrady, eds., *Christine de Pizan: A Casebook* (New York: Routledge, 2003).
34. Susan Groag Bell, *The Lost Tapestries of the City of Ladies* (Berkeley: University of California Press, 2004).
35. Sandra Penketh, "Women and Books of Hours," in *Women and the Book: Assessing the Visual Evidence*, ed. Jane H. M. Taylor and Lesley Smith (Toronto: University of Toronto Press and the British Library, 1997), pp. 266–80; and Susan Groag Bell, "Medieval Women Book Owners: Arbiters of Lay Piety and Ambassadors of Culture," *Signs* 7 (1982), pp. 742–68.
36. *The Hours of Mary of Burgundy*, ed. Erik Inglis (London: Harvey Miller Publishers, 1995).
37. Madeline Caviness suggests that this is the case in the *Hours of Jeanne d'Evreux*. See her "Patron or Matron: A Capetian Bride and a Vade Mecum for Her Marriage Bed," *Speculum* 68 (1993), pp. 333–62.
38. Flora Lewis, "The Wound in Christ's Side and the Instruments of the Passion: Gendered Experience and Response," in *Women and the Book*, ed. Taylor and Smith, p. 206.

39. Michael Camille, *The Medieval Art of Love: Objects and Subjects of Desire* (New York: Harry N. Abrams, 1998); Martha Easton, "'Was It Good for You, Too?, Medieval Erotic Art and Its Audiences," in *Different Visions*, ed. Rachel Dressler, http://www.differentvisions.org (accessed May 3, 2010).
40. Roberta Gilchrist, "Medieval Bodies in the Material World: Gender, Stigma, and the Body," in *Framing Medieval Bodies*, ed. Sarah Kay and Miri Rubin (Manchester and New York: Manchester University Press, 1996), pp. 43–61. See also Roberta Gilchrist, *Gender and Material Culture: The Archaeology of Religious Women* (London and New York: Routledge, 1994); Jane Tibbetts Schulenburg, "Gender, Celibacy, and Proscriptions of Sacred Space: Symbol and Practice," in *Women's Space*, ed. Raguin and Stanbury, pp. 185–205.
41. For a thorough investigation of the evidence for Derbforgaill's role, see Jenifer Ní Ghrádaigh, "'But What Exactly Did She Give?': Derbforgaill and the Nuns' Church and Clonmacnoise," in *Clonmacnoise Studies: Seminar Papers 1998*, ed. Heather A. King (Dublin: Dept. of Environment Heritage and Local Government, 2003).
42. John Carmi Parsons, ed., *Medieval Queenship* (New York: St. Martin's, 1993).
43. On female rulers and regents and their representation, see Anne-Marie Legaré, ed., *Livres et lectures des femmes en Europe entre moyen âge et renaissance* (Turnhout: Brepols, 2007); and Kathleen Wilson-Chevalier, ed., *Patronnes et mécènes en France à la Renaissance* (St-Étienne: Presse Universitaire de St-Étienne, 2007).
44. Ralph V. Turner, *Eleanor of Aquitaine: Queen of France, Queen of England* (New Haven and London: Yale University Press, 2009), pp. 169, 311–13.
45. Kathleen Nolan, *Queens in Stone and Silver: The Creation of a Visual Imagery of Queenship in Capetian France* (New York: Palgrave Macmillan, 2009), p. 98.
46. Ibid., p. 111.
47. Ibid., p. 121.
48. Ibid., pp. 129–31.
49. Rachel Gibbons, "Isabeau of Bavaria, Queen of France (1385–1422): The Creation of an Historical Villainess," *Transactions of the Royal Historical Society* (6th ser.), 6 (1996), pp. 51–73.
50. Elizabeth L'Estrange, "Sainte Anne et le mécénat d'Anne de France" in *Patronnes et mécènes*, ed. Wilson-Chevalier, pp. 135–54.

BIBLIOGRAPHY

Abels, Richard, and Ellen Harrison. 1979. "The Participation of Women in Languedocian Catharism." *Mediaeval Studies* 41: 215–51.

Aberth, J. 2001. *From the Brink of the Apocalypse: Confronting Famine, War, Plague, and Death in the Later Middle Ages*. New York: Routledge.

Abreu-Ferreira, Darlene. 2002. "Work and Identity in Early-modern Portugal: What Did Gender Have to Do With it?" *Journal of Social History* 35: 859–87.

Abulafia, David. 1988. *Frederick II: A Medieval Emperor*. London: Penguin.

Alan of Lille. 1981. *The Art of Preaching*, trans., with an introduction, Gillian R. Evans. Kalamazoo: Cistercian Publications.

Alberti, Leon Battista. 1969. *I libri della famiglia*, trans. Renée Neu Watkins as *The Family in Renaissance Florence*. Columbia: University of South Carolina Press.

Albert the Great. 2008. *Questions Concerning Aristotle's On Animals*. Fathers of the Church: Medieval Continuation, vol. 9, trans. Irven M. Resnick and Kenneth F. Kitchell, Jr. Washington, DC: Catholic University of America Press.

Albuquerque, Martim de, and Eduardo Borges Nunes, eds. 1988. *Ordenações del-Rei D. Duarte*. Lisbon: Fundação Calouste Gulbenkian.

Alcock, N. W. 2003. "The Medieval Peasant at Home: England, 1250–1550." In *The Medieval Household in Christian Europe, c. 850–c. 1550: Managing Power, Wealth, and the Body*, ed. Cordelia Beattie, Anna Maslakovic, and Sarah Rees Jones. Turnhout: Brepols.

Almeida, Manuel Lopes de, Idalino da Costa Brochado, and António Dias Dinis, eds. 1960–74. *Monumenta Henricina*. 15 vols. Coimbra and Lisbon: Comissão Executiva do V Centenário da Morte do Infante D. Henrique.

Altmann, Barbara K., and Deborah L. McGrady, eds. 2003. *Christine de Pizan: A Casebook*. New York: Routledge.

Álvares, João. 1960. *Obras*, ed. Adelino de Almeida Calado. Coimbra: Acta Universitatis Conimbrigensis.

Ambrose, Kirk. 2006. *The Nave Sculpture of Vézelay: The Art of Monastic Viewing*. Studies and Texts 154. Toronto: Pontifical Institute of Mediaeval Studies.

Amt, Emilie, ed. 1993. *Women's Lives in Medieval Europe: A Sourcebook*. New York: Routledge.

Anne of France. 2004. *Lessons for my Daughter*, ed. Sharon Jansen. Cambridge: D. S. Brewer.

Anonymous. n.d. "The Misericords and History of Bristol Cathedral, the Holy and Undivided Trinity." Available at: http://www.misericords.co.uk/bristol.html. Accessed June 9, 2011.

Aquinas, Thomas. 1955–58. *Summa theologiae*. Rev. ed., 5 vols. Madrid: La Editorial Catolica.

Aristotle. 1943. *Generation of Animals*, trans. A. L. Peck. London: William Heinemann.

Aristotle. 1910. *Historia animalium*. In *The Works of Aristotle Translated into English*, ed. W. D. Ross. 12 vols., vol. 4, trans. D. W. Thompson. Oxford: Oxford University Press.

Arnade, Peter. 1996. *Realms of Ritual: Burgundian Ceremony and Civic Life in Late Medieval Ghent*. Ithaca: Cornell University Press.

Arrizabalaga, Jon. 2002. "Problematizing Retrospective Diagnosis in the History of Disease." *Asclepio* 54: 51–70.

Asser. 1983. "Life of Alfred the Great." In *Alfred the Great: Asser's life of Alfred and Other Contemporary Sources*, ed. and trans. Simon Keynes and Michael Lapidge. Harmondsworth: Penguin.

Aston, Margaret. 1984. *Lollards and Reformers: Images and Literacy in Late Medieval Religion*. London: Hambledon.

Aston, Margaret. 1980. "Lollard Women Priests?" *Journal of Ecclesiastical History* 31: 441–61.

Aston, Margaret. 1990. "Segregation in Church." In *Women in the Church*, ed. W. J. Sheils and Diana Wood. Studies in Church History 27. Oxford: Blackwell.

Audisio, Gabriel. 1999. *The Waldensian Dissent: Persecution and Survival, c. 1170–1570*. Cambridge: Cambridge University Press.

Augustine. 1992. "From the Literal Meaning of Genesis." In *Woman Defamed and Woman Defended: An Anthology of Medieval Texts*, ed. Alcuin Blamires. Oxford: Oxford University Press.

Augustine. 1999. *The Works of St. Augustine*, ed. D. G. Hunter, trans. Ray Kearney. New York: New York City Press.

Azevedo, Pedro de, ed. 1915–34. *Documentos das Chancelarias Reais Anteriores a 1531 Relativos a Marrocos*. 2 vols. Lisbon: Academia das Sciências.

Bacon, Roger. 1920. *Opera hactenus inedita Rogeri Baconi, Fasc. V. Secretum Secretorum cum glossis et notulis*, ed. Robert Steele. Oxford: Oxford University Press.

Baert, Barbara. 2010. "'Who Touched my Clothes?': The Healing of the Woman with the Haemorrhage (Mark 5: 24–34; Luke 8: 42–48 and Matthew 9: 19–22) in Early Medieval Visual Culture." *Konsthistorisk Tidskrift/Journal of Art History* 79: 65–90.

Bailey, Michael D. 2003. *Battling Demons: Witchcraft, Heresy, and Reform in the Late Middle Ages*. University Park: Pennsylvania State University Press.

Bailey, Michael D. 2001. "From Sorcery to Witchcraft: Clerical Conceptions of Magic in the Later Middle Ages." *Speculum* 76: 960–90.

Baird, Joseph L., and John R. Kane. 1974. "*La Querelle de la Rose*: In Defence of the Opponents." *French Review* 48: 298–307.

Baird, Joseph L., and John R. Kane, eds. 1978. *La Querelle de la Rose: Letters and documents*. Chapel Hill: North Carolina Studies in the Romance Languages and Literatures.

Baldwin, John W. 1970. *Masters, Princes and Merchants: The Social Views of Peter the Chanter and his Circle*. 2 vols. Princeton, NJ: Princeton University Press.

Bardsley, Sandy. 2001. "Debate—Women's Work Reconsidered: Gender and Wage Differentiation in Late Medieval England—Reply." *Past & Present* 173: 199–202.

Bardsley, Sandy. 2006. *Venomous Tongues: Speech and Gender in Late Medieval England*. Philadelphia: University of Pennsylvania Press.

Bardsley, Sandy. 1999. "Women's Work Reconsidered: Gender and Wage Differentiation in Late Medieval England." *Past & Present* 165: 3–29.

Barlow, Frank, ed. and trans. 1992. *Life of King Edward who Rests at Westminster*. 2nd ed. Oxford: Oxford University Press.

Barron, Caroline M. 1996. "The Education and Training of Girls in Fifteenth-century London." In *Courts, Counties and the Capital in the Later Middle Ages*, ed. Diana E. S. Dunn. Stroud: Sutton.

Barron, Caroline M. 1989. "The 'Golden Age' of Women in Medieval London." *Reading Medieval Studies* 15: 35–58.

Barrow, G.W.S. 1990. "A Kingdom in Crisis: Scotland and the Maid of Norway." *Scottish Historical Review* 69: 120–41.

Barstow, Anne Llewellyn. 1985. "Joan of Arc and Female Mysticism." *Journal of Feminist Studies in Religion* 1: 29–42.

Bartlet, Suzanne. 2009. *Licoricia of Winchester: Marriage, Motherhood and Murder in the Medieval Anglo-Jewish Community*. London: Vallentine Mitchell.

Baumgarten, Elisheva. 2004. *Mothers and Children: Jewish Family Life in Medieval Europe*. Princeton, NJ: Princeton University Press.

Beach, Alison. 2000. "Claustration and Collaboration between the Sexes." In *Monks and Nuns, Saints and Outcasts*, ed. Sharon Farmer and Barbara H. Rosenwein. Ithaca: Cornell University Press.

Beach, Alison. 2004. *Women as Scribes: Book Production and Monastic Reform in Twelfth-century Bavaria*. Cambridge: Cambridge University Press.

Beattie, Cordelia. 2010. "Economy." In *A Cultural History of Childhood and Family: In the Early Modern Age*, ed. Sandra Cavallo and Silvia Evangelisti. Oxford: Berg.

Beattie, Cordelia. 2007. *Medieval Single Women: The Politics of Social Classification in Late Medieval England*. Oxford: Oxford University Press.

Beattie, Cordelia, and Kirsten A. Fenton, eds. 2011. *Intersections of Gender, Religion and Ethnicity in the Middle Ages*. Houndmills: Palgrave Macmillan.

Bede. 1991. *Ecclesiastical History of the English People*, ed. and trans. D. H. Farmer, Ronald E. Latham, and Leo Shirley Price. Harmondsworth: Penguin.

Beier, Lucinda. 1987. *Sufferers and Healers: The Experience of Illness in Seventeenth-century England*. London: Routledge.

Bell, Rudolph M. 1987. *Holy Anorexia*. Chicago: University of Chicago Press.

Bell, Susan Groag. 2004. *The Lost Tapestries of the City of Ladies*. Berkeley: University of California Press.

Bell, Susan Groag. 1982. "Medieval Women Book Owners: Arbiters of Lay Piety and Ambassadors of Culture." *Signs* 7: 742–68.

Belo, C. 2009. "Some Considerations on Averroes' Views Regarding Women and Their Role in Society." *Journal of Islamic Studies* 20: 1–20.

Benadusi, Giovanna. 2004. "Investing the Riches of the Poor: Servants and Their Last Wills." *American Historical Review* 109: 805–26.

Ben-Amos, Ilana Krausman. 1991. "Women Apprentices in the Trades and Crafts of Early Modern Bristol." *Continuity and Change* 6: 227–52.

Benedictow, Ole. 2004. *The Black Death, 1346–1353: A Complete History*. Woodbridge: Boydell.

Bennett, H. S. 1937. *Life on the English Manor: A Study of Peasant Conditions 1150–1400*. Cambridge: University of Cambridge Press.

Bennett, Judith M. 1996. *Ale, Beer, and Brewsters in England: Women's Work in a Changing World 1300–1600*. New York: Oxford University Press.

Bennett, Judith M. 1997. "Confronting Continuity." *Journal of Women's History* 9: 73–94.

Bennett, Judith M. 1999. *A Medieval Life: Cecilia Penifader of Brigstock, c. 1295–1344*. Boston: McGraw-Hill College.

Bennett, Judith M. 1991. "Misogyny, Popular Culture, and Women's Work." *History Workshop Journal* 31: 166–88.

Bennett, Judith M. 2008. "Two Women and Their Monumental Brass, *c.* 1480." *Journal of the British Archaeological Association* 161: 163–84.

Bennett, Judith M., and Amy M. Froide, eds. 1999. *Singlewomen in the European Past, 1250–1800*. Philadelphia: University of Pennsylvania Press.

Benson, Robert L., and Giles Constable, with Carol D. Lanham, eds. 1982. *Renaissance and Renewal in the Twelfth Century*. Oxford: Clarendon Press.

Benyovsky, Irena. 2003. "Noble Family Clans and Their Urban Distribution in Medieval Trogir." In *The Medieval Household in Christian Europe, c. 850–c. 1550: Managing Power, Wealth, and the Body*, ed. Cordelia Beattie, Anna Maslakovic, and Sarah Rees Jones. Turnhout: Brepols.

Beresford, Maurice, and John Hurst. 1990. *Wharram Percy: Deserted Medieval Village*. New Haven and London: Yale University Press.

Berman, Constance. 1995. "Cistercian Nuns and the Development of the Order: The Abbey of Saint-Antoine-des-Champs outside Paris." In *The Joy of Learning and the Love of God: Studies in Honor of Jean Leclercq*, ed. E. Rozanne Elder. Kalamazoo: Cistercian Publications.

Bernard of Clairvaux. 1862. "Opera." In *Patrologiae Cursus Completus*, ed. J.-P. Migne. Vol. 182. Paris: Migne.

Bernhardt, John W. 2002. *Itinerant Kingship and Royal Monasteries in Medieval Germany, c. 936–1075*. Cambridge: Cambridge University Press.

Biller, Peter. 1997. "Cathars and Material Women." In *Medieval Theology and the Natural Body*, ed. Peter Biller and Alastair Minnis. York: York Medieval Press.

Biller, Peter. 2000. *The Measure of Multitude: Population in Medieval Thought*. Oxford: Oxford University Press.

Binski, Paul. 1996. *Medieval Death: Ritual and Representation*. Ithaca: Cornell University Press.

Biscoglio, Frances M. 1995. "'Unspun' Heroes: Iconography of the Spinning Woman in the Middle Ages." *Journal of Medieval and Renaissance Studies* 25: 163–84.

Bitel, Lisa M. 1996. *Land of Women: Tales of Sex and Gender from Early Ireland*. Ithaca: Cornell University Press.

Bitel, Lisa M. 2002. *Women in Early Medieval Europe, 400–1100*. Cambridge: Cambridge University Press.

Blamires, Alcuin. 1997. *The Case for Women in Medieval Culture*. Oxford: Clarendon Press.

Bloch, R. Howard. 1987. "Medieval Misogyny." *Representations* 20: 1–24.

Bloch, R. Howard. 1991. *Medieval Misogyny and the Invention of Western Romantic Love*. Chicago: University of Chicago Press.

Blumenfeld-Kosinski, Renate. 1990. *Not of Woman Born: Representations of Caesarean Birth in Medieval and Renaissance Culture*. Ithaca: Cornell University Press.

Blumenfeld-Kosinski, Renate, and Timea Klara Szell. 1991. *Images of Sainthood in Medieval Europe*. Ithaca: Cornell University Press.

Borland, Jennifer. 2011. "Violence on Vellum: Saint Margaret's Trangressive Body and its Audience." In *Representing Medieval Genders and Sexualities in Europe: Construction, Transformation, and Subversion, 600–1530*, ed. Elizabeth L'Estrange and Alison More. Aldershot: Ashgate.

Bothwell, J. S. 2008. "The More Things Change: Isabella and Mortimer, Edward III, and the Painful Delay of a Royal Majority (1327)." In *The Royal Minorities of Medieval and Early Modern England*, ed. Charles Beem. New York: Palgrave Macmillan.

Bouchard, Constance Brittain. 2002. "Eleanor's Divorce from Louis VII: The Uses of Consanguinity." In *Eleanor of Aquitaine: Lord and Lady*, ed. Bonnie Wheeler and John Carmi Parsons. New York: Palgrave Macmillan.

Boyle, Leonard E. 1985. "The Fourth Lateran Council and Manuals of Popular Theology." In *The Popular Literature of Medieval England*, ed. Thomas J. Heffernan. Knoxville: University of Tennessee Press.

Branham, Joan. 2002. "Bloody Women and Bloody Spaces: Menses and the Eucharist in Late Antiquity and the Early Middle Ages." *Harvard Divinity Bulletin* 30: 15–22.

Braunstein, Philippe. 1988. "Toward Intimacy: The Fourteenth and Fifteenth Centuries." In *A History of Private Life*, ed. Georges Duby. Vol. 2, *Revelations of the Medieval World*, trans. Arthur Goldhammer. Cambridge, MA, and London: Belknap Press of Harvard University Press.

Brooke, Christopher N. L. 1978. "'Both Small and Great Beasts': An Introductory Study." In *Medieval Women*, ed. Derek Baker. Dedicated and presented to Rosalind M. T. Hill, Studies in Church History, Subsidia 1. Oxford: Basil Blackwell.

Brown, Peter. 1988. *The Body and Society: Men, Women, and Sexual Renunciation in Early Christianity*. New York: Columbia University Press.

Browning, Jennifer, and Tim Higgins, with contributions from Patrick Clay, Paul Courtney, Angela Monckton, and Deborah Sawday. 2003. "Excavations of a Medieval Toft and Croft at Cropston Road, Anstey, Leicestershire." *Transactions of the Leicestershire Archaeological and Historical Society* 77: 65–81.

Bruce, J. Douglas, ed. 1903. *Le Morte Arthur: A Romance in Stanzas of Eight Lines*. Early English Text Society, extra ser. 88. London: Trübner.

Brundage, James A. 2002. "The Canon Law of Divorce in the Mid-twelfth Century: Louis VII c. Eleanor of Aquitaine." In *Eleanor of Aquitaine: Lord and Lady*, ed. Bonnie Wheeler and John Carmi Parsons. New York: Palgrave Macmillan.

Brundage, James A. 1987. *Law, Sex, and Christian Society in Medieval Europe*. Chicago: University of Chicago Press.

Brundage, James A., and Elizabeth A. Makowski. 1994. "Enclosure of Nuns: The Decretal of *Periculoso* and its Commentators." *Journal of Medieval History* 20: 143–55.

Bryce, Judith. 2005. "Les Livres des Florentines: Reconsidering Women's Literacy in Quattrocento Florence." In *At the Margins: Minority Groups in Premodern Italy*, ed. Stephen J. Milner. Minneapolis: University of Minnesota Press.

Bullough, Vern L. 1973. "Medieval Medical and Scientific Views of Women." *Viator* 4: 485–501.

Burke, Peter. 1997. "Unity and Variety in Cultural History." In *Varieties of Cultural History*, ed. Peter Burke. Cambridge: Polity.

Burke, Peter. 2004. *What is Cultural History?* Cambridge: Polity.

Burns, E. Jane. 2002. *Courtly Love Undressed: Reading through Clothes in Medieval French Culture*. Philadelphia: University of Pennsylvania Press.

Burns, E. Jane. 1992. "Knowing Women: Female Orifices in the Old French Fabliaux." *Exemplaria* 4: 81–104.

Burns, R. I. 1962. "The Parish as Frontier Institution in Thirteenth-century Valencia." *Speculum* 37: 244–51.

Burrow, J. A. 1988. *The Ages of Man: A Study in Medieval Writing and Thought*. Oxford: Clarendon Press.

Butler, Judith. 1990. *Gender Trouble: Feminism and the Subversion of Identity*. New York: Routledge.

Butler, Sara M. 2007. *The Language of Abuse: Marital Violence in Later Medieval England*. Leiden: Brill.

Bynum, Caroline Walker. 1992. " '. . . And Woman His Humanity': Female Imagery in the Religious Writing of the Later Middle Ages." In *Fragmentation and Redemption: Essays on Gender and the Human Body in Medieval Religion*. New York: Zone Books.

Bynum, Caroline Walker. 1987. *Holy Feast and Holy Fast: The Religious Significance of Food to Medieval Women*. Berkeley: University of California Press.

Bynum, Caroline Walker. 1982. *Jesus as Mother: Studies in the Spirituality of the High Middle Ages*. Berkeley: University of California Press.

Byrd, Lesley Simpson, ed. 2006. *Celestina: A Fifteenth-century Spanish Novel in Dialogue*. Berkeley: University of California Press.

Cabellero-Navas, Carmen. 2008. "The Care of Women's Health and Beauty: An Experience Shared by Medieval Jewish and Christian Women." *Journal of Medieval History* 34: 146–63.

Cabré, Montserrat. 2008. "Women or Healers? Household Practices and the Categories of Health Care in Late Medieval Iberia." *Bulletin of the History of Medicine* 82: 18–51.

Cadden, Joan. 1993. *Meanings of Sex Difference in the Middle Ages: Medicine, Science, and Culture*. Cambridge: Cambridge University Press.

Caesarius of Arles. 1994. *Césaire d'Arles. Oeuvres monastiques, II, Oeuvres pour les moines*, ed. A. de Vogüé and J. Courreau. Paris: CERF.

Caesarius of Arles. 1960. *Rule for Nuns of St. Caesarius of Arles: A Translation with a Critical Introduction*, ed. M. C. McCarthy. Washington, DC: Catholic University Press of America.

Camille, Michael. 1998. *The Medieval Art of Love: Objects and Subjects of Desire*. New York: Harry N. Abrams.

Camille, Michael. 1998. *Mirror in Parchment: The Luttrell Psalter and the Making of Medieval England*. London: Reaktion Books.

Carlson, C. L., and A. J. Weisl, eds. 1999. *Constructions of Widowhood and Virginity in the Middle Ages*. New York: St. Martin's Press.

Carpenter, Christine, ed. 1996. *Kingsford's Stonor Letters and Papers, 1290–1483*. Cambridge: Cambridge University Press.

Carpenter, Jennifer, and Sally-Beth MacLean, eds. 1995. *Power of the Weak: Studies on Medieval Women*. Urbana: University of Illinois Press.

Carrasco, Magdalena Elizabeth. 1990. "Spirituality in Context: The Romanesque Illustrated Life of St. Radegund of Poitiers (Poitiers, Bibl. Mun., Ms 250)." *Art Bulletin* 72: 414–35.

Carus-Wilson, Eleanora M. 1987. "The Woollen Industry." In *The Cambridge Economic History of Europe*, ed. M. M. Postan, Edward Miller, and Cynthia Postan. Vol. 2, *Trade and Industry in the Middle Ages*. Cambridge: Cambridge University Press.

Casagrande, Carla. 1992. "The Protected Woman," trans. Clarissa Botsford. In *A History of Women in the West*, ed. Christiane Klapisch-Zuber. Vol. 2, *Silences of the Middle Ages*. Cambridge, MA: Belknap Press.

Cavallo, Sandra. 2007. *Artisans of the Body in Early Modern Italy: Identities, Families and Masculinities*. Manchester: Manchester University Press.

Caviness, Madeline. 2009. "Anglo-Saxon Women, Norman Knights, and a 'Third Sex.'" In *The Bayeux Tapestry: New Interpretations*, ed. Karen Overby and Martin Foys. Woodbridge: Boydell.

Caviness, Madeline. 1998. "Artist: To See, Hear, and Know All at Once." In *Voice of the Living Light: Hildegard of Bingen and Her World*, ed. Barbara Newman. Berkeley: University of California Press.

Caviness, Madeline. 1998. "Hildegard as Designer of the Illustrations to her Works." In *Hildegard of Bingen: The Context of Her Thought and Art*, ed. Charles Burnett and Peter Dronke. London: Warburg Institute.

Caviness, Madeline. 1993. "Patron or Matron? A Capetian Bride and a Vade Mecum for her Marriage Bed." *Speculum* 68: 333–62.

Caviness, Madeline. 2001. *Visualizing Medieval Women in the Middle Ages: Sight, Spectacle, and Scopic Economy*. Philadelphia: University of Pennsylvania Press.

Caxton, William. 1890. *Caxton's Blanchardyn and Eglantine, c. 1489*, ed. Leon Kellner. Early English Text Society, extra ser. 58. London: Trübner.

Cazelles, Brigitte, ed. 1991. *The Lady as Saint: A Collection of French Hagiographic Romances of the Thirteenth Century*. Philadelphia: University of Pennsylvania Press.

Chapelot, Jean, and Robert Fossier. 1985. *The Village and House in the Middle Ages*, trans. Henry Cleere. London: B. T. Batsford.

Chaucer, Geoffrey. 1987. *The Riverside Chaucer*, ed. Larry D. Benson. 3rd ed. Oxford and Boston: Oxford University Press and Houghton Mifflin.

Chaucer, Geoffrey. 1992. "The Wife of Bath's Prologue," trans. David Wright. In *Woman Defamed and Woman Defended: An Anthology of Medieval Texts*, ed. Alcuin Blamires. Oxford: Oxford University Press.

Cheyette, Frederic L. 2001. *Ermengarde of Narbonne and the World of the Troubadours*. Ithaca: Cornell University Press.

Chibnall, Marjorie. 1991. *The Empress Matilda: Queen Consort, Queen Mother and Lady of the English*. Oxford: Blackwell.

Chojnacki, Stanley. 1992. "Measuring Adulthood: Adolescence and Gender in Renaissance Venice." *Journal of Family History* 17: 371–95.

Citrome, Jeremy. 2007. *The Surgeon in Medieval English Literature*. Basingstoke: Palgrave Macmillan.

Clanchy, M. T. 1984. "Learning to Read and the Role of Mothers." In *Studies in the History of Reading*, ed. Greg Brooks and A. K. Pugh. Reading: Centre for Teaching of Reading.

Clark, David. 2000. "The Shop Within? An Analysis of the Architectural Evidence for Medieval Shops." *Architectural History* 43: 58–87.

Clark, Elaine. 1982. "Some Aspects of Social Security in Medieval England." *Journal of Family History* 7: 307–20.

Clark, Robert L. A. 2001. "Jousting without a Lance: The Condemnation of Female Homoeroticism in the *Livre des Manières*." In *Same Sex Love and Desire among Women in the Middle Ages*, ed. Francesca C. Sautman and Pamela Sheingorn. New York: St. Martin's.

Classen, Albrecht. 2011. *Sexual Violence and Rape in the Middle Ages: A Critical Discourse in Premodern German and European Literature*. Berlin: De Gruyter.

Cockayne, Emily. 2007. *Hubbub: Filth, Noise and Stench in England, 1600–1770*. New Haven: Yale University Press.

Coelho, Maria Helena da Cruz. 1990. "A Mulher e o Trabalho nas Cidades Medievales Portuguesas." In *Homens, Espaços e Poderes: Séculos XI–XVI*. Vol. 1, *Notas do Viver Social*. Lisbon: Livros Horizonte.

Coelho, Possidónio Laranjo, ed. 1943. *Documentos Inéditos de Marrocos: Chancelaria de D. João II*. Lisbon: Imprensa Nacional.

Cohn, Samuel K., Jr. 2003. *The Black Death Transformed: Disease and Culture in Early Renaissance Europe*. London: Arnold.

Cohn, Samuel K., Jr. 1999. "Piety and Religious Practice in the Rural Dependencies of Renaissance Florence." *English Historical Review* 114: 1121–42.

Cohn, Samuel K., Jr. 1998. "Women and Work in Renaissance Italy." In *Gender and Society in Renaissance Italy*, ed. Judith C. Brown and Robert C. Davis. London and New York: Longman.

Cohn, Samuel K., Jr. 1996. "Women in the Streets, Women in the Courts, in Early Renaissance Florence." In *Women in the Streets: Essays on Sex and Power in Renaissance Italy*. Baltimore and London: Johns Hopkins University Press.

A Collection of Ordinances and Regulations for the Government of the Royal Household. 1790. London: Society of Antiquaries.

Condrau, Flurin. 2007. "The Patient's View Meets the Clinical Gaze." *Social History of Medicine* 20: 525–40.

Conklin, George. 1997. "Ingeborg of Denmark, Queen of France, 1193–1223." In *Queens and Queenship in Medieval Europe*, ed. Anne J. Duggan. Woodbridge: Boydell.

Constable, Giles. 1981. "Aelred of Rievaulx and the Nun of Watton: An Episode in the Early History of the Gilbertine Order." In *Medieval Women*, ed. Derek Baker. Oxford: Blackwell.

Constable, Giles. 1995. *Three Studies in Medieval Religious and Social Thought*. Cambridge: Cambridge University Press.

Contamine, Philippe. 1988. "Peasant Hearth to Papal Palace: The Fourteenth and Fifteenth Centuries." In *A History of Private Life*, ed. Georges Duby. Vol. 2, *Revelations of the Medieval World*, trans. Arthur Goldhammer. Cambridge, MA, and London: Belknap Press of Harvard University Press.

Cooke, Jessica. 1997. "Nice Young Girls and Wicked Old Witches: The 'Rightful Age' of Women in Middle English Verse." In *The Court and Cultural Diversity: Selected Papers from the Eighth Triennial Congress of the International Courtly Literature Society, the Queen's University of Belfast, 26 July–1 August 1995*, ed. Evelyn Mullally and John Thompson, Cambridge: D. S. Brewer.

Cooter, Roger. 2007. "After Death/After-'Life': The Social History of Medicine in Post-postmodernity." *Social History of Medicine* 20: 441–64.

Corbet, Patrick. 1986. *Les saints ottoniens. Sainteté dynastique, sainteté royale et sainteté féminine autour de l'an mil*. Sigmaringen: Thorbecke.

Correia, Fernando da Silva. 1942. "A Causa da Morte da Infanta Santa Joana: uma História Clínica do Século XV." *A Medicina Contemporânea* 23–24, offprint.

Correia, Fernando da Silva, and Júlio Dantas. 1943. "O Julgamento da Rainha D. Leonor: Seguido de Três Relatórios Médicos." *Occidente*, offprint.

Costa, José Pereira da, ed. 1998. *Vereações da Câmara Municipal do Funchal: Primeira Metade do Século XVI*. Funchal: Secretária Regional de Turismo e Cultura/Centro de Estudos de História do Atlântico.

Coulton, G. C., trans. 1972. *From St. Francis to Dante, Translations from the Chronicle of the Franciscan Salimbene, 1221–1288*. Philadelphia: University of Pennsylvania Press.

Cowen, Janet M., and Jennifer C. Ward. 2003. "'Al myn array is bliew, what nedith more?': Gender and the Household in *The Assembly of Ladies*." In *The Medieval Household in Christian Europe, c. 850–c. 1550: Managing Power, Wealth, and the*

Body, ed. Cordelia Beattie, Anna Maslakovic, and Sarah Rees Jones. Turnhout: Brepols.

Cullum, Patricia, and Goldberg, Jeremy. 2000. "How Margaret Blackburn Taught Her Daughters: Reading Devotional Instruction in a Book of Hours." In *Medieval Women: Texts and Contexts: Essays for Felicity Riddy*, ed. Jocelyn Wogan-Browne, Rosalynn Voaden, Arlyn Diamond, Ann Hutchison, Carol Meale, and Lesley Johnson. Turnhout: Brepols.

Cunningham, Andrew. 2002. "Identifying Disease in the Past: Cutting the Gordian Knot." *Asclepio* 54: 13–34.

Cyprian, Saint. 1958. "The Dress of Virgins." In *Saint Cyprian: Treatises*, ed. and trans. Roy J. Deferrari. Washington, DC: Catholic University of America Press in association with Consortium Books.

Damico, Helen. 1984. *Beowulf's Wealhtheow and the Valkyrie Tradition*. Madison: University of Wisconsin Press.

Dangler, Jean. 2001. *Mediating Fictions: Literature, Women Healers and the Go-between in Medieval and Early-modern Iberia*. Cranbury, NJ: Associated University Presses.

Dark, Patricia A. 2007. " 'A Woman of Subtlety and a Man's Resolution': Matilda of Boulogne in the Power Struggles of the Anarchy." In *Aspects of Power and Authority in the Middle Ages*, ed. Brenda M. Bolton and Christine E. Meek. Brepols: Turnhout.

Darnton, Robert. 1984. *The Great Cat Massacre and Other Episodes in French Cultural History*. New York: Vintage.

Davidoff, Leonore, and Catherine Hall. 1987. *Family Fortunes: Men and Women of the English Middle Class, 1780–1850*. Chicago: University of Chicago Press.

Davis, Natalie Zemon. 1987. *Fiction in the Archives: Pardon Tales and Their Tellers in Sixteenth-century France*. Stanford: Stanford University Press.

Davis, Norman, ed. 1971–76. *Paston Letters and Papers of the Fifteenth Century*. 2 vols. Oxford: Oxford University Press.

Davis, Robert C. 1998. "The Geography of Gender in the Renaissance." In *Gender and Society in Renaissance Italy*, ed. Judith C. Brown and Robert C. Davis. London: Longman.

D'Avray, D. L. 2005. *Medieval Marriage: Symbolism and Society*. Oxford: Oxford University Press.

D'Avray, D. L. 1985. *The Preaching of the Friars: Sermons Diffused from Paris before 1300*. Oxford: Clarendon Press.

D'Avray, D. L., and M. Tausche. 1981. "Marriage Sermons in *ad status* Collections of the Central Middle Ages." *Archives d'histoire doctrinale et litteraire du Moyen Age* 47: 71–119.

Day, Véronique. 2004. "Recycling Radegund: Identity and Ambition in the Breviary of Anne De Prye." In *Essays in Honor of Sandra Hindman*, ed. David S. Areford and Nina A. Rowe. Aldershot: Ashgate.

DeAragon, R. C. 2002. "Wife, Widow and Mother: Some Comparisons between Eleanor of Aquitaine and Noblewomen of the Anglo-Norman and Angevin World."

In *Eleanor of Aquitaine: Lord and Lady*, ed. John Carmi Parsons and Bonnie Wheeler. New York: Palgrave MacMillan.
de Cantimpré, Thomas. 1989/1997. *The Life of Christina Mirabilis*, trans. Margot H. King. Toronto: Peregrina.
de La Roncière, Charles. 1988. "Tuscan Notables on the Eve of the Renaissance." In *A History of Private Life*, ed. Georges Duby. Vol. 2, *Revelations of the Medieval World*, trans. Arthur Goldhammer. Cambridge, MA, and London: Belknap Press of Harvard University Press.
de la Tour Landry, Geoffroy. 1971. *The Book of the Knight of the Tower*, ed. M. Y. Offord, trans. William Caxton. Early English Text Society, supplementary ser. 2. London: Oxford University Press.
de Lorris, Guillaume, and Jean de Meun. 1994. *The Romance of the Rose*, ed. and trans. Frances Horgan. Oxford: Oxford University Press.
de Metz, Guillebert. 1804. *Description de la Ville de Paris au XVe Siècle*, ed. Le Roux de Lincy. Paris: Auguste Aubrey.
de Pisan, Christine. 1985. *The Treasure of the City of Ladies, or The Book of the Three Virtues*, trans. Sarah Lawson. Harmondsworth: Penguin.
de Pizan, Christine. 1977. *Ditié de Jehanne d'Arc*, ed. Angus J. Kennedy and Kenneth Varty. Oxford: Society for the Study of Mediaeval Languages and Literature.
de Pizan, Christine. 1983. *The Book of the City of Ladies*, trans. Earl Jeffrey Richards. London: Pan.
de Pizan, Christine. 1989. *A Medieval Woman's Mirror of Honor: The Treasury of the City of Ladies*, ed. Madeleine Pelner Cosman, trans. Charity Cannon Willard. New York: Persea.
de Pizan, Christine, et al. 2010. *Debate of the* Romance of the Rose, ed. and trans. David F. Hult. Chicago: University of Chicago Press.
de Tournai, Guibert. ca. 1481–83. *Sermones*. Louvain: Johannes de Westfalia.
DeVries, Kelly. 1999. *Joan of Arc: A Military Leader*. New York: Sutton.
de Wailly, Natalis, ed. 1876. *Récits d'un Ménestrel de Reims au treizieme siècle*. Paris: Renouard.
Dhuoda. 2007. *Handbook for Her Warrior Son*, ed. and trans. Marcelle Thiébaux. Cambridge: Cambridge University Press.
Dias, João José Alves, ed. 1998–2002. *Chancelarias Portuguesas: D. Duarte*. 4 vols. Lisbon: Centro de Estudos Históricos, Universidade Nova.
Dias, João José Alves, ed. 1982. *Livro dos Conselhos de El-Rei D. Duarte (Livro da Cartuxa)*. Lisbon: Editorial Estampa.
Dias, José João Alves. 2004–6. *Chancelarias Portuguesas: D. João I*. 11 vols. Lisbon: Centro de Estudos Históricos, Universidade Nova de Lisboa.
Dockray-Miller, Mary. 1998. "The Masculine Queen of Beowulf." *Women and Language* 21: 31–38.
Dolan, Brian. 2010. "History, Medical Humanities and Medical Education." *Social History of Medicine* 23: 393–405.
Dove, Mary. 1986. *The Perfect Age of Man's Life*. Cambridge: Cambridge University Press.

Dronzek, Anna. 2001. "Gendered Theories of Education in Fifteenth-century Conduct Books." In *Medieval Conduct*, ed. Kathleen Ashley and Robert L. A. Clark. Minneapolis: University of Minnesota Press.

Dronzek, Anna. 2006. "Private and Public Spheres." In *Women and Gender in Medieval Europe: An Encyclopedia*, ed. Margaret Schaus. New York: Routledge.

Duarte, Luís Miguel. 1999. *Justiça e Criminalidade no Portugal Medievo (1459–1481)*. Lisbon: Fundação Calouste Gulbenkian.

Duby, Georges. 1992. "Affidavits and Confessions." In *A History of Women in the West*, ed. Christiane Klapisch-Zuber. Vol. 2, *Silences of the Middle Ages*. Cambridge, MA: Belknap Press.

Duby, Georges. 1988. "The Aristocratic Households of Feudal France." In *A History of Private Life*, ed. Georges Duby. Vol. 2, *Revelations of the Medieval World*, trans. Arthur Goldhammer. Cambridge, MA, and London: Belknap Press of Harvard University Press.

Duby, Georges. 1988. "Introduction: Private Power, Public Power." In *A History of Private Life*, ed. Georges Duby. Vol. 2, *Revelations of the Medieval World*, trans. Arthur Goldhammer. Cambridge, MA, and London: Belknap Press of Harvard University Press.

Duby, Georges. 1983. *The Knight, the Lady, and the Priest: The Making of Modern Marriage in Medieval France*, trans. Barbara Bray. New York: Pantheon.

Duby, Georges. 1978. *Medieval Marriage: Two Models from Medieval France*, trans. Elborg Foster. Baltimore: The Johns Hopkins University Press.

Duby, Georges. 1997–98. *Women of the Twelfth Century*. 3 vols. Chicago: University of Chicago Press.

Duden, Barbara. 1991. *The Woman beneath the Skin: A Doctor's Patients in Eighteenth Century Germany*, trans. Thomas Dunlap. Cambridge, MA: Harvard University Press.

Duffin, Jacalyn. 2009. *Medical Miracles: Doctors, Saints and Healing in the Modern World*. Oxford: Oxford University Press.

Duffy, Eamon. 1990. "Holy Maydens, Holy Wyfes: The Cult of Women Saints in Fifteenth and Sixteenth Century England." In *Women in the Church*, ed. W. J. Sheils and Diana Wood. Oxford: Basil Blackwell.

Duggan, Anne J., ed. 1997. *Queens and Queenship in Medieval Europe*. Woodbridge: Boydell.

Dyer, Christopher. 1989. *Standards of Living in the Later Middle Ages: Social Change in England, c. 1200–1520*. Cambridge: Cambridge University Press.

Earenfight, Theresa. 2010. *The King's Other Body: María of Castile and the Crown of Aragon*. Philadelphia: University of Pennsylvania Press.

Earenfight, Theresa, ed. 2005. *Queenship and Political Power in Medieval and Early Modern Spain*. Aldershot: Ashgate.

Easton, Martha. 1994. "Saint Agatha and the Sanctification of Sexual Violence." *Studies in Iconography* 16: 83–118.

Easton, Martha. 2008. "'Was it Good for You, Too?' Medieval Erotic Art and its Audiences." *Different Visions: A Journal of New Perspectives on Medieval Art* 1. Available at: http://www.differentvisions.org. Accessed May 3, 2010.

Easton, Martha. 2009. "Why Can't a Woman Be More Like a Man? Transforming and Transcending Gender in the Lives of Female Saints." In *The Four Modes of Seeing: Approaches to Medieval Imagery in Honor of Madeline Harrison Caviness*, ed. Evelyn Staudinger Lane, Elizabeth Carson Pastan, and Ellen M. Shortell. Burlington: Ashgate.

Egan, Geoff. 1998. "Miniature Toys of Medieval Childhood." *British Archaeology* 35: 10–11.

Ehrenschwentner, Marie Luise. 1997. " '*Puellae litteratae*': The Use of the Vernacular in the Dominican Convents of Southern Germany." In *Medieval Women in Their Communities*, ed. Diane Watt. Cardiff: University of Wales Press.

Eichmann, Raymond, and John DuVal, eds. and trans. 1994. *The French Fabliau: B.N. Ms 837*. 2 vols. New York: Garland.

Elliott, Dyan. 1999. "The Priest's Wife: Female Erasure and the Gregorian Reform." In *Fallen Bodies: Pollution, Sexuality, and Demonology in the Middle Ages*. Philadelphia: University of Pennsylvania Press.

Elsakkers, Marianne. 2001. "In Pain You Shall Bear Children: Medieval Prayers for a Safe Delivery." In *Studies in the History of Religions*, ed. Anne-Marie Korte. Leiden: Brill.

Emmerson, R. K., and P.J.P. Goldberg. 2000. " 'The Lord Geoffrey Had Me Made': Lordship and Labour in the Luttrell Psalter." In *The Problem of Labour in Fourteenth-century England*, ed. James Bothwell, P.J.P. Goldberg, and W. M. Ormrod. York: York Medieval Press.

Enright, Michael J. 1996. *Lady with a Mead Cup: Ritual, Prophecy and Lordship in the European Warband from La Tène to the Viking Age*. Dublin: Four Courts Press.

Erler, Mary C. 2002. *Women, Reading, and Piety in Late Medieval England*. Cambridge: Cambridge University Press.

Erler, Mary C., and Maryanne Kowaleski. 2003. "Introduction: A New Economy of Power Relations: Female Agency in the Middle Ages." In *Gendering the Master Narrative: Women and Power in the Middle Ages*, ed. Mary C. Erler and Maryanne Kowaleski. Ithaca: Cornell University Press.

Farmer, Sharon. 1999. " 'It Is Not Good That [Wo]man Should Be Alone': Elite Responses to Singlewomen in High Medieval Paris." In *Singlewomen in the European Past, 1250–1800*, ed. Judith M. Bennett and Amy M. Froide. Philadelphia: University of Pennsylvania Press.

Farmer, Sharon. 1986. "Persuasive Voices: Clerical Images of Medieval Wives." *Speculum* 61: 517–43.

Farmer, Sharon. 2002. *Surviving Poverty in Medieval Paris: Gender, Ideology, and the Daily Lives of the Poor*. Ithaca: Cornell University Press.

Farmer, Sharon, and Carol Braun Pasternak. 2003. *Gender and Difference in the Middle Ages*. Minneapolis: University of Pennsylvania Press.

Fawtier, Robert S. 1960. *The Capetian Kings of France: Monarchy and Nation, 987–1328*, trans. Lionel Butler and R. J. Adam. London: Macmillan.

Federico, Sylvia. 2001. "The Imaginary Society: Women in 1381." *Journal of British Studies* 40: 159–83.

Fernández, Mercedes Borrero. 1998. "Peasant and Aristocratic Women: Their Role in the Rural Economy of Seville at the End of the Middle Ages." In *Women at Work in Spain: From the Middle Ages to Early Modern Times*, ed. Marilyn Stone and Carmen Benito-Vessels. New York: Peter Lang.

Ferreira, Vitaline Cardoso. 2006. "A Presença da Mulher na Legislação Medieval Portuguesa." MA diss., 2 vols., University of Lisbon.

Ferro, João Pedro. 1989. "Para o Estudo da População Portuguesa Medieval: o Caso de Alenquer." *História* 122: 38–65.

Finucane, Ronald. 1995. *Miracles and Pilgrims: Popular Beliefs in Medieval England.* 2nd ed. New York: St. Martin's Press.

Fiorenza, Elisabeth Schüssler. 1983. *In Memory of Her: A Feminist Theological Reconstruction of Christian Origins*. New York: Crossroads.

Fissell, Mary. 2008. "Introduction: Women, Health and Healing in Early-modern Europe." *Bulletin of the History of Medicine* 82: 1–17.

Fissell, Mary. 2004. "Making Meaning from the Margins: The New Cultural History of Medicine." In *Locating Medical History: The Stories and Their Meanings*, ed. Frank Huisman and John Harley Warner. Baltimore: Johns Hopkins University Press.

Fissell, Mary. 1991. *Patients, Power and the Poor in Eighteenth-century Bristol.* Cambridge: Cambridge University Press.

Flanagan, Sabina. 1989. *Hildegard of Bingen (1098–1179): A Visionary Life*. London: Routledge.

Fletcher, Eric. 1980. "The Influence of Merovingian Gaul on Northumbria in the Seventh Century." *Medieval Archaeology* 24: 69–86.

Fonseca, Luís Adão da. 2005. *João II*. Lisbon: Círculo de Leitores.

Foot, Sarah. 2006. *Monastic Life in Anglo-Saxon England, c. 600–900*. Cambridge: Cambridge University Press.

Forsyth, Ilene. 2002. "Narrative at Moissac: Schapiro's Legacy." *Gesta* 41: 71–93.

Forsyth, Ilene. 1972. *The Throne of Wisdom: Wood Sculptures of the Madonna in Romanesque France*. Princeton, NJ: Princeton University Press.

Fradenburg, Louise Olga, ed. 1993. *Women and Sovereignty*. Edinburgh: Edinburgh University Press.

Fraioli, Deborah A. 2005. *Joan of Arc and the Hundred Years War*. New York: Greenwood.

Fraioli, Deborah A. 2002. *Joan of Arc: The Early Debate*. Woodbridge: Boydell.

Freeman, Elizabeth. 2006. "Cistercian Nuns in Medieval England: Unofficial Meets Official." In *Elite and Popular Religion*, ed. Kate Cooper and Jeremy Gregory. Studies in Church History 42. Woodbridge: Boydell Press for the Ecclesiastical History Society.

Freeman, Elizabeth. 2004. " 'Houses of a Peculiar Order': Cistercian Nunneries in Medieval England, with Attention to the Fifteenth and Sixteenth Centuries." *Cîteaux: Commentarii Cistercienses* 55: 244–51.

French, Katherine L. 2008. *The Good Women of the Parish: Gender and Religion after the Black Death*. Philadelphia: University of Pennsylvania Press.

French, Katherine L. 1997. "Parochial Fund-raising in Late Medieval Somerset." In *The Parish in English Life, 1400–1600*, ed. Katherine L. French, Gary G. Gibbs, and Beat A. Kümin. Manchester: Manchester University Press.

French, Katherine L. 2001. *The People of the Parish: Community Life in a Medieval English Diocese.* Philadelphia: University of Pennsylvania Press.

French, Katherine L. 2005. "The Seat under Our Lady: Gender and Seating in Late Medieval English Parish Churches." In *Women's Space: Patronage, Place, and Gender in the Medieval Church*, ed. Virginia Chieffo Raguin and Sarah Stanbury. Albany: State University of New York Press.

French, Katherine L. 2006. "Women Churchwardens in Late Medieval England." In *The Parish in Late Medieval England*, ed. Clive Burgess and Eamon Duffy. Donington, Lincolnshire: Shaun Tyas/Paul Watkins Publishing.

Froide, Amy M. 2005. *Never Married: Singlewomen in Early Modern England.* Oxford: Oxford University Press.

Galen, Claudius. 1968. *Galen on the Usefulness of the Parts of the Body*, ed. and trans. Margaret Tallmadge May. 2 vols. Ithaca: Cornell University Press.

Gardiner, Mark. 2008. "Buttery and Pantry and Their Antecedents: Idea and Architecture in the English Medieval House." In *Medieval Domesticity: Home, Housing and Household in Medieval England*, ed. Maryanne Kowaleski and P.J.P. Goldberg. Cambridge: Cambridge University Press.

Garver, Valerie L. 2009. *Women and Aristocratic Culture in the Carolingian World.* Ithaca: Cornell University Press.

Gathagan, Laura. 1999. "The Trappings of Power: The Coronation of Mathilda of Flanders." *Haskins Society Journal* 13: 21–39.

Gavitt, Philip. 1996. "Infant Death in Late Medieval Florence: The Smothering Hypothesis Reconsidered." In *Medieval Family Roles: A Book of Essays*, ed. Cathy Jorgensen McItnyre. New York: Garland.

Geaman, Kristen. 2010. "Queen's Gold and Intercession: The Case of Eleanor of Aquitaine." *Medieval Feminist Forum* 46: 10–33.

Gee, Loveday Lewis. 2002. *Women, Art, and Patronage from Henry III to Edward III, 1216–1377.* Woodbridge: Boydell.

Gennaro, Clara. 1996. "Clare, Agnes, and Their Earliest Followers: From the Poor Ladies of San Damiano to the Poor Clares." In *Women and Religion in Medieval and Renaissance Italy*, ed. Daniel Bornstein and Roberto Rusconi, trans. Margery J. Schneider. Chicago: University of Chicago Press.

Gentilcore, David. 2006. *Medical Charlatanism in Early-modern Italy.* Oxford: Oxford University Press.

Ghrádaigh, Jenifer Ní. 2003. "'But What Exactly Did She Give?': Derbforgaill and the Nuns' Church and Clonmacnoise." In *Clonmacnoise Studies: Seminar Papers 1998*, ed. Heather A. King. Dublin: Dept. of Environment Heritage and Local Government.

Gibbons, Rachel. 1996. "Isabeau of Bavaria, Queen of France (1385–1422): The Creation of an Historical Villainess." *Transactions of the Royal Historical Society* (6th ser.) 6: 51–73.

Gibson, Gail. 1996. "Blessing from Sun and Moon: Churching as Women's Theatre." In *Bodies and Disciplines: Intersections of Literature and History in Fifteenth Century England*, ed. Barbara A. Hanawalt and David Wallace. Minneapolis: University of Minnesota Press.

Gilchrist, Roberta. 1999. *Gender and Archaeology: Contesting the Past.* London: Routledge.

Gilchrist, Roberta. 1994. *Gender and Material Culture: The Archaeology of Religious Women.* London and New York: Routledge.

Gilchrist, Roberta. 1993. "Medieval Bodies in the Material World: Gender, Stigma and the Body." In *Framing Medieval Bodies*, ed. Sarah Kay and Miri Rubin. Manchester: Manchester University Press.

Gilchrist, Roberta, and Marilyn Oliva. 1993. *Religious Women in Medieval East Anglia.* Norwich: Centre of East Anglian Studies.

Gilligan, Carol. 1987. "Woman's Place in Man's Life Cycle." In *Feminism and Methodology: Social Science Issues*, ed. Sandra Harding. Bloomington/Milton Keynes: Indiana University Press/Open University Press.

Gilsdorf, Sean, ed. and trans. 2004. *Queenship and Sanctity: The Lives of Mathilda and the Epitaph of Adelheid.* Washington, DC: Catholic University of America.

Girouard, Mark. 2000. *Life in the French Country House.* London: Cassell and Co.

Givens, Jean, Karen Reeds, and Alain Touwaide. 2006. *Visualizing Medieval Medicine and Natural History, 1200–1550.* Aldershot: Ashgate.

Gold, Penny Schine. 1985. *The Lady and the Virgin: Image, Attitude, and Experience in Twelfth–century France.* Chicago: University of Chicago Press.

Gold, Penny Schine. 1984. "Male/female Cooperation: The Example of Fontevrault." In *Distant Echoes: Medieval Religious Women*, ed. John A. Nichols and Lillian Thomas Shank. Kalamazoo: Cistercian Publications.

Goldberg, Jeremy [P.J.P.]. 2007. *Community Discord, Child Abduction, and Rape in the Later Middle Ages.* New York: Palgrave.

Goldberg, P.J.P. 1991. "The Public and the Private: Women in the Pre-plague Economy." In *Thirteenth Century England III*, ed. Peter R. Coss and S. D. Lloyd. Woodbridge: Boydell.

Goldberg, P.J.P., ed. and trans. 1995. *Women in England, c. 1275–1525.* Manchester: Manchester University Press.

Goldberg, P.J.P. 1992. *Women, Work, and Life Cycle in a Medieval Economy: Women in York and Yorkshire c. 1300–1520.* Oxford: Clarendon Press.

Golden, Judith K. 2002. "Images of Instruction, Marie de Bretagne, and the Life of St. Eustace as Illustrated in British Library Ms. Egerton 745." In *Insights and Interpretations: Studies in Celebration of the Eighty-fifth Anniversary of the Index of Christian Art*, ed. Colum Hourihane. Princeton, NJ: Princeton University in association with Princeton University Press.

Gomes, Rita Costa. 2003. *The Making of a Court Society: Kings and Nobles in Late Medieval Portugal*, trans. A. Aiken. Cambridge: Cambridge University Press.

Gomes, Saúl António. 1999. "Higiene e Saúde na Leiria Medieval." In *III colóquio sobre a história de Leiria e da sua região.* Leiria: Câmara Municipal.

Gonçalves, Iria. 2007. "Regateiras, Padeiras e Outras Mais na Lisboa Medieval." In *Lisboa Medieval: Os Rostos da Cidade*, ed. Luís Krus, Luís Felipe Oliveira, and João Luís Fontes. Lisbon: Livros Horizonte.

Goodich, Michael E. 1989. *From Birth to Old Age: The Human Life Cycle in Medieval Thought, 1250–1350*. Lanham: University Press of America.

Goodman, Jennifer. 1998. *Chivalry and Exploration, 1298–1630*. Woodbridge: Boydell.

Gower, John. 1900. *The English Works of John Gower*, ed. G. C. Macaulay. London: Oxford University Press.

Grassby, Richard. 2005. "Material Culture and Cultural History." *Journal of Interdisciplinary History* 35: 591–603.

Grauer, Anne. 1991. "Life Patterns of Women from Medieval York." In *The Archaeology of Gender*, ed. Dale Walde and Noreen Willows. Calgary: Department of Archaeology, University of Calgary.

Grauer, Anne, and Patricia Stuart-Macadam, eds. 1998. *Sex and Gender in Paleopathological Perspective*. Cambridge: Cambridge University Press.

Gravdal, Kathryn. 1991. *Ravishing Maidens: Writing Rape in Medieval French Literature and Law*. Philadelphia: University of Pennsylvania Press.

Green, Monica H. 2010. "Bibliography on Medieval Women, Gender and Medicine (1989–2009)." *Digital Library of Sciència.cat*, Universitat de Barcelona. Available at: http://www.sciencia.cat/biblioteca/ documents/Green_CumulativeBib_Feb2010.pdf. Accessed August 15, 2012.

Green, Monica H. 2005. "Bodies, Gender, Health, Disease: Recent Work on Medieval Women's Medicine." *Studies in Medieval and Renaissance History* (3rd ser.), 2: 1–46.

Green, Monica H. 2005. "Flowers, Poisons and Men: Menstruation in Medieval Western Europe." In *Menstruation: A Cultural History*, ed. Andrew Shail and Gillian Howie. Basingstoke: Palgrave Macmillan.

Green, Monica H. 2008. "Gendering the History of Women's Healthcare." *Gender & History* 20: 487–518.

Green, Monica H. 2009. "Integrative Medicine: Incorporating Medicine and Health into the Canon of Medieval European History." *History Compass* 7: 1218–45.

Green, Monica H. 2008. *Making Women's Medicine Masculine: The Rise of Male Authority in Pre-modern Gynaecology*. Oxford: Oxford University Press.

Green, Monica H., ed. 2001. *Trotula: A Medieval Compendium of Women's Medicine*. Philadelphia: University of Pennsylvania Press.

Green, Monica H. 2000. *Women's Healthcare in the Medieval West: Texts and Contexts*. Aldershot: Ashgate.

Green, Monica H., and David Smail. 2008. "The Trial of Floreta d'Ays (1403): Jews, Christians and Obstetrics in Later Medieval Marseille." *Journal of Medieval History* 34: 185–211.

Gregory of Tours. 1974. *The History of the Franks*, ed. and trans. Lewis Thorpe. Harmondsworth: Penguin.

Grenville, Jane. 1997. *Medieval Housing*. London: Leicester University Press.

Griffiths, Fiona J. 2007. *The Garden of Delights: Reform and Renaissance for Women in the Twelfth Century*. Philadelphia: University of Pennsylvania Press.

Grossman, Avraham. 2004. *Pious and Rebellious: Jewish Women in Medieval Europe*, trans. Jonathan Chipman. Hanover: University Press of New England.

Grundmann, Herbert. 1995. *Religious Movements in the Middle Ages*, trans. Steven Rowan. Notre Dame, IN: Notre Dame University Press.

Hajnal, John. 1983. "Two Kinds of Pre-industrial Household Formation." In *Family Forms in Historical Europe*, ed. Richard Wall, in collaboration with Jean Robin and Peter Laslett. Cambridge: Cambridge University Press.

Hall, Edwin. 1994. *The Arnolfini Betrothal: Medieval Marriage and the Enigma of Van Eyck's Double Portrait*. Berkeley: University of California Press.

Hallissy, Margaret. 1993. *Clean Maids, True Wives, Steadfast Widows: Chaucer's Women and Medieval Codes of Conduct*. Westport, CT: Greenwood Press.

Hamburger, Jeffrey F. 1997. *Nuns as Artists: The Visual Culture of a Medieval Convent*. Berkeley: University of California Press.

Hanawalt, Barbara A. 1987. "Golden Ages for the History of Medieval English Women." In *Women in Medieval History and Historiography*, ed. Susan Mosher Stuard. Philadelphia: University of Pennsylvania Press.

Hanawalt, Barbara A. 1986. *The Ties That Bound: Peasant Families in Medieval England*. Oxford: Oxford University Press.

Hareven, Tamara K., and Kathleen J. Adams, eds. 1982. *Ageing and Life Course Transitions: An Interdisciplinary Perspective*. London: Tavistock.

Harkness, Deborah. 2008. "A View from the Streets: Women and Medical Work in Elizabethan London." *Bulletin of the History of Medicine* 82: 52–85.

Harper, April, and Caroline Proctor, eds. 2008. *Medieval Sexuality: A Casebook*. New York: Routledge.

Harper, Stephen. 2003. *Insanity, Individuals and Society in Late-medieval English Literature: The Subject of Madness*. New York: Edwin Mellen.

Harris, Barbara J. 1990. "Women and Politics in Early Tudor England." *The Historical Journal* 33: 259–81.

Harrison, Ann Tukey, ed. 1994. *Danse Macabre of Women: Ms. fr. 995 of the Bibliothèque Nationale*. Kent, OH: Kent State University Press.

Harrison, Ann Tukey. 1989. "Fifteenth-century French Women's Role Names." *French Review* 62: 436–44.

Harvey, Barbara. 1993. *Living and Dying in England 1100–1540: The Monastic Experience*. Oxford: Oxford University Press.

Hatcher, John. 2001. "Debate—Women's Work Reconsidered: Gender and Wage Differentiation in Late Medieval England." *Past & Present* 173: 191–98.

Hatcher, John. 1994. "England in the Aftermath of the Black Death." *Past & Present* 144: 3–35.

Hatcher, John. 1986. "Mortality in the Fifteenth Century: Some New Evidence." *Economic History Review* (2nd ser.), 39: 19–38.

Hector, L. C., and Barbara Harvey, eds. and trans. 1982. *Westminster Chronicle 1381–1394*. Oxford: Oxford University Press.

Helle, Knut. 1990. "Norwegian Foreign Policy and the Maid of Norway." *Scottish Historical Review* 69: 142–56.

Henderson, John. 2006. *The Renaissance Hospital: Healing the Body and Healing the Soul*. New Haven: Yale University Press.

Hentsch, Alice A. 1903. *De la littérature didactique au moyen âge, s'addressant spécialement aux femmes*. Cahors: Coueslant.

Herlihy, David. 1995. *Women, Family, and Society in Medieval Europe: Historical Essays 1978–1991*, ed. A. Molho. Providence: Berghahn.

Herrad of Landsberg. 1977. *Hortus Deliciarum (Garden of delights)*, commentary and notes by A. Straub and G. Keller, ed. and trans. Aristide D. Caratzas. New Rochelle, NY: Caratzas Brothers Publishers.

Herrer, Hipólito Rafael Oliva. 2003. "The Peasant *Domus* and Material Culture in Northern Castile in the Later Middle Ages." In *The Medieval Household in Christian Europe, c. 850–c. 1550: Managing Power, Wealth, and the Body*, ed. Cordelia Beattie, Anna Maslakovic, and Sarah Rees Jones. Turnhout: Brepols.

Hicks, Michael. 2004. "Elizabeth (*c.* 1437–1492)."In *Oxford Dictionary of National Biography*. Oxford: Oxford University Press. Available at: http://www.oxforddnb.com/view/article/8634. Accessed September 1, 2011.

Hildegard of Bingen. 1855. *Sanctae Hildegardis Abbatissae Opera Omnia*. Patrologia Latina, ed. J.-P. Migne, vol. 197. Paris, Migne.

Hildegard of Bingen. 1990. *Scivias*, trans. Mother Columba Hart and Jane Bishop. New York: Paulist Press.

Hildegard of Bingen. 2001. *Selected Writings*, ed. and trans. Mark Atherton. Harmondsworth: Penguin.

Hilton, R. H. 1975. *The English Peasantry in the Later Middle Ages*. Oxford: Clarendon Press.

Hilton, R. H. 1982. "Lords, Burgesses and Hucksters." *Past & Present* 97: 3–15.

Hilton, R. H. 1984. "Women Traders in Medieval England." *Women's Studies* 11: 139–55.

Hindman, Sandra L. 1994. "The Illustrations." In *The Danse Macabre of Women: Ms. fr. 995 of the Bibliothèque Nationale*, ed. Ann Tukey Harrison. Kent, OH: Kent State University Press.

Hobbins, Daniel, ed. and trans. 2007. *The Trial of Joan of Arc*. Cambridge, MA: Harvard University Press.

Hoeniger, Cathleen. 2006. "The Illuminated *Tacuinum Sanitatis* Manuscripts from Northern Italy *c.* 1380–1400: Sources, Patrons and the Creation of a New Pictorial Genre." In *Visualizing Medieval Medicine and Natural History, 1200–1550*, ed. Jean Givens, Karen Reeds, and Alain Touwaide. Ashgate: Aldershot.

Holladay, Joan. 1994. "The Education of Jeanne d'Evreux: Personal Piety and Dynastic Salvation in Her Book of Hours at the Cloisters." *Art History* 17: 585–611.

Holladay, Joan. 2006. "Fourteenth-century French Queens as Collectors and Readers of Books: Jeanne d'Evreux and Her Contemporaries." *Journal of Medieval History* 31: 69–100.

Horden, Peregrine. 2008. "Family History and Hospital History in the Middle Ages." In *Hospitals and Healing from Antiquity to the Later Middle Ages*. Aldershot: Ashgate.

Horrox, Rosemary, ed. 1994. *The Black Death*. Manchester: Manchester University Press.

Howell, Margaret. 1998. *Eleanor of Provence: Queenship in Thirteenth-century England*. Oxford: Blackwell.

Howell, Margaret. 1987. "The Resources of Eleanor of Aquitaine as Queen Consort." *English Historical Review* 102: 372–93.

Howell, Martha C. 1996. "Fixing Movables: Gifts by Testament in Late Medieval Douai." *Past & Present* 150: 3–45.

Hufton, Olwen. 1974. *The Poor of Eighteenth-century France, 1750–1789*. Oxford: Clarendon Press.

Huisman, Frank, and John Harley Warner, eds. 2004. *Locating Medical History: The Stories and Their Meanings*. Baltimore: Johns Hopkins University Press.

Humbert of Romans, Gilbert of Tournai, and Stephen of Bourbon. 1978. *Prediche alle donne del secolo XIII: Testi di Umberto da Romans, Gilberto da Tournai, Stefano di Borbone*, ed. Carla Casagrande. Milan: Bompiani.

Huneycutt, Lois L. 2006. "Intercession." In *Women and Gender in Medieval Europe: An Encyclopedia*, ed. Margaret Schaus. New York: Routledge.

Huneycutt, Lois L. 1995. "Intercession and the High-medieval Queen: The Esther Topos." In *Power of the Weak: Studies on Medieval Women*, ed. Jennifer Carpenter and Sally-Beth MacLean. Urbana: University of Illinois Press.

Huneycutt, Lois L. 2003. *Matilda of Scotland: A Study in Medieval Queenship*. Woodbridge: Boydell.

Hunt, Lynn, ed. 1989. *The New Cultural History*. Berkeley: University of California Press.

Hunter, David G. 1987. "Resistance to the Virginal Ideal in Late-fourth-century Rome: The Case of Jovinian." *Theological Studies* 48: 45–64.

Hutton, Diane. 1985. "Women in Fourteenth-century Shrewsbury." In *Women and Work in Pre-industrial England*, ed. L. Charles and L. Duffin. London: Croon Helm.

Inglis, Erik, ed. 1995. *Hours of Mary of Burgundy*. London: Harvey Miller Publishers.

Isidore of Seville. 2006. *The Etymologies of Isidore of Seville*, trans. Stephen A. Barney, W. J. Lewis, J. A. Beach, and Oliver Berghof. Cambridge: Cambridge University Press.

Jackson, Richard A. 1984. *Vive le roi: A History of the French Coronation from Charles V to Charles* X. Chapel Hill: University of North Carolina Press.

Jacquart, Danielle, and Claude Thomasset. 1988. *Sexuality and Medicine in the Middle Ages*, trans. Matthew Adamson. Cambridge: Polity Press.

James, Edward. 1988. *The Franks*. Oxford: Basil Blackwell.

Jerome, Saint. 1991. *Select Letters of St. Jerome*, ed. and trans. F. A. Wright. London: Loeb Classical Library.

Jochens, Jenny. 1996. *Old Norse Images of Women*. Philadelphia: University of Pennsylvania Press.

Johns, Susan M. 2003. *Noblewomen, Aristocracy and Power in the Twelfth-century Anglo-Norman Realm*. Manchester: Manchester University Press.

Johnson, Penelope D. 1991. *Equal in Monastic Profession: Religious Women in Medieval France*. Chicago: University of Chicago Press.

Johnson, Willis. 1998. "The Myth of Jewish Male Menses." *Journal of Medieval History* 24: 273–95.

Jones, Malcolm. 1990. "Folklore Motifs in Late Medieval art II: Sexist Satire and Popular Punishments." *Folklore* 101: 69–87.

Jones, Peter Murray. 2006. "Image, Word, and Medicine in the Middle Ages." In *Visualizing Medieval Medicine and Natural History, 1200–1550*, ed. Jean A. Givens, Karen M. Reeds, and Alain Touwaide. Aldershot: Ashgate.

Jones, Peter Murray. 1984. *Medieval Medical Miniatures*. London: British Library.

Jones, Peter Murray. 1998. *Medieval Medicine in Illuminated Manuscripts*. London: British Library.

Jordan, Erin L. 2006. *Women, Power, and Religious Patronage in the Middle Ages*. New York: Palgrave.

Jussen, Bernhard. 2002. " 'Virgins-Widows-Spouses': On the Language of Moral Distinction as Applied to Women and Men in the Middle Ages." *History of the Family* 7: 13–32.

Karras, Ruth Mazo. 1996. *Common Women: Prostitution and Sexuality in Medieval England*. Oxford: Oxford University Press.

Karras, Ruth Mazo. 2003. *From Boys to Men: Formations of Masculinity in Late Medieval Europe*. Philadelphia: University of Pennsylvania Press.

Karras, Ruth Mazo. 1992. "Gendered Sin and Misogyny in John of Bromyard's Summa Predicantium." *Traditio: Studies in Ancient and Medieval History, Thought, and Religion* 47: 233–57.

Karras, Ruth, Mazo. 1990. "Holy Harlots: Prostitute Saints in Medieval Legend." *Journal of the History of Sexuality* 1: 3–32.

Karras, Ruth Mazo. 1996. "Prostitution in Medieval Europe." In *Handbook of Medieval Sexuality*, ed. Vern L. Bullough and James A. Brundage. New York: Garland.

Karras, Ruth Mazo. 1989. "The Regulation of Brothels in Later Medieval England." In *Sisters and Workers in the Middle Ages*, ed. Judith M. Bennett, Elizabeth A. Clark, Jean F. O'Barr, B. Anne Vilen, and Sarah Westphal-Wihl. Chicago: University of Chicago Press.

Karras, Ruth Mazo. 1999. "Sex and the Singlewoman." In *Singlewomen in the European Past 1250–1800*, ed. Judith M. Bennett and Amy M. Froide. Philadelphia: University of Pennsylvania Press.

Karras, Ruth Mazo. 2005/2011. *Sexuality in Medieval Europe: Doing unto Others*: New York: Routledge.

Karras, Ruth Mazo. 2004. " 'This Skill in a Woman is by no Means to be Despised': Weaving and the Gender Division of Labor in the Middle Ages." In *Medieval Fabrications: Dress, Textiles, Clothwork, and Other Cultural Imaginings*, ed. E. Jane Burns. New York: Palgrave.

Kelleher, Marie. 2010. *The Measure of Women: Law and Female Identity in the Crown of Aragon*. Philadelphia: University of Pennsylvania Press.

Kelly, Kathleen Coyne. 2000. *Performing Virginity and Testing Chastity in the Middle Ages*. London: Routledge.

Kempe, Margery. 1985. *The Book of Margery Kempe*, trans. B. A. Windeatt. Harmondsworth: Penguin.

Kempe, Margery. 2001. *The Book of Margery Kempe*, ed. Lynn Staley. New York: Norton.

Kerber, Linda. 1988. "Separate Spheres, Female Worlds, Woman's Place: The Rhetoric of Women's History." *Journal of American History* 75: 9–39.

Kettle, Ann. n.d. "Review of Georges Duby, *Women of the Twelfth Century*" (review 73). *Reviews in History*. Available at: https://www.history.ac.uk/reviews/review/73. Accessed September 1, 2011.

King, Helen. 1998. *Hippocrates' Woman: Reading the Female Body in Ancient Greece*, trans. M. B. Debvoise. London: Routledge.

King, Margot. 1983. "The Desert Mothers: A Survey of the Female Anchoritic Tradition in Western Europe." *Fourteenth Century Mystics Newsletter* 9: 12–25.

Klapisch-Zuber, Christiane. 1985. *Women, Family, and Ritual in Renaissance Italy*, trans. Lydia G. Cochrane. Chicago: University of Chicago Press.

Klapisch-Zuber, Christiane. 1986. "Women Servants in Florence during the Fourteenth and Fifteenth Centuries." In *Women and Work in Preindustrial Europe*, ed. Barbara A. Hanawalt. Bloomington: Indiana University Press.

Klein, Stacy S. 2006. *Ruling Women: Queenship and Gender in Anglo-Saxon Literature*. Notre Dame: Notre Dame University Press.

Kleinberg, Aviad. 1992. *Prophets in Their Own Country: Living Saints and the Making of Sainthood in the Later Middle Ages*. Chicago: University of Chicago Press.

Knighton. Henry. 1995. *Knighton's Chronicle*, ed. and trans. G. H. Martin. Oxford: Oxford University Press.

Knox, Lezlie. 2000. "Audacious Nuns: Institutionalizing the Franciscan Order of Saint Clare." *Church History* 69: 42–47.

Kowaleski, Maryanne. 1999. "Singlewomen in Medieval and Early Modern Europe: The Demographic Perspective." In *Singlewomen in the European Past 1250–1800*, ed. Judith M. Bennett and Amy M. Froide. Philadelphia: University of Pennsylvania Press.

Kowaleski, Maryanne. 1986. "Women's Work in a Market Town: Exeter in the Late Fourteenth Century." In *Women and Work in Preindustrial Europe*, ed. Barbara A. Hanawalt. Bloomington: Indiana University Press.

Kowaleski, Maryanne, and Judith M. Bennett. 1989. "Crafts, Gilds, and Women in the Middle Ages: Fifty Years after Marian K. Dale." In *Sisters and Workers in the Middle Ages*, ed. Judith M. Bennett, Elizabeth A. Clark, Jean F. O'Barr, B. Anne Vilen, and Sarah Westphal-Wihl. Chicago: University of Chicago Press.

Kowaleski, Maryanne, and P.J.P. Goldberg. 2008. "Introduction. Medieval Domesticity: Home, Housing and Household." In *Medieval Domesticity: Home, Housing and Household in Medieval England*, ed. Maryanne Kowaleski and P.J.P. Goldberg. Cambridge: Cambridge University Press.

Krueger, Roberta L. 2001. "'Nouvelles choses': Social Instability and the Problem of Fashion in the *Livre du Chevalier de la Tour Landry*, the *Ménagier de Paris*, and Christine de Pizan's *Livre des trois vertus*." In *Medieval Conduct*, ed. Kathleen Ashley and Robert L. A. Clark. Minneapolis: University of Minnesota Press.

Kuehn, Thomas. 1998. "Person and Gender in the Laws." In *Gender and Society in Renaissance Italy*, ed. Judith C. Brown and Robert C. Davis. London and New York: Longman.

Kümin, Beat. 1997. "The European Perspective." In *The Parish in English Life: 1400–1600*, ed. Katherine L. French, Gary G. Gibbs, and Beat Kümin. Manchester: Manchester University Press.

Kupfer, Marcia. 2003. *The Art of Healing: Painting for the Sick and the Sinner in a Medieval Town*. University Park: Pennsylvania State University Press.

La danse macabre. 1486. Paris: Guy Marchant. Available at: http://gallica.bnf.fr/ark:/12148/btv1b2200008n. Accessed June 3, 2011.

La danse macabre. 1491. Paris: Guy Marchant. Available at: http://gallica.bnf.fr/ark:/12148/btv1b2200006t. Accessed May 7, 2011.

Lagorio, Valerie M. 1984. "The Medieval Continental Women Mystics: An Introduction." In *An Introduction to the Medieval Mystics of Europe*, ed. Paul Szarmach. Albany: SUNY Press.

Laiou, Angeliki E., ed. 1998. *Consent and Coercion to Sex and Marriage in Ancient and Medieval Societies*. Washington, DC: Dumbarton Oaks.

Lambert, Malcolm. 1998. *The Cathars*. Oxford: Blackwell.

Lambert, Malcolm. 1992. *Medieval Heresy: Popular Movements from the Gregorian Reform to the Reformation*. Oxford: Blackwell.

Lansing, Carol. 1998. *Power and Purity: Cathar Heresy in Medieval Italy*. New York: Oxford University Press.

Larson, Wendy R. 2003. "Who is the Master of this Narrative? Maternal Patronage of the Cult of St. Margaret." In *Gendering the Master Narrative: Women and Power in the Middle Ages*, ed. Mary C. Erler and Maryanne Kowaleski. Ithaca: Cornell University Press.

Lawless, Elaine. 2003. "Transforming the Master Narrative: How Women Shift the Religious Subject." *Frontiers: A Journal of Women Studies* 24: 61–75.

Lawrence, C. H. 2001. *Medieval Monasticism*. 3rd ed. London: Longman.

Layher, William. 2010. *Queenship and Voice in Medieval Northern Europe*. New York: Palgrave.

Laynesmith, J. L. 2004. *The Last Medieval Queens*. Oxford: Oxford University Press.

Lee, Becky R. 2002. "A Company of Women *and* Men: Men's Recollections of Childbirth in Medieval England," *Journal of Family History* 27: 92–100.

Lee, Becky R. 2002. "Men's Recollections of a Woman's Rite: Medieval English Men's Recollections Regarding the Rite of the Purification of Women after Childbirth." *Gender & History* 14: 224–41.

Lee, Becky R. 1995–96. "The Purification of Women after Childbirth: A Window onto Medieval Perceptions of Women." *Florilegium* 14: 43–55.

Legaré, Anne Marie. 2007. *Livres et lectures des femmes en Europe entre moyen âge et renaissance*. Turnhout: Brepols.

Leguay, Jean-Pierre. 2000. "Urban Life." In *The New Cambridge Medieval History*, ed. Michael Jones. Vol. 6, *c. 1300–c.1415*. Cambridge: Cambridge University Press.

Lelwica, Mary Michelle. 2002. *Starving for Salvation: The Spiritual Dimensions of Eating Problems among American Girls and Women*. New York: Oxford University Press.

Lemarquand, Grant. 2004. *An Issue of Relevance: A Comparative Study of the Story of the Bleeding Woman (Mk 5:25–34; Mt 9:20–22; Lk 8:43–48) in North Atlantic and African Contexts*. New York: Peter Lang.

Lemos, Maximiano. 1921. *O Auto dos Físicos de Gil Vicente: Comentârio Médico*. Oporto: Tipografia Enciclopédia Portuguesa.

Lester, Anne E. 2009. "From the Margins to the Center: Religious Women and the Cistercian Order in Thirteenth-century Northern France." Unpublished paper presented at Brown University, March 2009.

L'Estrange, Elizabeth. 2008. *Holy Motherhood: Gender, Dynasty and Visual Culture in the Later Middle Ages*. Manchester: Manchester University Press.

L'Estrange, Elizabeth. 2007. "Sainte Anne et le mécénat d'Anne de France" and "Le mécénat d'Anne de Bretagne." In *Patronnes et mécènes en France á la Renaissance*, ed. Kathleen Wilson-Chevalier. St-Étienne: Presse Universitaire de St-Étienne.

Lewis, Flora. 1996. "The Wound in Christ's Side and the Instruments of the Passion: Gendered Experience and Response." In *Women and the Book: Assessing the Visual Evidence*, ed. Jane H. M. Taylor and Lesley Smith. London: The British Library.

Lisbon, Arquivos Nacionais da Torre do Tombo. *Chancelaria de D. Afonso V*. Book 19, fol. 91 (1439).

Lisbon, Arquivos Nacionais da Torre do Tombo. *Chancelaria de D. Afonso V*. Book 15, fol. 99 (1454).

Lisbon, Arquivos Nacionais da Torre do Tombo. *Chancelaria de D. João III*. Book 46, fol. 144v (1522).

Lisbon, Arquivos Nacionais da Torre do Tombo. *Chancelaria de D. Manuel*. Book 25, fol. 165v (1517).

Little, Lester K. 1979. *Religious Poverty and the Profit Economy*. Ithaca: Cornell University Press.

Livingstone, Amy. *Out of Love for My Kin: Aristocratic Family Life in the Lands of the Loire, 1000–1200*. Ithaca: Cornell University Press.

Lopes, Célia Rodrigues. 2001. "As Clarissas de Coimbra dos Séculos XIV a XVII: Paleobiologia de uma Comunidade Religiosa de Santa Clara-a-Velha." MA diss., University of Coimbra.

Lopes, Fernão. 1963–68. *Crónica de D. João I*. 2 vols. Oporto: Livraria Civilização.

López de Ayala, Pedro. 1991. *Crónicas*, ed. José Luis Martín. Barcelona: Planeta.

LoPrete, Kimberly. 2007. *Adela of Blois: Countess and Lord (c. 1067–1137)*. Dublin: Four Courts.

LoPrete, Kimberly. 2003. "Historical Ironies in the Study of Capetian Women." In *Capetian Women*, ed. Kathleen Nolan. New York: Palgrave Macmillan.

Luongo, Thomas. 2006. *The Saintly Politics of Catherine of Siena*. Ithaca: Cornell University Press.

MacKinney, Loren, ed. 1965. *Medical Illustrations in Medieval Manuscripts*. Berkeley: University of California Press.

Madahil, António Gomes da Rocha, ed. 1939. *Crónica da Fundação do Mosteiro de Jesus de Aveiro e Memorial da Infanta Santa Joana Filha del Rei D. Afonso V*. Aveiro: Francisco Ferreiro Neves.

Madden, T. F. 2007. *The New Concise History of the Crusades*. New York: Barnes and Noble.

Mâle, Emile. 1978. *Religious Art in France: The Twelfth-century, a Study of the Origins of Medieval Iconography*, trans. Marthiel Matthews. Princeton, NJ: Princeton University Press.

Mandler, Peter. 2004. "The Problem with Cultural History." *Cultural and Social History* 1: 94–117.

Manzalaoui, M. A., ed. 1977. *Secretum Secretorum: Nine English Versions*. Early English Text Society, original ser. 276. Oxford: Oxford University Press.

Marbod of Rennes. 1992. "The Femme Fatale" *(De meretrice)* and "The Good Woman" *(De matrona)*, from "The Book with Ten Chapters" *(Liber decem capitulorum)*. In *Woman Defamed and Woman Defended: An Anthology of Medieval Texts*, ed. Alcuin Blamires. Oxford: Oxford University Press.

Martin, Therese. 2005. "The Art of a Reigning Queen as Dynastic Propaganda in Twelfth-century Spain." *Speculum* 80: 1134–71.

Martin, Therese. 2006. *Queen as King: Politics and Architectural Propaganda in Twelfth-century Spain*. Leiden: Brill.

Martins, Mário. 1969. "O Bispo-Menino, o Rito de Salibúria e a Capela Real Portuguesa." In *Estudos de Cultura Medieval*. 3 vols. Lisbon: Editorial Verbo.

Mate, Mavis E. 1998. *Daughters, Wives and Widows after the Black Death: Women in Sussex, 1350–1535*. Woodbridge: Boydell.

Mate, Mavis E. 1999. *Women in Medieval English Society*. Cambridge: Cambridge University Press.

Mattoso, José. 1987. "Saúde Corporal e Saúde Mental na Idade Média Portuguesa." In *Fragmentos de uma Composição Medieval*. Lisbon: Estampa.

Mayer, Hans Eberhard. 1972. "Studies in the History of Queen Melisende of Jerusalem." *Dumbarton Oaks Papers* 26: 94–182.

Mays, Simon. 1999. "A Biomechanical Study of Activity Patterns in a Medieval Human Skeletal Assemblage." *International Journal of Osteoarchaeology* 9: 68–73.

McCarthy, Conor. 2004. *Marriage in Medieval England: Law, Literature and Practice*. Woodbridge: Boydell Press.

McCash, June Hall, ed. 1996. *The Cultural Patronage of Medieval Women*. Athens: University of Georgia Press.

McClanan, Anne, and Karen Rosoff Encarnación, eds. 2002. *The Material Culture of Sex, Procreation and Marriage in Pre-modern Europe*. New York: Palgrave.

McCleery, Iona. 2009. "Both 'Illness and Temptation of the Enemy': Understanding Melancholy in the Writings of King Duarte of Portugal (1433–38)." *Journal of Medieval Iberian Studies* 1: 163–78.

McCleery, Iona. 2006. "Isabel of Aragon (d. 1336): Model Queen or Model Saint?" *Journal of Ecclesiastical History* 57: 668–92.

McCleery, Iona. 2011. "Medical 'Emplotment' and Plotting Medicine: Health and Disease in Late Medieval Portuguese Chronicles." *Social History of Medicine* 24: 125–41.

McCleery, Iona. 2005. "*Multos ex Medicinae Arte Curaverat, Multos Verbo et Oratione*: Curing in Medieval Portuguese Saints' Lives." In *Signs, Wonders, Miracles: Representations of Divine Power in the Life of the Church*, ed. Kate Cooper and Jeremy Gregory. Studies in Church History 41. Woodbridge: Boydell.

McCleery, Iona. 2005. "Saintly Physician, Diabolical Doctor, Medieval Saint: Exploring the Reputation of Gil de Santarém in Medieval and Renaissance Portugal." *Portuguese Studies* 21: 112–25.

McCracken, Peggy. 1998. *The Romance of Adultery: Queenship and Sexual Transgression in Old French Literature*. Philadelphia: University of Pennsylvania Press.

McCracken, Peggy. 2002. "Scandalizing Desire: Eleanor of Aquitaine and the Chroniclers." In *Eleanor of Aquitaine: Lord and Lady*, ed. John Carmi Parsons and Bonnie Wheeler. New York: Palgrave MacMillan.

McDonald, Nicola. 1988. "Fragments of *(Have Your) Desire*: Brome Women at Play." In *Medieval Domesticity: Home, Housing and Household in Medieval England*, ed. Maryanne Kowaleski and P.J.P. Goldberg. Cambridge: Cambridge University Press.

McLaughlin, Megan. 1998. "The Bishop as Bridegroom: Marital Imagery and Clerical Celibacy in the Eleventh and Early Twelfth Centuries." In *Medieval Purity and Piety: Essays on Medieval Clerical Celibacy and Religious Reform*, ed. Michael Frassetto. New York: Garland.

McNamara, Jo Ann. 1995. "Canossa and the Ungendering of the Public Man." In *Render unto Caesar: The Religious Sphere in World Politics*, ed. Sbrina Petra Ramet and Donald W. Treadgold. Washington, DC: American University Press.

McNamara, Jo Ann. 1994. "The *Herrenfrage*: The Restructuring of the Gender System, 1050–1150." In *Medieval Masculinities*, ed. Clare A. Lees. Minneapolis: University of Minnesota Press.

McNamara, Jo Ann. 1983. *A New Song: Celibate Women in the First Three Christian Centuries*. New York: Institute for Research in History and Haworth Press.

McNamara, Jo Ann. 1996. *Sisters in Arms: Catholic Nuns through Two Millennia*. Cambridge, MA: Harvard University Press.

McNamara, Jo Ann. 2003. "Women and Power through the Family Revisited." In *Gendering the Master Narrative: Women and Power in the Middle Ages*, ed. Mary C. Erler and Maryanne Kowaleski. Ithaca: Cornell University Press.

McNamara, Jo Ann, and Suzanne Wemple. 1973/1988. "The Power of Women through the Family." *Feminist Studies* 1: 126–41. Reprinted with minor revisions in *Women and Power in the Middle Ages*, ed. Mary Erler and Maryanne Kowaleski. Athens: University of Georgia Press.

McSheffrey, Shannon. 1995. *Gender and Heresy: Women and Men in Lollard Communities, 1420–1530*. Philadelphia: University of Pennsylvania Press.

McSheffrey, Shannon, ed. and trans. 1995. *Love and Marriage in Late Medieval London*. Kalamazoo: Medieval Institute Publications.

McSheffrey, Shannon. 2006. *Marriage, Sex, and Civic Culture in Late Medieval London*. Philadelphia: University of Pennsylvania Press.

McSheffrey, Shannon. 2004. "Place, Space, and Situation: Public and Private in the Making of Marriage in Late-medieval London." *Speculum* 79: 960–90.

McVaugh, Michael. 1993. *Medicine before the Plague: Patients and Practitioners in the Medieval Crown of Aragon, 1285–1345*. Cambridge: Cambridge University Press.

Ménagier de Paris, Le. 2009. *The Good Wife's Guide: A Medieval Household Book*, ed. and trans. Gina L. Greco and Christine M. Rose. Ithaca: Cornell University Press.

Mendonça, Manuela. 2004. "A Reforma da Saúde no Reinado de D. Manuel." In *1as Jornadas de História do Direito Hispânico: Actas*. Lisbon: Academia Portuguesa da História.

Mertes, Kate. 1988. *The English Noble Household, 1250–1600: Good Governance and Politic Rule*. Oxford: Basil Blackwell.

Miller, Edward, and John Hatcher. 1978. *Medieval England: Rural Society and Economic Change 1086–1348*. London: Longman.

Miller, Edward, and John Hatcher. 1995. *Medieval England: Towns, Commerce and Crafts 1086–1348*. London: Longman.

Miller, Maureen C. 2003. "Masculinity, Reform, and Clerical Culture: Narratives of Episcopal Holiness in the Gregorian Era." *Church History* 72: 25–52.

Millett, Bella, ed. 1982. *Hali Meidhad*. Early English Text Society, original ser. 284. London: Oxford University Press.

Millett, Kate. 1970. *Sexual Politics*. New York: Doubleday.

Minnis, Alastair, and Eric J. Johnson. 2000. "Chaucer's Criseyde and Feminine Fear." In *Medieval Women: Texts and Contexts in Late Medieval Britain: Essays for Felicity Riddy*, ed. Jocelyn Wogan-Browne, Rosalynn Voaden, Arlyn Diamond, Ann Hutchison, Carol Meale, and Lesley Johnson. Turnhout: Brepols.

Minnis, A. J., with V. J. Scattergood and J. J. Smith. 1995. *The Shorter Poems*. Oxford Guides to Chaucer. Oxford: Clarendon Press.

Moi, Toril. 1999. *What Is a Woman? and Other Essays*. Oxford: Oxford University Press.

Moita, Irisalva. 1992. *V Centenário do Hospital de Todos os Santos*. Lisbon: Correios de Portugal.

Mol, Annemarie. 2002. *The Body Multiple: Ontology in Medical Practice*. Durham: Duke University Press.

Moore, R. I. 1994. *The Origins of European Dissent*. 2nd ed. Medieval Academy Reprints for Teaching, 30. Toronto: University of Toronto Press.

Moorman, John. 1968. *A History of the Franciscan Order*. Oxford: Oxford University Press.

Morganstern, Anne McGee. 2000. *Gothic Tombs of Kinship in France, the Low Countries, and England*. University Park: The Pennsylvania State University Press.

Morris, Colin. 1972/1987. *The Discovery of the Individual, 1050–1200*. Toronto: Medieval Academy of America.

MS Fonds français 995. Bibliothèque nationale de France, Paris [late fifteenth century].

MS Harleian 6815, fol. 25r–41v. The British Library, London [mid-sixteenth century from a late-fifteenth century original].

Mulder-Bakker, Anneke. 2003. "Jeanne of Valois: The Power of a Consort." In *Capetian Women*, ed. Kathleen Nolan. New York: Palgrave Macmillan.

Mulder-Bakker, Anneke B., and Jocelyn Wogan-Browne. 2005. "Introduction Part II: Medieval Households." In *Household, Women, and Christianities in Late Antiquity and the Middle Ages*, ed. Anneke B. Mulder-Bakker and Jocelyn Wogan-Browne. Turnhout: Brepols.

Mundy, John Hine. 1999. *Men and Women at Toulouse in the Age of the Cathars*. Toronto: Pontifical Institute of Mediaeval Studies.

Munkhoff, Richelle. 1999. "Searchers of the Dead: Authority, Marginality, and the Interpretation of Plague in England, 1574–1665." *Gender & History* 11: 1–29.

Munro, John H. 2003. "Medieval Woolens: Textiles, Textile Technology, and Industrial Organisation, *c.* 800–1500." In *The Cambridge History of Western Textiles*, ed. David Jenkins. Vol. 1. Cambridge: Cambridge University Press.

Murray, Jacqueline. 1998. "Gendered Souls in Sexed Bodies: The Male Construction of Female Sexuality in Some Medieval Confessor's Manuals." In *Handling Sin: Confession in the Middle Ages*, ed. Peter Biller and A. J. Minnis. Woodbridge: York Medieval Press.

Murray, Jacqueline. 1996. "Twice Marginal and Twice Invisible: Lesbians in the Middle Ages." In *Handbook of Medieval Sexuality*, ed. Vern L. Bullough and James A. Brundage. New York: Garland.

Mussachio, Jacqueline Marie. 1999. *The Art and Ritual of Childbirth in Renaissance Italy*. New Haven and London: Yale University Press.

Mustanoja, Tauno F. 1948. *Good Wife Taught Her Daughter, the Good Wife Wold a Pylgremage, the Thewis of Gud Women*. Helsinki: Suomalainen Tiedeakatemia.

Myers, A. R., ed. 1985. *Crown, Household and Parliament in Fifteenth Century England*. London: Hambledon.

Myers, A. R., ed. 1969. *English Historical Documents, 1327–1485*. London: Eyre and Spottiswoode.

Myers, A. R., ed. 1959. *The Household of Edward IV*. Manchester: Manchester University Press.

The National Archives, Kew Early Chancery Proceedings, C 1/63/138 (1480-3), C 1/82/64 (1486).

Nelson, Janet L. 1986. *Politics and Ritual in Early Medieval Europe*. London: Hambledon.

Nelson, Janet L. 1978. "Queens as Jezebels: The Careers of Brunhild and Balthild in Merovingian History." In *Medieval Women*, ed. Derek Baker. Oxford: Basil Blackwell for the Ecclesiastical History Society.

Nelson, Janet L. 1999. *Rulers and Ruling Families in Early Medieval Europe: Alfred, Charles the Bald, and Others*. Aldershot: Ashgate.

Newman, Barbara. 1987. *Sister of Wisdom: St. Hildegard's Theology of the Feminine*. Berkeley: University of California Press.

Newman, Barbara, ed. 1998. *Voice of the Living Light: Hildegard of Bingen and Her World*. Berkeley: University of California Press.

Nicholas, David. 1985. *The Domestic Life of a Medieval City: Women, Children, and the Family in Fourteenth-century Ghent*. Lincoln and London: University of Nebraska Press.

Nicholson, Helen J. 2004. "'La roine preude femme et bonne dame': Queen Sybil of Jerusalem (1186–1190) in History and Legend 1186–1300." *Haskins Society Journal* 15: 110–25.

Nicolas, Nicholas Harris, ed. 1830. *Privy Purse Expenses of Elizabeth of York. Household Accounts of Edward the Fourth*. London: W. Pickering.

Nolan, Kathleen, ed. 2003. *Capetian Women*. New York: Palgrave Macmillan.

Nolan, Kathleen. 2009. *Queens in Stone and Silver: The Creation of a Visual Imagery of Queenship in Capetian France*. New York: Palgrave Macmillan.

Noomen, Willem, and Nico van den Boogaard, eds. 1983–98. *Nouveau Recueil Complet des Fabliaux*. 10 vols. Assen, the Netherlands: Van Gorcum.

Norwich, John Julius. 1992. *The Normans in Sicily: The Magnificent Story of the "Other" Norman Conquest*. Harmondsworth: Penguin.

Nunes, José Joaquim, ed. 1918–19. "Livro que Fala da Boa Vida que Fez a Reynha de Portugal, Dona Isabel." *Boletim da Segunda Classe da Academia das Sciências de Lisboa* 13: 1293–1384.

Nyberg, Tore. 2000. "On Female Monasticism and Scandinavia." *Medieval Scandinavia* 13: 181–97.

O'Callaghan, Joseph F. 2005. "The Many Roles of the Medieval Queen: Some Examples from Castile." In *Queenship and Political Power in Medieval and Early Modern Spain*, ed. Theresa Earenfight. Aldershot: Ashgate.

Oexle, Otto Gerhard. 2001. "Perceiving Social Reality in the Early and High Middle Ages: A Contribution to a History of Social Knowledge." In *Ordering Medieval Society: Perspectives on Intellectual and Practical Modes of Shaping Social Relations*, ed. Bernhard Jussen, trans. Pamela Selwyn. Philadelphia: University of Pennsylvania Press.

Ogg, F. A., ed. 1907. *A Source Book of Mediaeval History*. New York: American Book Company.

Oliva, Marilyn. 1998. *The Convent and the Community in Late Medieval England: Female Monasteries in the Diocese of Norwich, 1350–1540*. Woodbridge: Boydell.

Oliveira, Cristóvão Rodrigues de. 1987. *Lisboa em 1551: Sumário em que Brevemente se Contêm Algumas Coisas assim Eclesiásticas como Seculares que Há na Cidade de Lisbon*, ed. José da Felicidade Alves. Lisbon: Livros Horizonte.

Oost, Stewart Irwin. 1968. *Galla Placidia Augusta: A Historiographical Essay*. Chicago: University of Chicago Press.

Orme, Nicholas. 1984. *From Childhood to Chivalry: The Education of the English Kings and Aristocracy 1066–1530*. London: Methuen.

Orme, Nicholas. 2001. *Medieval Children*. New Haven: Yale University Press.

Orme, Nicholas. 2006. *Medieval Schools: From Roman Britain to Renaissance England*. New Haven: Yale University Press.

Otis, Leah Lydia. 1986. "Municipal Wetnurses in Fifteenth Century Montpellier." In *Women and Work in Preindustrial Europe*, ed. Barbara A. Hanawalt. Bloomington: Indiana University Press.

Otis, Leah Lydia. 1985. *Prostitution in Medieval Society: The History of an Urban Institution in Languedoc*. Chicago: University of Chicago Press.

Ovid. 1914. *Heroides and Amores*, trans. Grant Showerman. Harvard: Loeb Classical Library.

Owst, G. R. 1966. *Literature and Pulpit in Medieval England*. Oxford: Oxford University Press.

Pain, Nesta. 1978. *Empress Matilda: Uncrowned Queen of England*. London: Weidenfeld & Nicolson.

Paino, Fiorelli. 2003. "The Palazzo of the da Varano Family in Camerino (Fourteenth–Sixteenth Centuries): Typology and Evolution of a Central Italian Aristocratic

Residence." In *The Medieval Household in Christian Europe, c. 850–c. 1550: Managing Power, Wealth, and the Body*, ed. Cordelia Beattie, Anna Maslakovic, and Sarah Rees Jones. Turnhout: Brepols.

Pais, Álvaro. 1988–98. *Estado e Pranto da Igreja*, ed. and trans. Miguel Pinto de Meneses. 8 vols. Lisbon: Instituto Nacional Investigação Científica.

Park, Katharine. 2006. *Secrets of Women: Gender, Generation and the Origins of Human Dissection*. New York: Zone Books.

Parsons, John Carmi. 1995. *Eleanor of Castile: Queen and Society in Thirteenth-century England.* New York: St. Martin's Press.

Parsons, John Carmi. 1995. "The Intercessory Patronage of Queens Margaret and Isabella of France." In *Thirteenth Century England*, vol. 6. Woodbridge: Boydell.

Parsons, John Carmi, ed. 1993. *Medieval Queenship*. New York: St. Martin's.

Parsons, John Carmi. 1993. "Mothers, Daughters, Marriage, Power: Some Plantagenet Evidence, 1150–1500." In *Medieval Queenship*, ed. John Carmi Parsons. New York: St. Martin's.

Parsons, John Carmi. 1996. "The Pregnant Queen as Counselor and the Medieval Construction of Motherhood." In *Medieval Mothering,* ed. John Carmi Parsons and Bonnie Wheeler. New York: Garland.

Parsons, John Carmi. 1995. "The Queen's Intercession in Thirteenth-century England." In *Power of the Weak: Studies on Medieval Women*, ed. Jennifer Carpenter and Sally-Beth MacLean. Urbana: University of Illinois Press.

Parsons, John Carmi. 1998. "Que Nos in Infancia Lactauit: The Impact of Childhood Care-givers on Plantagenet Family Relationships in the Thirteenth and Early Fourteenth Centuries." In *Women, Marriage, and Family in Medieval Christendom: Essays in Memory of Michael M. Sheehan, C.S.B*, ed. Constance M. Rousseau and Joel T. Rosenthal. Kalamazoo: Western Michigan University.

Paviot, Jacques. 1999. "Les *Honneurs de la Cour* d'Éleonore de Poitiers." In *Autour de Marguerite d'Écosse: Reines, Princesses et Dames du XVe Siècle*, ed. Geneviève Contamine and Philippe Contamine. Paris: Champion.

Paviot, Jacques, ed. 1995. *Portugal et Bourgogne au XVe Siècle*. Lisbon and Paris: Centre Culturel Calouste Gulbenkian/Commission Nationale pour les Commémorations des Découvertes Portugaises.

Payer, Pierre J. 1993. *The Bridling of Desire: Views of Sex in the Later Middle Ages.* Toronto: University of Toronto Press.

Pearsall, D. A., ed. 1962. *Floure and the Leafe and the Assembly of Ladies*. London: Nelson.

Pelling, Margaret. 1998. *The Common Lot: Sickness, Medical Occupations and the Urban Poor in Early Modern England*. London: Longman.

Penketh, Sandra. 1997. "Women and Books of Hours." In *Women and the Book: Assessing the Visual Evidence*, ed. Jane H. M. Taylor and Lesley Smith. Toronto: University of Toronto Press and the British Library.

Penn, Simon A. C. 1987. "Female Wage-earners in Late Fourteenth-century England." *Agricultural History Review* 35: 1–14.

Percy, Thomas, ed. 1827. *The Regulations and Establishment of the Household of Henry Algernon Percy at his Castles of Wreshill and Likinfield in Yorkshire.* London: W. Pickering.

Pereira, Fernando Jasmins, ed. 1990. *Documentos Sobre a Madeira no Século XVI Existentes no Corpo Cronológico: Análise Documental.* 2 vols. Lisbon: Arquivo Nacional da Torre do Tombo.

Pernoud, Régine, trans. 1955/ 2007. *The Retrial of Joan of Arc: The Evidence for Her Vindication.* New York, reprint San Francisco: Ignatius Press.

Pernoud, Régine, and Marie Véronique Clin. 1999. *Joan of Arc: Her Story*, trans. Jeremy duQuesnay Adams. New York: Palgrave.

Peroux, Catherine. 2000. "The Leper's Kiss." In *Monks and Nuns, Saints and Outcasts*, ed. Sharon Farmer and Barbara H. Rosenwein. Ithaca: Cornell University Press.

Perroy, E. 1955. "Wage Labour in France in the Later Middle Ages." *Economic History Review* (2nd ser.), 8: 234–36.

Perry, Mary Elizabeth. 1980. *Crime and Society in Early Modern Seville.* Hanover: University Press of New England.

Perry, Mary Elizabeth. 1985. "Deviant Insiders: Legalized Prostitutes and a Consciousness of Women in Early Modern Seville." *Comparative Studies in Society and History* 27: 138–58.

Petroff, Elizabeth Alvilda. 1994. *Body and Soul: Essays on Medieval Women and Mysticism.* New York: Oxford University Press.

Phillips, Kim M. 2000. "Bodily Walls, Windows, and Doors: The Politics of Gesture in late Fifteenth-century English Books for Women." In *Medieval Women: Texts and Contexts in Late Medieval Britain: Essays for Felicity Riddy*, ed. Jocelyn Wogan-Browne, Rosalynn Voaden, Arlyn Diamond, Ann Hutchison, Carol Meale, and Lesley Johnson. Turnhout: Brepols.

Phillips, Kim M. 2005. "The Invisible Man: Body and Ritual in a Fifteenth-century Noble Household." *Journal of Medieval History* 31: 143–62.

Phillips, Kim M. 1999. "Maidenhood as the Perfect Age of Woman's Life." In *Young Medieval Women*, ed. Katherine J. Lewis, Noël James Menuge, and Kim M. Phillips. Stroud: Sutton.

Phillips, Kim M. 2004. "Margery Kempe and the Ages of Woman." In *A Companion to* The Book of Margery Kempe, ed. John H. Arnold and Katherine J. Lewis. Cambridge: D. S. Brewer.

Phillips, Kim M. 2003. *Medieval Maidens: Young Women and Gender in England, 1270–1540.* Manchester: Manchester University Press.

Phillips, Kim M. 2000. "Written on the Body: Reading Rape from the Twelfth to the Fifteenth Centuries." In *Medieval Women and the Law*, ed. Noël James Menuge. Woodbridge: Boydell and Brewer.

Phillips, Kim M., and Barry Reay. 2011. *Sex Before Sexuality: A Premodern History.* Cambridge: Polity.

Pierce, Joanne. 1999. "'Green Women' and Blood Pollution: Some Medieval Rituals for the Churching of Women after Childbirth." *Studia Liturgica* 29: 191–215.

Pierpont Morgan Library. n.d. "Descriptions of Medieval and Renaissance Manuscripts: MS M.0813." Available at: http://corsair.morganlibrary.org/msdescr/BBM0813.htm. Accessed May 12, 2011.

Pilcher, Jane. 1995. *Age and Generation in Modern Britain.* Oxford: Oxford University Press.

Pina, Rui de. 1977. *Crónicas*, ed. Manuel Lopes de Almeida. Oporto: Lello & Irmão.

Pomata, Gianna. 1998. *Contracting a Cure: Patients, Healers, and the Law in Early Modern Bologna.* Baltimore: Johns Hopkins University Press.

Porter, Dorothy Carr. 2001. "The Social Centrality of Women in Beowulf: A New Context." *Heroic Age* 5. Available at: http://www.heroicage.org. Accessed September 1, 2011.

Porter, Roy. 1985. "The Patient's View: Doing Medical History from Below." *Theory and Society* 14: 175–98.

Potter, K. R., ed. 1976. *Gesta Stephani.* Revised by R.H.C. Davis. Oxford: Oxford University Press.

Prusak, B. P. 1974. "Woman: Seductive Siren and Source of Sin? Pseudepigraphal Myth and Christian Origins." In *Religion and Sexism: Images of Woman in the Jewish and Christian Traditions*, ed. Rosemary R. Ruether. New York: Simon and Schuster.

Pseudo-Albertus Magnus. 1992. *Women's Secrets: A Translation of Pseudo-Albertus Magnus's* De Secretis Mulierum *with Commentaries*, ed. and trans. Helen Rodnite Lemay. Albany: State University of New York Press.

Pugh, T. B. 2004. "Grey, Thomas, First Marquess of Dorset (*c.* 1455–1501)." In *Oxford Dictionary of National Biography.* Oxford: Oxford University Press. Available at: http://www.oxforddnb.com/view/article/11560. Accessed September 1, 2011.

Queirós, Isabel Ribeiro de. 1999. "Theudas e Mantheudas: a Criminalidade Feminina no Reinado de D. João II Através das Cartas de Perdão (1481–1485)." MA diss., 2 vols., University of Oporto.

Quirk, Kathleen. 2001. "Men, Women and Miracles in Normandy, 1050–1150." In *Medieval Memories: Men, Women and the Past, 700–1300*, ed. Elisabeth Van Houts. Harlow: Longman.

Randolph, Adrian. 2004. "Gendering the Period Eye: *Deschi da Parto* and Renaissance Visual Culture." *Art History* 27: 538–62.

Rankin, Alisha. 2008. "Duchess Heal Thyself: Elisabeth of Rochlitz and the Patient's Perspective in Early-modern Germany." *Bulletin of the History of Medicine* 82: 109–44.

Rawcliffe, Carole. 2009. "A Marginal Occupation? The Medieval Laundress and Her Work." *Gender & History* 21: 147–69.

Rawcliffe, Carole. 1995. *Medicine and Society in Later Medieval England.* Stroud: Sutton.

Rees Jones, Sarah, and Felicity Riddy. 2005. "The Bolton Hours of York: Female Domestic Piety and the Public Sphere." In *Household, Women, and Christianities in Late Antiquity and the Middle Ages*, ed. Anneke B. Mulder-Bakker and Jocelyn Wogan-Browne. Turnhout: Brepols.

Reid, Norman. 1982. "Margaret, 'Maid of Norway' and Scottish Queenship." *Reading Medieval Studies* 8: 75–96.

Reilly, Bernard F. 1982. *The Kingdom of Leon-Castilla under Queen Urraca: 1109–1126.* Princeton, NJ: Princeton University Press.

Remnant, G. L. 1969. *A Catalogue of Misericords in Great Britain.* Oxford: Clarendon Press.

Resende, Andre de. 2000. *Aegidius Scallabitanus: Um Diálogo sobre Fr. Gil de Santarém*, ed. Virgínia Soares Pereira. Lisbon: Fundação Calouste Gulbenkian.

Resnick, Irven. 2000. "Medieval Roots of the Myth of Jewish Male Menses." *Harvard Theological Review* 93: 241–63.

Reveney, Denis. 2003. "Household Chores in *The Doctrine of the Hert*: Affective Spirituality and Subjectivity." In *The Medieval Household in Christian Europe, c. 850–c. 1550: Managing Power, Wealth, and the Body*, ed. Cordelia Beattie, Anna Maslakovic, and Sarah Rees Jones. Turnhout: Brepols.

Reyerson, Kathryn L. 1992. "The Adolescent Apprentice/worker in Medieval Montpellier." *Journal of Family History* 14: 353–70.

Reynolds, Philip L., and John Witte, Jr., eds. 2007. *To Have and to Hold: Marrying and its Documentation in Western Christendom, 400–1600*. Cambridge: Cambridge University Press.

Rezak, Brigitte Bedos. 1988. "Women, Seals, and Power in Medieval France, 1150–1350." In *Women and Power in the Middle Ages*, ed. Mary Erler and Maryanne Kowaleski. Athens: University of Georgia Press.

Richardson, Amanda. 2003. "Gender and Space in English Royal Palaces *c.* 1160–*c.* 1547: A Study in Access Analysis and Imagery." *Medieval Archaeology* 47: 131–65.

Riddy, Felicity. 2008. "'Burgeis' Domesticity in Late-medieval England." In *Medieval Domesticity: Home, Housing and Household in Medieval England*, ed. Maryanne Kowaleski and P.J.P. Goldberg. Cambridge: Cambridge University Press.

Riddy, Felicity. 2003. "Looking Closely: Authority and Intimacy in the Late Medieval Urban Home." In *Gendering the Master Narrative: Women and Power in the Middle Ages*, ed. Mary C. Erler and Maryanne Kowaleski. Ithaca: Cornell University Press.

Riddy, Felicity. 1996. "Mother Knows Best: Reading Social Change in a Courtesy Text." *Speculum* 71: 66–86.

Riddy, Felicity. 1996. "'Women Talking about the Things of God': A Late Medieval Sub-culture." In *Women and Literature in Britain, 1150–1500*, ed. Carol M. Meale. 2nd ed. Cambridge: Cambridge University Press.

Rieder, Paula. 2006. *On the Purification of Women: Churching in Northern France, 1100–1500*. New York: Palgrave Macmillan.

Rigby, Stephen. 2000. "Gendering the Black Death: Women in Later Medieval England." *Gender & History* 12: 745–54.

Riley, Denise. 1988. *"Am I That Name?" Feminism and the Category of "Women" in History*. Houndmills: Macmillan.

Roberts, Charlotte, and Margaret Cox. 2003. *Health and Disease in Britain: From Prehistory to the Present Day*. Stroud: Sutton.

Robertson, Elizabeth. 1993. "Medieval Medical Views of Women and Female Spirituality in the *Ancrene Wisse* and Julian of Norwich's *Showings*." In *Feminist Approaches to the Body in Medieval Literature*, ed. Linda Lomperis and Sarah Stanbury. Philadelphia: University of Pennsylvania Press.

Robinson, J. M. 2001. *Nobility and Annihilation in Marguerite Porete's* Mirror of Simple Souls. Albany: SUNY Press.

Rodrigues, Ana Maria. 2007. "Entre a Sufocação da Madre e o Prurido do Pénis: Género e Disfunções Sexuais no *Thesaurus Pauperum* de Pedro Hispano." In *Rumos e Escrita da História*, ed. Maria de Fátima Reis. Lisbon: Edições Colibri.

Rodrigues, Ana Maria. 1989. "A População de Torres Vedras em 1381." *Revista de História Económica e Social* 25: 15–46.

Rollins, Hyder E. 1919. "Concerning Bodleian Ms. Ashmole 48." *Modern Language Notes* 34: 340–51.

Rollo-Koster, Joëlle. 2002. "From Prostitutes to Brides of Christ: The Avignonese 'Repenties' in the Late Middle Ages." *Journal of Medieval and Early Modern Studies* 32: 109–44.

Romano, Dennis. 1989. "Gender and the Urban Geography of Renaissance Venice." *Journal of Social History* 23: 339–53.

Roque, Mário da Costa. 1979. *As Pestes Medievais Europeias e o 'Regimento Proveitoso Contra ha Pestenença.'* Paris: Fundação Calouste Gulbenkian/Centro Cultural Português.

Rose, Mary Beth. 1986. "Introduction." In *Women in the Middle Ages and the Renaissance: Literary and Historical Perspectives*, ed. Mary Beth Rose. Syracuse, NY: Syracuse University Press.

Rossi, Alice S. 1980. "Life-span Theories and Women's Lives." *Signs* 6: 4–32.

Rossi, Patrick. 2006. *Danse macabre de La Chaise-Dieu: abbatiale Saint-Robert: é́ude iconographique d'une fresque du XVe siècle.* Le Puy-en-Velay: Éditions Jeanne d'Arc.

Rubin, Miri. 2009. *Mother of God: A History of the Virgin Mary.* New Haven: Yale University Press.

Rudge, Lindsay. 2006. "Texts and Contexts: Women's Dedicated Life from Caesarius to Benedict." PhD thesis, University of St. Andrews.

Rudolf of Fulda. 1995. "The Life of St. Leoba." In *Soldiers of Christ: Saints and Saints' Lives from Late Antiquity and the Early Middle Ages*, ed. Thomas Noble and Thomas Head. University Park: Pennsylvania State University Press.

Rudolf of Fulda. 1954. "The Life of St. Leoba, by Rudolf, a Monk of Fulda." In *The Anglo-Saxon Missionaries in Germany, Being the Lives of SS. Willibrord, Boniface, Leoba and Lebuin Together with the* Hodoepericon *of St. Willibald and a Selection from the Correspondence of St. Boniface*, ed. and trans. C. H. Talbot. London: Sheed and Ward.

Rushton, Peter. 1983. "Purification or Social Control? Ideologies of Reproduction and the Churching of Women after Childbirth." In *The Public and the Private*, ed. Eva Gamarnikov, David H. J. Morgan, June Purvis, and Daphne Taylorson. London: Heinemann.

Russell, Josiah Cox. 1948. *British Medieval Population.* Albuquerque: University of New Mexico Press.

Salisbury, Joyce E. 1991. *Church Fathers, Independent Virgins.* London: Verso.

Saunders, Corinne J. 2001. *Rape and Ravishment in the Literature of Medieval England.* Cambridge: D.S. Brewer.

Schlief, Corine. 2005. "Men on the Right—Women on the Left: (A)symetrical Spaces and Gendered Places." In *Women's Space: Patronage, Place, and Gender in the Medieval Church*, ed. Virginia Chieffo Raguin and Sarah Stanbury. Albany: State University of New York Press.

Schmitt, Jean-Claude. 1983. *The Holy Greyhound: Guinefort, Healer of Children since the Thirteenth Century.* Cambridge: Cambridge University Press.

Schowalter, Kathleen S. 2003. "The Ingeborg Psalter: Queenship, Legitimacy, and the Appropriation of Byzantine Art in the West." In *Capetian Women*, ed. Kathleen Nolan. New York: Palgrave.

Schulenberg, Jane Tibbetts. 2001. *Forgetful of Their Sex: Female Sanctity and Society, ca. 500–1100.* Chicago: University of Chicago Press.

Schulenberg, Jane Tibbetts. 2005. "Gender, Celibacy, and Proscriptions of Sacred Space: Symbol and Practice." In *Women's Space: Patronage, Place, and Gender in the Medieval Church*, ed. Virginia Chieffo Raguin and Sarah Stanbury. Albany: State University of New York Press.

Scott, James C. 1990. *Domination and the Arts of Resistance: Hidden Transcripts.* New Haven: Yale University Press.

Scott, Joan Wallach. 1996. "Introduction." In *Feminism and History*, ed. Joan Wallach Scott. Oxford: Oxford University Press.

Scott, Joan Wallach. 1983. "Women in History: The Modern Period." *Past & Present* 101: 141–57.

Scottus, Sedulius. 2008. *De Rectoribus Christianis (On Christian Rulers): An Edition and English Translation*, ed. and trans. R. Dyson. Woodbridge: Boydell.

Sears, Elizabeth. 1986. *The Ages of Man: Medieval Interpretations of the Life Cycle.* Princeton, NJ: Princeton University Press.

Seidel, Linda. 1999. *Legends in Limestone: Lazarus, Gislebertus, and the Cathedral of Autun.* Chicago: University of Chicago Press.

Sekules, Veronica. 2002. "Spinning Yarns: Clean Linen and Domestic Values in Late Medieval French Culture." In *The Material Culture of Sex, Procreation, and Marriage in Premodern Europe*, ed. Anne L. McClanan and Karen Rosoff Encarnación. New York: Palgrave.

Shadis, Miriam. 2003. "Blanche of Castile and Facinger's 'Medieval Queenship': Reassessing the Argument." In *Capetian Women*, ed. Kathleen Nolan. New York: Palgrave.

Shadis, Miriam. 2009. *Political Women in the High Middle Ages: Berenguela of Castile and Her Family.* New York: Palgrave.

Shahar, Shulamith. 1997. *Growing Old in the Middle Ages: "Winter Clothes Us in Shadow and Pain."* London: Routledge.

Shahar, Shulamith. 2001. *Women in a Medieval Heretical Sect: Agnes and Huguette the Waldensians.* Woodbridge: Boydell.

Shaw, Diane. 1996. "The Construction of the Private in Medieval London." *Journal of Medieval and Early Modern Studies* 26: 447–66.

Sheehan, Michael. 1997. *Marriage, Family and Law in Medieval Europe: Collected Studies*, ed. James K. Farge. Toronto: Toronto University Press.

Sheingorn, Pamela. 1993/ 2003. "'The Wise Mother': The Image of St. Anne Teaching the Virgin Mary." *Gesta* 32: 69–80. Reprinted, in *Gendering the Master Narrative: Women and Power in the Middle Ages*, ed. Mary C. Erler and Maryanne Kowaleski. Ithaca: Cornell University Press.

Sigal, Pierre-André. 1985. *L'Homme et le Miracle dans la France Médiévale, XIe–XIIe siècle*. Paris: Cerf.

Silleras-Fernandez, Nuria. 2008. *Power, Piety, and Patronage in Late Medieval Queenship: Maria de Luna*. New York: Palgrave.

Silva, Filomeno Soares da, ed. 2001. *Cartulário de D. Maior Martins: seculo XIII*. Arouca: Associação da Defesa do Património Arouquense.

Simeti, Mary Taylor. 2001. *Travels with a Medieval Queen*. New York: Farrar, Straus and Giroux.

Simons, Walter. 2001. *Cities of Ladies: Beguine Communities in the Medieval Low Countries, 1200–1565*. Philadelphia: University of Pennsylvania Press.

Sivan, Hagith. 2011. *Galla Placidia: The Last Roman Empress*. New York: Oxford University Press.

Sivéry, Gérard. 1999. "Social Change in the Thirteenth Century: Rural Society." In *The New Cambridge Medieval History*, ed. David Abulafia. Vol. 5, *c. 1198–c.1300*. Cambridge: Cambridge University Press.

Smith-Rosenberg, Carol. 1975. "The Female World of Love and Ritual: Relations between Women in Nineteenth-century America." *Signs* 1: 1–29.

Solomon, Michael. 1997. *The Literature of Misogyny in Medieval Spain*. New York: Cambridge University Press.

Sommer, H. O., ed. 1908–16. *Vulgate Version of the Arthurian Romances Edited from Manuscripts in the British Museum*. 8 vols. Washington, DC: Carnegie Institute.

Soranus. 1991. *Gynecology*, ed. Oswei Tempkin. Baltimore: Johns Hopkins University Press.

Stafford, Pauline. 2006. *Gender, Family, and the Legitimisation of Power*. Aldershot: Ashgate.

Stafford, Pauline. 1997. *Queen Emma and Queen Edith: Queenship and Women's Power in Eleventh-century England*. Oxford: Blackwell Press.

Stafford, Pauline. 1983. *Queens, Concubines and Dowagers: The King's Wife in the Early Middle Ages*. Athens: University of Georgia Press.

Stafford, Pauline. 1978. "Sons and Mothers: Family Politics in the Early Middle Ages." In *Medieval Women*, ed. Derek Baker. Oxford: Basil Blackwell for the Ecclesiastical History Society.

Stanbury, Sarah, and Virginia Chieffo Raguin. 2005. "Introduction." In *Women's Space: Patronage, Place, and Gender in the Medieval Church*, ed. Virginia Chieffo Raguin and Sarah Stanbury. Albany: State University of New York Press.

Steele, Robert, ed. 1898. *Three Prose Versions of the Secreta Secretorum*. Early English Text Society, extra ser. 74. London: Kegan Paul, Trench, Trübner & Co.

Steinberg, S. H. 1938. "A Portrait of Constance of Sicily." *Journal of the Warburg Institute* 1: 249–51.

Stell, P. M., and Louise Hampson, eds. 1999. *Probate Inventories of the York Diocese, 1350–1500*. York: York Minster Library.

Stolberg, Michael. 2011. *Experiencing Illness and the Sick Body in Early Modern Europe*, trans. Leonhard Unglaub and Logan Kennedy. Basingstoke: Palgrave Macmillan.

Strohm, Paul. 1992. "Queens as Intercessors." In *Hochon's Arrow: The Social Imagination of Fourteenth-century Texts*. Princeton, NJ: Princeton University Press.

Stuard, Susan Mosher. 1995. "Ancillary Evidence for the Decline of Medieval Slavery." *Past & Present* 149: 3–28.

Stuard, Susan Mosher. 2010. "The Three-decade Transformation: Medieval Women and the Course of History." In *Considering Medieval Women and Gender*, ed. Susan Mosher Stuard. Aldershot: Ashgate.

Stuard, Susan Mosher, ed. 1987. *Women in Medieval History and Historiography*. Philadelphia: University of Pennsylvania Press.

Swan, Laura. 2001. *The Forgotten Desert Mothers: Sayings, Lives, and Stories of Early Christian Women*. New York: Paulist Press.

Swanson, Jenny. 1990. "Childhood and Childrearing in *ad status* Sermons by Later Thirteenth Century Friars." *Journal of Medieval History* 16: 309–31.

Talbot, Mary Alice, trans. 1996. *Holy Women of Byzantium: Ten Saints' Lives in English Translation*. Washington, DC: Dumbarton Oaks Research Library.

Tanner, Heather J. 2002. "Queenship: Office, Custom, or ad hoc? The Case of Queen Matilda III of England (1135–1152)." In *Eleanor of Aquitaine: Lord and Lady*, ed. Bonnie Wheeler and John Carmi Parsons. New York: Palgrave Macmillan.

Tanner, Norman P. 1984. *The Church in Late Medieval Norwich, 1370–1532*. Toronto: Pontifical Institute of Mediaeval Studies.

Tellenbach, Gerd. 1966. *Church, State, and Christian Society in the Time of the Investiture Controversy*, trans. R. F. Bennett. Oxford: Basil Blackwell.

Tertullian. 1885. "On the Apparel of Women." In *The Ante-Nicene Fathers*, ed. A. Roberts and J. Donaldson. Vol. 4. Buffalo: The Christian Literature Publishing Co.

Thibodeaux, Jennifer. 2006. "Man of the Church or Man of the Village? Gender and the Parish Clergy in Medieval Normandy." *Gender & History* 18: 380–99.

Thomson, J.A.F. 1965. *Later Lollards, 1414–1520*. Oxford: Oxford University Press.

Thorold Rogers, James E. 1866–1902. *A History of Agriculture and Prices*. 7 vols. Oxford: Clarendon Press.

Thrupp, Sylvia L. 1962. *The Merchant Class of Medieval London, 1300–1500*. Ann Arbor: University of Michigan Press.

Tilly, Louise. 1987. "Women's History and Family History: Fruitful Collaboration or Missed Connection?" *Journal of Family History* 12: 303–15.

Toms, Jonathan. 2009. "So What? A Reply to Roger Cooter's 'After Death/After-"Life": The Social History of Medicine in Post-postmodernity.' " *Social History of Medicine* 22: 609–15.

Traub, Valerie. 2002. *The Renaissance of Lesbianism in Early Modern England*. Cambridge: Cambridge University Press.

Trevisa, John. 1975–88. *On the Properties of Things: John Trevisa's Translation of Bartholomæus Anglicus* De Proprietatibus Rerum. *A Critical Text*, ed. M. C. Seymour et al. 3 vols. Oxford: Clarendon Press.

Turner, Ralph V. 2002. "Eleanor of Aquitaine in the Governments of Her Sons Richard and John." In *Eleanor of Aquitaine: Lord and Lady*, ed. John Carmi Parsons and Bonnie Wheeler. New York: Palgrave MacMillan.

Turner, Ralph V. 2009. *Eleanor of Aquitaine: Queen of France, Queen of England.* New Haven and London: Yale University Press.

Underhill, Frances A. 1996. "Elizabeth de Burgh: Connoisseur and Patron." In *The Cultural Patronage of Medieval Women*, ed. June Hall McCash. Athens: University of Georgia Press.

Unger, Richard W. 2004. *Beer in the Middle Ages and the Renaissance.* Philadelphia: University of Pennsylvania Press.

Vale, Malcolm. 2001. *The Princely Court: Medieval Courts and Culture in North-west Europe, 1270–1380.* Oxford: Oxford University Press.

Vallet de Vireville, M., ed. 1859. *Chronique de la Pucelle, ou Chronique de Cousinot*, trans. Belle Tuten. Paris: Adolphe Delahaye.

Vanlandingham, Marta. 2002. *Transforming the State: King, Court, and Political Culture in the Realms of Aragon (1213–1387).* Leiden: Brill.

Vasconcelos, João, ed. 1996–98. *Romarias: Um Inventário dos Santuários de Portugal.* 2 vols. Lisbon: OLHAPIM.

Ventura, Margarida Garcez. 1997. *Igreja e Poder no Século XV: Dinastia de Avis e Liberdades Eclesiásticas (1383–1450).* Lisbon: Edições Colibri.

Vereações. Books 5 (1475–85) and 6 (1485–88). Arquivo Histórico Municipal, Oporto.

Vernarde, Bruce L. 1997. *Women's Monasticism and Medieval Society: Nunneries in France and England, 890–1215.* Ithaca: Cornell University Press.

Vickery, Amanda. 1993. "Golden Age to Separate Spheres? A Review of the Categories and Chronology of English Women's History." *The Historical Journal* 36: 383–414.

Vitalis, Orderic. 1969–85. *The Ecclesiastical History of Orderic Vitalis*, ed. and trans. Marjorie Chibnall. 6 vols. Oxford: Clarendon Press.

Wahrman, Dror. 2008. "Change and the Corporeal in Seventeenth- and Eighteenth-century Gender History; or, Can Cultural History be Rigorous?" *Gender & History* 20: 584–602.

Ward, Jennifer C. 1997. "English Noblewomen and the Local Community in the Later Middle Ages." In *Medieval Women in Their Communities*, ed. Diane Watt. Toronto: University of Toronto Press.

Ward, Jennifer C. 1992. *English Noblewomen in the Later Middle Ages.* London: Longman.

Warr, Cordelia. 1996. "Painting in Late Fourteenth-century Padua: The Patronage of Fina Buzzacarini." *Renaissance Studies* 10: 139–55.

Warren, Florence, ed. 1931. *Dance of Death Edited from MSS. Ellesmere 26/A.13 and B.M. Lansdowne 699, Collated with the Other Extant MSS.* With introduction, notes, etc., by Beatrice White. Early English Text Society, original ser. 181. London: Humphrey Milford.

Warren, Kim. 2007. "Separate Spheres: Analytical Persistence in United States Women's History." *History Compass* 5: 262–77.

Webb, Diana M. 2005. "Domestic Space and Devotion in the Middle Ages." In *Defining the Holy: Sacred Space in Medieval and Early Modern Europe*, ed. Andrew Spicer and Sarah Hamilton. Aldershot: Ashgate.

Webb, Diana M. 1990. "Woman and Home: The Domestic Setting of Late Medieval Spirituality." In *Women in the Church*, ed. W. J. Sheils and Diana Wood. Studies in Church History, 27. Oxford: Blackwell.

Weinstein, Donald, and Rudolph M. Bell. 1982. *Saints and Society: The Two Worlds of Western Christendom, 1000–1700*. Chicago: University of Chicago Press.
Weisz, George. 2006. "Making Medical History." *Bulletin of the History of Medicine* 80: 153–59.
Wemple, Suzanne Fonay, 1981. *Women in Frankish Society: Marriage and the Cloister 500–900*. Philadelphia: University of Pennsylvania Press.
Wemple, Suzanne F., and Denise A. Kaiser. 1986. "Death's Dance of Women." *Journal of Medieval History* 12: 333–43.
Werckmeister, O. K. 1972. "The Lintel Fragment Representing Eve from Saint-Lazare, Autun." *Journal of the Warburg and Courtauld Institutes* 35: 3–7.
Wheatley, Henry B., ed. *Merlin, or The Early History of King Arthur*. 1973. Early English Text Society, original ser. 10, 21, 36, and 112. Reprinted as 2 vols. Liechtenstein: Kraus.
Wheeler, Bonnie, and Charles T. Wood, eds. 1996. *Fresh Verdicts on Joan of Arc*. New York: Routledge.
Wilkinson, Louise J. 2003. "The *Rules* of Robert Grosseteste Reconsidered: The Lady as Estate and Household Manager in Thirteenth-century England." In *The Medieval Household in Christian Europe, c. 850–c. 1550: Managing Power, Wealth, and the Body*, ed. Cordelia Beattie, Anna Maslakovic, and Sarah Rees Jones. Turnhout: Brepols.
William of Malmesbury. 1988–99. *Gesta Regum Anglorum*, ed. and trans. R.A.B. Mynors, R. M. Thomson, and M. Winterbottom. 2 vols. Oxford: Clarendon Press.
William of Tyre. 1943. *A History of Deeds Done beyond the Sea*, ed. and trans. Emily Atwater Babcock and A. C. Krey. 2 vols. New York: Columbia University Press.
Wilson-Chevalier, Kathleen, ed. 2007. *Patronnes et mécénes en France â la Renaissance*. St-Étienne: Presse Universitaire de St-Étienne.
Winer, Rebecca Lynn. 2008. "Conscripting the Breast: Lactation, Slavery and Salvation in the Realms of Aragon and Kingdom of Majorca, *c.* 1250–1300." *Journal of Medieval History* 34: 164–84.
Winer, Rebecca Lynn. 2006. *Women, Wealth and Community in Perpignan, c. 1250–1300: Christians, Jews and Enslaved Muslims in a Medieval Mediterranean Town*. Aldershot: Ashgate.
Winstead, Karen A. 1997. *Virgin Martyrs: Legends of Sainthood in Late Medieval England*. Ithaca: Cornell University Press.
Witte, John, Jr. 1997. *From Sacrament to Contract: Marriage, Religion, and Law in the Western Tradition*. Louisville, KY: Westminster John Knox Press.
Wogan-Browne, Jocelyn. 2001. *Saints' Lives and Women's Literary Culture, c. 1150–1300: Virginity and its Authorizations*. Oxford: Oxford University Press.
Wolbrink, Shelley Amiste. 2003. "Women in the Premonstratensian Order of Northwestern Germany, 1120–1250." *Catholic Historical Review* 89: 387–408.
Woodcock, Thomas, and John Martin Robinson. 1988. *The Oxford Guide to Heraldry*. Oxford: Oxford University Press.
Woolf, Virginia. 1929. *A Room of One's Own*. London: Grafton.
Woolgar, C. M. 2010. "Food and the Middle Ages." *Journal of Medieval History* 36: 1–19.
Woolgar, C. M. 1999. *The Great Household in Late Medieval England*. New Haven: Yale University Press.

Wright, Thomas, ed. 1860. *Songs and Ballads with Other Short Poems, Chiefly of the Reign of Philip and Mary, Edited from a Manuscript in the Ashmolean Museum.* London: J. B. Nichols and Sons.

Wright, W. A. 1873–78. *Generydes: A Romance in Seven-line Stanzas.* Early English Text Society, original ser. 55 and 70. London: Trübner.

Wyatt, David R. 2009. *Slaves and Warriors in Medieval Britain and Ireland, 800–1200.* Leiden: Brill.

Yorke, Barbara. 2003. *Nunneries and the Anglo-Saxon Royal Houses.* London: Continuum.

Youngs, Deborah. 2006. *The Life Cycle in Western Europe, c. 1300–c. 1500.* Manchester: Manchester University Press.

Zurara, Gomes Eanes de. 1992. *Crónica da Tomada de Ceuta*, ed. Reis Brasil. Mem Martins: Europa-América.

CONTRIBUTORS

Sandy Bardsley is Cohen Professor in the Humanities at Moravian College in Bethlehem, Pennsylvania. She is the author of *Venomous Tongues: Speech and Gender in Late Medieval England* (2006), *Women's Roles in the Middle Ages* (2007), and several articles and book chapters on medieval women and work.

Cordelia Beattie is Senior Lecturer in Medieval History at the University of Edinburgh. She is author of *Medieval Single Women: The Politics of Social Classification in Late Medieval England* (2007) and co-editor, with Anna Maslakovic and Sarah Rees Jones, of *The Medieval Household in Christian Europe, c. 850–c. 1550: Managing Power, Wealth and the Body* (2003) and, with Kirsten A. Fenton, of *Intersections of Gender, Religion, and Ethnicity in the Middle Ages* (2011). She is also the medieval editor of Manchester University Press's Gender in History series.

Marian Bleeke is Associate Professor of Art History at Cleveland State University. Her research interests include Romanesque and Gothic sculpture; issues involving women, gender, and the body in medieval art; and histories and theories of reception and response. Her recent publications include "The Eve Fragment from Autun and the Emotionalism of Pilgrimage" in *Crying in the Middle Ages: Tears of History* (2011); "Considering Female Agency: Hildegard of Bingen and Francesca Woodman," *Woman's Art Journal* 31.2 (November 2010): 39–46; and "Versions of Pygmalion in the Illuminated Roman de la Rose (Oxford, Bodleian Library, MS Douce 195): The Artist and the Work of Art," *Art History* 33 (February 2010): 28–53.

Jennifer Borland is Assistant Professor of Art History at Oklahoma State University. She specializes in medieval art and architecture with specific interests in medieval theories of corporeality and vision, audience and reception, medical and scientific imagery, cross-cultural exchange, and issues of gender and representation. Her publications include "Violence on Vellum: Saint Margaret's Transgressive Body and Its Audience" in *Representing Medieval Genders and Sexualities in Europe: Construction, Transformation, and Subversion, 600–1530*, ed. L'Estrange and More (2011); "Audience and Spatial Experience in the Nuns' Church at Clonmacnoise" in *Different Visions: A Journal of New Perspectives in Medieval Art* (2011); and "The Forested Frontier: Commentary in the Margins of the Alhambra Ceiling Paintings" in *Medieval Encounters* 14.3 (2008). She is currently working on a study of several illustrated manuscripts of Aldobrandino of Siena's *Régime du corps,* a late-medieval health guide.

Rachel Dressler is Associate Professor of Art History at the University at Albany, State University of New York. She has published on fourteenth-century English tomb effigies, including the book *Of Men and Armor in Medieval England: The Chivalric Rhetoric of Three English Knights' Effigies* (2004), and authored several articles on the same subject. She is currently researching the use and significance of curtained spaces in sacred and secular images. In addition to her own research, Professor Dressler is the founder and editor in chief of *Different Visions: A Journal of New Perspectives on Medieval Art* (http://www.differentvisions.org).

Martha Easton received her PhD in 2001 from the Institute of Fine Arts, New York University, and she is currently Assistant Professor of Art History and Museum Studies in the Department of Communication and the Arts at Seton Hall University. She has taught at Bryn Mawr College, New York University, and the Cooper Union, and worked at the Cloisters and the Metropolitan Museum of Art. Her publications focus on gender, eroticism, and sanctity in medieval visual culture, including "Transforming and Transcending Gender in the Lives of Female Saints" in *The Four Modes of Seeing*, ed. Pastan, Shortell, and Lane (2009); "The Wound of Christ, the Mouth of Hell: Appropriations and Inversions of Female Anatomy in the Later Middle Ages" in *Tributes to Jonathan J.G. Alexander*, ed. L'Engle and Guest (2006); "Pain, Torture and Death in the Huntington Library *Legenda aurea*" in *Gender and Holiness*, ed. Riches and Salih (2002); "Saint Agatha and the Sanctification of Sexual Violence," in *Studies in Iconography* 16 (1994); and "Uncovering the Meanings of Nudity in the 'Belles Heures' of Jean, Duke of Berry" in *The Meanings of Nudity in Medieval Art*, ed. Lindquist (2012).

Katherine L. French is the J. Frederick Hoffman Chair of Medieval English History at the University of Michigan–Ann Arbor. She is the author of *The People of the Parish: Community Life in a Late Medieval Diocese* (2001) and *The Good Women of the Parish: Gender and Religion after the Black Death* (2008). She is also the coauthor with Allyson Poska of *Women and Gender in the Western Past* (2 vols.) (2007) and many articles on medieval women and religion.

April Harper is Assistant Professor of History at the State University of New York, Oneonta. She received her PhD in History from the University of St. Andrews in 2003, and her primary research is on images of sexuality in medieval literature, law, science, and theology. She has published on food and adultery in Old French literature and is editor, with Caroline Proctor, of *Medieval Sexuality: A Casebook* (2008).

Lois L. Huneycutt is Associate Professor of History at the University of Missouri, Columbia. Her many publications include articles on European queenship and the roles of royal and noble women in the eleventh and twelfth centuries. She is the author of *Matilda of Scotland: A Study of Medieval Queenship* (2003) and is now engaged in a comparative study of the Anglo-Norman queens of England (1066–1154).

Elizabeth L'Estrange is Lecturer in History of Art at the University of Birmingham. She obtained her PhD from the University of Leeds in 2003 and has held postdoctoral fellowships from the Leverhulme Trust and the Belgian Fonds national de la recherche scientifique at the University of Liège in Belgium. Her main research interests are illuminated manuscripts, especially books of hours, and women as subjects and consumers of art objects especially in late-medieval and early modern France. She has published a number of articles on Anne of Brittany and Anne of France, and her first book, *Holy Motherhood: Gender, Dynasty and Visual Culture in the Later Middle Ages* (2008), won the Society for Medieval Feminist Scholarship's first book prize in 2010.

Iona McCleery is Lecturer in the School of History at the University of Leeds and was previously Wellcome Fellow in the History of Medicine at the University of Durham. She is running a Wellcome Trust–funded three-year public engagement project, *You Are What You Ate*, which uses historical food to encourage public reflection on the modern diet. She is writing a monograph on the history of practitioners and patients in late-medieval Portugal and is part of an international team translating the chronicles of Fernão Lopes into English, to be published by Boydell in 2014. Her most recent publications are an article on medicine and health in chronicles for *Social History of Medicine* 24.1 (2011) and an article on melancholy and patient narratives for *Journal of Medieval Iberian Studies* 1.2 (2009).

Kim M. Phillips is Senior Lecturer in History at the University of Auckland. She is the author of *Medieval Maidens: Young Women and Gender in England, 1270–1540* (2003); coauthor with Barry Reay of *Sex before Sexuality: A Premodern History* (2011); co-editor of essay collections on medieval women, sexual histories, and cross-cultural encounters; and author of numerous articles in these fields. Her latest book, *Before Orientalism: Asian Peoples and Cultures in European Travel Writing, c. 1245–c. 1510*, is forthcoming with The University of Pennsylvania Press.

INDEX

Adam, 7, 12, 64, 137, 181–2
Adela, Countess of Blois, 68, 171
Adelaide, St., 174
Adelaide of Maurienne, 164
Admont, 66
adolescence, 17, 20, 129
adultery, 79, 185, 195
Aelfthryth, 159
Aelgyva, 194–5
Afonso, Caterina, 97
Afonso V, King, 97–8, 104
Agatha, St., martyr, 187, 213
age of reason, 26, 130
ages of man, 15–17, 20, 25, 37, 219n10
Agnes, Abbess of Clonmacnoise, 206
Agnes, St., 72
Agnes Awmbler of Barroby, 77
Agnes of Merania, 164
Agnolella, 197
Ahasuerus, 197
Aidan, Bishop, 173
Alan of Lille, 27, 28
Alaric, 158
Alberti, Giannozzo, 121
Albertus Magnus, 22, 26, 29, 91
Alexander the Great, 17
Alexander III, King of Scotland, 170
Alfonso I of Aragon, 166
Alfonso VIII, 208
Alfonso X, 164–5
Alfonso XI, King of Castille, 95
Alfred the Great, 162
Álvaro Pais, Bishop of Silves, 103
Amazons, 11
Ambrose, St., 25–6
Anastaise, 202
Anastasius IV, Pope, 175
Anchorites, 5, 133, 135, 172
Andre, brother, 100
Anes, Margarida, nun, 98
Anes, Margarida, servant, 102
Angela of Foligno, 74
Angevin Empire, 45
Anjou, 67
Anne, St., 78, 134, 180, 185–6, 196, 199, 211, 213
Anne of Bohemia, 171
Anne of Brittany, 186, 203, 211
Anne of France, 94, 199, 206, 211
annulment, 164–6
  see also divorce; marriage
Anselm of Canterbury, St., 159, 171
Aquinas, Thomas, St., 26, 41, 43, 53
Aragon, 81, 115, 164

Aristotle, 6, 16–17, 19, 21–2, 40–2
Arnold, Matthew, 3
ascetics/asceticism, 25, 59, 68, 81, 98, 172, 175–6, 191
The Assembly of Ladies, 115
Asser, 162
Ataulf, 158
Athelwold, Bishop of Winchester, 159
attack on the Castle of Love, 205
Augustine, St., 6, 7, 12, 25–6, 41–3, 66, 71, 112
Augustinian, 71
Autun, 181
Autun Eve, 182–4
Aveiro, 97, 99
Averroes, 41
Avignon, 176

Baden, 122
Baker, Derek, 4
Baldwin II, 165
Baldwin, John, 25
"Ballad of the Tyrannical Husband," 137
Baptism, 18, 78
Barbara, St., martyr, 187
Barbero, Francesco, 122
Barking Abbey, 136
Barron, Caroline M., 142
Barthélemy, Dominique, 13
Bartholomaeus Anglicus, 6–7
Bathsheba, 185
Battle of Fraga, 162
Bayeux Tapestry, 180, 194, 200
Beach, Alison, 66
Beatrice of Rethel, 169
Beatrice of Toulouse, 81
Beatriz of Castile, 96
Bede, 173
beguines, 73–4, 82, 133
Bell, Susan Groag, 134
Bell, Rudolph, 176
Belles Heures of Jean de France, Duc de Berry, 187
Benedictine Rule, 69, 72
Benedictines, 65, 72, 136, 202
Bennett, Judith M., 9, 142
Beowulf, 115, 159
Berenguela, of Spain, 164
Berkeley, Elizabeth, 117
Bernard of Clairvaux, 69, 165, 174, 207
Berneuil, 66, 69
Bertrada of Montfort, 168, 261n8
Bible moralisée, 209
Biller, Peter, 90–2
Birth of St. John the Baptist, 186, 199
Blackburn, Margaret, 199
Blamires, Alcuin, 9–12
Blanche of Castile, 11, 149, 156, 164, 180, 206, 208–10, 213
Bloch, R. Howard, 9
Blysa, 68
Boccaccio, 55, 118
body, 7, 18–21, 40–4, 47, 49–51, 57–8, 80, 86, 88, 90, 100, 101, 104, 106, 117, 119, 192, 122, 153–4, 172, 177, 180–4, 192–3, 213, 221n42
  diseased, 66
  male, 6, 74, 189, 195, 202
  maternal, 43–4
  and prostitutes, 54
  sexual, 43, 49
  and suffering, 74, 98, 175–6
Bollschwell, 68
Bologna, 72
Bolton Hours, 199
Bonaventure, 26
Boniface, Archbishop, 174
Boniface VIII, Pope, 74
Book of Margery Kempe, 120
Book of the Knight of the Tower, 129, 133
Boswell, John, 50, 230n41
Bourbon, Stephen, 78
Bourbourg, 65
Bracciolini, Poggio, 122
Brásia, 102
Brittany, 8, 67
Brooke, Christopher N. L., 4
Brundage, James, 74

Brunhilde, 158
Bugalho, João, 102
Burke, Peter, 3
Burkhardt, Jacob, 3
Burrow, J. A., 17
Butler, Judith, 13
Buzzacarini, Fina, 187
Bynum, Caroline Walker, 12, 60, 176

Cabellero-Navas, Carmen, 94
Cabré, Montserrat, 94
Caesarea, 172
Caesarius of Arles, 48
Camerino, 121
Casola, Pietro, 122
Castile, 97, 109, 115
Cathars, 80–2
Catherine, St., 177
Catherine of France, 171
Catherine of Siena, 73–4, 146, 176
Catherine of Valois, 116, 171
Cavallo, Sandra, 88
Cavendish, John, 125
Cecilia, St., 136
Cecily, Duchess of York, 115, 135
Celestina, 88, 102
celibacy, 25–6, 61–2, 91, 194
Chaucer, Alice, Duchess of Suffolk, 115
Chaucer, Geoffrey, 7, 9, 55, 90, 115, 124
Charles the Bald, 162
Charles VI, of France, 170, 210
Charles VII, King of France, 177, 210
Charles VIII, King of France, 199, 211
Charlemagne, 161, 174
chastity, 9–11, 25–28, 48–9, 69, 73, 98, 121, 154
Chibnall, Marjorie, 46
childbirth, 58, 60, 77–8, 86, 88, 93, 97, 100, 103–4, 115–16, 122, 130, 140–1, 146, 149, 180, 190, 195, 199, 243n60, 246n98
childhood, 17, 19, 35, 129, 141, 146
Chilperic I, King of Neustria, 158
Chojnacki, Stanley, 35
Christian, 11–12, 54, 58, 61, 66, 76, 78, 82–3, 100–3, 106, 121, 136, 154–5, 157, 161, 164, 172, 176, 187–8
Christianity, 26, 60, 61, 63, 74, 83, 120, 154, 161, 177, 188, 190
Christianization, of Europe, 161
Christians, 25, 164, 173
Christina Mirabilis, 175–6
Chrystosom, John, St., 48
churching, 78–9, 96–7, 103, 130
Church of the Innocents, 22
Cistercians, 69, 165
Cîteaux, 65
Clare of Assisi, 135
see also Offreduccio, Clare
Clementia of Burgundy, 65
Cleophas, Mary, 78
Clonmacnoise, Ireland, 206
Clothar I, King of the Franks, 173, 190
clothing, 18, 29, 32, 53, 90, 94, 120, 124, 138, 140, 146–7, 149
Clovis, 161
Clunbury, 78
Clungonford, 78
Cluniac, 68
Cluny, 65, 68–9
Cnut, King, 195
Cohn, Samuel, 123, 252n74
Coimbra, 99–100
Constance of Sicily, 169–70
Constantine the African, 6
Constantine the Great, 187, 199
Constantius III, Emperor, 158
Cooke, Jessica, 21
Corvyger, William, 78
Council of Constance (1414), 122
Coventry, 82
Criseyde, 9, 124
cross-dressing, 135, 190
Crown of Aragon, 92
Cyprian of Carthage, 25

Damian, Peter, St., 63
d'Andalo, Diana, 72
Dansa de la mort, 22

danse macabre, 22, 35
Danse macabre des femmes, 22
Danse macabre des hommes, 22
Dante, 16, 112
d'Arbrissell, Robert, 67–8, 79
David, King, 185
Davis, Natalie Zemon, 99
Davis, Robert C., 122–3
de Bretagne, Marie, 134
de Bryene, Alice, 117
de Burgh, Elizabeth, 117, 150
de Cantimpré, Thomas, 176
de Condet, Alice, 134
de Fougères, Etienne, 50
de Gúzman, Dominic, 71–2
de Lisboa, Pedro, 95
de Laurac, Blanche, 81
de Lisle, Robert, 16, 21
de Lorris, Guillaume, 2, 203
de Menabuoi, Giusto, 186
de Meun, Jean, 2, 203–4
de Pizan, Christine, 1–3, 5, 9, 12, 14, 32, 35, 112, 124, 132, 148, 177, 180, 202–4, 210, 213
de Queimado, Domingos, St., 98
Derbforgaill, 206
de Santarém, Gil, 85, 100, 104
De secretis mulierum, 19, 21
Desert Fathers, 172
Desert Mothers, 42, 172
de Voragine, Jacobus, 47, 185
d'Evreux, Jeanne, 94
Dhuoda, 154
Dives, 193
Dives et Pauper, 12
divorce, 44, 157, 164–6, 207
  see also annulment
Domes, 78
Domingas, Maria, 85–6, 99–100, 103–4
Dominicans, 71–3, 82, 85, 100, 104, 171, 176
Dove, Mary, 17, 20, 37
Dronzek, Anna, 106, 132–3
Duarte, King of Portugal, 96–7
Duby, Georges, 106–7, 115, 117, 178
Duchié, Jacques, 112
Du con qui fu fez a la besche, 39, 58
Dünnwald, 68

Earenfight, Theresa, 164
Edgar, King of England, 159
Edith of Wessex, 169
Edward the Confessor, 169, 195
Edward I, King of England, 170–1
Edward II, King of England, 149
Edward III, King of England, 149, 171
Edward IV, King of England, 118, 135, 149, 171
Edwin of Northumbria, King, 173
Egil's Saga, 159
Eichstätt, 121
Eirik Bloodaxe, 159
Elaine, 55
Eleanor de Poitiers, 96
Eleanor of Aquitaine, 44–5, 67, 164, 167, 206–8, 213, 228n17
Eleanor of Aragon, 81
Eleanor of Castile, 171, 208
Eleanor of Provence, 167
Elizabeth, St., 180, 185–7,196
Elizabeth of Hungary, 206
Elizabeth of York, 117
Elovsdatter, Ingrid, 73
employment, 31, 128
enclosure, 68, 69, 74, 108, 124, 194
England, 18, 45–6, 50, 65, 67, 76–7, 80, 82, 99, 114, 118, 127, 137, 139–41, 144, 149–50, 159–62, 165, 167, 169–71, 173, 177,194, 207, 261n8
Ermengard of Narbonne, 162
essentialism, 5
Esther, 159, 197
Eugenia, St., 190–1
Eugenius III, Pope, 175
Eve, 7–9, 12–13, 42, 45, 49, 57, 63–4, 82, 91, 131, 137, 180–5, 192, 212
Exeter, 147

Fawtier, Robert, 164
Federico, Sylvia, 125

Felipa, 97
feminine, 2, 6, 9–11, 17, 26, 37, 64, 106, 112–25 passim, 177, 90
anti-, 2, 13
femininity, 6–7, 9, 13, 42, 46, 49, 61–2, 64, 71, 83, 106, 119, 131
feminism, 12, 14, 46
anti-, 11–12, 218n35
feminist, 5, 14, 218n37
historians, 13
philosophy, 2, 13
Fernando, Prince, 96
Ferrour, Johanna, 125
Fissell, Mary, 86
FitzCount, Brian, 45–6, 229n21
Fletcher, Eric, 173
Florence, 77, 112, 122
Fontevraud, 67, 70, 81, 207–8
Foucault, Michel, 87
Fourth Lateran Council, 26, 69, 72, 76
France, 1, 65, 67, 71, 81, 96, 99, 114–15, 144, 158, 164, 169–70, 177, 180, 207–8, 210–11, 262n13
Franciscans, 6, 22–3, 28, 71–3, 97–8, 103, 224n85
Francis of Assisi, 71–2, 79
Fredegunde, 158
Frederic Barbarossa, Emperor, 175
Frederick II, Emperor, 169–70
Fulk of Anjou, 165
Fulk of Neuilly, 71

Galehaut, 57
Galen, 19, 40–1
Galla Placidia, 158
Galswintha, 157–8
Gamen, Katherine, 125
Gardiner, Mark, 115
Geaman, Kristen, 160
Gentilcore, David, 88
Germany, 67, 162, 169–70, 174
Ghent, 113
Gibraltar, 92
Gilchrist, Roberta, 117
Giles of Rome, 19
Gilligan, Carol, 15, 37
Giustiniano, Marino, 111
Godstow Abbey, 136
Goldberg, P.J.P., 110, 142
golden age, 142
Gomes, Rita Costa, 96
Gonçalves, João, 102
Goodman (*Ménagier*) of Paris, 132
"The Good Wyfe Wold a Pylgremage," 32–3
Governaunce of Prynces, 20, 35
Gower, John, 50
Grauer, Anne, 92
Great Dunmow, Essex, 77
Green, Monica H., 86, 94
Gregorian reform, 61–4, 67–8, 76
Gregory VII, Pope, 61, 162
Gregory XI, Pope, 176
Grey, Thomas, 149
Guibert of Tournai, 27
guilds, 46, 113, 123–4, 130–1, 145–7
Guinefort, St., 78
Guinevere, 55–7, 205

Hadewijch of Antwerp, 74
Hajnal, John, 31
Hales, John, 125
Hanawalt, Barbara, 5, 109–11, 129
Hanseatic League, 73
Harfleur, 79
"Harleian Ordinances," 118
Harold Godwinson, 194
Harris, Barbara J., 150
Harrison, Anne, 23, 33
Hartlepool, 173
Hartley, L. P., 4
Hatcher, John, 144
health, 17, 40, 83, 86–102 passim, 104, 130, 140, 154, 195, 196, 241n45
and men, 89, 144
see also prostitute; *Tacuinum Sanitatis*
Henry I, King of England, 46, 159, 163, 165, 171

Henry II, King of England, 44–5, 50, 67, 165, 167, 207
Henry III, King of England, 167
Henry IV, Emperor, 61, 162
Henry V, King of England, 171
Henry VI, Emperor, 169
Henry VI, King of England, 116
Henry of France, 170
Henry the Fowler, 174
heresy, 51, 73, 76, 79, 81–2, 177
heretic, 53, 59–60, 71, 79, 80, 82–3
hermaphrodite, 40
Herrad of Hohenbourg (Lansberg), 66, 136, 202
heterosexual, 50, 64
Hildegard of Bingen, 51, 66, 174–6, 180, 200–2, 213
Hild of Streonshal, 173
Hiltigard, 174
Hilton, R.H., 143
Hindman, Sandra, 24
Hippocrates, 17
Hirsau reform, 136
Holland, Sir John, 119
Hours of Louis XII, 185
Hours of Mary of Burgundy, 203
"Household Book," 118
housewives, 59
Hugh, Abbot of Cluny, 68
Hugh of Jaffa, 165
Hugh of St. Cher, 121
Hugh of St. Victor, 12
Huizinga, Johan, 3
humors, 21, 40
Hundred Years' War, 171, 177
Hussites, 80

Ida of Louvain, 74
infant, 17, 26, 29, 139, 149, 154, 182
Ingeborg of Denmark, 164–5
inheritance, 47, 85, 161, 195, 229n27
Innocent III, Pope, 164
Innocent IV, Pope, 72
intersexual, 40
Ipswich, 73
Isabeau of Bavaria, 180, 210
Isabel, Duchess of Burgundy, 96, 98, 104
Isabel, Queen, 100–1
Isabella, 166
Isabella of Castile, 206
Isabella of France, 149
Isabelle of France, 209
Isidore of Seville, 5–7, 17, 19, 43, 57, 89
Italy, 73, 81, 88, 93, 123, 158, 162, 170, 176

James the Great, St., 78, 186
James the Less, St., 78, 186
Jean le Bon, King of France, 204
Jeanne of Flanders, 162
Jerome, St., 25–6, 42, 48–9, 57
Jerusalem, 46, 165
Jesi, 169
Jew/Jewish, 5, 12, 53–4, 78, 79, 100–1, 103
Joan, Countess of Flanders, 206
Joana, Princess, 97–9
Joanna of Naples, 206
Joan of Arc, 130, 155, 176–7
Joan of Navarre, 117
João I, King of Portugal, 96
João II, 97–8
John, King of England, 167
John of Gaunt, 119, 125
Johnson, Eric, 9
John the Baptist, 93, 185–7
John the Evangelist, 78, 186
Jones, Peter Murray, 93
Jordan, Erin, 162
Jose, St., 78
Joseph, 198
Jovinian, 25
Juan, king of Castile, 96
Jude, St., 78, 186
Jussen, Bernhard, 25

Karras, Ruth Mazo, 33, 53, 149
Kempe, Margery, 90
King, Margot, 172

"king's wife," 162
Kitab sirr al-asrar, 17
Knight of la Tour Landry, 94
Knighton, Henry, 119
Kuehn, Thomas, 124

"Labors of Adam and Eve," 137
La Compileison, 26, 29
la Cousature, Gilbertra, 79
La-Joie, 69
Lamego, 98
Lancaster, Elizabeth, 119
Lancelot, 55–7, 205
Langtoft, Rose, 111
Lansing, Carole, 80
Laynesmith, J. L., 161
Lazarus, St., 103, 185, 193
Le chevalier qui fi st parler les cons, 57
Le Fee, Morgan, 55
le Fèvre, Jehan, 9
le Noir, Bourgot, 204
le Noir, Jean, 204
Leoba, St., 103, 174, 175
Leonor, Queen, 100
Leonor of Aragon, 97
Le Roman de la Rose, 1, 203–4
lesbian, 230n41
  see also same-sex desire
Lester, Anne, 69
life cycle, 15, 17, 26, 31, 33, 37, 92, 96
Life of Macrina, 172
Life of St. Leoba, 174, 175
Life of Saint Radegund, 191
Li jugemenz des cons, 57
Lincoln, 77
Lisbon, 96, 99–101
literacy, 3, 28, 55, 82, 129, 131, 133–5
Lollards, 80, 82
Lombard, Peter, 12
London, 106, 111, 128–9, 131, 133, 145–7, 150
Lopes, Fernão, 96
Louis, Count of Loos, 176
Louise of Savoy, 211
Louis VI, 163–4
Louis VII, King of France, 164, 207
Louis VIII, King of France, 164, 208
Louis IX, King of France, 149, 164, 209–10
Louis XII, King of France, 211
Louis the Pious, 155
Lourenço, Afonso, 95
Lourenço, Diego, 99
Luis, Catalina, 95
Luttrell, Sir Geoffrey, 114
The Luttrell Psalter, 114
Lyon, 78

Mabilia, 81
McDonald, Nicola, 118
Mackinney, Loren, 93
McLaughlin, Megan, 62
McNamara, Jo Ann, 26, 62, 64, 156, 167
Maconnais, 68
Macrina, St., 172
McSheffrey, Shannon, 80, 106
Madeira, 99, 101
maid-wife-widow model, 24–5, 28, 35, 37
maiden/maidenhood, 18, 20–1, 28–9, 33, 47, 48, 113, 117, 119, 122, 130, 136, 198, 222–3n67, 251n52, 252–3n78
maidenhead, 88, 113
majority, age of, 164–5, 229n27
Makowski, Elizabeth, 74
Malehaut, Lady, 57
Marbod of Rennes, 8–9, 39
Marcigny, 68
Margaret, Countess of Flanders, 206
Margaret of Anjou, 117, 206
Margaret of Antioch, St., 77–8, 177, 181, 188–90, 196
Margaret of Austria, 203, 211
Margaret of Scotland (Maid of Norway), 170
Margaret of York, 206
Marguerite of Hainault, 162
Maria, 166

Marian, 57, 77, 90, 197
  and paradox, 43
Maria of Castile, 164
Marie Narrette of Douai, 77
Marina, 190
marriage, 17, 25–37, 45, 47, 49, 64–5, 76, 80–1, 94, 97, 106, 153–4, 157–8, 161, 168–9, 171–3, 176, 180, 187, 190, 208, 211
  and clerics, 61–4, 159
  intermarriage, 97
  partners, 147–50
  and prostitutes, 51–4
  remarriage, 44, 207
  representations, 196–8
  and same-sex intimacy, 49–51
  see also annulment; divorce; Eleanor of Aquitaine
Martha, 103
Martins, Isabel, 100
Martins, Maria, 101
martyrs/martyrdom, 10, 25, 47, 78, 96, 98, 135, 180, 187–8, 190
Mary Magdalene, 103, 180, 184–5
Mary of Brittany, Abbess of Fontevraux, 206
Mary of Egypt, 42
Mate, Mavis E., 143
Matheolus, 112
Matilda, Abbess, 174
Matilda, Empress, 45, 163, 168
Matilda, Queen, 159, 163
Matilda of Boulogne, 163
Matilda of England, 165, 170
Matilda of Flanders, 149
Matilda of Quedlinburg, Abbess, 174
Matilda of Ringelheim, 174
Matilda of Scotland, 169
Matilda of Tuscany, 162
maturity, 16–17, 22, 35, 37, 47, 151
Meer, 67
Melisende, 165, 166
mendicants, 71, 73, 79
menstruation, 6, 13, 58, 86, 91–2, 103–4
Mertes, Kate, 115
Metz, Guillebert de, 112
Michael, St., 177
midwife/midwifery, 78, 97, 101, 141, 146, 195
Miller, Maureen, 62
Minnis, Alastair, 9, 11
misogynist, 2, 7, 9, 64, 83, 92, 97
misogyny, 9, 11, 61, 203
Moissac, 192
Mol, Anne-Marie, 104
Mons, 115
Montemor-o-Velho, 100
Montpellier, 131
Moore, R. I., 62, 75
Mortimer, Katherine, 197–8
Mortimer, Roger, 149
Moulins Triptych, 199–200, 211
Murray, Jacqueline, 50
Muslim, 5, 54, 95
Mussachio, Jacqueline, 93
mystics/mysticism, 59, 73–4, 176–7
  see also body and suffering

Nicholas, David, 113
Nolan, Kathleen, 94, 168–9
Norbert of Xanten, 67
Norfolk, 109
Norway, 170
Norwich, 73
nunneries, 31, 81, 98–9, 135–6, 153, 206
nuns, 5, 23, 27, 48–9, 66–70, 91, 98–9, 103, 133, 135–6, 170–4 passim, 200, 202, 208
  Dominican, 73
  Franciscan, 72
  Ste.-Croix, 190–1
  see Radegunde/Radegund of Thuringia
Nuns' Church, 206

Odo of Bayeux, Bishop, 200
Offreduccio, Clare, St., 71–2, 100, 135
old age, 16–18, 20–2, 35, 102, 185
Olibrius, 188
Oporto, 101

Orme, Nicholas, 135
Orvieto, 81
Otto III, Emperor, 174
Ovid, 1, 39, 58
Oxford University, 82

Padua, 186–7, 199
Paris, 22, 112, 131, 133, 204
Pascal II, Pope, 171
Paston, Margaret, 90
Patients and Physicians, 196
Paul, St., 7, 12, 43
Paviot, Jacques, 96
Payer, Pierre, 26
peaceweaver, 159, 171
Pearl Maiden, 47
peasantry, 59
peasants, 78, 107–10, 127–33, 137–41, 147, 149, 175, 177
Pelling, Margaret, 88
penitential of Theodore, 51
Penn, Simon A. C., 143
Pepin, King of the Franks, 174
perfect age
  for men, 18, 47
  for women, 18, 20–1, 37, 47
Peter of Poitiers, 51
Petrarch, 112
Petroff, Elizabeth, 72
Petronilla of Chemillé, 67
Philip, Roman prefect, 190
Philip I, King of France, 168
Philip II "Augustus," 164–5
Philip IV, King of France, 170
Philippa, of Portugal, 96–7
Philippa of Foix, 81
Philippa of Hainault, 171
Phillips, Kim M., 18, 29, 47
Pietro, 197
Pina, Rui de, 97, 104
plague, 90, 95–7, 101
Plague, the, 90, 96, 141, 143–4
Poitou, 67
Poor Clares, 72
Poor of Lyons, 80
Porete, Marguerite, 73
Porter, Roy, 87–8, 90, 92, 102
Portugal, 95–6, 99–101, 103
Portuguese Algarve, 103
postplague, 123, 142–4
Pouchere, Julia, 125
poverty, 62, 66–7, 69–73, 79–81, 172
pregnancy, 49, 86, 92, 96, 169–70, 182
Premonstratensians, 66–8
Prémontré, 67
prostitute, 23, 33, 42, 49, 51–4, 71, 88, 124, 145–7, 180, 185
  see also body; health
prostitution, 53–4, 146–7
Proto-Evangelium of James, 185
Psalter and Hours of Bonne de Luxembourg, 204
Psalter-Hours of Yolande de Soissons, 189
Pseudo-Aristotle, 17
public/private, 125, 156

Quedlinburg Abbey, 174
Queen's Manuscript, 210
Querelle de la Rose, 1
Quintianus, 187

Radegunde/Radegund of Thuringia, 157, 173, 190–2
  see also nuns, Ste.-Croix
Raguin, Virginia Chieffo, 126
Ranworth, 77
Raymond IV of Toulouse, 44, 81
Récits d'un Ménestrel de Reims, 44
Reconquista, 75
Reformation, 80
Reims, 69
reproduction, 17, 154, 195
Rezak, Bridgitte Bedos, 168
Richard I, King of England, 67, 167, 207
Richard II, King of England, 171, 207
Riddy, Felicity, 32, 106, 112, 132
Riley, Denise, 13–14
Robert of Flanders, 66
Roger II, King, 169

Romano, Dennis, 122, 124
Rome, 62, 168, 176
Rose, Mary Beth, 4
Rougiers, 108–9
Rowley, Alice, 82
Rudge, Lindsay, 48
Rudolf of Fulda, 174
rural
  employment, 31
  households, 109, 129
  men, 144
  occupations, 143, 145, 148
  parishes, 79
  population, 108, 247n9
  religion, 76, 78–9, 81

St. Denis, Paris, 169, 174, 210
Ste.-Croix, Poitiers, 190–1
St. Jacques, 77
Saint-Lazarus, Autun, 181
St. Mary's Warwick, 197–8
Saint-Pierre, Moissac, 192, 194
Saint-Pierre, Poitiers, 207
St. Radegund Heals a Woman, 192
St. Walburg, 121, 202
Saladin, 44
Salic law, 170
Salome, Mary, 78
same-sex desire, 50–2
  see also lesbian; sexuality
San Damiano, 71–2
Santa Clara de Coimbra, 98
Santa Maria, Milan, 72
Santa Maria de Cantú, 68
Sant' Andrea a Comaggiano, 77
Santarém, Portugal, 85, 104
Schäftlarn, 66
Scivias, 201
Scotland, 169–70
Scott, James C., 136
Scottus, Sedulius, 161
Sears, Elizabeth, 17
Secretum secretorum, 17–21, 33, 35, 37
Sens, 69
Seville, 144
sex
  acts, 50–3
  appearance of, 6, 41, 190
  differences, 6–7, 19, 40–1
  stronger, 5–6, 67, 121, 144, 155
  weaker, 7, 67, 155
  see also "third sex"
sexual
  access, 157, 161
  activity, 43–4, 49, 58, 91, 106, 154
  advances, 6, 130
  ardor, 7, 20
  craving, 55–6
  desire, 57, 74, 119
  equality, 12
  intercourse, 22, 80, 119, 154
  nature, 43, 49, 74
  partners, 53, 157
  sin, 27, 182, 193
  status, 37, 45
  see also body; Eleanor of Aquitaine; maturity; status; virgins
sexuality, 3, 39, 40–58 passim, 64, 74, 80, 106, 117, 154–5, 180, 185, 192, 194–5, 212, 229n26, 261n8
  see also heterosexual; intersexual; lesbian; same-sex desire
Shadis, Miriam, 164
Shahar, Shulamith, 18–19, 81
Shaw, Diane, 106
Sibylla, 166
Sicily, 169
Sigebert, 158
Simon, St., 78, 186
Skänninge, 73
Smyth, Joan, 82
Soeiro, Maria, 100
Soissons, 66, 69
Soranus, 41
Spain, 67, 73, 123, 158, 208
Stanbury, Sarah, 126
status, 12–13, 58, 63, 69, 131, 142, 150–1, 156–7, 159, 162, 180, 207, 210, 218n37, 252n74
  class, 47

economic, 47
high, 24, 29, 82, 93, 100,117, 120, 122, 129, 133, 144, 146–7, 198
legal, 61, 148
low, 32–3, 35, 77, 99, 114, 124, 129, 143, 147, 164
marital, 13, 24, 30, 33, 35, 37, 79, 197
noble, 134
royal, 168
social, 3, 13, 24, 29, 35, 37, 82, 92, 123–4, 127, 137, 150
sexual, 37
Statutes of Labourers, 143
Stephen, King of England, 45, 163, 165
Stephen-Henry of Blois, Count, 171
Stonor, Sir William, 92
Stuard, Susan Mosher, 4
Stubbes, John, 112
Sudbury, Simon, 125
Suger of St. Denis, Abbot, 174, 207
Swanson, Jenny, 28
Sweden, 73
Sybil of Jerusalem, 46
Syon, 136

Tacuinum Sanitatis, 88, 109
Tancred, 169
Tauberbischofsheim, 174
Taylbos, William, 111
The Temptation of Eve, 182
Tertullian, 39
Theodosius the Great, 158
Theophanu, 174
"third sex," 49
Thomas, St., shrine at Canterbury, 90
Thomas Beauchamp, Earl of Warwick, 197–8
Thomas of Chobham, 120
Throne of Wisdom, 182–4
Tierra de Campos, Castile, 109
Tornabuoni, Francesca, 199
Tornabuoni, Giovanni, 199
Touraine, 67
Treaty of Troyes, 170, 210
Très Petites Heures, 211–12
Trevisa, John, 7
Troilus, 124–5

university, 26, 71–2, 82
University of Paris, 26
unmarried, 28–9, 32, 43–4, 68, 79, 99, 112, 117, 145, 197
Urban IV, Pope, 72
Urraca of Leon-Castile, 166

Vaz, João, 99
Venice, 35, 122–4
Veronica, 103
Verrocchio, Andrea, 199
Vicente, Gil, 102
Vickery, Amanda, 105–6
Vincent of Beauvais, 19
violence, 205
domestic, 5, 95
public, 173
virgin, 23–33 passim, 43, 47–9, 53, 56, 63–4, 67, 161, 173, 180
martyrs, 10, 135, 180, 187–8, 190
saints, 191
see also maid-wife-widow model; virgin-widow-spouse model
Virgin and Child, 183, 203
Virgin and Child as Throne of Wisdom, 183
Virgin and Child in Majesty, 184
virginity, 18, 26–9, 32–3, 117, 119, 172, 190
Virgin Mary, 9, 11, 18, 43, 47, 63–4, 68, 78–9, 93, 134, 159, 180, 182–5, 192, 198, 203, 210
virgin-widow-spouse model, 25, 37
virtue/virtues, 2, 6, 9–12, 21, 26, 28, 35, 48, 64, 68, 132, 136, 159, 218n27
Visigoth, 157–8

Wagner, Roy, 3
Wahrman, Dror, 103
Waldensians, 80–3
Waldes, Peter (Waldo), 80, 81
Watton, the Nun of, 49

wealth, 28, 31, 62, 65, 67, 69, 71, 76, 79–80, 82, 87, 94, 108, 131, 133, 147, 150, 154, 157–9, 162, 172, 180, 190–1
Wemple, Suzanne, 156, 167
Wessex, 162
Westminster, 77
Wharram Percy, 108, 145
"What the Goodwife Taught Her Daughter," 32, 132
Whitby, 173
Whyting, John, widow of, 109
widower, 176
widowhood, 26–7, 35, 37, 44–5, 158, 168, 172, 250n43
widows, 23–8, 33, 35, 43–4, 47–9, 63, 66–8, 77, 81, 109, 124, 173–4, 198–9, 210, 226n118
  and work, 113, 131, 139, 145, 150, 245n88
  see also maid-wife-widow model; virgin-widow-spouse model
wife, 11–12, 18–19, 23–35 passim, 46, 49, 53, 56, 58, 99, 120, 125, 132, 136, 138–40, 148, 55, 161, 164, 197–8
  see also maid-wife-widow model; virgin-widow-spouse model
wifehood, 19
Wife of Bath, 7, 90
William of Auvergne, 91
William of Malmesbury, 169
William of Tyre, 165
William the Conqueror, 68, 149, 163, 171, 194–5
wives, 1–2, 11, 13, 24, 27–8, 33, 43, 68, 94, 106, 122, 129, 132, 139–40, 143, 145, 148, 157, 161, 163, 195–9, 245n88, 261n8
  see also marriage and clerics
Woodville, Elizabeth, 94, 117–18, 149, 171
Woolf, Virginia, 2–3
Wyclif, John, 82
Wymondham, Norfolk, 109

Yonge, James, 20, 21, 35
York, 111, 145
Yorke, Barbara, 173
Youngs, Deborah, 15, 20

Zurara, Gomes Eanes, 96